Ladies of the Western

Ladies of the Western

Interviews with Fifty-One More Actresses from the Silent Era to the Television Westerns of the 1950s and 1960s

MICHAEL G. FITZGERALD *and* BOYD MAGERS

with forewords by Kathryn Adams, Mala Powers and Marion Shilling

McFarland & Company, Inc., Publishers
Jefferson, North Carolina, and London

ALSO BY BOYD MAGERS AND
MICHAEL G. FITZGERALD

*Westerns Women: Interviews with 50 Leading Ladies of Movie
and Television Westerns from the 1930s to the 1960s*
(McFarland, 1999)

*The present work is a reprint of the illustrated case bound
edition of* Ladies of the Western: Interviews with Fifty-
One More Actresses from the Silent Era to the Television
Westerns of the 1950s and 1960s, *first published in 2002 by
McFarland.*

LIBRARY OF CONGRESS CATALOGUING-IN-PUBLICATION DATA

Fitzgerald, Michael G., 1950–
Ladies of the western : interviews with fifty-one more
actresses from the silent era to the television westerns of the 1950s
and 1960s / Michael G. Fitzgerald and Boyd Magers ; with forewords
by Kathryn Adams, Mala Powers and Marion Shilling.
p.   cm.
Includes index.

ISBN 0-7864-2656-X (softcover : 50# alkaline paper) ∞

1. Western films.   2. Western television programs.
3. Actresses—United States—Interviews.
I. Magers, Boyd, 1940–   II. Title.
PN1995.9.W4F56   2006   791.43'028'0820973—dc21   2001044779

British Library cataloguing data are available

Manufactured in the United States of America

On the front cover:
Left: Beverly Garland in *Badlands of Montana* (1957)
Right: Kathleen Hughes in *Dawn at Socorro* (1954)

*McFarland & Company, Inc., Publishers
Box 611, Jefferson, North Carolina 28640
www.mcfarlandpub.com*

To my son, Alan Magers.

To Jon David Fitzgerald, who loves movies, old and new.

Acknowledgments

No book of this type could be written without assistance in a great variety of ways. We are quite sure some of those listed here are completely unaware of the part they played in the making of this book. But, whether their contributions were large or small, they are all important. For that we are deeply appreciative.

Thanks, then, to Eugene Blottner, Rand Brooks, Bobby Copeland, Edith Correale, Jean Fowley, Alex Gordon, Tommy and Kathy Hildreth, Dorothy Julius, Gordon Kay, Tom Land, Harris Lentz, Erik Madden, Dick Madigan, Jack Mathis, Bill McDowell, Tim Neeley, Francis M. Nevins, Ray Nielsen, Bob Pontes, Jim Shoenberger, Gale Storm, Neil Summers, Marshall Terrill, Tom Weaver, Nick Williams, Beverly Witney and Tinsley Yarbrough.

And an extra special thank you to Donna Magers, without whose computer expertise this book would surely have remained handwritten.

Of course, we thank the 51 western ladies interviewed—for their time, patience, consideration and memories.

Briefer versions of the following interviews originally appeared in these publications: Kathryn Adams, *Western Clippings* 35 (May-June '00); Claudia Barrett, *Western Ladies* 2 (Nov. '96); Reno Browne, *Western Ladies* 2 (Nov. '96); Phyllis Coates, *Western Ladies* 4 (March '99); Louise Currie, *Western Clippings* 16 (March-April '97); Frances Dee, *Western Ladies* 4 (March '99); Edith Fellows, *Western Ladies* 1 (Nov. '95); Barbra Fuller, *Western Ladies* 2 (Nov. '96); Lisa Gaye, *Western Ladies* 4 (March '99); Jane Greer, *Western Ladies* 3 (Nov. '97); Kathleen Hughes, *Western Clippings* 14 (Nov.-Dec. '96); Anne Jeffreys, *Western Ladies* 4 (March '99); Suzanne Kaaren, *Western Clippings* 21 (Jan.-Feb. '98); Elyse Knox, *Western Ladies* 1 (Nov. '95); Virginia Lee, *Classic Images* 227 (May '94); Adele Mara, *Western Ladies* 4 (March '99); Joyce Meadows, *Western Ladies* 4 (March '99); Colleen Miller, *Western Clippings* 26 (Nov.-Dec. '98); Dorothy Morris and Caren Marsh, *Western Clippings* 24 (July-Aug. '98); Noreen Nash, *Western Clippings* 34 (Mar.-Apr. '00); Gigi Perreau, *Western Clippings* 36 (July-Aug. '00); Mala Powers, *Western Clippings* 33 (Jan.-Feb. '00); Kasey Rogers, *Western Ladies* 4 (March '99); Jean Rouverol, *Western Ladies* 4 (March '99); Karen Sharpe, *Western Ladies* 4 (March '99); Marjorie Stapp, *Western Clippings* 29 (May-June '99); Olive Sturgess, *Western Clippings* 39 (Jan.-Feb. '01); Ruth Terry, *Western Clippings* 25 (Sept.-Oct. '98); Martha Tibbetts, *Western Ladies* 4 (March '99); June Vincent, *Western Ladies* 1 (Nov. '95); Beverly Washburn, *Western Clippings* 28 (March-April '99); Marie Windsor, *Western Clippings* 31 (Sept.-Oct. '99); Jane Withers, *Western Clippings* 27 (Jan.-Feb. '99). All of the interviews have been revised and updated.

Table of Contents

Foreword

BY KATHRYN ADAMS

"Mom," my daughter Kristy announced one day over a year ago, "I got an interesting letter from a man named Michael Fitzgerald. He wants to know where you are! Shall I tell him?"

I laughed a bit, because I had just moved to Mankato, Minnesota, from Northfield in the same state, and I wasn't sure exactly where I was myself! But I read the letter with interest and answered it. In the days and weeks that followed, a wonderful journey into my long-ago past began—my past as an actress at Universal Studios in the early '40s—sixty long years ago. I had been given the professional name "Kathryn Adams" and with marriage and children and several intervening careers, I had almost entirely forgotten my identity as a "starlet," as we were called in those days.

Michael wanted to know if I would be willing to be interviewed by him about my memories of those distant years. At first, I couldn't believe anyone in the whole world would remember or be interested in my brief career. But I was so intrigued by the idea that I agreed to his request.

There followed long telephone conversations in which Michael's obvious and genuine interest, as well as his gentle probing, quickened a flood of memories and appreciation. Names, faces, places, incidents came back to me with surprising vividness and fondness—actors, directors, film crews, the streets of Universal—the back lot across the road against the empty hills, the dust and rocks in location spots out beyond Chatsworth, the horses and mud puddles—riding a buckboard!

The journey into my past turned out to be an important and wonderful experience for me. In looking back, I learned much about those days I hadn't quite realized before. I was struck by how the times, the film techniques and the whole culture have changed. Interestingly enough, I also learned some things about me as I recalled who I was then! (I won't go into what I learned!)

Michael Fitzgerald's appreciation of the film industry's history and the people who made it live led me to an appreciation and enjoyment of my own nearly forgotten, short-lived career. It helped me realize again the impact our industry has had on so many lives throughout the years.

Michael is a most considerate and perceptive interviewer, and as you read these pages, I know you will catch his spirit as well as glimpses of the personalities he has written about.

1

Foreword

BY MALA POWERS

Hurrah for Michael Fitzgerald and Boyd Magers for focusing on the long overlooked contribution of women in westerns and the actresses who portrayed them.

The classical western movie has given us our unique American folklore that embodies the pioneer spirit of this nation. Westerns also embody and characterize the basic moral forces of both the male and the female. While the hero contributes the physical action that slays the ever-threatening dragons, it is the heroine who carries the civilizing values that lead us into the future. Without her, the western becomes one-sided and easily slips into violence just for the sake of violence.

In his insightful and comprehensive article *Saloon Girls and Rancher's Daughters: The Woman in the Western*,* Blake Lucas writes, "It's time to see the Western in a different light—not as a masculine genre but as one supremely balanced in its male/female aspect and one of the finest places for women characters in all of cinema."

I love western films. Whether watching them or acting in them, I have expe-

rienced what a little-known poet, William Frederick Hopkins (1890–1943), expressed in the following stanzas†:

> I'm sure that I'm right when I'm
>   making the claim
> That cowboys and romance are one
>   and the same....
> For daring and thrills and a life full of zest,
> There's nought to compare with the
>   glamorous West.
>
> Where truth will assist you in
>   making the grade,
> Where man is a man, and a spade is a spade.
> Where nature has toiled with her
>   magical touch.
> Where ladies are ladies and treated as such.

And most of the "ladies" we remember are heroines in differing ways. Each of them, however—from the Saloon Girl or Madam with a generous heart, to the idealized, romantic, seemingly passive beauty—cause our hero to reveal a deeper aspect of himself and to become more than he was when our story began.

As an actress, I had the opportunity to portray several western women who were

---

That article, copyright © 1998 Blake Lucas, appears in the book, The Western Reader, *edited by Jim Kitses and Gregg Rickman and published by Limelight Editions, New York.*
  †*Taken from his poem "Home Education" and used by permission.*

2

complicated, challenging, physically active and true to that frontier spirit so magically represented on the screen. They were women who also developed in strength and understanding as they overcame challenges and helped their men to grow.

I thoroughly enjoyed preparing for my western roles. The weeks of learning to ride and to shoot, prior to the filming of my first Western, *Rose of Cimarron*, are still vivid in my memory. Before that time, my experiences with the horse species had been limited to pony rides and the only gun I had ever touched was a cap gun. Luckily, I was given expert teachers, great stuntmen like Dave Sharpe and Tom Steele. And, at the old Ace Hudkins Stables in the San Fernando Valley, real cowboys turned movie wranglers patiently rode with me for hours every day. With gentle humor, they regaled me with western lore which they said would give me "horse sense." And I loved *almost* every minute of my training—and I got right back on that horse that threw me! Next day, I was riding him again—my bruises, aches and pains smothered with the strongest, and most pungent, liniment I could find.

I relished the actual filming of westerns as well, although it is definitely not all fun and games for actresses or for actors. There are long hours on horseback, physical fights, the fording of rivers and streams, runaway horses or wagon teams, scrambling up rocky mountains, stumbling and tumbling around in all kinds of terrain or mud as the script demands. Then there are the weather conditions— scorching sun or bone-chilling wind, sudden cloudbursts and dust storms. But the heroines had the added burden of having to look good ... no matter what! All of these obstacles and many more take their toll on both the body and the emotions. Although I, personally, have never had any truly dangerous experiences, I really believe that many of the actresses who have given us such pleasure in westerns had to actually be as heroic as the characters they portrayed.

Yet, as you read further, you'll find that most of us former rancher's daughters, saloon girls, mail order brides and scheming femme fatales wouldn't have missed those Golden Western days for anything and are delighted by this recognition. Happy reading!

Foreword

BY MARION SHILLING

The crisp air scented with sage and pine, the sun just rising over distant hills. Amid flower-filled meadows, our motion picture company is ready for another big day...

The joy and the camaraderie we felt, the *fun*, is somehow conveyed by those early westerns. Perhaps that's one of the main reasons that they're ever-growing in popularity. The fans find in them a refreshing contrast to today's sordid films.

Boyd Magers and Michael Fitzgerald, in producing their volume of leading lady recollections, provide an avalanche of memories of those wholesome "oaters." On reading them, our spirits are uplifted.

The love that went into those long-ago movies is infectious, isn't it?

As the senior of the group, the most "superannuated," I send greetings to my younger associates. I'm certain you share my gratitude in having enjoyed the privilege of being among the western screen leading ladies.

Introduction

In this, our second volume of interviews with half a hundred leading ladies from the silent movie era to the television westerns of the 1950s and 60s, we once again explore not only their careers but the problems these women encountered in making movies, especially westerns.

Conditions were often arduous, locations were harsh and pay was minimal. Often, an actress was the only female on location, required to provide her own wardrobe and do her own makeup. Then, there were often the unwanted advances of over-affectionate male co-workers. Often, just getting the job without the aid of the very real casting couch was a job in itself. Then they had to deal with image. An actress who had done B westerns was often looked down on when trying for roles in A films.

But, as so many of the ladies repeat over and over, "It was fun." It was another era of filmmaking, an era that will never come again.

Read the stories they relate with appreciation for the hardships and long hours these women endured to bring us hours of screen entertainment. You'll see how these varied problems were overcome by the jubilant spirit and excitement of making the films. Whatever the problems, the interviewees, to a woman, look back on it as a time well remembered.

As in our first volume, *Westerns Women*, no claim is made that these are the most popular or prolific actresses in westerns. We have tried to present a diverse mixture of better-known leading ladies along with several who are not quite so well known but who, nevertheless, have fascinating stories to relate. We have mixed it up with actresses from B westerns, A westerns and the television era— even one who made westerns strictly in the silent era. Together they present a clear picture of how western filmmaking and "the business" changed, and how it remained the same, over fifty years.

THE INTERVIEWS

Kathryn Adams

Cowgirl Psychology

Beautiful, talented Kathryn Elizabeth Adams had a brief but memorable career in motion pictures. Born July 15, 1920, in New Ulm, Minnesota, down the road 30 miles from Mankato ("which is famous for the slaughter of 33 Sioux Indians," she laughs), she got into pictures after being encouraged to enter a contest.

"In 1939, *Lux Radio Show* had a 'Gateway to Hollywood' program. The winners would get a contract with RKO Radio. A scout was sent to Minnesota, but nobody would enter. We were suspicious of Hollywood [*laughs*]. I was attending a small college in the Twin Cities, and my drama teacher said to go on and see what it's like. I won the midwest tryouts, although I lost the national finals. A big director, Gregory La Cava, was one of the judges who voted for me. He found out the contest was rigged and signed me for the second lead in *Fifth Avenue Girl* [1939] with Ginger Rogers! [Famous dress designer] Howard Greer was doing the clothes for this little hayseed from Minnesota! Tim Holt played my brother—this was before he was a big cowboy star. He felt uneasy about doing this picture. It was not his style, but he was fine, and a really nice person. He later worked with Hugh Beaumont, my first husband. Everybody in the picture business was so warm and hospitable. There was a makeup man who wanted to make *me*, but generally I got along fine with everybody. I could tell you a story about my mother—a Methodist minister's wife—and W. C. Fields, but I'm saving it for my memoirs, which I have just completed."

Kathryn is a published author, with several short stories appearing in various children's magazines. Asked about her writing, she reveals her works have appeared in *Pocket* and in *The Friend*, a Mormon magazine. "I write under my current married name, Kathryn Doty."

An early credit for Kathryn was a small role in *The Hunchback of Notre Dame* (1939). "I was supposed to play Esmeralda—then Charles Laughton, who was signed to play the Hunchback, cabled he was bringing Esmeralda with him from Ireland. It turned out to be Maureen O'Hara, as they had just worked together in *Jamaica Inn* [1939]. Maureen and I became good friends. The RKO backlot, or ranch, where it was filmed, was very interesting. William Dieterle, the director, was very tall and imposing. He was an ardent astrologer—he believed in it. He would start filming on the exact hour and exact day. He also wore white gloves. Charles Laughton took hours to be made up, and one time, Dieterle didn't get to start filming when the horoscope charts said he should, so he had to start all over, finding out the exact hour and day to shoot this and that [*laughs*]!"

Kathryn with her three-time cowboy hero, Alabama-born Johnny Mack Brown, in *Arizona Cyclone* (1941).

Her RKO musical short, *Molly Cures a Cowboy* (1940), starred Ray Whitley. "Ray was a very good singer—we shot it quickly, and they didn't let me sing in it, although I wish I had!"

When asked how she got over to Universal, Kathryn relates an unusual tale. "RKO didn't use me properly. I could sing, but they never let me sing in a picture. I had a small role in a Kay Kyser movie, *That's Right—You're Wrong* (1939). David Butler was the director. When he found out RKO was going to drop me, he said, 'I'm doing a Bing Crosby picture [*If I Had My Way*, 1940] over at Universal. I'll tell them to put you under contract and I'll use you in the film.' That was that—I never had a screen test or anything. It was

all too easy for me! As a result, I didn't appreciate it at the time. I never had an agent. Although Myron Selznick did represent me for awhile, he didn't do anything."

Kathryn co-starred with Donald Woods in Universal's *Sky Raiders* (1941), advertised as "The most sensational sky-serial ever made." "Donald was really, really nice. So relaxed. I remember the many stock shots they used. One time, the airplane plunges into water [Chapter Eleven]—they used a stock shot to show it. Although no one could have survived, in the next chapter, I *did* survive and am rescued, being seen sitting in a ship captain's quarters. There was another scene where they got a bear [Chapter Ten]—now that

Billy Halop and Robert Armstrong greet Kathryn and Donald Woods coming off the ship in a scene from Chapter 12 of *Sky Raiders* (1941).

was scary!" Kathryn also had an unbilled bit as a girl on the street in Chapter One of *Junior G-Men of the Air*, 1942.

Asked about interacting with the special effects, Kathryn relates, "Don Brown, a producer at Universal at the time, filled me in on off-screen stories and showed me how they put it all together. That was fascinating!" *Sky Raiders* co-director Ray Taylor (with Ford Beebe) was "a director from Perham, Minnesota. He was a very cordial to me. Ray was a great, wonderful man; very easy; so great. We Minnesotans stood together [*laughs*]. I had a flair for acting—but had so little experience. I was ahead of my time in that I was college-educated before getting into the business. I was less interested in glamour and being 'sexy' and more into sub-

stance, but I only got the type of roles in style at the time. When watching the beginning of *Sky Raiders* recently, I decided I wasn't as unprofessional as I remembered [*laughs*]. It's fun! [Actress] Helen Parrish was a good friend. I was at her wedding to [actor-writer] Charles Lang. The Andrews Sisters sang 'Apple Blossom Time.' I'd worked with them in *Argentine Nights* [1940]. Another one I was close to was Evelyn Ankers, but we weren't as close as Helen and I."

Director Taylor also guided Adams through the first two of her three leading lady roles opposite Johnny Mack Brown at Universal. "Horses! I was not a horsewoman. The horses knew more about filming westerns than I did, so I just 'hung on' and they did the work! I knew nothing about horses—I was told, 'Don't worry. Just get on the horse. Hang on to the pummel.' When those movie horses heard 'Action,' they would back right out of the post, gallop down the street and do their part—well. The director always had someone close to me, so I wouldn't jiggle off—or if I did, they would catch me before I fell off! Johnny Mack Brown was very nice; gracious and helpful. 'Please be careful!' That was my most oft-repeated farewell line to Johnny Mack Brown [*laughs*]. When saying goodbye to Johnny, I put my hand on his shoulder, which is a normal, natural thing to do. 'No, you can't do that! You can't *touch* him! We will have to shoot it over' [*laughs*]. Nell O'Day did more of the tomboy stuff. In the first picture, *Bury Me Not on the Lone Prairie* [1941], remember the scene in the buckboard where I am riding? Well, it was not easy to gallop! There was nothing but the seat to hang onto—I thought I would jiggle down. There was *no double* for that, either! But, Nell O'Day—she was a fine horsewoman. She was a little tiny person [5'3"], yet her horse was a huge Irish jumper chestnut, 17 hands. Such a large horse for a little person. Nell was down to earth, a nice person. She entered horse shows all over the area. I saw her perform in many of them. She did jumps and everything!"

In *Rawhide Rangers* (1941), Nell sings and Kathryn plays the piano. "That was me; I could play piano as well as sing. On loanout from Universal, I was even supposed to be Gene Autry's leading lady in some of those musical westerns he did at Republic, but at 5'7" I was told I was too tall [*laughs*]!"

Another of her leading men was Richard Arlen, with whom she co-starred in Universal's coal mining adventure, *Black Diamonds* (1940). "Richard was another one from Minnesota. He was very nice and considerate. The difference in our ages

didn't seem to matter. Andy Devine was a sweetheart, and Mayor of Van Nuys!"

Asked about her retirement, Kathryn says, "I married Hugh Beaumont, who was in the 'Gateway to Hollywood' contest with me, in 1941. Our marriage, at first, was like the Janet Gaynor-Fredric March *A Star Is Born* [1937]. My career was eclipsing his at that time. I did return to pictures in 1946, in PRC's *Blonde for a Day*, to play opposite Hugh's Michael Shayne, but that was because Cheryl Walker, who was playing his girlfriend Phyllis, was expecting a child, and then later miscarried. So I stepped in for that one time only. When Hugh and I were getting married, Universal wanted us to actually get married on film, for the marriage scene sequence in Irene Dunne's *Unfinished Business* [1941]. This was some stunt of Richard Birdwell, publicity agent for Jean Harlow. They thought it would be great publicity! I was horrified! I used various excuses to not have this happen, but they kept coming up with a reply. I told them we had no place to live right now and they said, 'We'll find you a place.' That sort of thing! I was aghast! Anyway, I did get out of that one! Hugh and I did marry in 1941 and had three children—Hunter, born in 1943; Kristan, born in 1945; and Mark, born in 1949. We bought an island in Minnesota, so we had a place to come every year with the children, just so they could see what it was like when I was growing up. I became a psychologist with the Footlight's Child Guidance Clinic at Hollywood Presbyterian Hospital. I was involved in that and never ever considered taking a role on *Leave It to Beaver* [in which Hugh starred], or anything else, for that matter. When I moved back to Minnesota, I continued as a psychologist. For the last 25 years, I have been Mrs. Fred Doty! Since retiring as a psychologist, I turned to writing—children's stories and also my memoirs. One of my very best

Al Bridge, Kathryn, Johnny Mack Brown, Frank Shannon and Nell O'Day in a quieter moment from the action-packed *Rawhide Rangers* (1941).

friends is Marge Raitt, who was married to singer John Raitt. So, I have known Bonnie Raitt all of her life!"

One final look back at her career and some of her co-stars: John Barrymore (*The Invisible Woman* [1941]): "He then needed prompts for his dialogue [*laughs*]! And Virginia Bruce who played the 'Invisible Woman' was another Minnesotan."

Although Kathryn found most everybody (with the exception of that one makeup man) great to work with, "Maria Montez was not a pleasant person. She was one of the exceptions [*laughs*]!"

About her career in general, Kathryn muses, "I didn't regret leaving it. I regret not appreciating it more—at the time. It all came so easy, I just didn't think of it then, like I do now. Hugh didn't ask me to

quit—I just quit to raise my children. It was a different world. Acting wasn't something I longed for—it just happened. I love the water and am a good swimmer. I also love the wilderness. I have a very good life now…. I sport a tiny hearing aid, have all my own teeth, and absolutely no face lifts with the exception of tiny pierces in my ears for those endlessly intriguing rings, which were not worn in westerns."

Kathryn Adams
Western Filmography

Movies: *Molly Cures a Cowboy* (1940 RKO short)—Ray Whitley; *Bury Me Not on the Lone Prairie* (1941 Universal)—Johnny Mack Brown; *Rawhide Rangers* (1941 Universal)—Johnny Mack Brown; *Arizona Cyclone* (1941 Universal)—Johnny Mack Brown.

Claudia Barrett

Shy Persistence

Claudia Barrett, one of Republic's latter-day leading ladies, was first under contract for a year to Warner Bros., where they changed her name from Imagene Williams. "I chose Claudia ... my agent handled George Brent, so he was thinking Brent ... my mother's maiden name is Benton, so I was thinking Benton ... Jack

Gorgeous Claudia Barrett was one of Republic's last leading ladies and one of the busiest women in television westerns of the 1950s.

Warner came up with Barrett. I liked the new name and took it legally."

Claudia was born in West Los Angeles, grew up in Sherman Oaks, graduated from Van Nuys High and went to the Pasadena Community Playhouse to study acting for a year. "I did a play in Encino. The drama coach at Warner Bros. saw me and gave me a screen test. I started studying acting when I was seven years old because I was a very shy little girl and my parents thought it would be helpful to me ... which it was."

During her year at Warner Bros. she did *White Heat* (1949), *Chain Lightning* (1950) and *The Great Jewel Robber* (1950). "Warner Bros. was fun because you worked with top directors. I was a little nervous working with big stars like Cagney, Bogart and David Brian, but they put you right at ease. David Brian was doing a picture with Bette Davis. I did all of the tests for that—where the star doesn't come in... I had to test all these people that were up for different parts." She really wanted the part in *Caged* (1950) which went to Eleanor Parker. "I had an interview with the director. At this time I was shy ... and didn't say a lot. He called me a mouse. It upset me so much I went to my dressing room and just cried and cried and cried. There were a couple of things that almost happened that would have made a difference. I almost got the lead from Ida

One of the nastiest screen villains in westerns, Myron Healey, with Claudia, Allan "Rocky" Lane and sidekick Chubby Johnson (who replaced regular Lane sidekick Eddy Waller for several films) in a tense moment from *Night Riders of Montana* (1951).

Lupino in *Outrage* [1950] when she was starting to direct. [Mala Powers eventually starred.] Sally Forrest got another [1951's *Hard, Fast and Beautiful*]. But, things happen in your life that change a lot of things."

To say Claudia was extremely discouraged when Warner Bros. didn't pick up her option is an understatement. "The day I found out, I was in an automobile accident, I was so upset! I was a very shy person and it was difficult for me after my contract was up to go on interviews. It took a couple of years for me to finally begin to relax when I went on an interview and start talking. My first job was at Republic, *Rustlers on Horseback* [1950]. I did three with Rocky Lane. My second was *Old Frontier* [1950] with Monte Hale.

Monte was a delightful person, very charming and sweet. Rocky sort of kept to himself … he was not friendly, but I thought he did a good job. I was watching one of the tapes you sent me and I was amazed the director kept shooting the back of my head. But they shot those fairly fast and the director wants to get everything in. They didn't do any closeups of me either, so I think he was just in a hurry. I was green… I didn't know too much other than approximately where the camera was [*laughs*]. I was not under contract to Republic—they were all individual pictures.

"I did a *Stories of the Century* ['Sontag and Evans' (1955)] and the director [Bill Witney] liked me very much and wanted me to meet Mr. Yates, head of

Republic. So I did get to say 'Hi.' I liked Bill so much. The lady who did all the costumes thought I was just built for those period clothes. The only one I got to know personally was character actor Chubby Johnson, who became friends with my ex-husband [actor Alan Wells]. We visited Chubby in Las Vegas when he lived there. My ex and I ran a poultry store when we were not acting. Chubby came in and helped us chop up chickens one night. Chubby was a darling man—very easy to know, wonderful sense of humor."

Unlike some leading ladies, Claudia always looked at home in the saddle. "I was a Brownie in the Girl Scouts. The Brownie Troop went to a big riding stable in Van Nuys. I learned English riding, however, which was more difficult than western."

Following her Republic days and the low-budget cult classic, *Robot Monster* (1953), the actress became very active on TV. "As I said, it took a couple of years before I got brave enough to talk on interviews. Finally, after I learned how to talk [*laughs*], I met a wonderful agent through Myron Healey, whom I'd met at Republic, and he got me working all the time. I think I did a couple hundred shows and most of them were through this one agent, Fred Katz.

"Quite often, as with *Wild Bill Hickok* [1951–1958], we did two shows at the same time. When we were on location, we did locations for both shows. *Roy Rogers* [1951–1957] and *Buffalo Bill Jr.* [1955–1956] episodes were shot one right after the other. I'd always wanted to go on location because I'd heard you got to travel and see places ... so my first *location* was [*laughs*] Apple Valley! That was *Buffalo Bill Jr.* Dick Jones was very nice. On lo-

cation, Flying-A [the production company] didn't have a makeup man or hairdresser so I had to do that myself. Notice, when I'm riding in that buckboard [*Black Ghost*, 1956], it looked as if my hair was going to come off as well as the hat. They did have a makeup person back at the studio when we did the inside shots. I was quite young when I did the *Hopalong Cassidy* episode ['Lawless Legacy,' 1952]. William Boyd was a real gentleman. Steve Rowland, who played my brother was just getting started. His father was a director.* The scene where I go to get the sheriff, I turned around and bumped right into Edgar Buchanan. We had to do that several times to get the timing right. I didn't realize at the time, Clayton Moore—the Lone Ranger—was in that. But I did the *Hopalong* before I did the *Lone Ranger* in 1953. I didn't really get to know these people very well, everyone was very busy."

Claudia worked on Roy Rogers' TV show in 1955. "They [Rogers and wife Dale Evans] were a delightful couple. He was sort of quiet ... didn't talk a lot. She was very outgoing ... very talented lady. She wrote a song right on the set they were gonna do. I did a religious picture right after I worked with Roy and Dale and I did a good job because of her, because she is so sincere in what she says and what she believes. It helped me a lot in my performance in this other picture. One thing I liked about the Roy Rogers shows, they always had a good moral."

We asked Claudia if she felt like she was doing the same ingenue role over and over again. "I was married when I was 18. I always felt like a woman, felt like an adult. Then I'm looking at the tapes you sent and I thought, 'Boy, I really was an in-

Roy Rowland directed Boys' Ranch *(1946),* The Outriders *(1950),* Bugles in the Afternoon *(1952),* Gun Glory *(1957) and many non-westerns. Steve was later a regular as one of the Clantons on* Wyatt Earp *(1955–1961).*

genue' [*laughs*]. Being small, I guess I was sort of typecast as an ingenue."

There's a dramatic change in her work, her style—even her hair color at times—from *Roy Rogers*, *Wild Bill Hickok*, all those shows, to when Claudia did *Lawman* (1960), *Colt .45* (1960), etc. She was getting much more depth into her performances. "I was older then. A lot of those early shows are when I was 18, 20, 22 years old. I was about 26 when I did *Colt .45* and *Lawman*. You grow up. I went through a divorce and after that I grew up very fast. My own personality changed a lot. As for *Colt .45*, I ran into Wayde Preston and [director] Lew Landers—together, as a matter of fact—not too long afterward in Palm Springs. There was a private airport. Wayde had his own plane, a little Cessna, and he took Lew Landers and me for a

scary ride where he turned the plane upside down ... but it was fun."

Actor turned director Marc Lawrence directed her in a *Lawman*. "I loved him as an actor and he was really easy to work with as a director. We got along fine."

As for her favorite roles: "I would love to see *Flowers for Jenny*, which I did with Dale Robertson. It was a property he owned and was thinking of doing as a feature film. [It aired on *Schlitz Playhouse* 8/3/56.] It was a very nice role and I enjoyed working with Dale, a very charming man. We shot a *Tales of Wells Fargo* in Modesto. Also I did a *Pony Express* [1959–1960] with Grant Sullivan that I would love to find. Playing a bad girl is much more fun."

Among her TVers was a *Gray Ghost* (1958) episode. "We shot that in Sonora.

Looks like Allan "Rocky" Lane is giving Claudia good advice not to smoke in *Night Riders of Montana* (1951).

It's a beautiful area. I ran into Tod Andrews later on. [His early death in 1972] was a shame. I also did a *Rough Riders* [1959] with Jan Merlin. We did a *Hallmark Hall of Fame* together. He played a young Oliver Wendell Holmes and I played his wife."

On *Seven Ways from Sundown* (1960), Audie Murphy was playful. "When I was trying to do my closeups he was making faces at me and it was very difficult to concentrate [*laughs*]. I don't think I rehearsed with Audie until we actually did the take."

Two of Claudia's close friends in the business were "Jan Shepard and her husband Dirk London, whose real name is Ray Boyle. He was on the *Wyatt Earp* [1955–1961] series." (London played Morgan Earp 1958–1961 and was in several other TV westerns. He later became an excellent artist. Shepard was seen in over 30 TV westerns, everything from *Sgt. Preston* [1955–1958] and *Circus Boy* [1956–1957] to *Rawhide* [1959–1965], *Gunsmoke* [1955–1975] and *The Virginian* [1962–1970].)

"I did seven shows with my ex-husband, Alan Wells, including *Cisco Kid* [1952–1956] and *Lone Ranger*. We had a great time working together. Alan and I were so busy for the seven years we were married, we didn't have time to have children."

Besides westerns, Claudia appeared on *Abbott and Costello* (1952–1953), *China Smith* (1952–1955), *Space Patrol* (1950–1955), *That's My Boy* (1954–1955), *Mr. and Mrs. North* (1952–1954), *Big Town* (1950–1956), *The Millionaire* (1955–1960), *The Lone Wolf* (1955), *G. E. Theater* (1953–1962), *Peter Gunn* (1958–1961), *Highway Patrol* (1955–1959), *Boston Blackie* (1952–1953) and others. "Troy Melton, who was the stuntman on *Boston Blackie*, was gonna make me a stuntwoman. When I fell off the building in one episode ... I did that myself. Troy thought I was just terrific

[*laughs*]. Such a nice guy. He helped me get on and off horses and ride."

Claudia tells us when she appeared in *Taggart* (1964), "Tony Young was married to Madlyn Rhue, but, while I was making the film, I talked more with Dan Duryea about his *China Smith* series."

Somewhere in the mid–1960s, Claudia disappeared from view. "I went through some personal problems and I just never came back. I loved acting ... but I went through a very bad period in my life. Since then I worked for 14 years at the Academy of Motion Picture Arts and Sciences. I was with the scientific and technical awards and all of the technical branches, which are very interesting. I worked with some really talented people. That was fun and exciting."

Shy, as she says, or not—the actress had the persistence to see it through where many others would have given up. "I do consider myself a professional and tried to conduct myself that way. One group had me in on all these interviews. It was between myself and somebody else ... and they didn't use me. This happened, like, three times. Finally, I told my agent, 'Look—this is ridiculous, they aren't going to hire me and I'm not going on their interviews.' He said, 'Please, please ... they want you, please go.' So I went and I finally got the job. Persistence does pay off. That was *Death Valley Days* [1952–1970]."

Does she think she's still shy? "I'm not easy to get to know. Strangers ... or people I don't know ... don't get to know me well usually. But I am outgoing in certain ways. In my work at the Academy, I handled a lot of meetings and a lot of people and I was very outgoing to them on the job."

Art, rather than acting, occupies Claudia's time these days. "When visiting Ireland in 1984, I took up watercolor painting. When I came home I started studying art. Although I miss acting, art has taken its place in my life. It's creative, enjoyable and most satisfying." Claudia has had her works reproduced on note cards and her prints and watercolors have been displayed at numerous southern California exhibitions.

Claudia Barrett
Western Filmography

Movies: *Rustlers on Horseback* (1950 Republic)—Allan Lane; *Old Frontier* (1950 Republic)—Monte Hale; *Nightriders of Montana* (1951 Republic)—Allan Lane; *Desperadoes' Outpost* (1952 Republic)—Allan Lane; *Seven Ways from Sundown* (1960 Universal-International)—Audie Murphy; *Taggart* (1964 Universal-International)—Tony Young.

Television: *Cowboy G-Men*, "Running Iron" (1952); *Cisco Kid*, "Raccoon Story" (1952); *Hopalong Cassidy*, "Lawless Legacy" (1952); *Cowboy G-Men*, "Silver Shotgun" (1953); *Cisco Kid*, "Vendetta" (1953); *Lone Ranger*, "Sheriff's Son" (1953); *Wild Bill Hickok*, "Mountain Men" (1953); *Heinz Studio 57*, "The Duel" (1954); *Lone Ranger*, "Colorado Gold" (1954); *Death Valley Days*, "Eleven Thousand Miners Can't Be Wrong" (1954); *Stories of the Century*, "Sontag and Evans" (1955); *Roy Rogers*, "Showdown" (1955); *Roy Rogers*, "Treasure of Paradise Valley" (1955); *Roy Rogers*, "Ranch War" (1955); *Buffalo Bill Jr.*, "Black Ghost" (1956); *Buffalo Bill Jr.*, "Hooded Vengeance" (1956); *Fury*, "The Baby" (1956); *Schlitz Playhouse*, "Flowers for Jenny" (1956); *Death Valley Days*, "Gold Is Where You Find It" (1956); *Tales of Wells Fargo*, "Ride with the Killer" (1957); *Californians*, "Panic on Montgomery Street" (1958); *Trackdown*, "End of the World" (1958); *Gray Ghost*, "Father and Son" (1958); *Death Valley Days*, "Stagecoach Spy" (1959); *Rough Riders*, "Paradise Gap" (1959); *Shotgun Slade*, "Little Sister" (1960); *Lawman*, "The Catcher" (1960); *Colt .45*, "Alibi" (1960); *Pony Express* (unknown episode) (1960); *Wagon Train* (unknown episode).

Reno Browne

Queen of Monogram

Monogram leading lady Reno Browne, born Josephine Ruth Clarke, April 20, 1921, was nicknamed after her hometown in Nevada. Reno was a popular rodeo performer in the early 1940s, twice becoming Queen of the Reno Rodeo. As a child, Reno was interested in ballet, piano and riding but, "I liked horses best." Over 25 trophies attest to her superb abilities.

Reno was educated at St. Thomas School in Reno and the Dominican Convent in San Rafael, California, for four years of high school. She then spent a year at the University of Nevada followed by two years at Actor's Laboratory in Los

GW-52-34

Comic sidekick Max Terhune, Monogram's most popular cowboy Johnny Mack Brown and Reno in *West of El Dorado* **(1949).**

Angeles and one year at the Pasadena Playhouse.

As to her entrance into show business, "I had an agent in Hollywood who was in a barber shop getting a haircut. Next to him was producer Scotty Dunlap, who was looking for a girl for Johnny Mack Brown westerns who could ride horseback. The girl he'd hired before had gotten on one side of the horse and fallen off the other. My agent told him about me and I went out for the interview and got the job."

In the mid–1940s, Reno was a leading lady to Johnny Mack Brown and Whip Wilson in six B-westerns each. "I found those two the most gentlemanly people I have ever met. I loved Johnny Mack Brown when he played the spoons. He used to get hold of a couple of spoons

and make rhythms against his leg. It was so much fun to sit around and listen to him. Johnny and Whip were entirely different people. Johnny was more eager and knew his craft very well since he had been active in westerns and motion pictures for years. Whip had a wonderful voice. He was fairly new to the business but was a quick learner. When he was hired, my boss asked me to take him out for a ride to see how he did. He rode pretty well except the horse ran away from him. After that though, he had no trouble whatsoever with the horse. He *was* on a strange horse when he was with me and I, of course, was on my own stallion. So I can't say he was a bad rider … although that was a funny little bit."

Reno started off as Reno Browne but

midway switched her last name to Blair. "When I first signed, I was working with Johnny Mack Brown and [Monogram] thought the public would think I was his daughter or something. So they made me use the name Blair. Funny though, his horse's name was Reno, so when I changed my last name to Blair they had to change his horse's name to Rebel." Incidentally, Reno's primary horse was named Major (Ora Plaza).

Although the 5'4" Reno was an expert horsewoman, she laughingly told us, "Once I fell off a rocking chair and dislocated my jaw. They teased me about it because I couldn't fall off a horse, but I could fall off a tipping rocking chair!"

Bearing in mind we all have good and bad days, I asked Reno what were the "worst" and "best" days of her life. "The worst was probably my first day on the set when I was wearing big rowel spurs and my spur got caught in another horse's stirrups. I twisted my leg and sprained my ankle. They had to cut the boot off which made me mad because they ruined a very good pair of boots. The best would be the start of any new picture. That was always good because you learned more and met new people. You learned your script and the next day everything on the script would be changed. So you didn't really memorize the lines because you knew the next day they would give you new words. But they gave you time and worked patiently with you. We made a film in five

A serious discussion from *Across the Rio Grande* (1949) with Dub "Cannonball" Taylor, Jimmy Wakely, Reno and Riley Hill.

Reno's expert horsemanship earned her roles in 13 Monogram B-westerns, including *Gunslingers* (1950) with perennial father Steve Clark and Whip Wilson.

days, or two in ten days. Sometimes you would go in a door with one outfit on and come back out and put another outfit on to go through the same door for a different picture. You didn't know which one you were working on sometimes!"

Her other co-star, in one film, was Jimmy Wakely. "Jimmy was such a charming, quiet man with good humor and he had a beautiful voice. He was very warmhearted to all he met, a grand human being. He looked larger than he was. One time we did a food show in San Jose with the Sons of the Pioneers and several others. I'd been on stage with a strange horse. Next day it came out in the newspaper, 'Reno Browne came to town, using her own pony. The pony she brought, needed

a pot, and that was no baloney!' [*laughs*]. Following this horse, one of the Pioneers came on stage, stepped right in it and slid all the way across the stage [*laughs*]. We cleaned it up before Jimmy came on stage.

"Another incident with Jimmy—the stuntmen were rehearsing a fight. Jimmy decided he wanted to do the shot. He did, and clipped the other guy right in the nose. Best leave it to the professionals."

Reno chuckles over another memory involving Holly Bane, who played heavies in many Monogram westerns. "Holly was in a scene where someone had gotten shot. He and another man were supposed to pick this shot man up and take him out. Holly had the feet, with his back to the camera and he had to bend over [*laughs*]. He didn't have any shorts on!"

Reno seemed to love the action part of filmmaking best. "That was the most enjoyable. One action scene I did was to ride a horse, bend down and pick up a package from the ground. The film I like the best is *Fence Riders* [1950] with Whip Wilson. I got to do some stunt things, and there was quite a bit of activity during the filming."

As for her family, Reno tells us, "I had two husbands—one was Lash LaRue. I didn't have any children. I have stepchildren—Lash LaRue's children by a previous marriage. They still call me Mom. Lash was quite a character! I'd rather not say more, and there is a lot more to say."

Besides her Monogram westerns, Reno tells us, "I had my own radio show, *Reno Rides the Range*. Whenever I was going into a new town, I would send 13 episodes of the radio show to be played before I got there. Also, I worked on several TV shows, like an episode of *Crossroads* [1955–1957] with Darren McGavin as the leading man. It took a lot of time, going to horse shows every Sunday of the year, openings for Pacific Coast Theaters and appearing at orphanages."

Reno believes westerns are no longer as popular as they once were "because there's very little sex in them; and, although everyone loves to see them, they were made with an extremely low budget. That is no longer possible. A picture at that time could be made for around $50,000. Today, people go to see big set movies."

Since leaving films, Reno travels. "I represented the United States government at the Peruvian World Fair for three weeks. I was presented to the King and Queen of England. Also, on a trip to Paris, France, I adopted an eight-year-old boy. I sent money every month to the Catholic convent for food—a wonderful experience. A good wind at your back."

Additionally, Reno was a pilot with the Civil Air Patrol, directed summer stock theatrical performances and was a concert pianist. She was named an honorary deputy sheriff in Washoe County and Clark County, Nevada, and received a war bonnet from the Paiute tribe, Washoe County, Nevada. She holds the distinction of being the only leading lady, other than Dale Evans, to have a comic book published in her name. Marvel Comics produced three issues in 1950.

Reno died May 15, 1991, of cancer.

Reno Browne
Western Filmography

Movies: *Under Arizona Skies* (1946 Monogram)—Johnny Mack Brown; *Gentlemen from Texas* (1946 Monogram)—Johnny Mack Brown; *Raiders of the South* (1947 Monogram)—Johnny Mack Brown; *Law Comes to Gunsight* (1947 Monogram)—Johnny Mack Brown; *Frontier Agent* (1948 Monogram)—Johnny Mack Brown; *Shadows of the West* (1949 Monogram)—Whip Wilson; *Across the Rio Grande* (1949 Monogram)—Jimmy Wakely; *West of El Dorado* (1949 Monogram)—Johnny Mack Brown; *Haunted Trails* (1949 Monogram)—Whip Wilson; *Riders of the Dusk* (1949 Monogram)—Whip Wilson; *Rangeland* (1949 Monogram)—Whip Wilson; *Fence Riders* (1950 Monogram)—Whip Wilson; *Gunslingers* (1950 Monogram)—Whip Wilson.

Virginia Carroll

Character Lady

"**A** man came into I Magnum's [a department store section of Los Angeles' Biltmore Hotel], where I was working as a model, and asked if I'd be interested in being in the movies—that I should go to RKO tomorrow. I asked him, 'How much would it pay?' When he said 'About $75 a week,' I immediately said, 'I'll be there!' [*laughs*]." This was how Virginia Elizabeth Carroll, born in Los Angeles, California, December 2, 1913, began her career. "I went in and was told I was too short to be a model. I'm only 5'5", and they were casting girls for the Technicolor fashion show sequence in *Roberta* [1935] with Irene Dunne and Randolph Scott. I came back for the next five days in a row, and finally they said I could be the sports model. So, *Roberta* was my very first picture."

Virginia's first western was *A Tenderfoot Goes West* (1936) with Jack LaRue. "Russell Gleason was in that, and I was friends with the family—his father Jimmy Gleason and his mother, Lucille Webster Gleason. Every Sunday, we'd go to their house in Beverly Hills for Sunday brunch. They were both darling people." As it was her first western, Virginia recalls, "I was not a good rider, but westerns were fun to do. They asked me if I could ride, and I said, 'Oh, sure,' but that's a joke! I still cannot ride very well. I did take riding lessons when I was at school in New York, but that was riding English saddle, which is

nothing like they want you to ride for the movies [*laughs*]. I could get on and off horses, but girls didn't have to do much in westerns. In fact, later on, both Gene Autry and Roy Rogers would kid me—they'd tell the studio to 'Give her the oldest nag you have' [*laughs*]. Typical western heroines were girls who couldn't ride but could smile pretty; smile at horses or the trees [*laughs*]!"

Billed below Virginia in that film was future star and her husband, Ralph Byrd. "He didn't mind, because he was about to become Dick Tracy! Chester Gould, who created the comic strip, saw Ralph on the lot at Republic one day and said, 'That's Dick Tracy!' It was that simple! Ralph and I met at a little theater in Beverly Hills. We were doing a play together, but I cannot recall its title. This was in 1935, and we married in 1936. I later had a tiny role in one of Ralph's serials, *Dick Tracy Returns* [1938]."

Virginia's second western, *Oklahoma Terror* (1939), was directed by Spencer Gordon Bennet. "A wonderful man; a very nice man!" The star was (Addison) Jack Randall, "who had a terrible reputation. But, he was nice to me [*laughs*]. We were on location at either Big Bear or Lake Arrowhead. I didn't have much to do in the picture, and I was there three or four days. He offered me the use of his car, just to drive around and see the scenery! 'Borrow

Badmen Marshall Reed and Bill Kennedy are caught at the windup to *Triggerman* (1948) by Johnny Mack Brown, sidekick Raymond Hatton and Virginia.

my car,' he stated, and he loaned me the car! I had no problems, but then, he knew Ralph [*laughs*]. So, Jack Randall left me alone!"

Asked about any other locations, Virginia states, "Oh, I went to Lone Pine and the Iverson Ranch; the common ones, but not too often. Actually, Ralph would go on tours, sometimes three or four months long. I went back east with Ralph in 1939—for a month! I also went with him in 1940, but by this time, our little girl was born, so I stopped going after that one. Then Ralph went into the service during World War II. Incidentally, I named our daughter Carroll Byrd, after my maiden name, spelling it the same. She is horse crazy, even today!"

In between the westerns, Virginia ap-

peared in at least seven serials, including the aforementioned *Dick Tracy Returns* and the original *Superman* in 1948. "I played the mother of Clark Kent, who would grow up to be Superman. Mason Alan Dinehart, III, played him as a child. I knew his father, character actor Alan Dinehart, fairly well. He was very talented." Her other serials were *Mysterious Dr. Satan* (1940); *G-Men Vs. the Black Dragon* (1943); *Daughter of Don Q* (1946); *The Crimson Ghost* (1946) and *The Black Widow* (1947).

Virginia's third western, *The Masked Rider* (1941), starred her frequent leading man, Johnny Mack Brown. "Johnny Mack was a wonderful guy; there was no trouble; he was extremely nice; very easy to work with!"

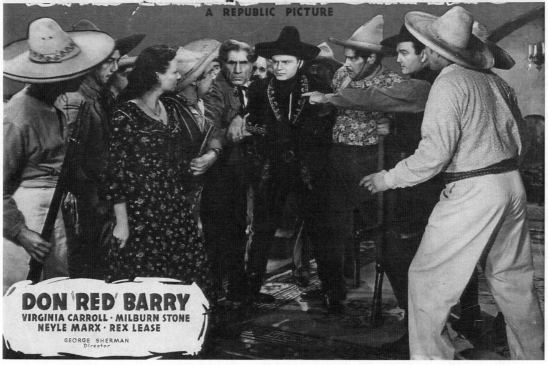

"THE PHANTOM COWBOY"

A REPUBLIC PICTURE

DON 'RED' BARRY

VIRGINIA CARROLL · MILBURN STONE
NEYLE MARX · REX LEASE

GEORGE SHERMAN
Director

Virginia confronts her "very difficult" leading man, Don Barry, in *The Phantom Cowboy* (1941). Milburn Stone (second from right) later became famous as "Doc" Adams on television's *Gunsmoke*.

Unfortunately, the same cannot be said for her next leading man, Don "Red" Barry of 1941's *The Phantom Cowboy*. "Don Barry was very difficult. A little man; a short man, with a very big disposition! He used to stand on a box when we did our scenes together! One day, he didn't have the box and I asked, 'Where's your box?' Now I didn't mean anything by it; I just wondered where it was, so we could shoot the scene. Don stormed to the main office, up to Herbert Yates' office, the head of Republic. 'That Miss Carroll doesn't take her work very seriously.' To which Yates replied, 'Don't ever worry about Virginia Carroll.' I was married to Ralph Byrd, a big star for Republic at the time [*laughs*]!

It struck me so funny. I didn't get mad about it! But that was Don Barry!"

The Phantom Cowboy was directed by "little Georgie Sherman. A nice little guy." Milburn Stone was the film's heavy. "Milburn was one of the funniest men you'd ever know. This was before he became famous on *Gunsmoke*. He'd wait until I would get ready for my closeup. Then he'd make faces; cross his eyes and roll his eyes, making them go around and around like Harry Ritz! He'd break me up! And I was supposed to be crying or doing something serious! Years later, I saw Milburn at a party and he was still doing those things [*laughs*]!"

Virginia's next oater was over at Co-

Tex Ritter and Virginia Carroll have the drop on land grabbers Tris Coffin and Joe McGuinn in *Prairie Gunsmoke* (1942).

lumbia, supporting "Wild Bill" Elliott and Tex Ritter in *Prairie Gunsmoke* (1942). "Bill Elliott was tall; also he was pretty quiet. I have a lot of stills of Bill and me and also of Johnny Mack and me. Tex Ritter was extremely nice; he's the father of John Ritter, the comedy actor!"

When making *Raiders of the West* in 1942, Virginia sighs, "The shooting was so fast, I hardly remember Lee Powell or the picture at all. A girl has so little to do—a couple of days and my part was finished!"

Beginning in the 1940s, Virginia began to mix leads with character/support roles, such as her part in the bigger budgeted *Bad Men of Tombstone* (1949). "That

was a small role—so I recall little about it. And I don't recall Whip Wilson [*Crashing Thru* (1949)] at all! If I was working, it was fine; if I didn't work, I didn't care. Some parts I might only work a couple of hours! I was not ambitious, and Ralph didn't want me to work. He was jealous." Nevertheless, Virginia continued to appear frequently, bridging the gap from movies to TV. Then her husband Ralph Byrd died in 1952 at the youthful age of 43. "The newspapers said he died of a heart attack, but actually he died of cancer in the Veterans Hospital in Sawtell."

Virginia did remarry, but reflects, "I've been widowed for most of my life.

From 1957 until his death in 1969, I was married to Lloyd McLean, who was a cameraman at 20th Century–Fox. He did mainly process work. Like Ralph, he also died of cancer."

As for friends in the industry, "I was friends with Gene Autry and Roy Rogers, and I was very good friends with Dale Evans. I did several movies and TV shows with Roy and Dale. In one of their TV things, 'Desert Fugitive,' I played the heavy! Dale and I had a fight scene in it. We both laughed so hard, because we were such good friends. Also because her brassiere broke when we were doing it! It was really awful [*laughs*]. She said, 'They'll have to do something about this!' [*laughs*]. Dale was full-breasted, you see. She had a great sense of humor!

"I loved Roy. My husband Ralph and Roy Rogers were under contract to Republic at the same time. Ralph came home one day and said, 'I made a test with a young kid, but he needs to change his name. His name is Leonard Slye!' Of course, his name *was* changed—to Roy Rogers. Everybody was so friendly in those days—there was no jealousy (except from Ralph in regards to my working!).

"Roy and Dale were attracted to one another from the beginning," Virginia remembers. "They had a tragic life, losing their only child, and two of their adopted ones were killed. It's unbelievable, the things that happened to them.

"My best friend back then was Maxine Doyle, who was married to director William Witney. I'm godmother to John Witney, their son," Virginia smiles. "Ralph and I, Maxine and Bill, and director John English and his wife, who wasn't in the business, palled around together. I'm still good friends with Bill and his current wife, Bev. There was another wife in between Bev and Maxine. Bev is wonderful! Bill's strokes have been so hard on her."

Where other actresses came and went, some relatively quickly, Virginia Carroll hung in there for 20 years, both in leads and support roles. A great compliment to a fine actress.

Virginia Carroll Western Filmography

Movies: *A Tenderfoot Goes West* (1937 Hoffberg)—Jack LaRue; *Oklahoma Terror* (1939 Monogram)—Jack Randall; *The Masked Rider* (1941 Universal)—Johnny Mack Brown; *The Phantom Cowboy* (1941 Republic)—Don Barry; *Raiders of the West* (1942 PRC)—Lee Powell, Art Davis, Bill Boyd; *Prairie Gunsmoke* (1942 Columbia)—Bill Elliott, Tex Ritter; *Heldorado* (1946 Republic)—Roy Rogers; *The Last Roundup* (1947 Columbia)—Gene Autry; *Spoilers of the Forest* (1947 Republic)—Rod Cameron; *Frontier Agent* (1948 Monogram)—Johnny Mack Brown; *Overland Trails* (1948 Monogram)—Johnny Mack Brown; *Triggerman* (1948 Monogram)—Johnny Mack Brown; *Bad Men of Tombstone* (1949 Allied Artists)—Barry Sullivan; *Crashing Thru* (1949 Monogram)—Whip Wilson; *Riders of the Whistling Pines* (1949 Columbia)—Gene Autry; *The Blazing Sun* (1950 Columbia)—Gene Autry.

Television: *Roy Rogers*, "Desert Fugitive" (1952); *Wild Bill Hickok*, "Cry Wolf" (1952); *Roy Rogers*, "Hard Luck Story" (1954); *Roy Rogers*, "Uncle Steve's Finish" (1955); *Roy Rogers*, "Quick Draw" (1955); *Roy Rogers*, "His Weight in Wildcats" (1956).

Phyllis Coates

Reporting on a Career

Although she's best known as reporter Lois Lane on TV's *Superman* series (which she played "like a horse with a bit in my mouth, hard driving") and as the star of the 1955 Republic serial, *Panther Girl of the Kongo*, Phyllis Coates has performed many roles in her acting career, including more than a few westerns.

"I was born in Wichita Falls, Texas, November 15, 1927. My father was a farmer and sheet metal worker. We later moved to Odessa, Texas, where I attended high school. It was so depressing, I couldn't wait to get out of there.

"When I was 16, my mother and I left Texas and I later attended college in California. My mother was hostess at a restaurant when we first came to California in 1942. Ken Murray was in there having lunch. I was there talking to my mother and he said, 'Hey, girlie. If you ever need a job, come around and see me. I'm Ken Murray and here's my card!' I'd never heard of Ken Murray. I didn't know what a vaudeville show was. My mother took me to the theater. Ken told me to pull up my skirt to see my legs and I almost fainted—prior to high school, I was in a convent at Catholic school. He poked me in the boob and said, 'Are those real?' I started to cry and he said, 'Oh, my God, what have I got here?' Anyway, I went to work for him and wore my graduation dress on stage until they made me a sexy, chorus girl-type dress. His Blackouts were, I think, the last of vaudeville. I was only 16 when I went to work for Ken, who'd been a stand-up comic. The show was loaded with vaudevillians—singers, dancers, acrobats, dog acts—you name it. And that did it. I decided to become an actress.

"Oh no, don't ask me that!" she exclaims when queried if Phyllis Coates is her real name. "My legal name is Gypsie Ann Evarts Stell. Can you imagine that? The nuns called me Ann but everyone who knows me well calls me Gypsie. My mother, poor dear, was crazy as a loon. Maybe Texas made her crazy. I was born when she was 15. She'd seen the name in a true confession magazine—a story about a horse named Gypsie. And the Ann Evarts part was after a girlfriend of my father's. The whole thing is bizarre but it's on the birth certificate. I went on an interview at MGM to see a producer. He asked, 'Where are you from?' I answered, 'Texas,' with my terrible accent. He asked, 'What's your name?' I said, 'Gypsie Ann Evarts Stell.' He said, 'Oh, shit! You can't go in to read with a name like that.' He looked through some books on his desk and said, 'Coates. Coates. Phyllis. Phyllis Coates. Tell them your name is Phyllis Coates.' He's the one that laid that awful name on me."

In the beginning, her first film work

Serial heavies John Day and Mike Ragan (who was also known as Holly Bane) have the drop on Phyllis—the *Panther Girl of the Kongo*—in Chaper Two of the 1955 Republic serial.

was in several Joe McDoakes one-reel comedies. "I'd done a play at an acting school. Based on my work there, I was offered a stock contract at Warner Bros. and they placed me in the series. The Joe McDoakes shorts were broad, slapstick comedy. That's where I really got the feel for comedy. I loved it. George O'Hanlon was a very funny man."

Since she was from Texas, could we assume Phyllis was a good rider, and ready for westerns? "No, I was a lousy rider. I only got on a horse when I had to, and got off as soon as I could. I liked stage work best. There is nothing like working to a live audience. For instance, making serials was just a job. Really, it was very hard

work. We had a tight schedule and limited budget. We had to work hard and fast."

Phyllis made over 15 B-westerns in the 1950s as well as three serials (*Jungle Drums of Africa* [1953]; *Gunfighters of the Northwest* [1954]; *Panther Girl of the Kongo*) but told us the difference in making them was very little. "We would shoot a western in about six days and a serial in about three weeks. Basically, they were the same type of film. Jock Mahoney was in one of those western serials. He was great! I'm sure everyone knows Jock is a fun-loving guy. I enjoyed working with him. He was a great stuntman and horseman."

She particularly recalls *Panther Girl of the Kongo.* "I have a picture of myself with

WILD BILL ELLIOTT in FARGO

with
PHYLLIS COATES
MYRON HEALEY
FUZZY KNIGHT

PRODUCED BY   DIRECTED BY
VINCENT M. FENNELLY · Lewis D. Collins
STORY AND SCREENPLAY BY
Jack DeWitt and Joseph Poland SILVERMINE PRODUCTION

Veteran sidekick Fuzzy Knight and "the best cowboy" (according to Phyllis), Bill Elliott, protect our leading lady from harm in *Fargo* (1952).

Emma, the elephant. She was great. I told the director [Franklin Adreon], 'Listen. Once I get up on this elephant, I'm not coming down. You may as well shoot everything you can today.' Those things have hairs on them about three or four inches long. They're like Brillo, and I had that short costume on. It was tough. I mean, they worked you to death."

Phyllis made the bulk of her westerns at Monogram with Johnny Mack Brown, Whip Wilson and Bill Elliott. "Most of the cowboys were great. Johnny Mack Brown was a very sweet, loving man, but probably the best cowboy, even better than some guys I'd worked with who were bigger names and better looking, was Wild Bill Elliott. He was the best cowboy. He

patterned himself after William S. Hart. The only cowboy I ever worked with that was no fun was that awful guy, Whip Wilson. All he had was his whip—and his ego. I would do two westerns back to back for Monogram. Then I'd have to take a week off and go to Palm Springs and recuperate. It was awful. They lit the horse—they didn't give a damn about the leading lady. You held onto your hat and sort of went with the flow. We shot over in that awful Monogram studio. It really was the ass-end of the world."

After nearly ten years toiling in B's, Phyllis began to receive better parts on TV and, finally, in an A-western, *Cattle Empire* (1958) with Joel McCrea. "I admired Joel McCrea. He and his wife, Frances

Dee, had a long and happy marriage. Joel was very cute. He asked me to go to dinner one night and you don't turn down the leading man. It was really funny. He said, 'I want to apologize to you.' I said, 'For what? Whatever could you have done to offend me?' He said, 'I wanted you to know I wouldn't offer to take you to bed.' Well, my jaw dropped down. I didn't know what to say. He said he was very much in love with his wife, and he always made that clear to his leading ladies. I thought I'd die."

In the Allan "Rocky" Lane film, *El Paso Stampede* (1953), Phyllis was blonde, and in a Whip Wilson movie she was a brunette. She told me, "It was because of my role in the *Superman* series. I didn't want people to see me in films and relate me to the Lois Lane character. So, I changed my hair style and color so I would not be typed as that character. Now as to the way I wore my hair as Lois Lane… [*Sour sounding*] Ooohhh … that had to do with Mrs. Bob Maxwell … Jessica Maxwell [*laughs*]. It was pretty funny, wasn't it? [*laughs*]." (Maxwell was the *Superman* series producer.)

The popular *Superman* TV series (1952–1957) starred George Reeves. "George was a very human sort of guy, complicated, but sweet. Also a heavy drinker. And his lady, Toni Mannix, was a great gal but a party animal. Unfortunately, he was typed as Superman and couldn't find work after the series. He took his own life. No one imagined the interest (in *Superman*) would last this long. It's like a cult." (Whether Reeves committed suicide or was murdered is still a subject of debate.) "When people start talking about it, I just have to get into a different mindset. It's out of their concern and their love for George that it bothers them. There's never been a closure for people who care. I don't know if there ever will be."

Phyllis' good looks and hard-driving realistic-reporter approach (along with her unparalleled blood-curdling scream when in danger) made the first-season *Superman* episodes far superior to those that followed with Noel Neill as Lois Lane. So why did Phyllis leave a successful series? "I had another life. I had a lot of personal problems and a child that was considered, at that time, a cripple. She was born with a congenital hip. At the time, there was rather a crude medical procedure to take care of her. She was in a cast for about a year and a half. I used to take her to the studio. The grips would help me care for her. It was like a big family in those days. Not like it is today. There was just so much going on. At the time we did *Superman* it was really the bottom of the barrel. When I first met George, he asked me to come to his dressing room, he made us a martini, proposed a toast and said, 'Well, Phyllis, to the bottom of the barrel.' That's the way television was considered at that time. But we both needed the work. Well, a little voice inside of me just said, 'Get out.' Also, the original producer, Bob Maxwell, left to do *Lassie*, and was replaced by Whit Ellsworth. Whit was kind of vanilla pudding compared to Maxwell. Whit came in and whipped the show up into a pudding. My contract had expired and they offered me about five times what I was getting to stay. Whit, George, everybody really pushed. But I signed to do a pilot with Jack Carson and Allen Jenkins. I'd always had the hots to play comedy. We did the pilot for MCA; shortly thereafter, Jack got sick, so it never followed through. That's why I left, not 'cause I was mad or anything like that. I loved George, I loved the crew. They offered me a large increase in salary to stay, but I really wanted out."

Noel Neill replaced Phyllis as Lois Lane but it was not an easy transition. "We never became friendly. I tried. George tried to introduce us. She took it more

Phyllis and Joel McCrea survey their *Cattle Empire* (1958). Joel was married to another of our Ladies of the Western, Frances Dee.

seriously I think than I did. She had it written into some kind of contract that she would never appear with me in person. I just backed off. It could have been a lot of fun. I don't understand that thinking, but, that's the way some people are."

Phyllis was on the *Superman* set one famous day when the wires broke holding George up in a flying position. "Yes, I saw this ... and it was the funniest visual... I got hysterical laughing! The only time George ever got mad at me, 'cause I couldn't stop laughing [*laughs*]. Everything came loose ... his rubber muscles... [*laughs*]. He wouldn't speak to me all day! It was the funniest sight ... but that was the end of the wires [*laughs*]! By the way, if anyone has a still from *Superman and the*

Mole-Men [1951], you might notice, the weapon the mole men used is an *Electrolux vacuum cleaner* [*laughs*]!

"While we were filming *Superman*, Robert Shayne, who played Inspector Henderson in the series, was arrested on the set for being a card-carrying Communist. One morning George and I were going down to the set and we could see Bob in the distance with two guys on either side of him. George said, 'That's the heat!' He meant law or police. Sure enough, it was two FBI agents. [Producer Robert] Maxwell, George and I got together and tried to save Bob. His career was wrecked for years. An ex-wife of his turned him in during the McCarthy thing. We all wrote letters and pleaded but it took years. This was during the McCarthy era and there was a big Communist scare. Bob and many other Hollywood personalities had their careers ruined."

Accidents on a set are rare, but they do happen, as Phyllis explains: "Once while filming, I missed my mark. We had marks on the floor to show us where to stop. In one of the [fight] scenes, I went too far and actually got slugged. It wasn't funny at the time, but we had a good laugh later."

Some of Phyllis' western TV work was for Gene Autry. "Gene's company produced *Death Valley Days* at the start [1952]. I did the first episode of that series ["How Death Valley Got Its Name"]. We shot in Death Valley in August! We lost a cameraman, an assistant director, some grips ... it was so hot, people were just falling over. But it was beautiful. And it was a good episode ... it was exciting. They put a lot of money into that first production. I got a note from Mr. Autry, because everybody had been passing out and had to be shipped back home. Other people had to come replace them. He said, 'Hang in there, girl.' I've still got the note!"

Every actor or actress has favorite pieces of work, and Phyllis is no different. "I enjoyed doing an *Untouchables* (1959–1963) with a French director. I was not as fortunate as some actors... I didn't get rehearsal time. At Monogram we made 'quickies.' We made an entire film in six days. There was no second take. If you took a second take, everybody pouted and got mad. They lit the cowboys and lit the cowboy's hat and the cowboy's horse [*laughs*]. It was that kind of quickie stuff. So, when I got to work with a good director on an *Untouchables* where he took time and went in for some fine points in acting ... I loved it!"

Phyllis worked on *Rawhide* (1959–1965) and lived in Carmel where Clint Eastwood was mayor. Surely she has some Eastwood stories. "If I told the Clint Eastwood stories, I'd have a lawsuit on my hands [*laughs*]! But he made a good mayor, everybody absolutely adores him. Carmel is overrun with people looking for Clint. He did what he went in to do [as mayor], got out and a friend of his is in now. I did two episodes of *Rawhide* ... Charles Marquis Warren directed. Actually, I didn't have any scenes with Clint. I did a play which Maggie Eastwood, Clint Eastwood's former wife, sponsored—*Love Letters* with Alan Young. It got great reviews and played to a big convention hall in Carmel."

Over the years, what co-worker did Phyllis respect the most? With a sigh, she states again, "I did low-budget things. But when you work with those directors ... Tommy Carr, George Blair, Lee Sholem ... they were guys who knew how to make a movie and knew what they were doing. They were all action guys. There was no time for analyzing or rehearsing. They got in and shot a movie. I liked 'em all. I did enjoy working with Ida Lupino as a director on an *Untouchables*. As far as actors, there were a lot of them ... George Reeves, Jock Mahoney, Walter Reed ... it's hard to pick out specific people. It was a combination of people that made things work."

Phyllis' marriage to director Norman Takar ended in 1965, leaving her to raise a 15-year-old daughter and eight-year-old son. She remarried a doctor but declined more film work. "My husband didn't understand the movie business, so I gave it up and helped him run his business." However, once again single, "After a few years I came out of a long retirement to resume my acting career. I completed a film called *Goodnight, Sweet Marilyn* where I played Marilyn Monroe's mother. It's a good part and I'm very pleased with my performance. I was Lois Lane's [Teri Hatcher] mom on the recent Superman series—*Lois and Clark* [1993–1997] ... and did some commercials. Right now I don't have any work planned. I just don't like to travel any more. If somebody came up with a good 'granny-gone-wrong' part, I'd love to do that. Maybe if they'd come up and shoot in the Carmel-Monterey area [*laughs*]."

Phyllis Coates
Western Filmography

Movies: *Outlaws of Texas* (1950 Monogram)—Whip Wilson; *Canyon Raiders* (1951 Monogram)—Whip Wilson; *Longhorn* (1951 Monogram)—Bill Elliott; *Man from Sonora* (1951 Monogram)—Johnny Mack Brown; *Nevada Badmen* (1951 Monogram)—Whip Wilson; *Oklahoma Justice* (1951 Monogram)—Johnny Mack Brown; *So You Want to Be a Cowboy* (1951 Warner Bros. short)—George O'Hanlon; *Stage to Blue River* (1951 Monogram)—Whip Wilson; *Canyon Ambush* (1952 Monogram)—Johnny Mack Brown; *The Gunman* (1952 Monogram)—Whip Wilson; *Fargo* (1952 Monogram)—Bill Elliott; *The Maverick* (1952 Allied Artists)—Bill Elliott; *Scorching Fury* (1952 Fraser)—Richard Devon; *Wyoming Roundup* (1952 Monogram)—Whip Wilson; *El Paso Stampede* (1953 Republic)—Allan "Rocky" Lane; *Marshal of Cedar Rock* (1953 Republic)—Allan "Rocky" Lane; *Topeka* (1953 Allied Artists)—Bill Elliott; *Blood Arrow* (1958 Regal/Fox)—Scott Brady; *Cattle Empire* (1958 20th Century–Fox)—Joel McCrea.

Serial: *Gunfighters of the Northwest* (1954 Columbia)—Jock Mahoney.

Television: *Cisco Kid*, "Wedding Blackmail" (1950); *Range Rider*, "Trail of the Lawless" (1951); *Cisco Kid*, "Haven for Heavies" (1951); *Cisco Kid*, "Phony Sheriff" (1951); *Cisco Kid*, "Uncle Disinherits Niece" (1951); *Death Valley Days*, "How Death Valley Got Its Name" (1952); *Range Rider*, "Pale Rider" (1952); *Lone Ranger*, "Stage to Estacado" (1953); *Lone Ranger*, "Perfect Crime" (1953); *Kit Carson*, "Riders of the Hooded League" (1954); *Kit Carson*, "Hermit of Indian Ridge" (1954); *Lone Ranger*, "Woman in the White Mask" (1955); *Frontier*, "King of the Dakotas" (1955); *Death Valley Days*, "Solomon in All His Glory" (1956); *Gunsmoke*, "Wild West" (1958); *Tales of Wells Fargo*, "Alias Jim Hardie" (1958); *Desilu Playhouse*, "Trial at Devil's Canyon" (1959); *Black Saddle*, "Client: Dawes" (1959); *Rawhide*, "Incident of the Judas Trap" (1959); *Sheriff of Cochise*, "Woman Escapes" (1959); *Rawhide*, "The Little Fishes" (1961); *Gunslinger*, "Johnny Sergeant" (1961); *Tales of Wells Fargo*, "Bitter Vengeance" (1961); *Death Valley Days*, "A Gun Is Not a Gentleman" (1963); *Death Valley Days*, "Lucky Cow" (1964); *Gunsmoke*, "Homecoming" (1964); *The Virginian*, "Smile of a Dragon" (1964); *Death Valley Days*, "Left Hand Is Damned" (1964).

Louise Currie

Serial Queen and Western Heroine

Louise Currie—the name conjures up images of a gorgeous blonde heroine, facing perils from the Scorpion and his henchmen in the classic 1941 *Adventures of*

Kirby Grant and Gene Garrick are with Louise in her favorite western role as Buckskin Jane Sawyer, complete with whip and gun, in *Gun Town* **(1946).**

Captain Marvel, considered by many the greatest serial ever made! Another chapterplay, *The Masked Marvel*, followed in 1943.

Educated at Sarah Lawrence College in Bronxville, New York, Louise decided she was interested in films. "Max Reinhardt, who had discovered so many famous stars, opened a workshop in Hollywood and I was very fortunate because he felt I had a certain amount of talent. I studied there for two years and he starred me in many of the shows at his theater."

The talented actress appeared in scores of films in the 1940s, finally leaving the business in the early 1950s. Between comedies with Lum and Abner and mysteries with Kent Taylor, there were westerns, with everybody from Bob Steele and Charles Starrett to Tim Holt, Gene Autry, Kirby Grant and Eddie Dean. The first, *Billy the Kid Outlawed* (1940), was followed only months later with *Billy the Kid's Gun Justice* (1940). "They weren't made simultaneously. It's just a coincidence. Bob Steele was sharp and busy; hustling, bustling. He was a real fighting cowboy, ready for a fight at a moment's notice. He was the opposite of Charles Starrett [*The Pinto Kid*, 1941]. Charles was a handsome cowboy, so good-looking. But he looked like an Eastern dude, not the cowboy type. He seemed to be having a hard time riding his horse, just like I was. I got to know him very well, but I felt he should have played the visiting Easterner, rather than being a cowboy. I felt the same for myself. I *was* an Eastern college girl, from Sarah Lawrence, so I was out-of-place as well."

Tim Holt starred in a well-mounted series of oaters at RKO, and one of his best was *Dude Cowboy* (1941). "Tim Holt was really kind of a lady killer. Very handsome, very personable. His riding was more realistic. He knew how to ride, he had his own ranch. It made him more comfortable in the saddle. He was a ladies' man cowboy—very attractive. Both Marjorie Reynolds and I got to flirt with Tim. I don't think either of us won him—the girls in westerns seldom did. And I liked Helen Holmes. She was so good. I got a kick out of her. She had been a big serial and western star back in silent days. That movie was fun, not just a rough-and-tumble western like the Bob Steele's. This one had a story to it."

As for *Stardust on the Sage* (1942), "My part was so 'ick.' I didn't have enough to do. It was one of those 'hanging on the garden gate' type of roles. Gene Autry was very professional—and it was a slick production. It's just I was not too keen on my part." When told Autry and Edith Fellows played tricks on one another, Louise stated, "I intimidated Gene. I held my ground. There was no nonsense with me—no romance either. I was more sophisticated than his other leading ladies, perhaps. Gene was very proficient; there were no tricks. How do you argue with success? He had a great business head. He knew what to sell and how to sell it. He sold himself extremely well—something that most of the others, unfortunately, never could do."

Concerning Hopalong Cassidy and 1944's *Forty Thieves*, "I had a good time with Jimmy Rogers. I was a friend of his sister Mary, from my days back east. So I got to know Jimmy quite well. I kept up with Mary for some time. She has since passed away, but because of her, I struck up a new friendship on the film with Jimmy. He was a very special person. Hopalong, I didn't get to know much. Isn't that awful!?"

Wild West (1946) was Louise's only color western. "I remember Eddie Dean—a nice-looking singer, and he had talent. He could sing—very well. And his sidekick Roscoe Ates could stutter with the best of them!"

Kirby Grant's *Gun Town* (1946) is probably the star's favorite western film. "I adored *Gun Town*. It was a chance to really do something! I was the Marjorie Main type—Buckskin Jane Sawyer. I learned to do things with the bullwhip; they taught me how—and that was wonderful. I worked the buckboard—I liked doing all of that. I had to bring this stagecoach in and come to a very abrupt stop. Then I realized the man, who's hanging on the side, is the hero. I have to grab my bullwhip and rescue him. Naturally, my double brought it up comparatively close in a dead run, then I had to get on it and bring the stagecoach up to where we stopped. That was quite a trick but I was young and healthy, fortunately. I was very lucky not to have any accidents. It was exciting and fascinating. I was part of the action. I was running that town with the bullwhip. Lyle Talbot was in it. I remembered him as a matinee idol in Oklahoma, my home state [she was born Louise Gunter in Oklahoma City on an April 7]. He came to the local theater in a play when I was a little girl. All the women thought he was just fabulous. Now here I was, a grown woman, playing in a picture with this man. *Gun Town* is really a special picture. It had more story—it wasn't just about chases and horses. Kirby Grant was an attractive young man—he was nice and fun to work with. Most of the westerns didn't mean anything, because I couldn't get my teeth sunk into them. But

William "Hopalong Cassidy" Boyd, Jimmy Rogers (son of Will Rogers), Louise and Robert Frazer console Andy Clyde, who has obviously made a mess of things in *Forty Thieves* (1944).

in *Gun Town*, and *Dude Cowboy*, I thought I really did a good job. The parts weren't superfluous. The others were kind of boring to do, and as a result, they are kind of a blur in my mind."

It is definitely the Tom Tyler chapterplay *Adventures of Captain Marvel* (1941) for which Louise is best remembered. "We worked fast with little or no time for retakes. Every actor was required to know his lines and be willing to work from early morning 'til late at night. The situations were exciting. I didn't do much except be a victim on most of the cliffhangers. Tom Tyler was a wonderful, but quiet man ... a nice fellow, attractive, a good person, but he was shy! Frank Coghlan, Jr., Billy Benedict and I had lots of

fun together, but Tom never seemed to join us in our good times. Those two boys were very talented, super to work with. They really knew what they were doing. Such fine young actors. We chatted, laughed and enjoyed working together. Tom stayed by himself, but again, he couldn't have been nicer. It's just too bad he didn't become pals like Frank and Billy and I did. Dave Sharpe did some doubling for me on *Captain Marvel*. He wasn't a tall man, so he could be put in women's clothes, then at a distance he would look the same. He was an incredible double and could do almost anything. He was so masculine, so virile, that it really makes you laugh if you think he might be a double for a woman. I also had a woman double but

Gene Autry, Louise and Bill Henry in *Stardust on the Sage* (1942). Henry was the husband of another of our Ladies of the Western, Barbara Knudson.

I don't recall her name." The serial had two directors, William Witney and John English. "One would be working on location and the other in the studio. I presume that was only to save Republic money by doing it faster."

Comparing A-films to the many serials and westerns she did, Louise says, "Obviously, they must get more quality in an A-picture. I was in a couple of A-pictures [such as *Citizen Kane*, 1941 and *Call Out the Marines*, 1942] and to me it was so slow it was almost excruciating to sit and sit for days to do one small scene when you could have done it in 15 minutes in a B movie. Sometimes you wonder if it isn't more spontaneous when you don't just go over and over a scene. I don't like to waste

time, so maybe that's why I enjoyed doing pictures that were fast."

Stuntman Tom Steele worked closely with Louise on Republic's serial *The Masked Marvel* (1943). "Tom Steele was a very handsome, energetic person—so charming, so pleasant and interesting to talk with. I enjoyed his company on the set! A really nice, nice, nice man. I played a secretary who tells people what to do—I enjoyed that part of the serial! In *Adventures of Captain Marvel*, Tom Tyler was always rescuing me and carrying me off [*laughs*]. Tom Steele, however, never did that. I didn't have those cliffhanger hazards on *The Masked Marvel*. Tom Steele and I just had dialogue together, and, as a result, I didn't get to see his stuntman prowess at work! I frankly thought all the young men favored each other [David Bacon, Rod Bacon, Richard Clarke, Bill Healy]; all of them were very attractive — and they were hired because of their resemblance to one another. Therefore, you were supposed to have trouble figuring out which one was the real Masked Marvel. They were trying to mix you up. But Tom Steele was much slimmer than David Bacon, who was supposed to be the Masked Marvel. Their physiques didn't match at all [*laughs*]."

"On a sad note, David Bacon was murdered, just after we completed the serial. He had picked up a hitchhiker, who stabbed him in the back and robbed him. The first few chapters were playing in the theaters, but he never got to see the ending. He was gone before the final chapters were sent to theaters!"

Spencer Gordon Bennet, who began as a director in the latter days of silents, helmed *The Masked Marvel*. Louise "liked him personally. I think maybe some of the young men had never acted before this, so Bennet had his hands full." She recalls a good time doing that serial. "It was too speedy for him to give me any direction, so I cannot compare him to other directors in that way. Spencer was fun."

Louise believes, "As an actress, I think my part in *Masked Marvel* was far better. I'm in almost all the scenes. My part is larger and it made a bit more sense. I wonder when you look at *Captain Marvel*, why I'm even in it. I guess they wanted a female to be rescued at the end of each chapter. But I think for the finished product, *Captain Marvel* was a better serial overall."

Married in 1948, she and her husband owned Louise Currie Interiors for years after her film work ended. Today, recently widowed (her husband, actor John Good, died in 1998), Louise frequently travels to Europe. Her best friend, actress Jane Randolph, sometimes accompanies Louise on her jaunts.

"I'm grateful for the life I've had and the continued interest fans have shown me. I believe it was because I made so many different types of films and played so many different roles that made it all fun."

Louise Currie
Western Filmography

Movies: *Billy the Kid Outlawed* (1940 PRC) — Bob Steele; *Billy the Kid's Gun Justice* (1940 PRC) — Bob Steele; *Dude Cowboy* (1941 RKO) — Tim Holt; *Pinto Kid* (1941 Columbia) — Charles Starrett; *Stardust on the Sage* (1942 Republic) — Gene Autry; *Forty Thieves* (1944 United Artists) — William Boyd; *Gun Town* (1946 Universal) — Kirby Grant; *Wild West* (1946 PRC) — Eddie Dean (reissue/edit — *Prairie Outlaws*).

Frances Dee

Mrs. Joel McCrea

Lovely Frances Dee is a legendary actress from Hollywood's Golden Age of the 1930s and 1940s. Born November 15, 1909, in Los Angeles, the star actually grew up elsewhere. "My father got a job in Illinois, so when I was a little girl we moved to Chicago, where I attended public schools, plus a year and two semesters at the University of Chicago."

Returning to California, Frances soon got work as a screen extra. "As did Joel. We both started that way. In his case, he began as a wrangler. When they'd shoot a movie across the street from where he lived, he'd ask to be hired on as wrangler. Then he'd get an extra's job as one of the posse."

Frances soon landed a contract at Paramount. "My first role was a bit in Buddy Rogers' *Follow Thru* [1930]. I had one line and had to dance, and I can't dance." Frances hit it big fairly early when assigned the leading role opposite Maurice Chevalier in *Playboy of Paris* (1930). The following year, she was seen opposite Richard Arlen in her first western, *Caught* (1931). "That was my second or third picture. I had signed at Paramount for $50 a week. There were no guild rules then—Screen Actors Guild hadn't been formed. So they could loan you out to another studio and work you 18 hours a day—and they did! I did *Caught* at Paramount in the day and was doing a picture with Douglas

Fairbanks, Jr., at Warner Bros. at night! I'd get up at four A.M. to get to makeup so we could leave the studio at five to go on location. I was slapping my face to get awake. I enjoyed very, very much the cast of *Caught*, especially Louise Dresser. She was such a professional. I'd sit and watch her and Tom Kennedy. I learned from them—practically the only acting I had done was in high school plays. *Caught* was shot in three weeks on location at the Paramount Ranch in the Valley, also used in *Wells Fargo* [1937]. It was still there a few years ago. In the day it was *hot* yet at night it was *cold*—I muddled through that picture. In fact, you can see breath coming from Richard Arlen and myself in one night scene! But, I thought it had an interesting ending to it."

After *Caught*, Frances wanted to perfect her craft. "After a couple of those squeaky-voice things, Paramount sent me to a vocal coach, to get rid of my midwestern accent and that high-pitched voice." Regarding her second western, *Wells Fargo*, Frances relates, "That was one of Paramount's biggest pictures, unlike *Caught*, which was one of its tiniest."

Frances was freelancing. "I left Paramount, went to RKO, then signed a three-picture pact with Paramount. *Wells Fargo* was the first picture Joel and I did together after we were married. Frank Lloyd, one of the best directors in Hollywood, was at the

Frances and husband Joel McCrea at home on their ranch.

helm. He had done *Mutiny on the Bounty* [1935] a couple of years earlier. Recently there was a party at the Hollywood Museum, and a little girl came up to my son Jody and told him she was Frank Lloyd's granddaughter. Alma Lloyd, Frank's daughter, was in *If I Were King* (1938) with me. I was deeply fond of Frank as a man as well as a director. He directed *If I Were King*. On *Wells Fargo*, Lloyd called everyone in and told us exactly what he had planned for the entire day. It made a tremendous difference to everyone—he was like a general. This went for extras, costume people, whomever. We respected Frank Lloyd; we all enjoyed everything, as everyone was a part of it. Joel said he had not seen this before—or since. There was a scene, shot at the Paramount ranch, where Joel brings in the mail. It's an important part of the story, a winter scene, but shot in the summer, and it was *hot!* I have a daughter in the picture, and she is a *big* girl—Lloyd wanted me to hold her up, and in that heat! I was wearing velvet—so I was really burning up!"

Asked specifically about working with Joel, Miss Dee smiles, "He didn't like working with me, although I enjoyed working with him. I'd get bossy [*laughs*]; I'd sneak over to his dressing room. I never felt he reached his potential, so I'd say, 'What if you did this or what if you did that?' I'd then go to the rushes—and see Joel had wiped me off the screen! I was so busy thinking about him I didn't think about myself! Joel never gave me any ideas—he thought it should be left up to the actor."

Some time after *Wells Fargo* was released, there was a screening at the studio. "We never took the boys to anything but the kiddie pictures, so we took them to see it—Jody was six and David four at this time. They sat quietly, and at the very end, David got to wiping his eyes. Daddy said, 'Are you all right?' David cried and cried. Joel picked him up—clinging him, but he was not consolable. We never knew what it was—unless it was our growing old at the end that upset him in some way. We generally didn't let them see our films—we thought it would confuse them."

Four Faces West (1948) was Frances' next western, and her next picture with Joel. "The director wanted me, not 'Papa.' [Producer] Harry Sherman was always busy doing things. The wardrobe man, Ivan, was Swedish, and new to this coun-

try. He would say ware-y instead of wear-y. Joel said Ivan told him, 'When Frances works with you, you are not so ware-y' [*laughs*]. Papa loved this. It became a family thing to say, from then on. I was not bossing so much on this one! We shot it on location for two months between Gallup and Grants, New Mexico—at 200-foot-tall Inscription Rock. 'Paso Por Aqui' [Passed This Way]—that inscription was on that rock—it's shown in the film, which was reportedly a true story [based on a *Saturday Evening Post* story]. The rest of it was shot at the California Studios, where Harry Sherman had his offices, across the street from Paramount. I also did *Private Affairs of Bel Ami* (1947) there; Ingrid Bergman's *Arch of Triumph* (1948) was shot there. It is now the Raleigh Studios." (Portions of several Hopalong Cassidy films were also lensed there.) "Good ol' 'Pop' Sherman," Frances grinned. "He was high on Joel; they loved westerns, and Sherman didn't think Paramount did right by Joel. Pop Sherman was rugged looking, with white hair. An outdoor man, an athlete—he was in those long bicycle marathons. He always liked bicycle riding—even in later years. He was charming, strong-looking, tall, and couldn't have been nicer to work with. He included everyone in on things. He was a very expansive kind of man. His personality suited his appearance."

Frances Dee's last feature to date is 1954's *Gypsy Colt*, shot in Technicolor. "I was four months along with my last child, Peter, who is 20 years younger than Jody! I loved working with Ward Bond and that darling little girl, Donna Corcoran. I could relate to that film—especially the water shortage. Someone was always out of water."

As for some personal data, Frances Dee met Joel McCrea at the beach, where Paramount had her doing publicity photos in January 1933 for June bathing suit

Joseph Calleia, Frances and Joel McCrea in a scene from *Four Faces West* (1948), shot at El Morro National Monument, better known as Inscription Rock, located between Grants and Gallup, New Mexico.

ads. "We were at Santa Monica Pier, and a tall tan man ran down to that cold water and jumped in! Someone said it was Joel McCrea, the RKO movie star, and they wanted to get a still taken of us both. As a coincidence, he had just seen me in a picture a few nights before and said he'd like to meet me. I teased him about all of this later—but he apologized because he had a light beard. He said he'd just gotten up at three in the afternoon, and was exercising his horses. I knew he went with the *in* crowd; I'd read he played polo with Will Rogers; so I was 'turned off.' He asked to come see me, but I held back. I thought I wouldn't know which fork to use. He wanted to bring a book by my house, a couple of weeks later, and he suggested a party. I still held back. Finally, a month later, we both were assigned to *Silver Cord*

[1933], with Joel opposite Irene Dunne and me paired with Eric Linden. We worked late one night, and Joel took me to dinner. We started seeing each other. I then learned he slept no later than 7:00— he lived at home and his mother would clear the table at 7:30. Joel wouldn't miss a meal! He took me to his ranch—which is where I still live today. What I had thought were polo ponies turned out to be two cow horses! I asked him about the polo, and he said, 'Those are Will's horses.' Incidentally, it was Will Rogers who challenged Joel to buy that ranch!" Shortly thereafter, the two stars were engaged. "Just after *Silver Cord*, I was doing *Little Women* [1933] with Katharine Hepburn— and during that film Joel proposed. We were married five months later."

Frances was on location in New York

for *Keep 'Em Rolling* (1934) with Walter Huston. "I had a week off and was staying at the Waldorf Astoria—it was the most exciting city in the world. We were married in Rye, New York, and were honeymooning until I had to go back to work. After our children were six or seven, every year Joel and I would go back to New York once a year—in the autumn. We would see some Broadway shows, and go up to Stonybrook, Long Island."

Frances says she and Joel were quite compatible. "We liked the same things, and I thought I'd like being on a ranch. The kids begged us to let them attend the little school, where they could ride their ponies to school. But the nearest neighbor was two miles away. I thought I was in exile! My children were spread out—Jody was born in 1934 [I was already showing when I had to do retakes on *Of Human Bondage* (1934)], David in 1937 and Peter in 1954! When you're older, you are more patient. On the ranch, I would make jelly … we'd associate with the other ranchers. I'd ride a horse to see Mabel, a good friend whose mother had homesteaded their place. Mabel taught me to make enchiladas. She had a good and true saying— 'Men are men—if you don't baby them, someone else will!'"

A lot of their Hollywood friends would come out to the ranch for the weekend. "Gary Cooper and his wife came; even Alfred Hitchcock! Hitch loved to come— and get butter! We made it ourselves!"

Did Frances *ever* get used to the ranch? "I still live there! When the kids were in high school, we moved to Beverly Hills. It was then I realized, 'I gotta get back to the real country!' Finally, we sold all the cattle and half of the ranch. When we moved to Conejo Valley, there were 90 people; now there are 90,000. Our cows were getting into other peoples' properties. The old house has been turned over to the city, as a park. I have moved into the old bunkhouse, which Joel used as his office."

About politics, she's quick to admit, "Joel was conservative, in the John Wayne way. He campaigned for conservatives. But that doesn't mean he *only* associated with them. Director John Berry [who was named a Communist along with 300 others in the 1950s], would often have lunch with Joel. Maybe Joel wanted to hear all about it [*laughs*]! The Cattlemen's Association wanted Joel to run for governor, but he didn't want the responsibility. Soon after that, Ronald Reagan got into politics!"

Asked about a John Wayne story, the star (who appears with "Duke" in 1941's *A Man Betrayed*, aka *Wheel of Fortune*) remembers, "There's a scene where we are at a nightclub and a big fight breaks out. John is supposed to put a tablecloth over me and carry me out. We thought it'd be fun if I did it—not a stunt double. I didn't think about it until we were actually doing it, but I was getting hit while he was carrying me! When the tablecloth was removed and the director saw I was under it, he was not at all pleased [*laughs*]!"

Remembering Joel McCrea's *This Is Your Life* induction into the Cowboy Hall of Fame in 1975, Frances smiles, "That was the highlight of his mature years. He was on the board for a long time, and president for two years. We'd go to Oklahoma twice a year for various duties. There was a wonderful artist who did his portrait.

"Joel preferred westerns," Frances continued, "He always wanted to do them. He'd say, 'If I have to do claptrap, I want to do it on a horse!' In fact, his two favorite pictures are *Ride the High Country* [1962] and *Stars in My Crown* [1950]. Whenever Joel was in a western, Jody would visit the set. He usually shows up as an extra. So, he's probably in *Four Faces West* [1948]."

Joel McCrea used a few horses over

Frances and Ward Bond, later the television star of *Wagon Train,* **in** *Gypsy Colt* **(1954).**

Beach pictures, which he found to be 'getting pretty silly,' Jody quit and went into ranching. Both borrowed the money to get started. Ranching, despite the Hollywood look at it, is long days and hard work with sometimes little or no profit—sort of like farming! Peter lives in Connecticut."

"Joel quit films after *Ride the High Country.* The Hays Office was gone and scripts were getting worse and worse. There would be new scripts coming in but Joel said he couldn't do that stuff. He did do *Mustang Country* (1974), a good clean picture, shot in Canada. He loved the story. He liked the director, and John Wayne's son, Patrick, was in it. It was not a moneymaker, however.

"Joel didn't change over the years," Frances laughs, "he just got more mellow. Women, however, get to be rascals [*laughs*]." The cowboys he liked? "John Wayne was first; then Gary Cooper—a friend since the 1930s; James Stewart and Randolph Scott, of course."

and over. "Yes, he had this big old horse, Diamond Jr.—he rode him a lot in pictures. I bought Diamond Jr. as a present. And Dollar—the favorite horse—he had a dollar sign on his hip—was in *Four Faces West,* among many others. Joel rode as a kid in Hollywood—in the canyons between Hollywood and the Valley. He and a friend would camp out. It was then, at age 16 or 17, he did a lot of wrangling and extra work, for pictures shooting near his house."

About her children, Frances relates, "David moved to New Mexico then Jody eventually settled there. This area is too grown-up for ranching. The brothers live 30 miles from each other, near Roswell. Jody has lots of dogs. After several of those

Other than ranching and acting, Frances says Joel always claimed, "'If I hadn't been a rancher, I'd have been a beach bum.' He loved body surfing. We went to Ventura, sometimes rented a beach house, and let the kids learn to surf. Typical Californians!" Joel McCrea was considered the best horseman in Hollywood, and he knew it. "That's because he was told it so often! He could do anything; he kept everything in tip-top shape. Although he's been gone eight years, I still have his old Chevy, which is in perfect condition!"

**Frances Dee
Western Filmography**

Movies: *Caught* (1931 Paramount)—Richard Arlen; *Wells Fargo* (1937 Para-mount)—Joel McCrea; *Four Faces West* (1948 United Artists)—Joel McCrea; *Gypsy Colt* (1954 MGM)—Ward Bond.

Edith Fellows

Child Actress

Of the dozens of child actresses to grace the silver screen, many critics proclaim the most talented was Edith Fellows, who is as fine a singer as she is a thespian! Debuting in a Charlie Chase silent, *Movie Nights* (1927), the star has appeared in dozens of pictures in a wide range of genres. She had her own series, the *Five Little Peppers*, while under contract to Columbia.

"I was born in Boston, Massachusetts, on May 20, 1923. My father had a job offer in Charlotte, North Carolina, so he, my grandmother and I went to Charlotte, when I was one year old. I was pigeon-toed and kept tripping myself, falling all the time. Doctors in 1925 didn't know what to do, but one doctor suggested I take dance lessons; [he felt] that the different positions would train my feet to go out."

"Then, when I was four, I was at Henderson's School of Dance, and I had my own one-woman show [*laughs*]. I sang, danced and did recitations! A guy was in the audience—he came backstage and told my grandmother that 'the child should be in show business'—that I should be in pictures. He said I was 'a natural.' But, he needed a $50 advance. People at the school took up a collection for Grandma and I to go to Hollywood.

"The guy had given us a card, with his address—but there was no such address! Surprise, surprise. Grandma turned to housework to keep us alive. She didn't want to go back defeated, so we stayed. When she was working, I was left with a neighbor, who had a little boy who did bits and extra work. One day, they had a call at the Hal Roach Studio for an interview, and she had to take me along. The little boy got the part, but then he came down with the measles! The studio told the woman, 'Okay, just bring his sister.' She explained that I was a neighbor child, not a sister, but I got the job anyway—and that was the Charlie Chase comedy *Movie Nights*."

There are a few excellent westerns in her repertoire. "We shot *Rider of Death Valley* [1932] way out on location in Calabasas. It was *hot*. Tom Mix, however, left no impression. I loved Tony—Mr. Mix put me up on top of Tony and rode me around. That was a thrill! Lois Wilson was the leading lady and she was the one who impressed me. I worked with her off and on through the years and she became one of my favorites ladies. Not a close friend—but a friend."

Unlike Tom Mix, it was Richard Dix who really made an impression. "I'll never forget what a most warm person he was. My earliest memories of him are on *Cimarron* [1931]. I was at the dinner table and I sat on someone's lap. Later, Mr. Dix was off the set, pacing up and down, learning his lines. He got to a spot and went blank. Well, I gave him his line. He came over to me, smiled and said 'Thank you.' He was wonderful. A lot of people would have gotten angry, but not Richard Dix. He didn't mind a little girl prompting him on his part!"

Asked about *Law and Lawless* (1932) with Jack Hoxie, she retorts, "I did that?" When Boyd Magers gave her a copy of the film to screen, Edith proclaimed, "I must have had amnesia. After watching it, I don't recall a thing. I don't know Majestic Studios. I do remember the name Jack Hoxie but not that I was in a picture with him. Actually, we had no scenes together. He was a bad actor, a little overweight. This movie wasn't released—it escaped!"

Regarding her two westerns with Gene Autry, *Heart of the Rio Grande* (1942) and *Stardust on the Sage* (1942), Edith recalls, "Gene Autry was a real camp, a great tease, a great practical joker. You had to be on your toes around him! In *Heart of the Rio Grande*, I'm the snotty rich girl. There's a scene where I'm supposed to be bucked off a horse. They loosened the ground and had a two-step ladder so I

Edith, one of the most talented child actresses of the 1930s and 1940s, as she appeared at 18 in the Chicago stock company of *Janie* in 1942.

could roll off. Well, Gene put horse stuff on the ground! I didn't know he was doing it—the crew knew it. When the makeup person turned me around to powder me—that's when Gene did his deed. Well, he had a beautiful rawhide makeup case. So I found some of Champion's manure and put it in Gene's cold cream jar! He loved it! He was a good guy, fun, with a great sense of humor. A real okay person. I liked playing the games. I have devilment in me—we acted like two kids. He liked me striking back. However, on the second picture, he didn't kid around as much. Gene was quieter and I don't remember pranks. I guess he tested me and knew he couldn't get away with anything. A neat guy to work with. I went to his memorial when he died. They held it at the museum and it was very nice. I went directly home and played *Heart of the Rio Grande* which is my favorite of the two films we did. Unfortu-

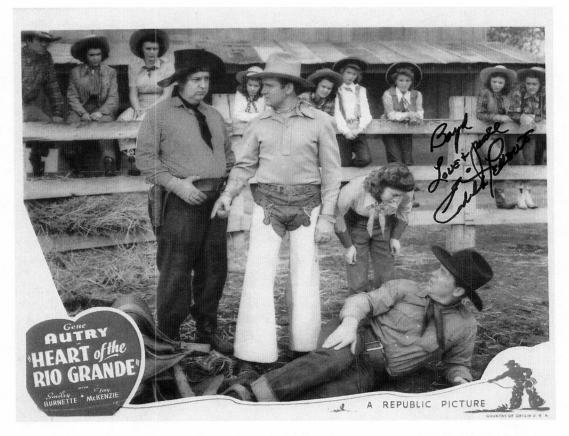

Edith is more concerned about William Haade's condition while Smiley Burnette and Gene Autry discuss who tampered with Haade's saddle, causing him to fall, in *Heart of the Rio Grande* (1942). That's Jean Porter (second from right) hanging on the fence. Jean was interviewed for our first volume, *Westerns Women*.

nately, I hadn't seen him in a long time. We didn't keep in touch because I moved to New York shortly after our pictures. When I came back out here, I just never did seem to run into him."

One of the Pepper pictures, *Out West with the Peppers* (1940), sounds as if it were a western but Edith says, "It wasn't. It had some logging sequences in it and a rescue on a raft. I was disappointed in all of the *Pepper* scripts. Andy Hardy was doing well at MGM and Columbia wanted to do the same. But they didn't live up to my expectations. I was released from Columbia in 1941 after spending six years there. It was like my home. It was a small lot. You could

walk from one side to the other in three minutes. I knew everybody—they were like family. It was heart-wrenching when I had to leave. It took a long, long time to get over the hurt."

Asked about her work in early television, she recalls, "I didn't do any westerns. I did do four *Tales of Tomorrow* (1951–1953) and an *Armstrong Circle Theater* called 'Gentle Rain' [1952], but it was a comedy. I was living on a farm and Cliff Robertson and Whit Bissell were fighting over me. That was kind of fun."

Edith recently received the Lifetime Achievement Award from the Laurel and Hardy Society. "I was in *The Devil's*

Edith appears ready for her beau to take her to the dance.

Brother (1933) with the boys, and that excited the society no end. Originally they only wanted people who worked with Laurel and Hardy, but they are harder to find now. So, they also include Our Gang kids, because they also worked for Hal Roach. I did a couple of those shorts, so I have two good connections."

Once a month, Edith meets with a group of ladies called Show Buddies. "That's always a real treat. Carol Bruce, Betty Garrett, Giselle McKenzie, Barbara Perry and others are involved. That's the closest I get to show business these days."

Edith Fellows
Western Filmography

Movies: *Cimarron* (1931 RKO)—Richard Dix; *Law and Lawless* (1932 Majestic)—Jack Hoxie; *Rider of Death Valley* (1932 Universal)—Tom Mix; *Heart of the Rio* Grande (1942 Republic)—Gene Autry: *Stardust on the Sage* (1942 Republic)—Gene Autry.
Television: *Father Murphy*, "The Robber" (1982).

Barbra Fuller

Soap Opera ... Reel and Real

Barbra Fuller, radio's Claudia on *One Man's Family* for 14 years, a contract player at Republic and Lash LaRue's sixth wife, first broke into Chicago radio at the tender age of 11.

Born Barbara Fuller ("I did the 'Barbra' spelling as an attention-getter—before Streisand") in Nahant, Massachusetts, she was three when her father died, and moved with her mother to St. Petersburg, Florida. Getting into radio behind the scenes, her mother moved to Chicago when Barbra was seven, appointing a friend in Denison, Ohio, Barbra's guardian until 1931 when she joined her mom in Chicago. "I used to go to the studio with her and sit and read a book. The head of production said to mother, 'Barbra always has a book with her. She obviously likes to read. I wonder how she reads aloud? Would you mind if I auditioned her?' And he cast me in a part—George Gobel's younger sister in *The Eye of Montezuma*, a children's program. The show only lasted about six months but it was a lot of fun. I think I got $12.50 a show and the adults got $25. But a lot of people were working for $5."

After working steady for about two years ("I occasionally did commercials for

Bill Elliott made a "tremendous impression" on Barbra. Publicity pose for *The Savage Horde* (1950).

Amos 'n' Andy."), everything suddenly ground to a halt. Her mother kept urging her on and when Barbra was about 13 she landed one radio role after another: *Road of Life*, *Stepmother*, *Scattergood Baines*, *Painted Dreams*, usually ingenue roles, all top Chicago soap operas.

"Later, [I played] opposite John Larkin, who was awfully good and loaded with animal magnetism. At the Tribune Tower, we were playing young sweethearts and across the street at the Wrigley Building, we were playing a young couple in the throes of a bitter divorce. We were playing opposite each other day after day after day. I thought, 'He has so much animal magnetism across the microphone, but I don't feel it at all when we're just sitting around the table.' Then one night at a party, he made a slight pass and I thought, 'My Lord, sitting at the table, drinking Coca Cola with the rest of the cast, he wasn't being romantic.' But at this party ... and he was married, and his wife was pregnant ... and I thought, 'I can't go back now.' I suddenly realized he was attractive. So I went to New York and stayed at a hotel for a couple of nights. I told my best friend, 'I have to get away from Chicago or I'm apt to fall in love with my leading man.' You can walk away from something like this but if you have to stand opposite a microphone and play love scenes with somebody you're beginning to feel something for, you can't do that. I went back to Chicago, resigned from all my shows, gave them two weeks notice and took off and moved to New York. At the time I left in 1942, I was doing 25 soap operas a week ... three shows, two of them had repeats. I stayed in New York about three years and did a lot of radio."

Coming to California in 1945 with an introduction to radio writer-director Carlton E. Morse from actress Mercedes McCambridge, Barbra soon wound up as Claudia on Morse's top-rated radio soap *One Man's Family*. "This was a classic radio program for 27 years. Strictly an upbeat, affirmative, high standard, warm and human program. They had never replaced a character, but I sounded just like Claudia. They supposedly killed off the character three years earlier, so they had no Claudia for three years. I played it from 1945 until it went off the air in 1959, 14 years. It was a fun part. Claudia was a good girl with interesting qualities. I was replaced one summer in 1949 because they moved the show back to New York to try to put it on television. I couldn't go be-

cause I was under contract to Republic. Just as well, because, of course, the show came right back to California."

Barbra was under contract to Republic for a year, beginning with *The Red Menace* (1949). "Republic wanted all new faces. I had told my agent, 'I don't care what I get paid, I'm willing to pay them just to get some film.' I was making more than in radio because, at Republic, it was by the week and on *One Man's Family*, it was by the show; so it depended on how many shows I did a week." Barbra did 13 films that year for Republic and continued her soap opera on radio. "It was a wonderful year. They did *Family* on weekends so I was able to do both, except when they went back to New York. Republic, like any studio, paid you for nine weeks out of 13. But the other four weeks, you were not loafing in the swimming pool, you were doing publicity layouts or interviews. So I was working constantly. But I loved it. They were wonderful to me. It was like being in a stock company, I played every kind of part there was. Mr. Yates [Republic boss Herbert J. Yates] sent me roses the first day of filming, on the first day of the contract. Needless to say, nobody figured there was any hanky panky going on because Vera Ralston was very much in control. And there wasn't. He just was being nice. I made $175 a week for nine weeks out of 13. By the time you figure it, you were unemployed for four months of the year. At the end of my first year, they had options. I would have been making some fairly good money by that time, but they started phasing out all of their people because they were discontinuing the studio."

Barbra smiles when reminded she co-starred in six mysteries with Robert Rockwell. "I couldn't say anything but good about him, but I didn't know him well at the beginning. At a festival, where we were together, I was asked who gave me my first screen kiss and I said Bob Rockwell.

Barbra tries to restrain gunman Bob Steele from shooting her fiancé while veteran heavies Roy Barcroft and Marshall Reed look on in *The Savage Horde* (1950).

They asked what it was like. And I said, 'Nothing.' And Bob echoed, 'That's right. You're thinking about your lines, you're thinking about the lights, the last thing in the world you're thinking about is the kiss.' Of course, it would have been difficult with someone like John Larkin [*laughs*]. They turned those things out so fast there was no time to sit around and get chummy. You learned your lines, went in, rehearsed, shot and that was it. I was delighted when Bob got the part of Mr. Boynton on *Our Miss Brooks* on radio as well as TV. He was perfect for it."

One of the Rockwell-Fuller crime dramas was *Alias the Champ* (1949), which co-starred pro wrestler Gorgeous George,

the flamboyant larger-than-life forerunner to all the ring superstars we are besieged with on television today. Barbra chuckles, "Gorgeous George was in person *exactly* the way he was in the wrestling arena. He had a wife who was with him at all times ... every little pin curl ... it was ridiculous. He was totally involved with being beautiful. Very definitely 'ham.' But it was tragic, he really didn't make much money in early television and he died in a sleazy hotel on Hollywood Boulevard. I'm sure he died broke."

As for her westerns, she was miserable on *Rock Island Trail* (1950). "I couldn't stand the way I looked and both Adrian Booth and Adele Mara looked great. Gor-

Barbra is protected by her on-screen fiancé, Noah Beery, Jr., in *The Savage Horde* (1950).

geous costumes and gorgeous makeup, and I didn't have anything to do. I never cared what I looked like if I had something to do. I had a hat I didn't like and clothes I wasn't terribly happy with. So that is not one of my favorite pictures. Speaking of Adrian Booth, when we were working together, she was in the throes of her romance with David Brian."

The Savage Horde (1950) was Barbra's favorite. "I liked Bill Elliott. He was very helpful. He was a little on the wolfish side, but I didn't have any trouble with him. One time I had to ride up to the camera and do a quick dismount. We did it two or three times. The wardrobe woman, afterwards, said to me, 'Did you notice Mr. Elliott ... he was standing right behind the camera, ready to grab the horse if you

had any problems.' This was the star of the picture who could have been loafing in his dressing room, but instead he was interested in being helpful to a newcomer. He was caring and it made a tremendous impression on me.

"Now, when I started the picture, I knew very little about western riding. I had ridden in Chicago, English saddle, but I'm not the world's greatest horsewoman. When they assigned me to the picture I said, 'I can ride a horse but I'm not terribly good.' They said, don't worry about it, we use the double for everything. Well, yes, they use a double, but you do it all first. Then, whatever you don't look right in, they use the double for. But you have to go through all of it first."

The turning point in Barbra's life

came during her 1951–1952 marriage to Lash LaRue. "We met at the Hotel Del Coronado at a publicity junket. I was there for Republic and he was down for Fawcett Publications [publishers of his comic books]. He came in suntanned, rugged-looking, all dressed in black, and I was very suntanned and all dressed in white … we made a nice combination. He was attractive and he was attracted, I guess, to me. He called me … I don't remember how long it took …we had one or two dates. Then all of a sudden, I didn't hear from him, but he was on tour. I didn't know that, he hadn't said anything about it. Then he called. So we had a couple more dates … and he kept disappearing … but after the first time, I knew why he was disappearing. Then he ran some of his pictures for me one day. Up until that time, all he had been to me was a date I enjoyed being with because he was kind of exciting. He played a twin brother in one film and I was impressed by how good he was. I thought, 'The man has talent.' That was the first time I really got interested in him. I don't even remember how it progressed but all of a sudden, he said, 'Let's get married.' I remember saying to my mother, 'I don't want to be somebody's fifth wife.' Because, at that point, he told me he'd been married four times. This was when he first proposed. Then he went on tour again, came back and he had married again! Actually, he remarried one of his previous wives! So it made me his sixth wife instead of his fifth wife, when I finally decided, oh, what the heck! We were married in February 1951.

"Basically, it just wasn't working out and I sued Lash for divorce in 1952. It took six months for it to become legal. I remember for much of that six months I was going around thinking, 'Am I making a mistake—should I or shouldn't I?' He couldn't make up his mind what he wanted but he kept coming back. Every time I'd turn around, he'd be ringing my doorbell again, which was very upsetting to say the least. I started looking around for an answer. I thought, it takes two to make a disaster. My mother was very much opposed to my marrying Lash because I was seeing another man at the same time, a man Mom thought the world of; she didn't think I'd be happy with Lash. I thought, it's either going to be the best thing that ever was or the worst thing that ever was. It turned out to be sort of the worst thing that ever was, except it *was* good for me because I thought, all right, I did something wrong too, it's not all his fault. I started looking and I had the feeling God is the answer. I finally latched on to Ernest Holmes' teachings and the Science of Mind … and then Dr. William Hornaday, who was Ernest's protégé and shining light. The first time I heard him, I thought, 'This is the answer. I'm not making a mistake—go ahead and get the divorce.' I have been closely involved with the church ever since, 44 years. I've always been grateful to Lash, because I would not have gotten so involved with the church if I hadn't been looking for an answer instead of blaming him. I started producing tapes of Dr. Hornaday's talks and handling his radio program.

"In the process [of the divorce], I lost track of our godson. Then I saw Lash after 40 years at the Memphis Film Festival. When I talked to him, the primary thing I was trying to do was find out where our godson, J.P. Sloane, was, which I did. His picture was on several of Lash's comic book covers [#31, 38, 40, 42]. He was just absolutely darling, thoughtful and caring. He said to me a couple of months ago, 'The trouble with Lash was, he just had hormone problems.'"

As to her appearance on *Trackdown: The Bounty Hunter* which was the 1958 pilot for *Wanted Dead or Alive*, "I remember thinking Steve McQueen was awful

... *both* of them, Robert Culp also, were terribly impressed with themselves. Then, of course, McQueen became a big, big star and Culp became a big star briefly. My only feeling was, jeepers, they really think they're something."

How would Barbra Fuller like to be remembered a hundred years from now? "Probably by the tapes, around the teachings of the philosophy of Dr. Ernest Holmes and Dr. William Hornaday. I think they are a more lasting thing than Barbra Fuller, the actress."

Barbra Fuller
Western Filmography

Movies: *Rock Island Trail* (1950 Republic)—Forrest Tucker; *Savage Horde* (1950 Rep.)—Bill Elliott; *Singing Guns* (1950 Republic)—Vaughn Monroe; *City of Badmen* (1953 Fox)—Dale Robertson.

Television: *Trackdown:* 'The Bounty Hunter" (1958); *State Trooper*, "Clever Man" (1958); *U.S. Marshal*, "Destination Nowhere" (1960); *Daniel Boone*, "Noblesse Oblige" (1970).

Beverly Garland

Frank Independence

She's frank, intense, self-driven and the personification of the independent woman. For the prefect portrait of Beverly Garland, watch her excellent work in the *Laramie* episode, "Saddle and Spur" (1960).

The harried heroine, star of many cult horror films of the 1950s and over 40 movie and TV westerns, was an only child born Beverly Lucy Fessenden one October 17. "An actress never reveals her true age," she laughs in her typical rollicking, bawdy fashion. Beverly was born in Santa Cruz, California, "where my parents were visiting friends. There was an earthquake and I arrived early! My mother told the

doctor to take me away, that I wasn't her child—her doctor had told her she would have a son, not a daughter. They finally assured her I was indeed her child and I hadn't gotten mixed up with one of the other newborns [*laughs*]!"

Beverly grew up in Glendale, California, but moved to Arizona during her high school years. "My mother and I both had horses, so I learned to ride. But riding for pleasure is different than riding in pictures—with the galloping and stunts they make you do. My movies were too cheap to hire a stunt girl, so I had to do them myself!"

The family moved back to California

Feisty Beverly Garland is a gun-slinging western lady in *Badlands of Montana* (1957).

where Beverly attended Glendale City College. "I did summer stock at Laguna where Ray Cooper, an agent-friend of my parents, spotted me and wanted to sign me. He got me an interview for *D.O.A.* [1949]. I met the director, Rudolph Maté, and tested. They liked what they saw and I got the part. It was that easy!"

However, *D.O.A.* nearly put a stop to Beverly's blossoming career. When a reporter interviewed her and asked if she thought the picture would win an Academy

Award, she expressed a frank opinion that there were "a lot of good pictures out." The producer, hearing the candid remark as flippant disloyalty, officially blacklisted her for the next couple of years. "I was a waitress and I worked in the dead letter office at Forest Lawn." Again the hearty laugh. Characteristically, her natural self-determination eventually came through. When she received an Emmy nomination for her *Medic* episode "White Is the Color" (1954) where she played a pregnant leukemia victim, her presence was suddenly much in demand.

As for her name change, "I didn't think Fessenden was a good name for the marquee, so I took a family name of Campbell. I used that name on an *I Married Joan* [1952–1955], a *Lone Ranger* [in 1950] and other early TV shows."

Beverly was given the *dreaded* line in that *Lone Ranger* episode. "I played the mother of a young child who asks me at the end of the show, 'Who was that masked man?' and I said, 'He's the *Lone Ranger*.' They said, 'No, you have to say it, 'He's the *Lone Ranger!*' So, I did it again, saying, 'He's the Lone *Ranger*.' Again they didn't like it. So I said—practically screaming, 'He's the LONE *RANGER!*' [*laughs*]. Clayton Moore, by the way, was such a nice guy—and good-looking, too."

Beverly's first feature western was *Bitter Creek* (1954) with Wild Bill Elliott. "I liked Bill Elliott. He was a very stiff actor; he never really changed his expression. But that was what they wanted in those days! Bill was a very big man who said very little. He was silent, big and quiet."

By this time she was acting under the name Beverly Garland. "I married Richard Garland, an actor, and used his last name—Garland is also another family name, and I liked it. We met doing a play at the Hollywood Players Ring Theater, *Dark of the Moon*. We were married for

four years. He was drinking more and more and we eventually divorced [in 1953] when he had an affair with my best friend. My career was going great—I won an Emmy for the pilot episode of *Medic* with Richard Boone and Lee Marvin. Because I had gotten a lot of publicity out of the name Beverly Garland, I didn't want to change it when we divorced."

"Later [1960], I met and married builder-developer Fillmore Crank, whose wife was killed in a car wreck. He had two children, Fillmore Jr., and Kathleen, who works in my hotel [Beverly Garland's 255-room Holiday Inn on Vineland Avenue in North Hollywood]. In 1964, Fillmore and I had a daughter, Carrington, and in 1968 we had a son, James. Fillmore died the last of March 1999, primarily of cancer. He was sick only two weeks!"

The Beverly Garland Hotel is widely known around the country as well as in Los Angeles. The idea to use her name "was a mutual thing. We originally had an agreement with Howard Johnson—a contract that lasted 20 years. But, no one was going to the Howard Johnson hotels, so we changed the name to the Beverly Garland Howard Johnson, with Howard Johnson in teeny print!" A few years ago, she became associated with Holiday Inn. Beverly and Fillmore bought the seven-acre property from Gene Autry (it was just a treeless seven-acre field overrun by chickens) for $100,000, which was a great deal. "Maybe it was just the down payment [*laughs*]! We've had it for 27 years now." The original intention was to build an apartment complex. It was good friend Casey Stengel, the late baseball manager, who toured the site and suggested to the pair that a hotel would prove more profitable. "Initially, people used to say, 'It's a shame you built a hotel here because there's nothing.' Now, they say, 'You're so smart to have built it there.'"

The typically strong, independent

Morris Ankrum, Wayne Morris and Beverly are concerned about a youngster in *Two Guns and a Badge* **(1954), the film many consider the "last B-western series film."**

women she plays on screen are, Beverly reveals, "like me. I can't play a wallflower; a clinging vine. I am a strong woman—not namby-pamby. In fact, because of the roles I often played, my agent didn't want to send me on the interview for Fred MacMurray's wife in *My Three Sons* [Beverly co-starred from 1969 to 1972]. He said, 'You've played alcoholics, sheriffs, tough broads, and you are not known for the typical housewife type.' I convinced him to at least send me, and I got the part! I went in, wearing a June Allyson–like dress with a Peter Pan circular collar [*laughs*]. The first show I did, Fred was teaching me to play golf. He said something to me and I barked back—in a Mary Tyler Moore to Dick Van Dyke kind of way—and they

said, 'No. You cannot talk to him that way.' So, I had to shoot it over, saying the lines more softly [*laughs*]!" June Haver, Mrs. MacMurray, "was on the set only once—during the wedding scene—otherwise, she never came."

In 1954, Beverly played in two westerns, *Desperado* and *Two Guns and a Badge*, with Wayne Morris. "I also was replaced [by Virginia Grey] in a movie called *Fighting Lawman* with Wayne. In that one, they wanted to shoot the last scene first, where I am supposed to gallop a horse as fast as I can, ride up to the rocks, get my rifle up, shoot the bad guy. I started to get on the horse and they said, 'That's the wrong side. Get on the other side.' So, I got on the horse, and it took off—over hill and dale. I was hanging onto the horn! I now saw why they put the horns on saddles [*laughs*]! Finally, the horse came back. By now, I was scared and had shaky legs. I tried it again but my hat fell off. So we had to try and do it again. I got on the horse, rode and bent down to pick up the rifle, which I was supposed to shoot! Nothing went right. The horse was looking at me, wondering who this was on its back. That horse couldn't believe I was in this movie [*laughs*]. The next time I tried it, instead of leaning to the side to pick up the rifle, I leaned forward—the horse threw his head back and did a belly laugh—and you could hear the crack! My nose was broken in three places. I got off the horse and they told me, 'Goodbye.' You had to do your own riding and I just couldn't do it right, at the time." As for Wayne Morris, "He was no longer a star. This was not Warner Bros.! He was nice, but heavy. He had to have a box to get on his horse! I didn't hang around with him so I didn't know about his drinking—but from his being puffy, I certainly suspected it."

In *Gunslinger* (1956), produced and directed by Roger Corman, "I played a sheriff—and had to do all the stunt work. I go into a bar to clean up the town. I have a hair-pulling fistfight with a madam (Allison Hayes). We did it inside, the last day of shooting. The following scene, however, was shot the day before. You see me running out of a building, leap onto a horse and ride out of town. I'm supposed to come down as fast as I can and get on this horse. 'Think high, think high' [*laughs*]. Well, I really twisted my ankle coming down the stairs. At home, I took off my Levis and boots. I put my leg in hot water, and it felt wonderful. The next day, it was three times its normal size! I couldn't walk on it! I called my boyfriend and asked him to get me to work. He told me to stay at home, but you can't stay at home, you have to go in, then you can go back home if the studio lets you! Otherwise, you're in big trouble! I told Roger, 'I can't do the stunts today.' Within one hour, a 'doctor' comes in with a big needle. He gives me five shots in my ankle. Wardrobe cut the Levis and boot to get the foot in them. It felt great—but they practically ruined my leg! I didn't walk for three months after that—but Roger always came through! But they got the stunt of my fighting with the madam [*laughs*].

"We made *Gunslinger* at Jack Ingram's location ranch. Very cold and very rainy. John Ireland and I have our only love scene up in a old, twisted tree, thank you Roger Corman, and the tree was the home of these very large ants. At 6 A.M. they were just getting up and they really resented the two of us who were sitting up in the branches trying to do this bloody love scene—going, 'Ouch'—being bitten alive. It was ridiculous! Also we had a wonderful dressing room. It was a shed with a dirt floor. Roger finally got us a little heater in there because we were freezing to death.

"Still more—beautiful Allison Hayes is riding up in the middle of town with John Ireland. The horses are stopped and we're talking about whether we should go to lunch or not. All of a sudden, Allison just collapses off her horse, right down on the ground and breaks her arm. I think because she *really* wanted to get off this terrible movie. Roger says, 'It's okay, Allison. We'll just bind it up and we'll film you so nobody knows your arm is broken.' So she went through the rest of the movie with a broken arm [*laughs*]."

Asked if she and Roger Corman were an *item*: "No. We went out to dinner a few times and became good friends. He even wanted to put me under contract, but I rejected the offer. Roger Corman is a *very* innovative man."

Were there any low-budget picture

directors who were helpful? "Most of them I worked with were quite good. But brilliant directors don't happen often. On *The Alligator People* [1959], for instance, Roy Del Ruth was superb!"

In 1999, Beverly attended the Memphis Film Festival along with Rex Reason, her leading man in *Badlands of Montana* (1957). "Rex looks wonderful! It was fun to see him again. He is a cute guy!"

Beverly's leading men in movies and the TV western series she guested on reads like a laundry list of who's who in westerns. Richard Boone, her *Medic* co-star and star of *Have Gun Will Travel* [1957–1963]: "Richard Boone was such a good actor—a special man. Just wonderful. He was not good-looking, he had bad skin and was very homely—but a brilliant actor. I was also called a good luck charm for 'pilots' as I did several, in addition to *Medic*, which eventually sold!"

The Saga of Hemp Brown (1958) and Rory Calhoun: "What an adorable guy—such a cutie. I couldn't keep my eyes off him! Yvette Vickers, who had a tiny role, also had a small part in the play *Dark of the Moon*. When we did *Hemp*, she had a wonderful figure."

Curucu, Beast of the Amazon, (1956) a non-western, starred John Bromfield (later the star of *U.S. Marshal*. "I had never met John Bromfield before, and I haven't seen him since. He's a terribly handsome man. He didn't care if he acted or not—he wanted to go fishing! Which is probably what he's doing these days. John was just a love; a very handsome, good-looking guy. Curt Siodmak, the director, could speak German, English, whatever. But John and I could only speak English. The rest of the cast spoke either Portuguese or German, whichever!"

Dick Powell: "Dick Powell could do *anything*! He was brilliant! And he had a good deal of charm."

Guy Madison on a *Zane Grey Theater*

in 1961: "Frankly, I don't recall much about him. He didn't impress."

Robert Loggia: "We did the Disney thing (*Nine Lives of Elfego Baca*, 1959); he was wonderful. Quiet; very intelligent. He had a lot of pizzazz."

Tom Tryon (*Texas John Slaughter*, 1958–1961): "He became a successful novelist—a good one—and was very handsome."

Jock Mahoney: "Jocko was a close friend; I knew him when he was still a stuntman. We did *Yancy Derringer* together in 1959. He was one of my favorite people."

Clint Eastwood (*Rawhide*, 1959–1965): "He was quiet; didn't say much; but even then, he had a presence."

Eric Fleming (*Rawhide*): "We did 'Happy Birthday' on the road with Miriam Hopkins. He was heavy then and was dieting. He always ate scrambled eggs and tomatoes! When we later did *Rawhide*, he looked great! Eric never wore shoes! He wore them when he worked, of course [*laughs*]. He was very spiritual."

Robert Culp (*Trackdown*, 1957–1959): "I am not mad for him! It was awful for me to work with him. He didn't give me anything. Very selfish. I can't work with someone who doesn't give something back. I need feedback for me to do my work. I was out on a limb. If you don't get something, you can't give something back. I don't know about others, but Robert Culp just didn't give me *anything*!"

Steve McQueen (*Wanted Dead or Alive*, 1958–1961): "I didn't do much with him, and I never witnessed, first hand, some of the wild stories that other people relate!"

Darren McGavin (*Riverboat*, 1959–1961): "A wonderful actor, very giving."

Dale Robertson (*Tales of Wells Fargo*, 1957–1962): "We got along great; everything was great; I like him very much."

Wayne Rogers (*Stagecoach West*, 1960–1961): "A sweetie."

Beverly asserts her displeasure over what Tom Tryon has done in a 1959 episode of Disney's *Texas John Slaughter*.

Jack Elam (*The Dakotas*, 1963): "A good friend, a long-time friend!"

James Arness (*Gunsmoke*, 1955–1975): "A favorite person of mine."

Neville Brand (*Laredo*, 1965–1967):

"We did a lot of stuff together, including a picture in Japan. I stayed home and he went out with the girls; then at three or four in the morning, he would tell me all about them. What a drinker!"

Robert Horton (*A Man Called Shenandoah*, 1965–1966): "We are still good friends. I talk to him at least once a week. His wife Marilyn is an incredibly wonderful girl. They live in George Montgomery's house, which he built when he was married to Dinah Shore."

Lloyd Bridges (*The Loner*, 1965–1966): "Always a favorite."

David Carradine: "We did *Kung Fu* in 1975. I remember his lying down in the middle of a street. I was not close to him [*laughs*]!"

Robert Conrad (*The Wild Wild West*, 1965–1969): "Thank goodness we didn't have any love scenes together. I am taller than Robert Conrad, but then, who isn't? He's a tiny man."

When Beverly is called a "star" for her well-known work on *My Three Sons* and *Scarecrow and Mrs. King* (1983–1987), she retorts, "A star is Ingrid Bergman, Bette Davis, Joan Crawford. I am a working professional actress. To me, acting is blood. To me, acting is like taking four quick pep pills. Acting is pleasure, excitement, abandonment. I get all that and security too."

Today, Beverly is well-known for hosting Ray Courts' Hollywood Collectors' Show at her hotel. "But I am not connected with it at all. It is all Ray's. He rents all my ballrooms and banquet rooms and has been tremendously successful! I've attended many of the shows, but less since my husband died."

Recently, Beverly was seen on the daytime drama *Port Charles*. "It's a spin-off of *General Hospital*. Although some characters switch back and forth between both shows, so far I have not. I worked four days in April [2000], and do not know where the character will be taken. If the part gets larger, that's great; but if the part is cut out, that's okay as well. There is always something over the horizon! I'm more mature. Not so terribly ambitious or self-driven. I wonder if there's anyone on earth I'd trade places with—and I can't think of anyone. That's security."

Beverly Garland Western Filmography

Movies: *Bitter Creek* (1954 Allied Artists)—Bill Elliott; *The Desperado* (1954 Allied Artists)—Wayne Morris; *Two Guns and a Badge* (1954 Allied Artists)—Wayne Morris; *Gunslinger* (1956 American Releasing)—John Ireland; *Badlands of Montana* (1957 20th Century–Fox)—Rex Reason; *The Saga of Hemp Brown* (1958 Universal-International)—Rory Calhoun; *Cutter's Trail* (1970 CBS-TV movie)—John Gavin.

Television: *Lone Ranger*, "Beeler Gang" (1950); *Frontier*, "Cattle Drive to Casper" (1955); *Zane Grey Theatre*, "Courage Is a Gun" (1956); *Zane Grey Theatre*, "Hanging Fever" (1959); *Nine Lives of Elfego Baca*, "Move Along, Mustangers" (1959); *Nine Lives of Elfego Baca*, "Mustang Man, Mustang Maid" (1959); *Texas John Slaughter*, "Killers from Kansas" (1959); *Texas John Slaughter*, "Showdown at Sandoval" (1959); *Yancy Derringer*, "Fair Freebooters" (1959); *Yancy Derringer*, "Wayward Warrior" (1959); *Trackdown*, "Hard Lines" (1959); *Man from Blackhawk*, "Logan's Policy" (1959); *Rawhide*, "Incident of the Roman Candles" (1959); *Zane Grey Theatre*, "A Small Town That Died" (1960); *Riverboat*, "Three Graves" (1960); *Laramie*, "Saddle and Spur" (1960); *Tales of Wells Fargo*, "Pearl Hart" (1960); *Wanted Dead or Alive*, "Prison Trail" (1960); *Stagecoach West*, "The Storm" (1960); *Zane Grey Theatre*, "Jericho" (1961); *Rawhide*, "Incident at Sugar Creek" (1962); *Rawhide*, "Incident of the Gallows Tree" (1963); *Dakotas*, "The Chooser of the Slain" (1963); *Gunsmoke*, "The Odyssey of Jubal Tanner" (1963); *Laredo*, "Lazyfoot, Where Are You?" (1965); *A Man Called Shenandoah*, "The Onslaught" (1965); *The Loner*, "Incident in the Middle of Nowhere" (1966); *Pistols 'n' Petticoats*, unknown title (1966); *The Wild Wild West*, "The Night of the Cut Throats" (1967); *Gallegher Goes West*, " Tragedy on the Trail" (Part 1–2) (1967); *Gunsmoke*, "The Victim" (1968); *Gunsmoke*, "Time of the Jackals" (1969); *Lancer*, "Devil's Blessing" (1969); *Gunsmoke*, "The Badge" (1970); *Kung Fu*, "Battle Hymn" (1975); *How the West Was Won*, "The Slavers" (1979).

Lisa Gaye

TV's Reigning Western Queen

The gorgeous 34-23½-36" star of innumerable movies and TV shows of the 1950s and 1960s, Lisa Gaye was born in Denver, Colorado, March 6, 1935. The youngest of three actress-sisters (Teala Loring and Debra Paget being her older siblings; kid sister Meg was a non-professional), the future star came to California with her family, when sister Teala received a Paramount contract and the name Judith Gibson.

There were so many TV shows Lisa appeared on, it's a wonder she was able to watch them all. "But I did—at least on the first run. In fact, on a local channel here in Houston, they still run *Have Gun Will Travel* [1957–1963] and *Wild, Wild West* [1965–1969]."

One of her television co-stars was Steve McQueen, with whom she appeared in *Wanted Dead or Alive* (1958–1961). "I loved working with him; he was generous and professional. He gave so much. Of course he was high-strung and pressed to the edge a little. We were shooting on the back lot and he asked me if I'd like a ride back to the soundstage, on his motorcycle. So I certainly said 'Sure.' I made a big mistake by getting on his motorcycle. We went all over that lot, and not at a slow pace! He didn't slow down—he was always on the cutting edge. We zoomed right up to the soundstage where the doors were closed. He had it arranged that someone inside would open them at the last minute, but I thought we were goners for sure. After that ride, I said, 'Thank you,' and never rode with him again [*laughs*]."

As for a preference for other actors, Lisa is quick to explain, "Each is different. I am a people person and got along great with everyone—except a couple of the directors, who were harsh. You spend so

Lisa Gaye was one of the most prolific actresses on television westerns in the 1950s and 1960s.

much time together, everyone pulls together like a team; there was no time for temperament on TV shows. I worked quite often with Michael Connors, when he was known as 'Touch'. One day he told my husband, 'Ben, I spend as much time with your wife as you do!'"

In between all those westerns, there was *Rock Around the Clock* (1956), in which Lisa danced fabulously. "Dancing was my first love; I planned to go on and do ballet. But, I was seen in a play—this resulted in a screen test and I was placed under contract to Universal-International when I was only 17! My first part was as one of the screaming crowd who surround James Stewart and June Allyson as they get out of their car in *The Glenn Miller Story* [1954]. My screen test was elaborate—they put all kinds of money into it. They had a new color film they wanted to try out, so I did singing and dancing as well as acting. Earl Barton, who danced with me in *Rock Around the Clock*, danced with me in the test! Universal-International was the only studio, at that time, where you were given lessons in drama, singing, dancing, fencing, horseback riding. It was awesome … and you got paid to learn! At the time I was there, they had 65 contract players—Rock Hudson, Tony Curtis, Julie Adams, David Janssen, Richard Long, the list is endless. I was contracted to be a back-up for Yvonne DeCarlo; Race Gentry was supposedly Rock Hudson's backup, but I could never see it [*laughs*]. I played a harem girl [like Yvonne often did] in *Yankee Pasha* [1954]."

Lisa also performed a very seductive Greek dance in the 1957 *Have Gun Will Travel* episode "Helen of Abajinian" (for which Gene Roddenberry won a Writers Guild award). Asked about acting and any technique she may have, Lisa states, "I just did it. It wasn't hard to memorize lines. It all was just a lot of fun. I was always happy to be working—but I didn't like to do the publicity. Give me a script and I'm happy."

The star was also able to play a wide range of parts. "I developed a lot of accents. I was in a lot of plays when I was a child; that helped a lot. Also, the idea to give each sister a different screen name was my mother's—she wanted names that were good for the marquee."

About any favorite directors, the answer comes as a surprise: "Robert Cummings! I played Collette DuBois on *The Bob Cummings Show* [1955–1959], or *Love That Bob* as it later became. Bob not only starred and played a couple of parts [photographer Bob Collins and Grandpa Collins], but he often directed as well. He was great! He was also a friend. He had terrific timing for comedy; he understood comedy. He knew what he wanted and sometimes there would be take after take until he got it. He taught me a lot! In 1958, I replaced Lori Nelson in the last 13 episodes of *How to Marry a Millionaire* at Fox. You paid your dues on TV. Often there was no makeup nor hairdresser—you did it yourself! But it was great training. The first show I did after Universal was *Annie Oakley* in 1956 with Gail Davis. Being in so many westerns, riding was a must."

Asked if she knew how to ride before Universal, the answer was, "Yes. Thanks to my mother. My brother Frank [Griffin] wanted a car, but my mother didn't want him to have one at his young age. So, she compromised and bought a horse. We are a big family, and I learned to ride on Frank's horse! It was that simple. We rode up in the Hollywood Hills."

Concerning her lone big-screen western co-star, Audie Murphy (*Drums Across the River* [1954]), who gave so many co-stars trouble, Lisa states, "He was a gentleman—always! Friendly. Of course, I was still a teenager when we worked together, but he was very nice, very protective of

Audie Murphy and Lisa take a break between scenes of *Drums Across the River* (1954).

me. Audie was like a big brother to me. He took care of me. Watched out for me. I was the only girl there besides the script girl. I received some lusty looks from some of the men, but I always handled myself where they knew not to put the make on me. It's how you handle it yourself. I had an attitude and I knew to 'always be aware of what goes on around you.' They knew I was a lady—they may have looked, but they didn't touch or say anything. If they had, Audie would have come to my rescue."

Another cast member in *Drums Across the River* was Walter Brennan. "He was a sweetheart, like a daddy to me."

When queried about any accidents that may have occurred, especially in regards to her frequent on-screen bouts with men who slapped her around, Lisa recalls, "Only one time did I get hurt, and it was my fault! I missed my mark on one of those *Death Valley Days* ['A General Without Cause' (1961)]. I couldn't bring myself to stop and we made contact. I was a half a step too close and was backhanded in the mouth by Jack Elam, who was very upset about it, especially since my lip bled! Jack had tears in his eyes! He kept apologizing and I kept saying it was all right—it was my fault, not his—I overstepped my mark. We had rehearsed and rehearsed. I was to run up to him—and he was to backhand me. I usually line myself up with a bush or something to find a mark. I was half a step past and when he went to swing his arm back—well, there was a great reaction in that shot [*laughs*]! My lip only bled a little bit—but Jack was such a sweet man about it."

Lisa also recalls a *Wild Wild West* with a falcon ("The Night of the Falcon" [1967]). "In pre-production, they told me they wanted me to ride and be on horseback with the falcon simultaneously. I told them I'll either ride the horse or be with the falcon, but *not* both. So, my stunt double had to work with the bird. Well, the falcon *was* a problem. It screeched, the horse reared up—and the stunt girl fell off the horse near the cliff! That falcon also attacked his trainer—chewed his face, but I didn't know about it until later. I just had a gut feeling about it. I love birds—but if I had done the riding shot with the falcon, I'd probably have gone over the cliff [*laughs*]! I later did the close-up with the bird; they sat me on a high ladder so it would look like I was up on a horse. I noticed its trainer—he looked like raw meat.

His face was solid stitches—I thought he'd gone through the windshield of a car! After I did the scene, they told me the falcon had attacked him and chewed him up! God watched over me during that time! On *Wild Wild West*, you had to play it tongue-in-cheek. It couldn't be any other way! Yet, [guest star] Robert Duvall tried to look serious. He was a really nice man; I always thought he was wonderful. It's nice when someone like that makes it big. Lots of the Universal guys did—Tony Curtis and Rock Hudson—they are icons!"

We asked Lisa who she felt best portrayed a cowboy. "Clint Walker! I did two *Cheyenne*s with him, and I did his screen test when he was signed at Universal. He was Chet back then, but he didn't stay long. He is big, slow-speaking and easygoing—he settled into the saddle better than anybody else. Clint was always after me to quit smoking [*laughs*], but he failed. I have since quit myself. Incidentally, Clint Eastwood was another Universal alumnus. I did his reading at Universal as well. His hair stood up like five fingers—a cowlick. He is a sweet guy to work with. I did do *Zorro* in 1958 with Guy Williams, but he was going out as I was going in [to Universal]; I never knew him too well. Jack Kelly and I did a *Maverick* [1957–1962]. We were both at Universal where, at one time, he had his leg in a cast and had to walk with a cane and I had a back brace. On Tuesday or Wednesday, the studio would show us classic movies and we'd have to break them down; critique them. Jack and I showed up with our casts [*laughs*]! Jack broke his leg on a movie set. As for me, I was going to show Teala's daughter what fun it is to do a backwards slide, down a slide [*laughs*]! I went 'Whoopee!' and slid onto the cement of a badminton court! I hit and cracked the lumbar of my back. The doctor said I could either be in a body cast for six months, or a brace for one year. I took the brace, even though it required daily heat and other treatments, because I would still be mobile. This was right after I signed with Universal. I was going to class, so it didn't matter as much. Right after I got out of the brace, I did the picture with Audie—and still had muscle spasms because I had been in that brace for so long. The brace went from the back of the neck to the tailbone; it was rigid, but I could walk."

Regarding some of her other TV Western leading men: "Richard Boone was one of my favorites—he wanted me to go to New York to study with a drama coach. He was very generous. I never desired to be a star—I just loved to work. Marriage was my first priority, so I didn't go."

Lisa guest starred on *Tombstone Territory* (1959–1960). "Pat Conway—poor Pat! I was terrible, kidding him about the size of his boots. He was a good sport; a good guy. 'What size *are* those boots, Pat?' [*laughs*]. Pat was a big, tall guy, and it was a running gag. We had fun; lots of laughter."

Keith Larsen: "Doing a show in color like *Northwest Passage* [1958–1959] was big in those days. Keith is a sweet guy; Buddy Ebsen was also in that. We'd be cutting up—Buddy Ebsen, a wonderful entertainer—we'd start tap dancing in those period clothes!"

Peter Breck of *Black Saddle* (1959–1960): "Peter knew what he wanted even in those days—he was very professional, always thinking and concentrating on what he was doing."

Wayde Preston, *Colt .45* (1957–1960): "My goodness, he was very, very nice."

Will Hutchins: "I loved him as an actor—he is a very handsome guy; *Sugarfoot* [1957–1961] was a great show. I adored it."

Gene Barry: "I later danced in a *Burke's Law* [1963–1966] set in a little Mexican town. But mostly, guest shots on that show were bits, so I only agreed to do one.

"On *Bat Masterson*, 'Sharpshooter' [1959], I was working with a mark shot sharpshooter, holding plates. I was rigged with wires so the rounds would explode around me. Gun powder on the plate exploded. Well, the gun powder burned a hole in my leg—I didn't say 'Ouch' because I didn't want to spoil the shot—and have to do it again! I was once on a trapeze swing on a *Whirlybirds* [1956–1959]. Up they go 60 feet! That was scary."

The name Scott Brady results in a good anecdote. "They say a lot of things against Scott, but he looked out for me! A still-working character actor said something disparaging about me. He said it at the commissary—loudly, on purpose, so I could hear. When I went back to the set, the man who had said something came looking for me. 'I need to apologize to you; I was set straight that you are a lady.' Scott Brady, who had such nice blue orbs [eyes], had set him straight all right!"

In the late 1960s, Lisa's booming career seemed to have come to a halt. "There were shows I never did—*Bonanza*, *Star Trek*—yet when I'd watch them on TV, I would say to myself, 'I could have done that!' I did a *Paladin* with Dan Blocker, but never a *Bonanza*; I did a pilot with long-time friend Leonard Nimoy—he and his wife always came to my New Year's Eve party, yet I never did his show. I couldn't walk though the door at Paramount—so I changed agents. Then, it was like I never worked again! Incidentally, I did a pilot with Leonard [*Stranded* with Richard Egan, Julie Adams, Peter Graves and Karen Sharpe] that was done at the same time as the pilot for *Star Trek*. It was released as a feature, *Valley of Mystery*, in 1967. Had our show sold, he never would have had to put on those funny ears each week [*laughs*] and become the superstar he did!"

DEATH VALLEY DAYS

FROM PUBLICITY DEPARTMENT · 20 MULE TEAM PRODUCTS DEPARTMENT · 630 SHATTO PLACE · LOS ANGELES 5 CALIFORNIA

A WOMAN WITH A REASON FOR LIVING AND A MAN WITH A REASON FOR DYING CHANGE THE LIFE OF "A GENERAL WITH-OUT CAUSE" IN TRUE DEATH VALLEY DAYS TALE.   4633

During our Civil War, the French were invading Mexico. The Union, attempting to aid the Mexicans, sent supply wagons south, but they were often plundered by outlaw bands before reaching the Army.

Wounded, Miles Owens (WILLIAM BOYETT), only survivor of a raid by bandit king, "General" Juan Cortina (JACK ELAM), attempts to make his way through the Mexican desert with the remaining supply wagon. With him is Dolores (LISA GAYE), a soldier-guide.

When one of the horses gives out, they hide the wagon and continue on horseback, but a chance mishap makes them Cortina's prisoners.

Cortina attempts to make the two reveal the hiding place, but no amount of torment can make them talk. Slowly, the outlaw "general" develops a grudging respect for their "principles", and his own life is affected by their loyalty.

LISA GAYE stars as a woman soldier whose assignment is nearly foiled by a "General Without A Cause", true DEATH VALLEY DAYS drama.   633/NO

Lisa as a woman soldier in the *Death Valley Days* episode "A General Without a Cause" (1961).

Lisa appeared in *Death Valley Days* (1952–1970) a total of nine times, more than any other actress. "I loved doing that show! I especially liked the fact the stories were all true! On one show, there was a plowing field—a Morgan horse had reins half way around my shoulders—rigged to the plow. They buried air hoses under the soil. The horse spooked and kept going. When the man hit the air hose, the horse ran away. The rein didn't break at first—when it should have. The horse kept dragging me, and my face got full of mud! My stunt double, a man, watched it all on the bus [*laughs*]. There was a wrangler who was supposed to catch the horse when it was spooked, but that horse ran over the wrangler—*and* the wrangler's horse!"

At one time, Dale Robertson was the host of *Death Valley Days*. "Dale is a friend of the family. He is like a big brother to me. Dale worked with Debbie in *The Gambler from Natchez* [1954]. Dale and I did a couple of his *Tales of Wells Fargo* shows. He also did a *Death Valley Days* with me. Most of the *Death Valley Days* were filmed in Kanab, Utah, but one, 'The Captain Dick Mine,' was done in Gallup, New Mexico. We stayed at the El Rancho, a very famous hotel whose rooms were named after various celebrities who had stayed there. In the episode, they shimmied me up the mountainside. As for myself, I fear nothing, but this big old rock had a crack on it! When I saw the show, it could have been *anybody* on that rock. It was like looking at two sticks the camera was so far away! The things I did—I really was kind of dumb! In that particular show, I played an Indian girl who tries to find a gold mine while avenging my husband's death! When I was in the Indian outfit and makeup, I needed to go to town to see the woman who made the costumes. The driver pulled up, and there were some *real* Indians hanging around. They said, 'Ya-Ta-Hay. Ya-Ta-Hay' [*laughs*]. The words mean whatever you want them to mean. The driver was hysterical—they were making a pass! They wanted to know who this squaw woman was!"

Asked about her life today, Lisa reveals, "I married Ben Ware in 1955. He passed away in 1979. I have one daughter and six grandchildren. I first came to Houston to help house sit for Debbie, who travels frequently. I later became a receptionist at Channel 14, the local religious TV station. I was there 19 years, but am now retired. I'm very much involved with the Church of Evangelistic Temple; I sing in the choir and occasionally sing in a trio—but never solo. I like living in Houston, it's quite different from Los Angeles. Here, most people seem to drive a truck, and they don't always wait for an off-ramp. They make their own ramps and veer off the freeway [*laughs*]. I do miss the ocean; the gulf is just not the same. But I enjoy it here in Houston, it's a nice place to live."

Lisa Gaye
Western Filmography

Movies: *Drums Across the River* (1954 Universal-International)—Audie Murphy.

Television: *Annie Oakley*, "Annie and the Lacemaker" (1956); *Jim Bowie*, "Trapline" (1956); *Jim Bowie*, "Spanish Intrigue" (1957); *Have Gun Will Travel*, "Helen of Abajinian" (1957); *Have Gun Will Travel*, "Gun Shy" (1958); *Zorro*, "Fall of Monasterio" (1958); *Tombstone Territory*, "Tin Gunman" (1958); *Northwest Passage*, "Gunsmith" (1958); *Northwest Passage*, "Surprise Attack" (1958); *Californians*, "Man Who Owned San Francisco" (1958); *Tombstone Territory*, "Grave Near Tombstone" (1959); *Black Saddle*, "Client: McQueen" (1959); *Bat Masterson*, "Sharpshooter" (1959); *Bat Masterson*, "Buffalo Kill" (1959); *Colt .45*, "Law West of the Pecos" (1959); *Sugarfoot*, "Trial of the Canary Kid" (1959); *Pony Express*, "Peace Offering" (1959); *Cheyenne*, "Outcasts of Cripple Creek" (1960); *Cheyenne*, "Counterfeit Gun" (1960); *Death Valley Days*, "Million Dollar Pants" (1960); *U.S. Marshal*, "Backfire" (1960); *Wanted Dead or Alive*, "Journey for Josh" (1960); *Rawhide*, "Incident of the Slavemaster" (1960); *Bat Masterson*, "Fatal Garment" (1961); *Death Valley Days*, "A General Without a Cause" (1961); *Maverick*, "State of Siege" (1961); *Shotgun Slade*, "Friends No More" (1961); *Wagon Train*, "Tiburcio Mendez Story" (1961); *Tales of Wells Fargo*, "Dowry" (1961); *Tales of Wells Fargo*, "Kelly's Clover Girls" (1961); *Laramie*, "Perfect Gift" (1962); *Bronco*, "One Evening in Abilene" (1962); *Death Valley Days*, "Other White Man" (1964); *Death Valley Days*, "Captain Dick Mine" (1965); *Death Valley Days*, "The Rider" (1965); *The Wild Wild West*, "Night of the Skulls" (1966); *Death Valley Days*, "Gypsy" (1967); *The Wild Wild West*, "Night of the Falcon" (1967); *Death Valley Days*, "Other Side of the Mountain" (1968); *Death Valley Days*, "Lottie's Legacy" (1968); *Death Valley Days*, "Tracy's Triumph" (1969).

Jane Greer

Westerns Gave Her Trouble

The term *"film noir"* brings to mind a beautiful and extremely talented actress, Jane Greer. Born Bettejane Greer September 9, 1924, in Washington, D.C., she began her career as a singer and model. Originally contracted in 1944 by the Hughes Tool Company, which meant she was placed under contract by Howard Hughes, she was later under contract with RKO, eventually starring with Robert Mitchum in two *film noir* classics, *Out of the Past* (1947), her favorite role, and *The Big Steal* (1949). "No one wanted to work with Bob after his drug bust, but when they asked me about doing *The Big Steal*, I jumped at it. Bob was so helpful. He was terrific."

Jane remembers, "When I first signed at RKO, I darkened my hair. And dark hair makes you look a bit sinister on the screen. Consequently, every part I got was 'the other woman.' Finally, I'd been there for years when a producer, Joan Harrison, wanted me for a normal person. RKO said, 'She plays a heavy.' But Joan told them I'll fix it, and she lightened by hair. Suddenly, I looked human. But I did have a hard time moving away from that 'other woman' image."

During the mid–1940s, Jane Greer had a brief, unhappy marriage to Rudy Vallee. "It lasted about a year, all told [*laughs*]." This didn't stop Howard Hughes from constantly harrying her. "Howard

Hughes was something else. One time, we were at Chi Chi's on Hollywood Boulevard. He had a sundae, and he spilled some chocolate sauce on his shirt. He excused himself to go to the bathroom. When he finally came back to the table, his shirt was all wet! He had washed that shirt in the restaurant bathroom [*laughs*]! When I married Eddie Lasker in 1947, it still didn't stop Howard from trying. It was years before he gave up!"

Jane managed to make a couple of westerns around the same time—one an "A," the other a "B." "*Sunset Pass* [1946] was really a funny picture. James Warren was the star, but we only had one scene at the train station. I never really got to know him very well, or John Laurenz for that matter. John played Chito Rafferty instead of Richard Martin. I don't know why. Dick was a very lovely man, married to a great gal, Elaine Riley. Steve Brodie was in it; also Robert Clarke. Both great guys I knew quite well at RKO. In fact, a few years ago, I was trying to round up a group of the RKO players and was having trouble getting to Steve. By the time we had the function, he had died. I did see Bob Clarke a couple of years ago at the Universal Reunion."

Asked about some of the production problems, Jane laughingly says, "We were up in Lone Pine where it was freezing that time of year, and I caught the flu. In the picture, my boyfriend, John Laurenz, and I went out. I wore a sort of dance-hall blouse while he strummed his guitar and sang a serenade to me. We both had ice in our mouths so the vapor wouldn't photograph. So he was singing with a mouth full of ice [*laughs*]. Needless to say, I got sick as a dog. Later, I was trying to do a scene on a train with James Warren and Nan Leslie, in which Nan has the line, 'We met on a train.' I started laughing and couldn't stop. For whatever reason, that line was the funniest, most stupid line I'd ever heard in my life. And every time she would start it, I would laugh hysterically! I knew this was costing the studio money, but I couldn't help it. I also felt lousy. Somebody finally called the studio nurse, who put a thermometer in my mouth, told me I had 104 degree temperature, said 'She's hallucinating' and had me sent home immediately. I was dizzy, so I went to bed. I still had three scenes to shoot, but they simply dropped all three! They filmed the rest of the picture without me! Now, in the scene when John Laurenz was singing to me, I went up in a tree to retrieve some mistletoe, and he rode away leaving me hanging there. At the end of the picture, someone says, 'Where is Conchita?' or whatever my name was, and it goes to a scene where I … my double…is still up a tree—four and a half feet high—and in someone else's dubbed-in voice you hear, 'Help, help, please help' [*laughs*]. It was ludicrous!"

Asked if *Station West* (1948) with Dick Powell was a better experience, the star states an emphatic, "No! Dick Powell was very nice, but the director, who was notorious in the business, Sidney Lanfield, was a real son of a bitch. He wanted Marlene Dietrich for the picture and he let me know it! He was terrible to me—in fact, terrible to any woman. Can you imagine, this guy had the audacity to say to Agnes Moorehead, 'Do you *think* when you read

Talented Jane Greer in an RKO publicity pose from the 1940s.

a line, hatchet-face?' She came back with, 'Mr. Lanfield, I've taken enough. The boat just sailed and you're on it.' She refused to work with him, came back to Los Angeles, so another director had to do her remaining scenes. As for me, I was a basket case—in tears! He'd say something ugly to me just before I started a scene. He'd say, 'I could go down on Hollywood Boulevard and find 15 actresses who can act better than you' and he'd go on and on. I was glaring and had tears, then he'd ask what was the matter with *me!* He was crazy! Finally, when we were back from location in Sedona, Arizona, he was told—'It's either you or her, and we have *her* under contract.' After that, I wasn't touched by him. And he was fired."

Asked about her co-stars, such as Raymond Burr: "I got to know Ray quite well at RKO. Because of everything that

Station West (1948) with Dick Powell was not one of Jane's best work experiences.

happened, he had to coach me for *Station West*. I certainly received no help from that director [*laughs*]."

Another actor in the film was John Kellogg. "He really let me have it [*laughs*]! We had worked together the year before, in *Out of the Past*. We were on location out in the Valley, and the guys taught me how to play poker. I liked it! Well, John Kellogg came in—and he starts playing. He asked me, 'Have you got anything better than two jacks?' I said 'Sure,' but of course I was bluffing. I wasn't about to let him know what I had in my hand. He said, 'Okay, take it.' Then he asked, 'What did you have?' I said, 'Nothing.' He came back with, 'But you took the pot!' He was ready to kill me [*laughs*]! He started swearing at me—and he took my money back! He then asked, 'What are you doing in this picture?' Of course, I told him I was the *star*!

I saw him years later, apparently when we did a *Zane Grey Theater*, and he brought up the poker incident again. Of course, I still remembered it!"

Incidentally, she's quick to assert that she did her own singing in both RKO westerns.

Jane had a life-threatening experience while appearing in *Run for the Sun* (1956), a loose remake of 1932's *The Most Dangerous Game* and 1945's *A Game of Death*. "We shot that on location in Mexico—around Acapulco, Puerto Vallarta and Mexico City. Richard Widmark, a darling to work with, and I were running, and I had grabbed his arm. He stopped—I kept running, fell and cracked my tailbone when I hit a rock! A week later, I had terrible pain. It became infected, but it would be four years before it was at the most serious state. I had gone to doctors and taken

Ann Rutherford (another of our Ladies of the Western), Jane (billed Bettejane Greer) and Tom Conway in a scene from Jane's screen debut, *Two O'Clock Courage* (1945).

crap like cortisone. Eventually, a doctor in La Jolla told me 'You have coxsackie B.' I couldn't find a doctor here, so I had to go to Michael DeBakey, who cured me. He did the operation where he removed the sac, which was strangling the heart! The sac had grown around my heart. It was attached to it. The only cure is to remove it! You only get this virus around swamps and places like that."

Asked about some of the TV westerns she did, Jane states she was especially fond of *Bonanza*'s "The Julia Bulette Story." "It was one of the first ones they did—in 1959, and it was a good part. I just saw it again recently. It was great. I also remember doing a western with Eddie Albert, directed by David Niven (*Zane Grey Theater*, "The Vaunted"). It was the first

thing David had directed and he was scared stiff. Eddie put him on all the time ... scaring David all the more. I also did a *Stagecoach West* with Wayne Rogers and another old RKO pal, Robert Bray. I saw it recently and enjoyed it very much. Too bad the series wasn't a hit—it holds up well."

Unlike many of her contemporaries, Jane Greer is still acting. She co-starred in *Against All Odds*, the 1984 so-called remake of *Out of the Past*. In 1982, she appeared as Tom Selleck's mother in *Shadow Riders*. "I just had a one-day job. We shot it up in the gold country and I did go on location. There's a scene where Tom sees me for the first time in years. He grabs me really hard and cracked my ribs, hugging me! You could hear the snap. The pain was killing me, but the director, Andrew Mc-Laglen, wanted one more take! So, I held my breath and let Tom grab me again [*laughs*]."

Jane, who died August 24, 2001, has been "immortalized" in best selling author Elmore Leonard's novels, as she's mentioned in nearly every one, even though she's never met Leonard. Jane Greer was a most gracious lady, with many good stories to tell. She was also a most welcome guest at film festivals.

Jane Greer
Western Filmography

Movies: *Sunset Pass* (1946 RKO)—James Warren; *Station West* (1948 RKO)—Dick Powell; *Shadow Riders* (1982 TV Movie)—Tom Selleck.

Television: *Zane Grey Theatre*, "A Gun for My Bride" (1957); *Zane Grey Theatre*, "The Vaunted" (1958); *Bonanza*, "Julia Bulette Story" (1959); *Zane Grey Theatre*, "Stagecoach to Yuma" (1960); *Stagecoach West*, "High Lonesome" (1960).

Marie Harmon

Making the Grade

"I would say I started entertaining at age five, speaking little pieces especially for my favorite uncle Lloyd. He made me the lead star at each family reunion and told everyone one day they would see my name in lights. Unfortunately, he was killed when a train hit his car coming around a blind corner. I was 13 years old. I always hoped when I succeeded, Lloyd would be watching from 'way up there.'"

The still beautiful, blonde Marie Harmon was born October 21, 1923, in Oak Park, Illinois, the only girl among five

brothers, four older, one younger. "My mom gave me elocution lessons so I could perform for the Kiwanis and Elks after their meetings. It gave me the experience of being in front of adult audiences. I enjoyed comedy to make people laugh. Our Carol Playground had a little theater group and, fortunately, I was able to get most lead parts in the summer plays such as *Pocahontas* [I had to scream a lot] and *Snow White*.

"When I attended Oak Park High, I became a small fish in a big pond! I was

Marie's first Republic film was *The El Paso Kid* (1946) with Sunset Carson.

turned down when I read for a school play which really hurt my feelings. To succeed, I had to show them what a mistake they'd made. I continued to do leads in the playground theater group and received notable publicity in *Oak Leaves*, an old established Village news magazine.

"The war started in December 1941, and I entered a contest for 'The Perfect Blind Date for a Serviceman' in the *Chicago Tribune* and won!"

With an "eye on Hollywood," Marie soon figured out working in an office for Coca-Cola in Chicago wasn't the way west. Switching to a waitress job in a bar, she made much more money to finance her way to California. "One evening before work, I met a girl in another club taking photos of patrons as they had a few drinks. She told me she was leaving shortly for

California, riding with a couple who were driving new cars west to be sold by car dealer Mad Man Muntz in Hollywood. I immediately asked my mom if I could go too. I would work in Hollywood but attend acting classes on the side. She helped me convince my dad it would be safe and we, my new friend Winnie and I, could get an apartment together and share expenses."

"We left Chicago in March 1942, and arrived five days later in Hollywood and found a modest hotel in the heart of town. Winnie got a job photographing couples in a club, the Florentine Garden, in the evening and I was hired as a car hop at Roberts Drive-In on Sunset Boulevard. One evening, La Verne Andrews of the Andrews Sisters came in with friends, of which one was a frequent customer, and they invited me on a double date. I had a great time because La Verne took all of us home to meet her parents. Much to La Verne's and my surprise, I would have the second lead in one of their movies a year and a half later at Universal, *Her Lucky Night* [1945]."

Situations changed fast back in those days and Marie found she had to work nights if she was to have acting exposure. "I did plays in the daytime and became a cigarette girl in an after-hours private club in the late evening. I changed from the drive-in to Eugene's on the Sunset Strip which catered to the studio crowd. I met Orson Welles one evening when he tipped me $10 for a deck of cards. Brian Donlevy came to sit out the wait of the birth of his baby. Busby Berkeley came in frequently when he wasn't shooting a musical. George Raft flirted with me one evening to the distaste of beautiful Betty Grable. Being a cigarette girl had its drawbacks. Some patrons seem to think cigarette girls should be available and I was not. So I left.

"Winnie heard Lou Costello was opening a new club called the Bandbox, so we both applied for a job of hostess, where we would do the seating for the shows. Lou was a sweet boss and he too was surprised a year later when I was cast in a bit part in one of his movies … but I ended up on the cutting room floor. We were friends right up to the time he died in the late '50s."

During this time, Marie obtained a good part in *Geneva* at the Bliss-Hayden Little Theatre in Beverly Hills, owned by Lela Bliss and Harry Hayden, established actors in film. "I will always be grateful to Harry for giving me that break because I had calls from Universal, Columbia and Warners when I closed. Universal put me in Deanna Durbin's picture *Hers to Hold* [1943] the very next week. That was my start and I would go back to the Bliss-Hayden Theatre to guest star in other plays.

"I went on to work with Loretta Young in *Ladies Courageous* (1944), doing only a bit part, but later to have my part rewritten through the script after doing one scene. Casting scout Milly Gussey was the one to discover me and went to bat to suggest me for different parts at Universal. She was my guiding light! I turned 20 during the filming of *Ladies Courageous* in 1943 and they gave a surprise birthday party for me after we were through shooting for the day. Many years later, the photo of the cast with me and the cake appeared in my home town paper, which I hoped would show my high school that I did make the grade after all. As I said, I was turned down in our school play many years back."

South of Dixie with Anne Gwynne and David Bruce followed. Then, trying to get a solid foothold on a career, Marie went out on everything just for the experience. "I made my first western, *Springtime in Texas*, with Jimmy Wakely at Monogram in 1945. My agent told the director I would do my own riding. On location there were doubles for all the male actors—but none for me. As we were shooting a scene with all of us on horses, Jimmy's double jumped from a porch onto his horse next to mine and accidentally knocked my saddle loose and my foot out of the stirrup. That caused a stampede. All the horses took off in a heated run with me holding on to my horse's neck as my saddle slid around with me slipping down and watching the ground coming up close. I truly thought it would be the end and I would be trampled to death. The good Lord opened the eyes of all the other cowboys and, fortunately, the stampede was brought to a halt. I was in shock and have never forgotten the experience."

Then it was on to Republic to play opposite Sunset Carson in *El Paso Kid* (1946). "I loved that studio because it seemed like home, just like Universal.

Sunset Carson and Marie in *The El Paso Kid* **(1946).**

Herb Yates called my agent in to talk contract, so she brought me along—a mistake! I signed a contract that day for $150 a week. I understood more money would be discussed after he saw how the picture and I were received. When time passed and nothing more was offered, I went to the Screen Actors Guild to break the contract. Milly Gussey, my 'guiding light,' said I should never have done that. One hundred fifty dollars was good money, but it was too late. I was 'blackballed' and didn't work anywhere for a whole year.

"Then Republic called me back to work—this time with Roy Rogers in *Night Time in Nevada* [1948]. Roy had just married Dale Evans. Since a cowboy may kiss his horse but must never kiss his girl on screen, the studio thought the public would never accept a married couple as leads in a western, Roy therefore needed a new leading lady and I was brought in to step into Dale Evans' shoes. Working with Roy was super—such a down-to-earth, thoughtful man, who was so happy with Dale. I told Roy I couldn't sing—not even carry a tune—but he said not to worry, my voice could be dubbed in. As it were, the part I had did not require any singing. Somewhat later, all the fans made it clear they would be happy to see Roy and Dale together again, so this opportunity disappeared."

After a few more auditions, Marie started to feel like "a has-been. After all, I was 24 and all the young girls coming in were in their teens, just as I was when I first started. I thought it was time for me to move on to other things.

Marie's first western was *Springtime in Texas* (1945) with Dennis Moore, Jimmy Wakely, old-time minstrel man Lee "Lasses" White and prolific character player Budd Buster.

"In 1951, I met and married a wonderful man, Don Currie, with an easygoing manner and a beautiful sense of humor. He was open to new ideas, so when I suggested a dress business, my other teenage dream, he was game and we opened the Dona-Rie Shops, selling ladies ready-to-wear in Hollywood and the San Fernando Valley for the next 23 years.

"We had four children, Sondra, my twins—Marie and Cherie—and a son, Don Anthony Currie. The girls have all appeared in films and on television. Sondra is well established working in many more pictures than I even came close to. My three daughters have all married into the entertainment field with Marie being the first, marrying Steve Lukather, the lead guitarist of ToTo fame, while Sondra

married producer-director Alan J. Levi and Cherie tied the knot to Robert Hays, the star of *Airplane* (1980) and other films. My son Don is a mortgage banker.

"In 1972 my husband and I decided to go our separate ways after 21 years of marriage. He has since passed away. In 1975 I married Dr. Wolfgang Kaupisch, a senior industrial advisor to the Government of Indonesia for the World Bank. We were stationed in Jakarta, the capital of Indonesia for three and a half years. While in Jakarta, I produced and directed plays for both the Women's International Club and the American Women's Club."

Upon their return to the States and her husband's retirement, "We met Roy Rogers [in 1981] when we found a photo of me among his leading ladies in his museum in Victorville. When Roy learned of my presence, we were invited to his private office above the museum by his secretary. Roy and my husband found a common interest: East Africa, where Roy hunted big game and my husband acted as economic advisor to the government of Tanzania. As we were about to leave, Roy entertained us by playing his guitar, singing and yodeling, all the while his German pointer yodeling along with him! What a charming man."

Today, Marie and her husband spend half their time in the south of Portugal, where they have a home on a four-acre orchard, the other half in southern California, where her children live.

Marie Harmon
Western Filmography

Movies: *Springtime in Texas* (1945 Monogram)—Jimmy Wakely; *El Paso Kid* (1946 Republic)—Sunset Carson; *Gunsmoke* (1946 Standard)—Nick Stuart; *Night Time in Nevada* (1948 Republic)—Roy Rogers.

Virginia Herrick

From Hoss Opera to Grand Opera

Virginia Herrick flashed by on the B-western and TV screen in a few short years, but she left an impact. She's led quite a life—from a secluded ranch in Washington to the opera halls of Spain. "I was born in Washington state on Olympic Peninsula. I had a view of Mount Olympus, when I was a child, from my bedroom window. It was covered with snow year-round. There were two other mountains and they had very unusual names, Little Mountain and Big Mountain. I was born in the valley, my grandfather homesteaded that property and there were these mountains around it. My daddy named Virginia Creek up in the high country, up in the mountains, after me. And a road's named after us too. As a little kid, I used to yodel, and hear echoing around the mountains. I would mimic the birds and sing. That's why my voice [became so strong]."

"But I wanted to be a concert pianist at age five or six. I was so lucky, I had so many miracles happen in my life. God did it ... nobody else. I know that. For instance, up in the mountains there, I had an upright piano that came from Seattle, from my folks' family.

"My father was head of the community there, and head of the school board. Now this was a community where your closest neighbor is a mile away. So he

Virginia admonishes Al "Fuzzy" St. John for grabbing a sandwich before the jailhouse table is set as Bud Osborne, Lash LaRue, Archie Twitchell (seated) and Clarke Stevens watch in Lash's last B-western *Frontier Phantom* (1952).

thought, I'll build a schoolhouse right here next to where my kids are being born. The first year in school, my teacher, a man, used to beat the kids and was very mean. He said I was stupid because I was so shy. It frightened me. So my dad got rid of him and got another teacher from Billingham, a lady, and she was a musician. She knew music, so she taught me piano, got me interested in it. I took to it like a duck to water. I loved the piano. I took piano lessons from her 'til I was about five or six, and she told my dad, 'I've taught her all I can, she's got to go to the city to get a teacher who can teach her.' That kind of ended my wanting to be a concert pianist, you had to have proper training, and I couldn't do it any more.

"About that time, I was getting interested in voice, because this teacher had the most beautiful contralto voice. She couldn't teach me voice because I was too young. I must have been around 12 or 13 and you should wait probably until you're 16. I couldn't study singing then, until I left the ranch and got to a city.

"About that time things got poor, there wasn't much money. We had to get a mortgage on the property and finally we lost it, because the state moved the highway from in front of our place where Dad and Mama had a little store and gasoline pump, down about a mile away. That was in 1929 or 1930. So we lost everything and my dad had to go out and work in the lumber mills and my mama stayed and looked after the ranch. My two older brothers left and went to get work.

"Now there were some people who had come in to the high country from Seattle and they said, 'This child should go to the city where she can have teachers who can teach her things she should be doing.' I was very small and they wanted to adopt me, but my mother would never let me go. Well, we never heard a word from them again until I graduated at 16 from high school. A letter came in the mail, just out of the blue. This is one of the miracles. The letter said, 'We'd like to have Virginia come and live with us.' Since then, they had adopted two little children. They said, 'We would take care of her and we'd like an au pair to look after the two little children. And Virginia can live with us.' I said, 'Oh, Mama, I was just sitting out on the front porch, thinking, "What am I going to do?" I'm through high school, everybody's gone from here, it's just you and I and I've got to get away and try to do something. Please let me go.' Shy and timid, never been to a city before. Never gone up in an elevator, I'd never seen airplanes, never been on a train, anything like that. This was an opportunity. So I got on the bus and went to Seattle, and I met the people again.

"I went to the university to study because a lot of people thought I should be a costume designer, a dress designer, because I started sewing when I was five years old, making my dolls wonderful wardrobes. I'd copy them from the catalogues [magazines] showing famous designer-made clothes for stars. I'd copy those for my dolls. I started sewing for myself at about nine years old, designed my clothes and made my first coat when I was about 10 or 11. Sewed all my clothes after that. People saw that and thought this girl ought to be a designer. That's kind of what I wanted to go into because I knew I could make more money.

"Unfortunately, I knew I couldn't stay at the university because I had to get my mom, who was ill, away from the ranch. She was all alone."

Virginia obtained a job with a company "cutting fudge in a store window." The company eventually took her to Spokane, then their new shop in Los Angeles. By this time, Virginia had saved enough money to send for her mother.

"Soon after, a man saw me in the window who was with the Harry Conover Agency and thought I'd photograph well. They did all kinds of ads. So I had to leave my mama in Los Angeles and go back to New York to be a model. I did quite a lot of work there. Pepsodent toothpaste, Clairol Hair ads, all kinds of ads that ran in *Colliers* and *Post* and all the major magazines, magazine covers, detective magazines—shooting a gun. I was pretty successful but I didn't think I should send for my mama—under those circumstances, it was too iffy. So I went back to Hollywood."

"Mama and I started taking in sewing, dress designing and so on. I got enough money so I could start studying singing very seriously, which I always wanted to do. That lasted for two or three years.

"A man literally stopped me on the street and said he wanted to take me to the studio, said he was an agent. I said, 'I don't want to go to the studios,' because I was so shy. I'd learned to pose, but I was still shy. I said, 'I don't want to go to the studios. I've heard about those producers. I've heard what they do during...' I really didn't want to go 'cause I wasn't interested in movies, I was interested in singing. That's what I wanted to do. Finally he said, 'There's a new program on TV and they need a girl to just stand there and hand the host things, and say hello.' So I did that and the very next day, the agent, Harold Svoerland, set up a deal.

They called me from Republic and I signed."

Virginia's first film was *Vigilante Hideout* (1950) with Allan "Rocky" Lane. "I was very shy and I didn't know too much about acting, but Svoerland helped me. I remember, one of the scenes, I had to do a stage whisper. I was scared to death, I didn't know what a stage whisper was. So Harold got with me and showed me how to do a stage whisper. I was so terribly nervous that my eyes swelled shut. My eyes used to swell shut in those days when I'd get nervous. So they had to photograph me from the side all during the first two days until the swelling went down. But I knew my lines, because I always learned them carefully and I never fluffed my lines. Other people did, but I never did.

"I remember they let me ride and I was very happy about that. I'd learned to ride in Washington. I had my own horse and I used to go out on the highway before they moved the highway down from our place. When the cars would come, I taught my pinto pony to rear up. He'd rear up when a car would come." As for riding, Virginia's expert horsemanship comes into play in her Columbia serial *Roar of the Iron Horse* (1950), where her horse rears up at least three times in one scene.

With that start, one western followed another. "A week or two weeks or maybe three weeks at the most and I'd be back on another picture. Svoerland was training me. At the last, he wanted to get me into big things, like MGM. I did do a Hallmark production with Richard Denning, *Why Men Leave Home*. That was good because I got to wear beautiful clothes, beautiful things. In that picture, I was supposed to be an elegant lady."

A Monogram Whip Wilson was her second western. "I remember I was fascinated with those whip tricks of his. Fascinated." Unfortunately, Virginia didn't realize Whip was a trained opera singer. "Oh, we could have sung! I would have loved to have sung with him ... but I never heard him sing."

"The serial, *Roar of the Iron Horse* was the third one, I think. With Jock Mahoney. We called him Jocko. There again, I stayed by myself. I'd eat by myself, I wouldn't eat with anyone or anything. I'd just go over and sit on a log, We were on location, so I'd go to my separate little cottage and stay there. I never came out. I was extremely shy. Extremely so. On the set, they'd talk about Jocko's good sense of humor. He was also a heck of a stuntman and a heck of a rider. I've never seen anybody mount a horse like him. Gosh, I used to watch that. He was fascinating. In one chapter, I actually jumped in his arms. That was a great thrill."

There's a wild wagon chase in the serial with Virginia in the wagon. "Yes, I did some of that." Although there was an obvious stunt man with a dark wig doubling her part of the time. "Yeah, but they had to do reaction shots up close. I was scared to death. But it was fun."

Myron Healey was one of the heavies in *Roar of the Iron Horse* as well as her later *Montana Desperado* (1951). "I was a great admirer of Myron. He was a wonderful actor, I learned a lot from him. He would help me with my lines. Because I'd get one picture after another, I thought, well, I'd better learn this trade if I'm going to do it. Know what I'm doing. So I tried then to learn, to get better, and I know toward the last I was getting a lot better because I was more easy about it. Myron was in several pictures with me and he was very helpful. He was kind and a very wonderful person.

"I don't think there were probably any directors that gave me any direction, other than, *stand there, come in here*, that kind of thing. Not 'til the one I did with Crash Corrigan [*Buckskin Rangers*, 1950].

In Chapter Five of the 1951 Columbia serial *Roar of the Iron Horse,* Jocko Mahoney holds a gun on badman Pierce Lyden, leaving Virginia a bit puzzled.

There was a good director. Frank Mc-Donald was his name. He tried to help me in some of the scenes, but that was the first person to ever try to help me, except Svoerland. And that's a pilot that's lost. I may have done a better job ... pretty good job on that. Because McDonald was very helpful."

I Killed Geronimo (1950) was independently produced by Jack Schwartz and starred Jimmy Ellison. "He was so nice. What I remember is that the men on those pictures were so nice to me. Of course, I was very shy and I guess they knew it. I never have gotten over my shyness completely. It's still there. But anyway, I didn't associate with them very much, I just kept to myself." Often Virginia would be the only girl on location. "On *I Killed Geron-imo*, there was not even a hairdresser. I was the hairdresser, the makeup and everything. That was the cheapest picture, I think, I ever did." The film incorporated a lot of stock footage from John Wayne's *Stagecoach* (1939). "Yes, they did. I like shooting, and I shot the gun in that. And I liked the stagecoaches and I loved riding the horses. Also, I have a very high voice. I did a scream in *I Killed Geronimo*. It was so high no one could believe it. They took me off in the field and had me scream and scream and scream. They recorded it and used my scream in many other movies."

However, being the only girl on location, with so many men around, can obviously lead to problems with someone being a bit forward with their affections.

Virginia has just met James Ellison in this scene from *I Killed Geronimo* (1950). Luther Crockett is the observing officer.

"If anyone ever did, I'll tell you this, all the people on the set, all the guys, would keep them away from me. That's the way they were. I was like their little sister and they were very protective. They treated me that way, with great respect. Someone tried to get close to me once, but they kept him away."

Virginia appeared on one Gene Autry TVer. "Yeah, he's singing to me and I was thinking... I don't like his voice. 'Cause I was studying opera. To me, he was kinda twangy ... but it fit the role."

As for other TV work, Virginia recalls, "By the time I got down to the TV shows, *The Cisco Kid*, I was more at ease, and I loved the riding I did in those. They let me ride to my heart's content. But my legs were so short, I'm so short, that I'd have to really get up in the stirrup, then I'd swing over real easily, but it was hard to get my foot into that stirrup ... my legs are so short. Those were both very nice men on *The Cisco Kid*, but it is a long time ago and so much water went under the bridge. It was just a job to me, I made the money, took it home and that was it."

For about two and a half years, Virginia had been dating Omar V. Garrison. "I was on an interview for a job, I went into the office to interview with the producer and there was this man in there. He just stared at me and wouldn't stop. It made me a little angry and I thought, well, I'm not going to stay here with him staring at me like that. I called the secretary,

I said, 'I have someplace else to go on the lot, I'll come back a little later.' Well, I stayed away at least a half hour, I thought he'll be gone by this time. I went back and the office was empty. I thought, oh, good, he's gone. But who comes walking out of the producer's office but this man ... and the producer was with him and he said, 'This is the man from the *Los Angeles News* and he wants to do a story on you.' So he interviewed me. I remember [it] so well. There was a kind of a bench and I sat down on that and he sat on the arm of a chair. I never looked up at him. He'd ask me questions and I'd answer them. I told him about the things I had done and he didn't believe me because he thought it was too fantastic a story, how I got to Hollywood and all that. Finally, he left but he called up and said, 'I need to have you sign a release for this because you've been a professional model and we can't use the pictures we took unless you sign.' So I talked to him and I thought, gee, that man had a beautiful voice, sort of English, he went to school in England and had a very beautiful voice and beautiful accent. I thought, he sounds nice, I'd like to talk to him more. So he came and I signed the release. He began to get me advertising jobs ... Zenith television ... and I modeled the star sapphire ... the largest star sapphire in the world. Every time he could use me in any way, he did, to promote my career.

"We started going together. I liked him, he was like a mother-father-sister-brother. I mean I could talk about anything to him. And I needed someone like that. He was about ten years older than I. He knew I was studying singing, very serious about that ... and one day he heard me and couldn't believe he'd heard this big voice coming out of this little frame. Couldn't believe it. From then on, he said, you've got to go to Italy to study because there aren't opportunities here. At that

time, there weren't many opportunities for a singer, or really, the good teachers.

"He had an assignment to go to Rome and he said, 'If you'll marry me, I have to be there a year, at least, you can study singing.' Well, by this time, my big brother had come to live with us, so I knew Mother was okay. I got married in September 1952. And went to Italy. And studied singing. For a year. I sang outside of Rome, where newcomers sing, after they've studied about a year. Then my teacher said, 'You're ready to sing ... why don't you go back to your country?'

"So we came back to America and he started working for the paper again. There was a new opera company starting in Los Angeles, and I did that.

"But my husband, such a strange man, never liked to stay in one place. I wanted to stay here and get a home. He always liked to live in England, that was his favorite place, said it was his second home. We'd stay in London for a while, then we'd go down to Spain and find some outlying village and stay there and he'd write his books." Omar V. Garrison wrote 14 books including *Howard Hughes in Las Vegas*, the forerunner of all accounts of Hughes' life, *Balboa, Conquistador* and *Tantra, the Yoga of Sex*, still in print, translated into several languages. "Then maybe we'd come back to America and we'd do a book tour. I got into an opera company and as he traveled down to Southern Spain, I sang there ... several operas. Then we would come back to England again, live there for a while, then we'd go back to Spain again, for a while ... it was just like that ... my married life, back and forth. His career was the important one. I admired him so much because he was such a good writer, so I thought that was the most important thing, but I still kept up my singing. I still studied. I did a lot of singing in Spain, in those big old churches. They'd have weddings and I'd sing. In Malaga, Spain, I did

Dona Anna and Don Giovanni, Mozart…"

Eventually, on a speaking tour in Utah, Virginia and Omar found the "interesting looking little town of Cedar City. The air was so good … six miles high. It just invigorates you. We both felt so good, we decided to settle down. We had that home for about 15 … going on 20 years. We made a lot of good Mormon friends. That's when I first started designing wedding gowns for the Mormon girls because they get married so young and they're so cute and pretty, with little, cute shapes. I became Alanna of Cedar City. I enjoyed it. It is a certain talent I have for designing … a seamstress."

The couple spent summers in Cedar City and wintered in Spain. "But then Omar got quite ill. I think he was having little strokes, so we wanted to get away from there."

A good friend persuaded the couple to relocate to Las Vegas, Nevada, in November 1996. Omar died in September 1997.

It was only a short time later, through her friend Dick Madigan's interest in her early career in films, that Virginia was "re-discovered." Since then, she's attended a film festival and found there are still many fans of the westerns she made. "I'm amazed. I absolutely cannot believe that. And I'd never seen any of these pictures. I saw *I Killed Geronimo* because it played, and played and played … for years it would come back to haunt me. I am just overwhelmed. I just cannot believe it. I look back now and I think, 'Well, gee, I really wasn't too bad.'"

Virginia Herrick Western Filmography

Movies: *Vigilante Hideout* (1950 Republic)—Allan "Rocky" Lane; *Silver Raiders* (1950 Monogram)—Whip Wilson; *I Killed Geronimo* (1950 Eagle Lion)—Jimmy Ellison; *Montana Desperado* (1951 Monogram)—Johnny Mack Brown; *Frontier Phantom* (1952 Western Adventure)—Lash LaRue.

Serial: *Roar of the Iron Horse* (1950 Columbia)—Jock Mahoney.

Television: *Gene Autry*, "Six Shooter Sweepstakes" (1950); *Buckskin Rangers*, unsold Ray Corrigan pilot (1950); *Cisco Kid*, "Hidden Valley" (1951); *Cisco Kid*, "Quarter Horse" (1952); *Cowboy G-Men*, "Rawhide Gold" (1953).

Kathleen Hughes

Western Scream Queen

Cult star Kathleen Hughes is perhaps best known for her two horror films, *Cult of the Cobra* (1955) and the 3D *It Came from Outer Space* (1953), but the Uni-

This very famous pose of Kathleen from *It Came from Outer Space* (1953) has been used innumerable times to sell books, magazines and videos

happened... I was supposed to have a scene the next day where I was up all night. I had an early call but I didn't want to *look* as if I had been up all night, so I told my escort, who took me to Ciro's, I needed to get home early. Well, he later returned to Ciro's and it turned out to be that famous night when Darryl F. Zanuck swung from the trapeze! The papers said I had a spat with my date, but that wasn't true. Once again, I blew it! I missed one of the great Hollywood happenings."

Of her *Dawn at Socorro* co-stars, the actress says, "Piper Laurie was very nice. I don't remember Alex Nicol much. I was not impressed with Lee Van Cleef, never thought he'd be a big star someday. Edgar Buchanan and Paul Brinegar didn't impress me one way or the other. As for Mara Corday, we were already friends, both under contract to the same studio. I like Mara; later she and Dick [Richard Long] came to parties at our house. Her fights with Dick are legend, but I never witnessed any such thing! They never fought around me! The one who impressed me in *Dawn at Socorro* was Skip Homeier! I thought he was great! I've loved everything I've ever seen him in, and that includes his very first, *Tomorrow the World* [1944], when he was still a young teenager." Asked about her *Dawn* director, Kathleen recalls, "Oh, it was George Sherman! He came to our house and we went to his. A lovely man. The producer was William Alland. I heard a rumor recently that he and I had an affair back then, but it was not true. I only knew him to say hello. We never even had lunch together!"

versal-International contractee does have westerns to her credit, including the 1954 Technicolor *Dawn at Socorro* and many western television episodes.

"I had gone to New York to see some of the current Broadway shows. It was 1953 and, in those days, everybody seemed to know where everybody was. I got a call from Sam Speigel to read for a part in a picture that would be shot in New York. I had just been told to report back to Universal on Monday to replace another actress in *Dawn at Socorro*. So I told Sam, 'No.' I thought to myself, 'A picture is a picture.' I was under contract to Universal, what would be the difference? The difference was, the picture Sam wanted me to do was the Eva Marie Saint part in *On the Waterfront* [1954], and the part Universal wanted me for was only the second lead in *Dawn at Socorro*! So, I blew it! But, I did enjoy making the film very much. Rory Calhoun was a very, very nice man, a joy to work with, a gentleman and nice to be around. I can't say that about everybody I worked with. Another funny thing

1759-15AD

Kathleen is saloon girl Clare in *Dawn at Socorro* (1954).

After leaving Universal, Kathleen freelanced and landed quite a few roles on television. About the *Tall Man* episode "A Scheme of Hearts" (1961), she retorts, "I got to kiss Clu Gulager [*laughs*]! I always loved doing costume pictures. As a little girl, I would read storybooks and dream of wearing those clothes. I was never very fond of fashions of the day. I always liked Barry Sullivan. He was very nice. We shot it, like *Dawn*, entirely on the backlot of Universal. Even the scene at the lake was at Universal."

About *Hotel de Paree* ("Only Wheel in Town") in 1959, "My husband, Stanley Rubin, produced the series for one season. Earl Holliman had worked for him in *Destination Gobi* [1953]. The series wasn't going well, and Earl asked for Stanley to come in as producer and maybe save it. We shot that at the old Fox western lot. I played a woman of ill repute. All of the girls in the show were jealous of Dyan Cannon because we felt she was the director's pet. We were really catty, tearing her apart behind her back with stories like, 'She must have put tissue under her breasts to get such cleavage!' It's not that she wasn't nice, and nice to us—it's just that she was that director's pet!" As for Earl Holliman, Kathleen says, "I love him. He's the most talented, nicest guy. We have the same tap class and the same singing class. He's one of the few I see fairly regularly."

Asked about other Stanley Rubin–produced shows in which she has appeared, Kathleen is quick to comment, "Stanley hates nepotism, so I had to read for every part I got that he produced. I read for the casting director, everybody. Stanley was afraid if he cast me and others weren't satisfied with my performance, they'd be angry at him!"

Kathleen appeared in the sci-fi classic, *It Came from Outer Space* (1953), which was set in the modern-day west. The star reveals, "I had read the script. I begged them for the part! I kept after them to cast me. They said it was too small a role, but when I found out it would be in 3D, I really kept on until they finally relented! I am quite glad I was persistent! A famous still of me screaming was even used on a calendar. I bought several of them and gave them to family and friends for Christmas presents!

"I did another film in 3-D—*The Glass*

Web (1953). I was the female lead; John Forsythe and Edward G. Robinson were the men. It was a murder picture, and I played a blackmailing, scheming actress!"

When told she only seemed to have nice things to say about people, Kathleen reveals, "Not about everybody. Do you know Francis D. Lyon, who directed *Cult of the Cobra* [1955]? Well, I hated him! And Rudy Maté, who directed *Sally and Saint Anne* [1952]—he sent me to an assistant director—actually a wannabe director. The guy gave me terrible line readings. When I did them for the film, Rudy screamed, 'Why are you doing the part like that?' The assistant director was right there but didn't say a word, and I was too shy to speak up for myself. Rudy had a tick—his head shook, like he was saying 'No.' He went to wardrobe where I was trying on a lot of gorgeous clothes. His head ticked no, or so I thought; I thought

Easy on the eyes Universal-International 1950s publicity pose of Kathleen.

he rejected the clothes. I had never seen him before that."

As to their current projects, Kathleen reveals, "Stanley and I both contributed one of the stories for a book, *Tales from the Casting Couch*, released in December 1996. These were stories about Marilyn Monroe edited by Michael Viner and Terry Frankel for Dove Books. Actually, I also wrote four anonymous stories—without credit. You'll enjoy it!"

Kathleen Hughes
Western Filmography

Movies: *Dawn at Socorro* (1954 Universal-International)—Rory Calhoun.
Television: *Hotel de Paree*, "The Only Wheel in Town" (1959); *G. E. Theatre*, "Journal of Hope" (1960); *The Tall Man*, "A Scheme of Hearts" (1961).

Lois January

Texas Lady

The leading lady in a dozen B-westerns of the 1930s is a true Texan, born October 5, 1912, in McAllen. "It's near the border. A few feet south and I would have been a Mexican [*laughs*]! It was a one-horse town then—but a resort town now! My mother wanted to be out here in California. We went for a visit, returned to Texas, then the family moved to California."

At the beginning of her career, Lois was a featured singer in the famous Rainbow Room in New York. She also appeared in many of the top nightclubs and cabaret rooms. In radio she appeared for four years on *Reveille Sweetheart* for CBS then two years on Mutual in *January's Calendar*. She was also host Jack Bailey's assistant on CBS' *County Fair* (1945–1950).

But it's film, and B-westerns in particular, for which Lois is best known. She landed a contract with Universal. "That's how I got the role in the Reb Russell western *Arizona Badman* [1935]. Universal farmed me out. They did those westerns on the back lot, way up in the hills of Canoga Park. I worked with the same cowboys over and over. They'd keep calling me back to do another picture.

"Universal taught you everything—I was in a lot of their big movies—but only in small parts. I never looked at show biz as a career. I never thought of it as a business. I had fun, fun, fun; otherwise, I could have gone further. But I enjoyed what I

Northwestern University football star turned cowboy hero Reb Russell, child star Tommy Bupp and Lois in her first western, *Arizona Badman* (1935).

was doing. I didn't drink, smoke or fool around. I lived with my family—they were supportive of me in every way."

Border Caballero (1936), Lois' second western, starred Tim McCoy. "I loved Tim; he was a very nice man and I liked working with him, but he was quite *old* even then! Tim had a thing for me. He really liked me. He was the first actor who invited me to his beautiful home [*laughs*], and I was crushed about that. I didn't play that game—so I was hurt. Noel Madison was another one—he tried to get me in his hotel room. I thought he was so nice, but he wanted *that*. Again, it crushed me. The casting couch is not a dream, it's real—I learned how to handle it. I'd kid with them and stay friends. You could tease them and

get their mind off it! Incidentally, Noel Madison was in the now–cult film, *Cocaine Fiends* [1937] with me. The working title, *The Pace That Kills*, was a better name. Of course, at Universal, Junior Laemmle [Carl Laemmle, Jr., son of the studio's founder and at the time, head of Universal's production] chased me. He was a little skunk. I hated him. You just take it in stride. Lucille Lund also had trouble with him—she asked me how I handled it, and I told her about joking with them."

Skull and Crown (1935) was a low-budget Bernard B. Ray production released by Reliable. "I didn't like the film, but I loved that dog, Rin Tin Tin, Jr. He was so beautiful. And I did enjoy making the movie; I had fun. I didn't have a steady

Townspeople watch as Ralph Byrd (husband of another of our Ladies of the Western, Virginia Carroll), Lois and Tim McCoy face the badmen in *Border Caballero* (1936).

agent, and you gotta have a good agent working for you. To me, it was all fun and games."

With so many westerns to her credit, there are bound to be accidents—no? "Not really. Being from Texas, I knew horses. I loved them and I was not afraid of them. I was not too happy with guns, however. In one of the movies—either with Fred Scott or Johnny Mack Brown—I was not able to handle a great white horse. I rode fast in front of a posse. I was supposed to pull the horse up at the door and get off. I couldn't make that horse stop! Because of time and budgets, you could only do one or two takes. I halfway slid off—it could have been a bad accident, but luckily I never had one."

Johnny Mack Brown was Lois' leading man in two westerns, *Bar Z Badmen* (1937) and *Rogue of the Range* (1937). "Like Reb Russell, Johnny used to be a big football star before he made movies. Johnny Mack was such a sweet guy—he loved being a western star—he was always the perfect gentleman. We were shooting a picture and he told the director, 'Why not have Lois in this scene where she will show up better?' He was building me up. I remained friends with his wife after he passed away."

Lois kept in touch with some of her other leading men throughout the years. "Bob Steele wouldn't let me come and see him when he was dying. He had emphysema and didn't look well. His wife said,

Lois wants to help Fred Scott, but Jimmy Aubrey suspects it's Fred's evil double, Killer Dane, in *Moonlight on the Range* (1937).

'He just looks terrible.' I'd seen him at parties, on the Universal lot, wherever, over the years."

As for Fred Scott, with whom she did her last two B-westerns in 1937, Lois recalls, "Fred was an opera singer. He was a wonderful guy—such a doll. We loved to sing together. I got to sing in *Moonlight on the Range* [1937], and he wanted me to do more singing, but on the other picture I didn't get to sing at all. I would get up before sunrise—and work into the dusk."

The westerns were peopled over and over with the same character actors, such as Charles King. "He was fun, but I went home after work and didn't socialize with any of these people." Fuzzy St. John: "I

loved him—he was so nice. The western stars were all normal, nice, wonderful guys. Those cowboys were just good, fun-loving guys. I like the feel of westerns; it felt like I was still back in Texas."

Lois worked at Paramount, MGM and RKO, with Universal "being my home." But in the late 1930s, she left Hollywood and went to New York, "where I did a Broadway show, *Yokel Boy* [1939], with Buddy Ebsen and another one, *High Kickers* [1941], with George Jessel and Sophie Tucker. Buddy looks weathered these days. I don't think he feels good.

"I sang on Meredith Willson's radio show—and had my own *Reveille Sweetheart* program on CBS—where I woke up the servicemen every morning. I'd get up at 4:30—to get to the 5:30–6:30 A.M. show. Arthur Godfrey followed me, and he took me on his show as well."

Early in her career, Lois appeared in a number of short subjects at Columbia and elsewhere. "I worked with Thelma Todd and ZaSu Pitts; Frankie Albertson and Lou Holtz, who was fabulous. Betty Grable was with me in some—she had a pushy mother—something I did not have."

Lois' most famous picture is *The Wizard of Oz* (1939) where she was the Emerald City woman with a cat. "I still get a lot of mail because of my part in *Oz*. In fact, I get more mail from that than from the westerns. We had no idea it would go like this when we made it. Judy Garland hated the commissary at MGM. So, she and I went to the Culver City Hotel, which was just across the street from Metro, and we'd sit in a cute little restaurant there. A few years ago, there was an Oz Film Fair held at the same hotel. I was on that movie for three months!"

Asked about her favorite westerns, Miss January hesitates, then explains, "I don't usually have favorites, but if I had to choose, I'd pick two: *Border Caballero* because I played a dance hall girl and I liked the story, and *Moonlight on the Range* because I got to sing on film."

When comparing one studio with another, Lois emphatically states, "They're all the same—they all go to the same locations. I couldn't tell which studio I was at."

The biggest studio to make a "B" western with Lois was Universal with *Courage of the West* (1937) starring Bob Baker. "Bob Baker was too pretty! He was nice, but didn't get friendly. He didn't want me to sing a song in his picture. That business is full of jealousy. It is an egotistical business; you have to have a pretty steady character to overcome it. I later got into metaphysics and philosophy."

These days, with a doctorate in metaphysics, she has her own cable TV show, *Take 5 with Lois January*. She uses her book of the same title for her show, which is seen on a variety of cable outlets in southern California.

Lois still receives residual checks from her long career. "I get checks from *Marcus Welby* [1969–1976], which is still running in syndication. I played a nurse at the hospital on that. I recently got a residual check for 69 cents for a European showing of *Polish Wedding* [1998]!" she laughs.

Lois January
Western Filmography

Movies: *Arizona Badman* (1935 Kent)— Reb Russell; *Skull and Crown* (1935 Reliable)— Regis Toomey; *Border Caballero* (1936 Puritan)—Tim McCoy; *Lightnin' Bill Carson* (1936 Puritan)—Tim McCoy; *Rogue of the Range* (1936 Supreme)—Johnny Mack Brown; *Lightnin' Crandall* (1937 Republic)—Bob Steele; *Bar Z Badmen* (1937 Supreme)—Johnny Mack Brown; *Trusted Outlaw* (1937 Republic)—Bob Steele; *Red Rope* (1937 Republic)—Bob Steele; *Courage of the West* (1937 Universal)—Bob Baker; *Moonlight on the Range* (1937 Spectrum)—Fred Scott; *The Roaming Cowboy* (1937 Spectrum)—Fred Scott.

Anne Jeffreys

White Cloud Moonhush

Anne Jeffreys certainly has had an all-media career. The perennially beautiful blonde, a famous John Robert Powers model at the start, played in nearly 50 movies, sang grand opera, starred in over 30 plays on Broadway and on tour (musicals, comedies, light opera), starred in the successful *Topper* television series (1953–1955) with husband Robert Sterling, then was on the soap opera *Bright Promise* in 1971. In between were a myriad of TV guest star appearances. She's been married since 1951 to former actor Robert Sterling. Born Anne Jeffreys Carmichael in Goldsboro, North Carolina, in 1923, she told us, "In spite of being a sickly child, my childhood was most pleasant, due to a wonderful mother and superior grandparents."

It's hard to believe Anne was ever sickly. At 78 she looks the picture of health. "Some people say 'phooey' to the golden years. But I say you can deter aging through diet, exercise and the right attitude. My mother started me on a lifetime routine of exercise, diet and vitamins. If you think young, dress youthfully, wear your hair in a becoming style, you can keep old age at bay. I also believe in living life by good thoughts—and in being kind to people."

As to why Anne became an actress, she replies, "Mostly because my mother wanted a career in singing for me. Thank goodness she steered me on my path of destiny. My first film was a Buster Crabbe western. Then I went under contract to MGM and did *Tarzan's New York Adventure* (1942) and *I Married an Angel* (1942) with my hero and heroine—Nelson Eddy and Jeanette MacDonald. Then I went under contract to Republic and didn't care for the roles of chorus girls or gangster molls they cast me in and requested to play a 'nice girl role'—hence the Wild Bill Elliott series.

"Bill Elliott was a very nice gentleman. He was originally a dress extra and somebody talked him into doing the Red Ryder series—probably Pappy Yates, who ran Republic. Bill was very tall—6'3", 6'4", and, of course, he had those boots, making him a giant. He was a man who knew what he wanted, smart business-wise. Everything was very well calculated and worked out in his career. He had it all planned what he was going to do and how he was going to do it. And he accomplished it. He became a big western star practically overnight. He was always sort of reserved and quiet, but fun…had a nice sense of humor. Of course, Gabby Hayes kept everything stirred up a bit [*laughs*]. He was such a sweetheart. We had a lot of laughs together. I learned to steal scenes anyway I could because, usually, the girl in those things was very incidental. The back of my head was in most shots. I used to wear a bow ribbon in my hair, so I wiggled

A winning team for Republic: Anne, Bill Elliott and Gabby Hayes. *The Man from Thunder River* (1943) is one of several they did together.

my bow ribbon, wiggled my ears ... anything to throw them off and get a little action in the camera. Bill always appreciated it.

"During the series with Bill, I once had to play an Indian girl [*laughs*]. They put a black wig on me, put dark makeup ... 'course, I had blue eyes. Put a headband around my forehead with a feather, buckskins and moccasins. The first day with all this getup on, I went in the commissary and was at the counter when my agent came in and sat right down beside me. I thought—he doesn't recognize me, so I didn't say anything. We must have eaten lunch beside each other for 15–20 minutes until I finally said, 'Could you pass the salt, please?' He looked around and gasped—'Annie?'

"Another thing—the crew were great pranksters. They were mischievous. I was the only girl and we were working in a phony cave on the backlot. It was one of those hot, dusty days. My name in the film [*Wagon Tracks West*, 1943] was Moonhush [*laughs*]. I was sitting in this canvas chair and did not see the cowboy sneak up behind me and tie my Indian fringe from my buckskins to the chair. Then someone hollered, 'Annie, they want you over here. Hurry, hurry.' I got up and took the chair with me! Here I was walking along dragging the chair behind me tied to the fringe of my buckskin! Another joke they played on me ... wearing these big old moccasins, I was always slipping my feet out and putting on comfortable shoes. They took them one time, put them behind my chair,

Bill Elliott, Anne Jeffreys as Moonhush, Tom Tyler as medicine man Clawtooth and Rick Vallin as college educated Fleetwing try to help Charles Miller as Brown Bear, who is stricken with a deadly fever in *Wagon Tracks West* (1943).

then hollered, 'Come on Annie, they want you now. Put on your moccasins.' I jumped into my moccasins and, unknowingly, they had filled them with talcum powder. Every time I stepped, these big white puffs [*laughs*] came flying all over the place. Whitecloud Moonhush they called me after that!

"Still another time, the Indians were in the cave supposedly drying fish over the fire and they had these smoked herring. Somebody took one of these smoked herring and put it in my Indian knapsack! It was a hot day and—phew, I couldn't figure out where the fish was. They're all walkin' 'round holding their noses—'Eeeuck—Annie!' It wasn't until lunch when I took the knapsack off that I realized what they'd done. I took it and hid it in the prop box but didn't tell the wranglers where I put it. I said, 'I found the fish fellas ... one of you has it in your knapsack.' They searched all day! 'Annie—now this isn't funny any more, it's real hot out here and that fish is smelling up something somewhere.' I said, 'No, no, you've got to find it.' For three days I let that fish foul up the prop box [*laughs*]. It was a lot of fun."

Anne starred with Randolph Scott in RKO's *Return of the Bad Men* (1948), which had an all star cast. "Gabby Hayes was an old friend from Republic, and Randy Scott, a fellow North Carolinian, was a true gentleman; but Robert Ryan is the one I remember most vividly. He was a very intense actor and murdered my character in both *Trail Street* [1947] and *Return of the Bad Men*. He choked me to

Robert Clarke, Gabby Hayes and Anne Jeffreys help Randolph Scott locate the outlaws in *Return of the Badmen* (1948).

death in one and shot me in the back in the other. He seemed to enjoy it, so I was a little leery of him [*laughs*]. However, he really was a very nice, warm person and a terrific actor."

The main things she will always remember about making western films are the dust and dirt—"and reflectors blinding me [*laughs*]."

There were primary differences between the lower budgeted Republic Bill Elliott B's and the A's with Randolph Scott and others at RKO. "Mostly you had more rehearsal time. Basically, they were the same—same horses, same wranglers, a lot of the same locations and a lot of the same actors. I enjoyed *Nevada* (1944). I liked working with Robert Mitchum and I had a good role for a western. We worked

on location, a beautiful spot near Mt. Whitney. We stayed in Lone Pine.

"All I desire—in my professional life," is what being an actress means to Anne. "I hope to continue acting as long as God allows me to. Sometimes I wasn't demanding enough or too choosy of my roles. I enjoyed acting, so I'd do any role the studio came up with. But the best days of my life were on Broadway. I did five Broadway shows. My first was *Street Scene*—opera, really. I was under contract to RKO but fell in love with New York theater. Then I did an operetta written especially for me. I did *Kiss Me Kate* for two years, then *Three Wishes for Jamie*. After that, *Kismet* with Alfred Drake at the Lincoln Center. I had about ten good years on Broadway, but kept going back to do films. When I left North Carolina, I studied music in New York. I was trained in opera and sang with the municipal opera company in New York as a 15 year old. I'm proud of all my stage work, which includes dozens of different shows, including *The King and I, Camelot, Sound of Music, Carousel, Destry* and *Bells Are Ringing*.

Topper was not the only TV series she and husband, Robert Sterling, made together. "We followed it with *Love That Jill* [1958], which was about the high fashion world. It only ran one season. He's done other series—*Ichabod and Me* [1961–1962], which he hated. I did *The Delphi Bureau* [1972–1973] and one season on *Finder of Lost Loves* [1984–1985], an ABC nighttime series. My husband no longer acts. I've also been on *Baywatch* recently. I love to travel and have done a lot of it. I have a wonderful husband and three great sons, and, at present count, three darling grandchildren. God has blessed me!"

Anne Jeffreys
Western Filmography

Movies: *Billy the Kid Trapped* (1942 PRC)—Buster Crabbe; *Calling Wild Bill Elliott* (1943 Republic)—Bill Elliott; *Bordertown Gunfighters* (1943 Republic)—Bill Elliott; *Man from Thunder River* (1943 Republic)—Bill Elliott; *Wagon Tracks West* (1943 Republic)—Bill Elliott; *Death Valley Manhunt* (1943 Republic)—Bill Elliott; *Overland Mail Robbery* (1943 Republic)—Bill Elliott; *Raiders of Sunset Pass* (voice only) (1943 Republic)—Eddie Dew; *Hidden Valley Outlaws* (1944 Republic)—Bill Elliott; *Mojave Firebrand* (1944 Republic)—Bill Elliott; *Nevada* (1944 RKO)—Robert Mitchum; *Trail Street* (1947 RKO)—Randolph Scott; *Return of the Bad Men* (1948 RKO)—Randolph Scott.

Television: *Wagon Train*, "Julia Gage Story" (1957); *Wagon Train*, "Mary Beckett Story" (1962); *Bonanza*, "Unwritten Commandment" (1966).

Linda Johnson

A Rose by Several Names

A stutter got Linda Johnson started in dramatics. Born Bertie May Linda Johnson in Oklahoma City, Oklahoma, "I never say my age out loud because I'm afraid I might overhear it and I don't want me to know," Linda tells us. "My mother died when I was five. Because of the trauma I suffered as a five year old losing a mother, I developed a terrible stutter. All through my school years, grammar school and even into junior high, I was just miserable because I couldn't read out loud

Bandits of Dark Canyon (1948) was the sixth of Linda's B-westerns.

in class. I struggled with that during my school years. I took speech arts in junior high school and a wonderful teacher got me over my stutter and got me interested in speech and drama. I started doing plays and winning prizes. Later, my father remarried and we moved to Texas. So the bad thing turned into something good."

From there, Linda went to New York for about a year and was accepted as a John Powers model.

Back living in Fort Worth, Texas, with her father, she read of the Jesse Lasky *Gateway to Hollywood* contest which was coming to Fort Worth. "They had open auditions. I remember about 200 or more people went. It was just kind of a fluky thing, somebody dared me to go, so I did. It was a process of elimination. It finally

got down to three boys and three girls. In the meantime, they sent out three Hollywood stars ... Johnny Mack Brown, Anita Louise and Wendy Barrie. I was in a skit with her. We had to be on the stage, at the local theater in Fort Worth, at least three performances a day for a week. They had applause machines and after your skit, we had to get up on the applause machine, three different times, once for appearance, once for talent, once for personality. Each time the audience would applaud. I was fortunate enough to win in Fort Worth. That meant I got to come to Hollywood. I didn't expect to win, I really didn't, but it was pretty exciting. Then my balloon was punctured a few weeks later because they found they had forgotten Dallas ... Dallas and Fort Worth are so close together ... they had forgotten to do Dallas. So I had to go to Dallas and go through the whole thing again, but fortunately, I won in Dallas also."

Linda came to Hollywood in October 1939 for the CBS radio finals of the *Gateway to Hollywood* contest. "It was like 13 weeks; a process of elimination. I was there for several weeks, but Gale Storm and Lee Bonnell were the two winners. However, I met my future husband, Joe Leighton, in the publishing department at CBS. [They married in 1941.] Gale is still fun and wonderful. We became friends right from the beginning and remained friends. We raised our children together. Our friendship is still enduring, which is wonderful."

Director Busby Berkeley was interviewing girls and Linda won her first part in *Forty Little Mothers* (1940) with Eddie Cantor. "From that, Busby Berkeley was doing *Strike Up the Band* [1940] and I was one of the lucky ones he chose to go into *Strike Up the Band*. It was my second movie. It was very exciting for me to have these two really big films in a row at MGM, just right off the bat. I thought, 'Oh, wow, this is great stuff!'"

Linda had entered the *Gateway to Hollywood* competition as Linda Johnson. "Somebody cautioned me that Bertie May wasn't quite right." Married in 1941, she was now Linda Leighton. But in her first westerns at Republic in 1942, she received billing as Melinda Leighton. "That was so funny the way that happened. I thought Leighton was such a beautiful name—in fact, I've told Joe that's why I married him, because Linda Leighton was so beautiful. But my agent said it was too theatrical sounding, it was too made-up sounding. That's why he said, 'We'll make it Melinda Leighton.' We did that for a while, but I didn't like it and so I switched back to Linda Johnson. I eventually switched again [during her later work on TV] to Linda Leighton because it was a pretty name and it's legitimate, but it was confusing.

"The first western I did was with Gene Autry... *Cowboy Serenade* [1942]. I did quite a few at Republic and they wanted to put me under contract but my husband was in the service, they were sending him to San Francisco, so it was kind of a choice. Do I stay here and do that or do I go with my husband? I went with my husband, so I was out for two or three years. When I came back, I kind of had to start all over again.

"Republic was not the most posh studio. I can remember doing an interior scene one time when it began to rain and the roof leaked. We had little drops of rain coming down, but we kept going [*laughs*].

"Gene Autry was very nice but he had a hard time getting off and on a horse, so they got a double for that. Of course, where *I* looked good was when a double was doing it [for me] [*laughs*]. I was able to handle it pretty well, I can't remember ever doing any riding before ... maybe some in Texas, but not extensively.

"When they ask you to do something in Hollywood, you just kind of grit your teeth and do it. I can remember one of the most difficult things I ever did in my whole life in a movie was when I was in Chicago on location, a movie I was doing with Kirby Grant. We were supposed to be contestants in some show. I had to hold two live chickens, by their feet, that were kicking around ... *that* was a very difficult thing to do. You never say no, you can't do something."

Linda's best work at Republic, and her favorite, is *Sundown Kid* (1942) starring Don Barry, where she plays a feisty reporter. "The part was more interesting, so I think I was more comfortable. I liked it because there was something to do. So many of them, you really don't have anything to do."

Eddy Waller, Bob Steele, Linda and John Hamilton (later to be editor Perry White on the *Superman* television series) in *Bandits of Dark Canyon* (1948).

For one scene in *Sundown Kid*, Linda had to give Don quite a slap in the face, which appeared quite realistic. "He deserved it. It was such a funny incident. These films were all out on location, no dressing rooms, you got up at the crack of dawn and went into the studio and then you get the makeup and so forth. Then they drive you out to location. On the way, we would always stop someplace and get doughnuts and coffee and have those on location. I still cannot pass a glazed doughnut without remembering, 'cause they tasted so wonderful when you got out there. Anyway, there was no place to sit, so you just sat in one of the limos and went over your lines. This is the first day and I had just met Don Barry. We were sitting in the car, going over our lines together

and he started making verbal passes at me. I said, 'My heavens, you sure work fast!' and in all seriousness, he said, 'Well I have to, it's just a five-day picture' [*laughs*]. I thought it was so funny. And he was so serious. I mean, it was just his routine. But he was a nice fellow, he didn't give me a bad time after that. I was just amused at him. So when I say he deserved the slap, he did. Anyway, I give myself a compliment for that film. It was definitely my favorite western.

"But my favorite western to work on, which I worked on for a long time, but I never made it to the screen, was *Red River* [1948] with John Wayne. I was on location in Nogales, Arizona, for three or four weeks. We all lived in tent cities they built for us. Howard Hawks was the director—

such a perfectionist. Every morning, we had to get up at the crack of dawn, get made up and in costume, everything. He had a thing about clouds, because everything was outdoors, it *was* a beautifully shot film. But we had to wait to see what the clouds were doing that day before they'd take a shot. But it was a long, long picture. I was one of maybe four or five girls. We were supposed to be the Donogal girls, that traveled with the wagon train, but anyway, we were all cut out. Then, all of the intrigue that went on on location; I really had my eyes opened. All the things you hear about location are true [*laughs*]. Mr. Hawks had his eye on Joanne Dru but she preferred John Ireland. Therefore, Hawks cut John's part quite a bit, more than it should have been ... in retribution. I think Hawks got divorced right after that, the cameraman got divorced right after that ... there was so much intrigue going on. I remember one girl, Abigail Adams [a.k.a. Tommye Adams], she was just a young girl, but she was dating the professional eulogizer, Georgie Jessel. He would come down but he was so much older than this young girl. And they had this thing going. It was the joke of the camp."

In 1947 Linda co-starred in her only serial, Columbia's *Brick Bradford*, starring Kane Richmond, who was no stranger to making action chapterplays. "The director, Spencer Bennet, was wonderful. He was very, very nice. I worked with him more than once. He was a very, very good director. Another director I liked was Derwin Abrams. We called him Abe. Personality makes a big difference.

"But the serial producer, Sam Katzman. I won't have anything nice to say about him. He was lecherous. Very. Not so much to me, because fortunately, somebody told me when I first started in that business, if you want to be treated like a lady, act like a lady. So I ... frankly, really

never had any problems. I never invited any problems. With Katzman, right off, no way. Anyway, there was a young girl, Helene Stanley, she was just darling and she was fairly young, and Sam was just after her all the time. I felt sorry for her because she didn't know how to cope with it. I don't mean anything serious happened but he was just ... crude. But the location was such fun, at Lone Pine. It really looks like the moon [which it was standing in for in the serial] ... and the craters. It's an incredible thing."

Linda's on-again, off-again career was in high gear while she did the second TV version of the popular radio soap opera *One Man's Family* (1954–1955). "They decided to make it into a TV show and started it in New York. Did it for just a short period of time in New York [in 1949]. It didn't work, or whatever, so they came to California and decided to try it again [as a daily 15-minute serial]. I would say we were almost one of the first soap operas. I played Hazel, the daughter. When I started out playing Hazel, she was the daughter on the show, she was 21. The show had been on radio for so long that the part I was playing as a young girl, Hazel, on television, the lady who was playing it on radio was a grandmother already! So the producer, Carlton E. Morse, had gone back to the very beginning for the television version. It was an interesting experience, because I had to get up at four in the morning to be at the studio to do rehearsals. We didn't have a teleprompter or anything. We had to learn everything. It was a long, long haul, but it was good, because at that time, I had two little children, so my husband would be there when I would leave at four in the morning and then the sitter would come in at eight or whatever, but I would be home by about one o'clock so I was there with my children.

"There was always some kind of con-

Riley Hill, Linda and Johnny Mack Brown at *The Haunted Mine* (1946).

troversy between NBC and Carlton E. Morse about contents of the show. There were a few things suggestive, which is absolutely ludicrous, when you see what's on television now. I remember one time I had to appear in a scene in a slip and there was a big meeting about that, you know, not fully clothed and everything. Any innuendoes or anything suggestive at that time were taboo."

Others have said they noticed an ego problem with Allan "Rocky" Lane. When Linda worked with him in 1947 she did also. "One other ego I can remember is Leo Carrillo. I did *The Cisco Kid* [1950–1956]. Somebody was always coming around powdering his nose and fixing his hair. He had an ego but he was pleasant and nice about it. Somehow, vanity is

more noticeable in a man, for some reason."

On the impressive side of the ledger for Linda were several people. "Raymond Burr. I did several *Perry Mason*s (1957–1966). He was just really nice. I was on the witness stand ["The Case of the Nimble Nephew," 1960] and it was the scene where Perry Mason was able to finally get the confession out of me. I was kind of proud of that scene. I got applause on the set when I finished and that's kind of thrilling. I also really enjoyed *Alfred Hitchcock* [1955–1962]. I was second lead, the female lead was Joan Fontaine. That was a fun one to work on. Then there were Brian Keith, James Whitmore, Eddie Albert and Robert Wagner on *Switch* [1975–1978]. That was kind of my swan song.

"I think one of the last things I did was that *Switch*. At that time, I was living down here [Dana Point, California] and it was a long drive. I think our last shot was on New Year's Eve and I had to drive all the way back. Then I did commercials and things after that."

Looking back over her career and life, Linda believes her best trait is "my ability to grow. I feel I'm still growing, and because of the experiences I've had that I can accept change and I can stay flexible, which I find I have to in life. There are two things I have that I try to work on—attitude and gratitude."

Linda Johnson
Western Filmography

Movies: *Cowboy Serenade* (1942 Republic)—Gene Autry; *Code of the Outlaw* (1942 Republic)—3 Mesquiteers; *The Sundown Kid* (1942 Republic)—Don Barry; *Wild Horse Rustlers* (1943 PRC)—Robert Livingston; *Haunted Mine* (1946 Monogram)—Johnny Mack Brown; *Bandits of Dark Canyon* (1947 Republic)—Allan "Rocky" Lane.

Television: *The Lone Ranger*, "Drink of Water" (1950); *The Cisco Kid*, "The Kid Brother" (1952); *The Cisco Kid*, "Mad About Money" (1952); *The Cisco Kid*, "The Commodore Goes West" (1953); *Sergeant Preston of the Yukon*, "Justice at Goneaway Creek" (1956); *Cimarron City*, "Cimarron Holiday" (1958); *Tales of Wells Fargo*, "The Town That Wouldn't Talk" (1959).

Suzanne Kaaren

The Exotic Mrs. Blackmer

Exotically beautiful Suzanne Kaaren is probably best known for her co-starring roles with Bela Lugosi in *The Devil Bat* (1941) and with the Three Stooges in some of their funniest shorts. But Miss Kaaren appeared in a couple of westerns—one with Tim McCoy and the other with Johnny Mack Brown. "I also knew Dale Evans before she married Roy. We'd go to a place in Santa Monica where she sang. We'd have dinner with friends and have a good time of it."

As for her first western leading man, Johnny Mack Brown, "I became friends with Johnny. We'd go to Will Rogers' Uplifters Club. They'd play polo and I awarded the cup to the winning team. Big Boy Williams also played, as did producer Walter Wanger. I even play, though not very well [*laughs*]. I loved horses, I like to wear boots. I even wore them in Central Park when we moved back to New York—the boots I wore in *Undercover Man* (1936). Johnny Mack was a great man, a

1930s publicity photo of Suzanne.

fun person. He taught me what to do when horses get out of hand, and how to get off when they do get out of hand! In the film, I got up on his horse and it started to run real fast! I looked up and was about to run right into the chow wagon. Well, I jumped off that horse and bruised my chest for weeks! It really hurt, so Johnny Mack told me how to roll off— to roll with the force and not get hurt. I experienced it later—visiting a friend in the valley. He had several spirited horses. There was a walnut grove—I got on this horse, loosened the grip, and he shot off like a bat out of hell, heading straight for those walnut trees! Remembering what Johnny Mack had told me, I rolled. My wristwatch was ten feet away and broken; my earrings were scattered, but I wasn't hurt at all! Incidentally, I did all my own stunts in *Undercover Man*; climbing out of that stagecoach onto the driver's side— everything! I am very athletic. I won the world title interscholastic high jumping

championship. I was a left-handed scissors jumper. *Undercover Man* was made in Kernville, where I did a lot of other films. I even got to kiss the cowboy—he kissed me and not his horse! Johnny Mack Brown and I became lifelong friends. He later visited us in North Carolina. He was promoting a movie and heard I lived in Salisbury, North Carolina, with my husband [Sidney Blackmer]. He loved to dance—we danced together at director Frank Borzage's when Johnny Mack's wife was pregnant with her second child. Irene, Johnny's wife, and I had a great deal in common—we are no-nonsense type of people. I was called 'the look, don't touch girl.' I was not looking for romance."

As to Tim McCoy in Suzanne's second western, *Phantom Ranger* (1938)— "He was wonderful. I was a debutante in Mexico; there were counterfeiters and I danced. It was a good part. Tim personally selected me for the film. There were some 200 girls up for the role! Tim loved the way I rode horses. It was a nice association. I also got to sit on Tim's lap—just like I did Johnny Mack's."

Suzanne also appeared, in a smaller role, in *Mexicali Rose* (1939) with Gene Autry. "Oh, that was funny. It was only a couple of days work, but Gene found out I blush easily. There were two blondes; we arrive and have a scene where we talk while eating. Autry, the director, the cameraman, all of them planned this joke. I was to be eating an avocado salad. Instead of that, they placed a woman's brassiere— with falsies—on my plate for me to pretend to be eating! I had to keep talking, as if everything was okay! It was a big joke [*laughs*].

"Another cowboy I met, but didn't work with, was John Wayne. I was in some little club down in Mexico with a group of people—and Wayne, who could drink with the best of them, came up and stated he wanted to dance with me. A Mexican

Tim McCoy defends Suzanne in a saloon scene from *Phantom Ranger* (1938). Badmen Karl Hackett and John Merton are to the left. Note that the girls on the right are wearing 1930s clothes and look very out of place. Suzanne explains they were just extras, not part of the scene, and should have been cropped out of this picture.

general I was with told him, 'No.' A big fight ensued, and the police came and took 'The Duke' away!"

Reflecting on her actor-husband, the distinguished Sidney Blackmer, Suzanne is quick to say, "It wasn't love at first sight—at least not with me. I originally met him at a going-away party. He grabbed my hand and wouldn't let go. I needed to leave for another cocktail party at Malibu Beach. Sidney said, 'Please, may I have your phone number?' I was shocked—I didn't believe in giving my number out to a stranger, so I said 'No.' Writer Garrett Fort [*Dracula* (1931), *Frankenstein* (1931), *The Mark of Zorro*

(1940), etc.] was in my party, and Sidney even asked Garrett—but I told Garrett to not give it out. He was very persistent, and eventually threw a party with his Chinese chef doing the cooking. Garrett was invited, and Sidney asked Garrett to bring me. I was a career girl and held my ground for some time, but Sidney eventually won me over. At the time, I had never seen him in a picture. I didn't go to movies much, until we started dating. Then we went all the time. He was a star, and a brilliant actor. Franchot Tone and others would ask his advice about things when they were on the stage. He studied technique and was someone you could learn a lot from. Such a dear man. When he was courting me, he'd walk my dog."

Regarding Suzanne's entrance into films, "I had been in *Americana* at the Schubert Theater on Broadway. From there I was one of the original Rockettes at Radio City Music Hall. I appeared in a short to be shown on experimental TV. Someone at Warners saw it, and I was eventually offered a contract. Since it was for less money than I was earning, I turned it down. Later, I was offered screen tests at Universal and Fox. A flip of the coin and I signed with Fox. I later did *Chicken Every Sunday* on Broadway with Sidney. I still have the large poster that stood outside the theater. Besides Fox, I was under contract to MGM. My favorite part is the first 30 minutes of *The Great Ziegfeld* [1936]. It's mostly me. What a prestigious picture! Frank Morgan, famous for his stuttering delivery, told me, 'I was half asleep and didn't remember my lines, so I did that stuttering. That's how that started!' My last picture at MGM was to be *Meet Me in St. Louis* [1944]. I was to play the girl next door, but I wanted to go back to New York with Sidney, so I asked for my release.

"I'm also proud of a Technicolor short I did at Warners, *Louisiana Purchase*, directed by Crane Wilbur. I played Josephine! I had a nice part as a Russian in *Trade Winds* [1938]. Fredric March was on the prowl for me. His trailer was on the set, and he told me his toilet seat was made of gold! He did that to get me in there. I told Fredric, 'For God's sake, are you on the make for me?' [*laughs*]."

The star also appeared with the Three Stooges. "What fun! *Disorder in the Court* [1936] is the biggest moneymaker of all the Stooge comedies. I only did it as a lark—I had a little time when Jules White saw me dancing and said, 'With those legs, you've gotta do it.' My favorite is *What's the Matador?* [1942]. I played a Spanish girl—with a very jealous husband. I had a Stooge under my bed, in the closet. It was a lot of fun. I went to the Stooge Convention in 1991."

As for recent times, Suzanne reveals, when her husband was dying of cancer, a crook stole all their money. "So, I went back to work—did a lot of extra parts, and then got a good role in *The Cotton Club* (1984) with Richard Gere. He played a gigolo and I was a wealthy woman who hired him. But before he was through, almost all of it was cut. Gere didn't want anybody's part upstaging his! There was a lot of pot smoking going on ... even a real murder happened on that film. They pumped smoke into the nightclub scene to make it look like cigarette smoke, and everybody got red eyes. At least some of my part remains in the film."

Suzanne Kaaren (her real name) was born March 21, 1916 ("I am an Aries and a Pisces mixed up") and lives today in an apartment that overlooks Central Park. "Donald Trump is my landlord! He tried to tear down the building, but the city refused because it's now considered a landmark!" She has two sons—Brewster Blackmer, "who lives in Spain," and Jonathan Blackmer, "who works for the Justice Department."

As for her cult-favorite leading man, Bela Lugosi, "What a gentleman. He always kissed my hand goodnight. He took the film [*The Devil Bat*, 1941] very seriously. What a distinguished man. Remember in the movie, when he gives the aftershave lotion to his next victim, they'd say 'Good night' and Bela would say '*Goodbye*.' Every night, as we were leaving the studio, we'd tell Bela 'Good night,' and he'd always tell us '*Goodbye*'" [*laughs*]!

Suzanne, Jean Carmen (who also appeared in many B-westerns) and Lola Jenson in the Three Stooges comedy *Yes, We Have No Bonanza* (1939).

Suzanne Kaaren
Western Filmography

Movies: *Undercover Man* (1936 Supreme)—Johnny Mack Brown; *Phantom Ranger* (1938 Monogram)—Tim McCoy; *Mexicali Rose* (1939 Republic)—Gene Autry; *Yes, We Have No Bonanza*—Three Stooges (1939 Columbia short).

Mary Ellen Kay

End of the Trail

Rex Allen was Republic's last singing cowboy. He starred in the last B-western series to lens at the once mighty Republic. By 1954, the rapid encroachment of television and the small screen western had spelled the demise of the theatrical Saturday afternoon program, or series, western. And Mary Ellen Kay was the last leading lady to make a definite mark on this unique brand of entertainment, costarring in six of Rex Allen's 19 westerns.

"I was born in Boardman, Ohio, which is like a little offshoot of Youngstown, August 29, 1929. The great fall, you know, the stock market. I was born that year.

"I was performing in school from the time I was a child, everything I could get into. It was just something natural. I wasn't one of those kids who was pushed into show business by their parents. I loved to sing and I led my parents in the direction I wanted to go. Everything that came up that was musical, I was on the stage singing. My grandparents on my mother's side were all musicians and singers and their relatives were still in vaudeville when I was born. My aunt was an opera singer in New York and my uncle was a lyric tenor. On my father's side, my grandfather was Swiss and German and played the guitar. I could hear my uncle's yodeling from way up in the hills in Pennsylvania, where he was skiing. I had already started

singing professionally in the middle 1940s, even though I was 15. My parents chaperoned me. I just loved to be on stage.

"When I first went to Hollywood, it was a different place. It was a little town and people were polite, lovely and helpful. Pretty close to my getting there, I got into doing stage work. From that I just kept growing. I did theater at the Glendale Center Theatre with interesting people, including Leonard Nimoy. I was enrolled at the Bliss-Hayden School of Theatre when a talent agent spotted me and offered me a screen test."

Mary Ellen's first film was *Girl's School* (1950) at Columbia. "I didn't have a very big part but I had a diving scene. Just like anything I was ever asked, 'Can you do it?' I would always say *sure*, and find out how to learn. I found an Olympic diving instructor by the name of Fred Cady and he taught me how to do a jackknife dive, because that's what they wanted.

"Also in 1950, I did *Tarzan and the Slave Girl* with Lex Barker at RKO. I played the slave girl that was engaged to the prince. Lex Barker [Tarzan] was very friendly, very nice to everybody. People were very nice in those days. I never saw any displays of temperament. I had such a good time. I met Edgar Rice Burroughs on that set and had a nice visit with him, I was so impressed. I was young. All I knew

Smiley Burnette, Charles Starrett as the Durango Kid, Mary Ellen and Don "Little Brown Jug" Reynolds in the showdown of *Streets of Ghost Town* **(1950).**

was he was this famous writer who had done all these wonderful Tarzan books."

It was then Mary Ellen moved into the field we know her best for—westerns. "My first western was *Streets of Ghost Town* [1950]. That was my love, because I loved horses long before I ever went to Hollywood. I always loved to dress cowboy. Whenever I'd visit my aunt, although she was an English rider, I donned her boots and clothes and just played cowgirl when I was young. Charles Starrett had such a fabulous background, he'd been making movies for a long time. I used to go to all the westerns when I was a little girl, in 1936, 1937, 1938. My favorite of the old-timers was Hopalong Cassidy. To me, he was like an angel, with his white hair. My

mother loved westerns. I can remember the first western she ever took me to see was *The Plainsman* [1936] with Gary Cooper and Jean Arthur. I loved her voice."

Mary Ellen was under contract to Republic from January 13, 1951, to January 12, 1952, and made ten features and a serial (*Government Agents Vs. Phantom Legion* [1951]) that year. "I got a phone call and it was an interview. My agent, William Morris at that time, sent me out to Republic. When I arrived I met George Blair, the director that was going to do my first film there, *Silver City Bonanza* [1951]. He put me in a buckboard with Rex and we rode around. Probably an hour and a half later, he simply said, 'I think you'll do.' George Blair was a honey—he was like a dad to me with a lot of good advice."

Mary Ellen nearly became Rex Allen's permanent leading lady, co-starring in six with him. "Rex was a wholesome young man. The perfect model for a cowboy—shy, handsome and a gentleman. He enjoyed what he did so much. He was like a kid who got to play cowboy and Indians for real. On the set, when things slowed down a bit between shots, he'd pick up his guitar and we'd sing together. He had such a wonderful voice."

Although the songs in B-westerns seem spontaneous and unrehearsed, there was actually a lot of preparation that went into the production of the musical numbers. "Rex had the most beautiful voice. It was so much fun. We did all of the singing in the studio. We never recorded anything on the set. You go in the studio where the orchestra was and Victor Young would direct us, put us in like phone booths. We'd put on earphones. Rex couldn't hear me and I couldn't hear him, but we could both hear the music. Then, they meshed things together. When we were on the set, we could hear the music as put together, then we'd just have to remember what the lyrics were, and that's how we did it. We *did* sing on the set but it wasn't going into the microphone. It was already recorded. All music was done that way."

George Blair directed her in two and Phil Ford in one before Mary Ellen made a string of three with Rex Allen under Bill Witney's tutelage. "Bill was just the best. He brought zip to everything. He could visualize what he wanted to see on the screen." They had completed *Colorado Sundown*, the first one, and then, as Mary Ellen explains, about three or four days into lensing *The Last Musketeer* (1952), "We didn't have too many days, 14 days and it's over, right? Bill Witney said, 'Do you think you could do a flying mount?' I looked at him and I just said, I could, I

would, that's what I said. And I would work on it. Well, every minute I had 'til we shot, about five days later, was hysterical. Slim Pickens and the guys would give me advice, and Rex would give me advice, tell me to relax and this is what you do and that's how you do it. I practiced—I fell under the belly of the horse … went all the way over … and finally I thought I was getting somewhere, but I didn't yet have confidence. When the day came, Bill said to me, 'Do you think you can do the mount today, because the scene's scheduled?' And I gulped, 'Yeah, I guess I can do it.' So later, he's lining up for the particular scene where I follow this young man that's in trouble. He's supposed to be my sweetheart and I know they're trying to kill him and so on and so forth. So when I'm supposed to mount the horse, I'm thinking, I have to back up just a tiny bit. Bill says to me, 'We're going to do a rehearsal, then we're going to do a take.' And I'm thinking, 'Two times! Oh, no!' I saw Bill lean toward the cameraman and they were talking back and forth. I could tell the cameraman was taking some instruction from him and finally Bill said to me, 'No, we're going to do it in one take. Let's just do it.' I said a prayer, 'Oh, Lord, help me.' I put my foot back on a little uprise with a rock and sort of pushed myself off. I had several yards to run, so I had a chance. The next thing I knew I was on the horse and we were galloping away. I felt so good and I know Bill was happy. Later, I found out, when I was at a film festival over 40 years later, I had never seen that movie, and when I saw the movie, it was so fast, Bill laughed and joked about it. He said, 'I just turned around to the cameraman and told him you better speed this up.' So you have to really look quick or you'll miss me [*laughs*]. It's just a once in a lifetime miracle, it was wonderful. I don't even know how I did it, but I did. I must

1804-52

Rex Allen and Mary Ellen recorded all their songs in a studio and listened to the playback on the set as they filmed the song scenes, such as here in *Silver City Bonanza*.

have had help spiritually, that's all I can say."

Mary Ellen didn't meet the head of Republic, Herbert J. Yates, until she'd been at the studio for ten months or so. "I thought I was going to play a joke on director Bill Witney. My hairdresser put me up to it. Bill Witney was the most focused director I'd ever met or that I'd ever worked with. He could see what he wanted and he knew how to have you do it. He just believed we could do it and he made us think we could. Anyway, I have dark hair. My hairdresser had a blonde wig on her work table, and she said, 'Why don't you try it on, see how it looks.' And I said, okay. We had just finished *The Last Mus-*

keteer. So I went out and paraded past Bill with this blonde wig, just sort of walked by him, and said 'Hi Bill,' made some remark about the day and 'I'll see you.' I knew we were going to start shooting the next movie pretty quickly, *Border Saddlemates* [1952]. I just had time to go to wardrobe and do whatever had to be done. Get the script and so on. Well, the next day I'm on the set and one of the fellows said, 'Gee, I'm sorry, I guess you're not going to be working on the next film.' Which didn't mean I wouldn't be working on something else, but I thought, Bill never said anything. I would imagine maybe he would say something because we'd just made two movies in a row. I thought to myself, 'Why didn't Bill tell me when he saw me walk by him?' He looked at me but he didn't say anything. But his mind was working, you can tell. Anyway, I went home and the next day I found out I wasn't doing the movie. Someone told me there was a phone call and Mr. Yates wanted to see me immediately. I trotted over to his office and went in and waited and waited and waited and finally he had me sit at his desk in front of him and handed me some sheets of script. He said, 'I want you to read the part of the girl and I'll read the part of the cowboy.' That's what he said! So he starts and then I read the girl and he reads the cowboy and I read the girl and he reads the cowboy and finally he says, 'Okay, that's enough. You can go now.' That was all. Well, I get home a little bewildered because I knew Republic was cutting down, that Roy and Dale had left and things were going to change. Right then, I get a phone call that says I was to report at a certain time tomorrow at wardrobe and to pick up my script. I thought, I bet he's forcing Bill to use me and that wasn't a good feeling. That was the impression I got."

Nothing was said about this incident during the lensing of *Border Saddlemates*, which turned out to be Mary Ellen's last film at Republic. It left her wondering for many years, until "around 42 years later I saw Bill for the first time again at the Knoxville Film Festival in 1994. On a celebrity panel, I finally got up enough nerve to bring it up. We'd never talked about it, we never discussed it, and that was the last western I made at Republic. So I just asked Bill, 'Back in 1952, why didn't you want me in *Border Saddlemates*? Did Mr. Yates have anything to do with my being in it?' Now Bill's taking all this in. I think he's going to reveal some big truth, because I'm sure he remembers and by George, you know what, he burst out into laughter and said, 'You didn't know?

No, Mr. Yates didn't make me do it. I just told him I couldn't have a blonde leading lady with a blonde cowboy. And we all had a good laugh [*laughs*]. Yates called me in just to check my hair color. I guess my little blonde wig joke really boomeranged."

Mary Ellen did, in fact, work as a blonde a couple of years later in a non-western, *The Long Wait* (1954), possibly her best work. It demonstrated her potential as an actress, where the B-westerns didn't give her that kind of opportunity. "I can remember working with Anthony Quinn. They bleached my hair blonde every other day, and they cut it, and if you put your fingers through my hair, it would just stand up. All I could think of in that last scene by the window, was, 'Oh my gosh, he's messing up my hair' [*laughs*]. So when I'm asked what was it like kissing Anthony Quinn, I don't remember, all I could think of was my hair. That just goes to show you, we actresses are so conscious of what's going on on the screen, that we don't really always get into it like we should."

Buddy Ebsen, fresh out of the service, had been Rex Allen's sidekick in Mary Ellen's first three Republic westerns, but a change was made for her last three—to rodeo comedian Slim Pickens. "When I first met Buddy, he and his sister still had their tap dancing school. But Buddy had some things coming up that looked good for him. And also, to tell you the truth, Republic was changing people quite frequently. Slim Pickens was a laugh a minute. He kept us in stitches when he'd get in the corral like an old rodeo clown with the bulls."

It's been proposed that Republic paired Rex and Mary Ellen in several films in order to establish another "Roy and Dale" co-starring team, but Mary Ellen discounts that idea. "No, they never, as far as the front office was concerned, I never heard anything. But it was a wonderful

Mary Ellen with Rex Allen and Bonnie De Simone in *Rodeo King and the Senorita* (1951).

experience. I was really kind of green, I was learning. I mean, some of those scenes are pretty bad, but then I've seen old westerns that are just as bad … but it was fun. It was for the kids."

The end of Rex Allen's B-westerns at Republic was, essentially, the end of 24 years of the Saturday matinee westerns for theaters—or *longer*, when you include the silent era. Television had arrived, bringing in the era of the so called "adult westerns." At the theaters, the longer, more maturely scripted A-western was coming into play, replacing the B-western. "I think with Wild Bill Elliott at Allied Artists it started to change. I had a little crush on Bill. He was really like a daddy, so sweet and I thought he was handsome. You know how young ladies are … but that was all. I don't think he knew that. I never told anybody that."

During the making of her one western with Bill Elliott, *Vigilante Terror* (1953), Mary Ellen had a frightening incident. "We were out on location and a hard riding scene was coming up. I declined having a stuntwoman ride for me because riding horses was a joy for me. I love horses. So off we went through the mountains—faster and faster. Suddenly, the shot was over and everybody reined in their horses—except me! I couldn't get my horse to stop running. I yelled, 'Loose horse! Loose horse!' Bill rode up beside me, grabbed the reins and stopped my horse exactly the way the hero would do in the westerns. He was *my* hero!"

Along with the six Allen titles, Mary Ellen co-starred in three with the inexplicable Allan "Rocky" Lane. "I didn't have the kind of situations Peggy Stewart and others had with Rocky. I just worked with a very nice person. 'Course, we never sat and talked. I did hear things from other people, but he was polite, on time, knew his lines. He wasn't really a people person. He was focused and professional. As I look back and think of Allan, I think he was shy and a loner. In scenes he always looked right in your eyes and smiled when he spoke to you, but afterwards he'd just go off on his own. I didn't see him mix with the guys. He was very good at what he did, but if you don't get to know the people you're working with, they think you are stuck up."

On the opposite side of the personality coin, "Lyn Thomas [another of Rex Allen's leading ladies] lived next door to me in those days. I hadn't seen her in 47 years. When we re-met, for her to remember my dog's name, Pattycake, and everything, just brought tears to my eyes. Just a delightful person! She's had open heart surgery but nothing can keep that woman down."

Besides the B-westerns, another of Republic's stalwart moneymakers over the years, and a genre they were the best at producing, was the serial. Mary Ellen co-starred with Walter Reed in *Government Agents Vs Phantom Legion* (1951). "It just seemed like I was at the desk all the time. Serials are shot out of sequence. I was on the set to shoot scenes for several different episodes in one day. I never read the whole script. I just knew what I had to do that day. Even then, they'd change the dialogue just before we were to shoot and I'd have to learn entirely new lines [*laughs*]. I'd be in the middle of a Rex Allen film and the next day I was told to report to building 21 to do lines for this serial. Luckily, I was a quick study. But most of the conversation would be between the guys about the plots and so on. Every now and then I'd say so and so is on the phone or whatever. It was just a part."

After a year at Republic, her option

was up, and her contract was not renewed. "There were some things outside that my agent wanted me to do and I was interested in television. I have a feeling Mr. Yates found out because he didn't want anybody being in television. That might have been part of it. And I *was* going on interviews for television shows about the end of my time at Republic."

Following her one year tenure at Republic, Mary Ellen began to freelance. "That was a strange time, because Republic was a family, you're there almost every day. Everybody is friendly and caring. I missed everybody. But then I really did get busy with television. I did something with Roy Rogers and Dale Evans and that was wonderful to be able to work with them. I worked on *Annie Oakley* [in 1956] and I did an episode of *The Lone Ranger* ["Outlaws in Grease Paint," 1957] where I played the part of a really bad gal, an actress who pretended to be two or three different kinds of people. That was fun.

"I loved TV in those days. When I would go on an interview for a television show, although most of what I did was filmed, it wasn't a cattle call. You had no more than maybe four or five people, but you wouldn't see them. It was done so discreetly in those days, in a sense that we're not going to put them all out there to intimidate each other. They were so thoughtful. I certainly made more money doing television than I did at Republic, so I was happy about that."

One of her movies in this period was *Yukon Vengeance* (1954) with Kirby Grant. "It was fun working with him. He was a very 'up' person. And his scenes were fun."

Mary Ellen was married in June 1954. "I went on tour for *The Long Wait* and got married when I came back. He was a cosmetics executive. Although we went back to New York where we had a beautiful home out in the country on 80 acres, we rented a house in the Palisades and would spend the winters there. It was really lovely and I got to know his two young sons, one was about 11 and the other was around six. We became great friends."

At some point in late 1954 or early 1955, Mary Ellen spent about four weeks "including costume fittings and so forth" on Cecil B. DeMille's epic *The Ten Commandments* (1956) to film a one-line scene, "Watch out for the alligators!" "We apparently went on a late honeymoon, but at any rate we were in San Francisco when I got a call from the studio. They said they wanted me to come in and read for *another* part. That would have made me appear twice in that movie, but I was wearing a wig for the first scene; it wouldn't have mattered. I turned it down. I just resigned myself to being married, although I did commute back to Hollywood for a few parts now and then."

Mary Ellen gave birth to a girl, Molly, who is now a singer in Nashville. But at the end of five years, the couple was divorced.

Toward the end of her marriage, Mary Ellen found work in the low-budget independent western *Buffalo Gun* (made in 1958, released in 1961) with country music singers Marty Robbins, Webb Pierce and Carl Smith forming a sort of latter-day Three Mesquiteers. "Oh, Marty Robbins, what a cutie he was. He was such a dear. He just made you smile. And of course, it was the funniest, worst movie I ever saw. Oh, it was funny! There would be a huge herd of stock footage buffalo running and you'd see these guys, acting like the Three Stooges. I just found it really funny. But when Marty was singing to me, I thought, next to Rex, that was the most beautiful voice I'd ever heard. Marty had such a sweetness about him, just was a darling human being. I was glad I had the opportunity to work with him. Wayne Morris was in it. He did a real super job

of acting. In this crazy movie, he just stood out like Superman.

"I met my second husband, Tim Ruffalo, shortly after I left New York. I went to Ohio to be close to my family. I had a little girl and I just wanted to be near my mother. I stayed in Ohio for three months, and kind of regrouped. Then I went out to Los Angeles and it had changed. It was a different place. The people had changed, the casting directors I knew were gone. It wasn't the same atmosphere. The kind of people they were looking for weren't the girl next door type. They were just more sex symbols. At least some of the scripts that I read, the language was changing and, you know, I just didn't feel comfortable."

Mary Ellen's second marriage in 1963 bore her a son, Bill. That marriage lasted for 30 years until Tim died in 1993 of a stroke following heart bypass surgery. The marriage also instigated a move to Phoenix, Arizona, where she now lives. "I hosted a Christian TV show off and on for six years. Here in Phoenix. But I did plays. I worked at the Sombrero Playhouse Dinner Theatre with Farley Granger in *Ring Around the Moon* and I did *Destry Rides Again*, different things like that. I made national commercials like Ford Truck where I'd be playing the part of 'Annie' and the good guy would be in white and the bad guy would be in black. We did like a 45-minute movie for Ford [dealer reps]."

Is there anything in her career Mary Ellen would have done differently? "I would have worked harder. I would have been more focused. But I was young, immature. I think I would have been a better actress had I probably stuck to it. I think my movies got better, as far as my acting is concerned, when Bill Witney started directing. I look back almost 50 years, and I'm saying, 'Isn't it wonderful that westerns are a lifestyle for a lot of these people that attend film festivals?'"

Mary Ellen Kay
Western Filmography

Movies: *Streets of Ghost Town* (1950 Columbia)—Charles Starrett; *Silver City Bonanza* (1951 Republic)—Rex Allen; *Thunder in God's Country* (1951 Republic)—Rex Allen; *Wells Fargo Gunmaster* (1951 Republic)—Allan "Rocky" Lane; *Rodeo King and the Senorita* (1951 Republic)—Rex Allen; *Fort Dodge Stampede* (1951 Republic)—Allan "Rocky" Lane; *Desert of Lost Men* (1951 Republic)—Allan "Rocky" Lane; *Colorado Sundown* (1952 Republic)—Rex Allen; *Last Musketeer* (1952 Republic)—Rex Allen; *Border Saddlemates* (1952 Republic)—Rex Allen; *Vigilante Terror* (1953 Allied Artists)—Wild Bill Elliott; *Yukon Vengeance* (1954 Allied Artists)—Kirby Grant; *Thunder Pass* (1954 Lippert)—Dane Clark; *Buffalo Gun* (1961 Globe)—Marty Robbins.

Television: *Roy Rogers*, "Pat's Inheritance" (1953); *Annie Oakley*, "Joker on Horseback" (1956); *Annie Oakley*, "The Mississippi Kid" (1956); *Circus Boy*, "The Little Gypsy" (1956); *Lone Ranger*, "Trouble at Tylerville" (1956); *Lone Ranger*, "Outlaws in Greasepaint" (1957); *Gray Ghost*, "Manhunt" (1958).

Elyse Knox

Anne Howe—And How!

The 1940s—the greatest decade in the history of motion pictures. One of the high spots of the era was lovely, blonde Elyse Knox. "I went to art school, then did modeling. I was a bride in a Vivian Donner fashion newsreel and it caught the attention of quite a few people. This led to a stock contract at Fox. I dated John Payne for a while, before he married Gloria De Haven. I'm still friends with his widow, Sandy."

One of Elyse's first leading roles was opposite Roy Rogers in *Sheriff of Tombstone* (1941). "Roy was a terrific person! I remember he'd just come back from a publicity tour and his station wagon was filled with initials his fans carved into the car. I always liked his singing a lot. I only regret I didn't do more than one picture with him. I wish we had Roy Rogers in present day time. He always represented the good guy—whenever he shot at somebody, he'd shoot the gun out of their hand, he wouldn't murder them. He was a lovely guy. We used to bump into each other every so often and he was always the same. A very real person. There were no airs. We need more good guys like Roy in films today, instead of all that other stuff."

In 1942, Elyse starred in her best-recalled vehicle, *The Mummy's Tomb* at Universal. "That was done on the back lot. Turhan Bey was in it. I saw him recently at a charity function. What a nice, lovely

Elyse, Sally Payne and Roy Rogers as the *Sheriff of Tombstone* (1941).

man. *The Mummy's Tomb* was my only horror film, so I remember it vividly. We had to work all night on the kidnapping and graveyard scenes. Lon Chaney, Jr., had a strap around his neck to support me. One arm was supposed to be paralyzed and he could only hold me with the other arm. I had this negligee with marabou—and one of the feathers somehow got under Lon's rubber mummy mask. He was one unhappy actor—because he couldn't get it out. After it was over, he thanked me for being petite. It seems some of my predecessors were a little on the *heavy* side [*laughs*]! The day of the kidnapping scene—where the Mummy takes me from my bed, the director told me, 'When you see him you really have to scream!' He thought

since I'd never done anything like that before, I wouldn't be able to do it. One look at Lon Chaney, Jr., coming at me and it wasn't hard to let out that scream at all!" (*laughs*).

Elyse co-starred with Don Terry in Universal's *Don Winslow of the Coast Guard* (1943) serial. "Mostly it was shot on the back lot. I was a nurse always dodging bullets and explosions. Don Terry and I previously did a feature, *Top Sergeant* [1942], although I don't recall much about him. But Walter Sande was always a very pleasant guy to be around."

When Elyse starred with Abbott and Costello in the 1943 smash *Hit the Ice*, the comedy team were already box office champions. "That was fun! I never knew

Elyse looks ready for a western barbecue in *Moonlight and Cactus* (1944).

Bud Abbott that well. Lou was more outgoing. My husband Tom [Harmon] and I had been close to Lou's family. He lived nearby. Lou was really a nice person. There's nobody around today who could replace him. Lou produced a movie for me, *A Wave, a WAC and a Marine* [1944]. Not a good film but some of the individual scenes turned out well. Lou looked at my scene with Ann Gillis as we were performing on a stage in uniform. I'm blind and she slaps me in the face. Lou came out of the projection room with tears in his eyes. Dear Lou kept telling me, 'You're gonna be the biggest star.' Lou was so enthusiastic for me—but the director was not good [Phil Karlson]. That director made Henny Youngman talk so fast even Henny couldn't understand himself [*laughs*]!"

Also in 1944, Elyse starred in the mu-sical-comedy-western *Moonlight and Cactus* back at Universal. "That had an enjoy-able cast and crew. It was a very happy set. Leo Carrillo was a charming man—I got to know him a little bit more than the others. The Andrews Sisters were great, very friendly. They used to come in to watch me when my hair and makeup was done." As for her leading man, "Tom Seidel was a nice man. He later married actress Jean Hagen and had a couple of kids. He left acting and became a carpenter while Jean won an Oscar nomination for *Singin' in the Rain* [1952] and later Emmys for *Make Room for Daddy* or *The Danny Thomas Show* [1953–1957]."

Elyse's last western was *Black Gold* (1947) with Anthony Quinn. "I enjoyed working with Anthony Quinn. He made it his business to know the people he worked

Jack Roper, Frank Jenks and Eddie Gribbon contemplate a meeting of Elyse, Joe Kirkwood, Jr. (as comic strip hero Joe Palooka) and Stanley Clements. Elyse brought Joe's comic strip girl-friend, Anne Howe, to life on the screen.

with. He was very supportive—very helpful. Such a good actor. You can't help but admire him. And his wife, Katherine De-Mille, was a beautiful gal. I didn't get to know her very well, but I loved her look." Also featured was Kane Richmond. "Kane was great, very professional and a very good-looking man." As for the director, Phil Karlson, "He was assistant to some big director earlier—this was only his eighth or ninth picture as a director. He was new and he was nice, but he was so emotional! He'd get into the scene himself. If it were a sad scene, he'd be crying! This threw me a little bit."

Monogram brought the Joe Palooka boxing champ comic strip to life for a se-

ries of films in 1946. Elyse essayed the role of Joe's love interest, Anne Howe, and recalls the films fondly, "Joe Kirkwood was the perfect choice to play Joe Palooka. He *was* Joe Palooka! But, he had no prior experience. On the first day of filming that first movie, he had a very difficult scene. We were walking down the street, and as we passed the various stores and shops, people would come out and he would greet them. That was a lot of dialogue—names—to remember, things like that, and he did have difficulty with it. I tried to put him at ease as much as possible. We have remained friends ever since. Leon Errol played Knobby. They were a lot of fun but at the time I had two children. I'm just a mother at heart, so I decided it was time to retire from the screen."

Speaking of sports, her husband was famous 1940 Heisman Trophy winner–sports announcer Tom Harmon. "We were married August 26, 1944, in a chapel on the campus of the University of Michigan. There was a lot of publicity about my wedding dress, since it was made from what remained of Tom's parachute. He had been shot down by the Japs and was missing 32 days! There was only about half of the parachute left—it took hours, taking the seams apart. It was quadruple reinforced and the panels had to be taken apart as well. Tom had played dead in that parachute—the Japs shot at him as he was descending, and the chute had two bullet holes in it! He was rescued by those friendly to us, dressed as a Coolie and taken from boat to boat until he got back to the Americans. He was badly burned, and they treated his burns with tea! So, this parachute had great sentimental value. *Life* magazine did a story—showing me with the chute. Fortunately, Tom was reassigned and taught at the Van Nuys Airport, but he was still in the service until the war ended. We had an early TV show, *At Home with the Harmons*, and did a lot of the *Pantomime Quiz* programs with Mike Stokey. We did Product 19 commercials together in the 1970s, and of course Tom was a sports announcer for many, many years. He died in 1987."

As to the possibility of a return to acting, Elyse states an emphatic, "No. I would hate to be around today. In my time you learned your craft with small roles. They always handed you a script and told you, 'This is your role.' Now, you have to read for a part, over and over. Two thousand people have to approve before you get anything. I liked my era, where you were groomed."

Quizzed about today, Elyse laughs, "I learned I'm an antique! My son Mark [actor Mark Harmon] found an old frame at a store, inside was a picture of me [*laughs*]! I'm back to painting, my first love. It's very fulfilling. That, and my family, make my life very complete."

Elyse Knox
Western Filmography

Movies: *Sheriff of Tombstone* (1941 Republic)—Roy Rogers; *Moonlight and Cactus* (1944 Universal)—Leo Carrillo; *Black Gold* (1947 Allied Artists)—Anthony Quinn.

Barbara Knudson

Aiming for a Star

Barbara Ann Knudson knew she'd be in show business from the beginning.

Born December 4, 1927, in Las Vegas, Nevada, she laughs, "I think I drove everybody crazy from the time I was five or six. I just thought I should be Shirley Temple. There was a theater billboard and whenever Shirley Temple was on that billboard, Mother literally had to walk me a different way because I would get so upset because Shirley was up there and I wanted to be. Mother tells the story that I literally threw rocks at the billboard. I would become uncontrollable because Shirley Temple was on that board. In bed at night, in the dark, I would pretend I was a starlet. Many years later, I realized anything you really set your mind out to do, somehow or another, it happens. I did become a starlet. But I did not know to ask to star [*laughs*]."

High school plays, cheerleading and Las Vegas little theater eventually led to Barbara being part of the Birdcage Theatre's stock company at the Last Frontier, which also included (imported from Hollywood) Isabel Jewell, King Donovan and Barbara's husband-to-be, Bill Henry. "Bill had been quite an up-and-coming actor with Robert Taylor, Loretta Young and that whole group. He'd been with 20th Century–Fox. He was 13 years older than me. Bill was quite a surfer and a swimmer. I think a lot of that came from Les Henry, his father, who was with the Los Angeles Athletic Club years and years ago. They had connections with the Olympics and Bill was kind of in that atmosphere as a young boy and actually lived in Hawaii for several years.

"Bill went in the service and when he came back, things weren't the same. But whatever it was in his life, he at least accepted things like that. So that's where I met him. We did the Birdcage Theatre thing; I got my first professional dollar bill from them and of course, joined SAG. Bill's brother was Thomas Browne Henry, who looked nothing like Bill as they had different fathers. Thomas Browne resembled his mother very, very much. He was older than Bill but I don't know how many

Barbara began her career at Paramount.

years. But they certainly were not similar in appearance.

"Now Thomas Browne was at Pasadena Playhouse, of all things, which is where I always wanted to go. When we stated doing rehearsals out at the Last Frontier, Bill would pick me up to take me to rehearsal, so we got to be friends. And he mentioned that his brother was at the Pasadena Playhouse because I told him I was saving my money to go there. Lo and behold, Bill decided to drive down, visit his parents who lived in Pasadena, and that I could go down and stay overnight with his mom and dad and go to the Pasadena Playhouse, to see it. But the whole time I'm watching this play, I'm sitting there so envious. I wanted to be up there.

"Well, about five to ten days later, we get a phone call from Thomas Browne Henry. He said two agents had contacted him, wanted to know who the girl was with Bill that night and was she an actress, was she interested in acting, where did she come from? Of course, we told them I was a local Las Vegas girl, and I was in the stock company there. Those two people happened to be talent scouts from Paramount and 20th Century–Fox. I didn't think anybody in the world even knew I was there. And now they were interested in testing me.

"I chose Paramount over Fox, for whatever reason. They thought I was a young Miriam Hopkins—that's what they were shooting for. When I saw my test, I was just sick! You know, you never like yourself on film. But—after I'd returned home to Las Vegas, I got a call that they were going to sign me to a contract. They wanted me down there by December of 1949, just before my twenty-first birthday. I was going with Bill by this time. He stepped in and we didn't go down 'til January.

"Also I should mention, Bill had quite a drinking problem. I didn't realize at that time at all. I thought it was just social drinking … but it presented itself to be a problem later. Anyway, he more or less would try to help with things with me not knowing how to respond, what to do.

"I used to want to change my name, because I had been this imaginary type of a child. I wanted so bad to have my name fancy. Different. Because you don't ever like your own name. But Paramount insisted on leaving it the same way when I first went there under contract. I was just so floored, all these things were happening, that I wasn't going to argue about that. But I often felt, had I been able to change my name, I could pretend to be somebody else. I'm very happy pretending to be somebody else. But now they'd say, here's Barbara Knudson … then I'd get stage fright. But if they'd said, 'Here comes Cherie LaSalle,' I'd have walked up and been her. But anyway, that was the beginning, all from accidental things, like being picked for the Birdcage Theatre, Bill

Henry happening to be there, his brother being at the Pasadena Playhouse, I happened to go to one performance, happened to be seen … then went to Paramount.

"I believe I was making $125 a week, which was big money in those days. I made it past the first year when they have options and they were starting to drop people. People that had been there longer than me and I thought were as talented, if not more so, were being dropped as the options came up. I remember passing through those options. Then when it came around to the third one, they dropped *me*. So I was there a little over two years.

"When I left Paramount, it was bad, because at that time, Bill had been called back and drafted into the Navy and being 36 years of age and drafted back into the Navy, that was quite a political move, I'm sure, by somebody. I do believe it was done through his family. His mother had quite a bit of pull and was very close friends with John Ford and John Ford had a lot of military pull.

"When Bill came back, Ford made Bill pay his penance. He was making Bill pay a penance for something … possibly … I remember Bill was here in Las Vegas, now this is before I went down to Hollywood. Ford wanted him to do a part in *She Wore a Yellow Ribbon* (1949) and he didn't want to do it. He didn't and John Ford made him pay for it. Ford was very rude to Bill and me when I first met him on the set one night but John Wayne came over and took care of it right away. He came over and babied me, kind of, and John Ford wasn't mean to me after that. He would see me, and call me the little one and he'd be kind.

"Bill was very happy in Las Vegas. He never wanted to go back to Hollywood. If it hadn't been for what happened to me, Bill Henry would never have gone back down there. He was perfectly happy and settled in here. He loved just being local. He was a lifeguard at the Last Frontier Hotel pool and he probably would have done great things in Vegas. He was so personable and everybody loved him. He would have been perfectly happy to stay here in Las Vegas. But when I went to Hollywood, he felt compelled to follow me."

Barbara and Bill were married in 1952 in a marriage that lasted just a few months over ten years. They had one son in 1958. "When I left Bill, our son Billy was two and a half. Bill Sr. never visited or played the role of a father, ever. In fact, he would send any literature that he had or anything to me, under Barbara Knudson instead of Barbara Henry. So Bill Jr. never did know his dad at all."

Bill's drinking problem was the reason for the break-up of the marriage. "He didn't have a problem, as far as he was concerned. Took a whole bunch of vitamin B and he was going to be fine. It just was one of those things, where I just had to leave … one day I realized he didn't really know what planet he was on. That was scary to me and I decided then I had to save one of them, either Bill Sr. or Bill Jr. and I decided to save my son. I feel badly, because all of us in the family still loved him as a person, he was really sick. He was his own worst enemy. It got to be where truly you could not live with that. I couldn't see raising a child and having him be afraid to bring people home. It's really very sad.

"Over the years, I kept wanting Bill Jr. to want to find his father. I have a neighbor who has quite a few connections and was going to do that when we read in *Variety* that he'd died … somewhere around 1982. He'd been transferred to the Motion Picture Home from another hospital within 24 hours before he passed away."

Barbara had a small role in Paramount's *Union Station* (1950) and then they allowed her to go on the road with

Barbara during her time at Universal-International.

Born Yesterday, playing the lead opposite Lon Chaney, Jr. "Lon was such a heavy drinker. He was very unpleasant that way. Of course, he was the star of the stars, and at rehearsal, the theaters were having him help direct. He directed me behind every piece of furniture there was. I remember complaining, after rehearsal, and they told me very nicely, very politely, but very definitely, that he was the star and that's the way he wanted it done. He'd been doing it all over the country and that's the way it would be staged. But I stole all the reviews. It just happened to be the right vehicle for me. He was just furious. The night after the reviews came out, he did everything he could possibly do, he'd start talking to me, under his breath as I was doing my lines. He would whisper something, off scene, or whatever, at me. Finally, I had about 15 or 20 minutes of that and I decided to get Lon at his own game. Every time he'd talk to me, I'd say, 'What?'

I'd look at him like, 'What did you say?' And he didn't know what to do. So he got in the middle of the card game scene. He'd always tell me a certain thing in the card game because that was such a highlight. But I knew it was wrong, I knew I was missing a big laugh and I refused to do that. I just did it the way I wanted and he got so unglued he practically forgot what he was doing. I just decided he wasn't going to do that to me any more."

A small party scene in one of Rock Hudson's films led to a contract with Universal-International. Roles in *Iron Man* (1951) and *Son of Ali Baba* (1952) followed. She was under contract there for two years; this was also the time period Barbara married Bill Henry. "Universal didn't really like someone to be married. I came back and that was the end of that, when the options came up. Tony Curtis and John Hudson were at Universal too. John was such a nice person, fine actor. The one you were afraid of all the time was Hugh O'Brian. God, talk about a strange person. He was friendly, but he was strange."

Moving to television—and several western series—was odd for Barbara because, "I was scared to death of horses! There was one scene in a *Lone Ranger* [1949–1957] where I had to ride out on a horse. Even though they had the wranglers like six feet away, I was scared. I got out there and I remember the director, Earl Bellamy, said to me, 'You earned your entire money in that last five minutes.' I said, 'Yes, I did!' I was scared to death of horses. I would have done a lot more westerns, had I not been afraid of horses."

Barbara also would have worked more if it had not been for her husband. "He would tell people that we were out of town. After I left him, I found this out. Casting people said, 'We wanted you but we knew you lived in Las Vegas and it was a quickie thing and we couldn't get you in town fast enough.' But we never lived in Las Vegas! Bill told people we had this ranch in Las Vegas. So he really did me more harm than good. I remember him telling me, screaming and hollering, he didn't want me to go down, the day I was going to start my contract at Paramount. He got so terribly drunk and he slept in front of our house and Mother was horrified. Bill said, 'I'm not going to be Mr. Barbara Knudson.' Agents would call up, he'd take the call and say, no, she's not available, she's out of town. He just had the jealousy thing, and I wasn't aware of it."

Of her early TV westerns, Barbara doesn't recall much about the *Hopalong Cassidy* episode she did in 1952. "I remember being fascinated with him, 'cause everybody always admired him. I just remember trying to keep my eyes open, because the lights were so bright out on the desert.

"I remember more about Gene Autry. I was a dance hall gal. Of course, everybody knew [because of Gene's drinking] that you better get the shots of Gene before noon [*laughs*]. That was kind of cute. He was always so pleasant and cheerful, but the funny thing was he could absolutely not remember the names of cities when he was filming. He would do this whole big line and he'd get to a town name and he'd forget it. And they'd say *cut*. [*laughs*] I was in this buckboard with Pat Buttram. Pat and I are in this overturned thing, and the shot is for Gene to jump over and help me out of this buckboard. I have to jump down about four and a half feet. Gene has to get me out of this thing. Prior to that, we left really early, early in the morning. I had grabbed my things, met the limo and gone out on location. We get ready for the scene and I have this big long dress and I put my shoes on but I'd brought two left shoes. So I thought, there wasn't anything that was so major that I couldn't wear those. Now, I had to

Las Vegas, Nevada, girl—Barbara Knudson.

jump out of this buckboard. Pat gets me out and we jump down and I have this left shoe on my right foot and it's just killing me. Autry does his line but forgets the town he has to say. 'Cut!' Then he'd do the next take. Gene would say 'They're on the road to … uh…' 'Cut!' About this time, my foot is killing me, my whole leg is out of joint because I'm jumping down on this left shoe. Finally, they ended up, practically saying 'thataway.' It was San Dimas, but he *could not* remember it [*laughs*]. That same day, I was sitting by the wardrobe trailer, touching up my makeup. I had this little pillbox hat, made out of cardboard. There was a big two-by-four, leaning against the trailer, and I guess people walking back and forth in the trailer rocked this board. It fell and hit me smack on the head. If it hadn't been for that hat, I don't know if I'd be here today. Running around with a foot in the wrong shoe and getting hit on the head with a board and everything else in the same film [*laughs*]. But I remember Gene, because we had a

lot of fun on the set, and Pat was such a wonderful person."

Barbara also worked on *Daniel Boone* (1964–1970). "Fess Parker was a sweetheart. We were close friends in a way. Fess was just starting out. Bill and I had a little apartment up in the Hollywood Hills. Fess had his guitar and would play music. He was living somewhere in a room, up a little further. He would walk by and we would invite him in to eat. We realized he really didn't have square meals every day, so we'd tell him, come in and play, as a joke, come in and play and we'll have dinner, but you've got to bring your guitar [*laughs*]. He was such a wonderful person and he still is."

Although Barbara still managed to do a few things in the business, she basically left and worked for Rand Brooks' ambulance service for a few years and then became a dental assistant. One of her last roles was in the Northwoods film Rand Brooks produced independently in 1961 for $178,000, *Legend of the Northwest* (originally filmed as *Bear Heart*). It was later purchased by a Texas company and released in 1979. "They wanted Jane Withers. She was all set for that, but she had an appendicitis attack at the last minute. Rand thought of me and we did it with Denver Pyle. Marshall Reed was in that too. I'd worked with him in the *Hopalong Cassidy*. He'd been around for all those years.

"I also remember Harry Lauter. I got caught with him driving a horse team. He couldn't drive horses worth a hoot. I thought sure we were going to go over a cliff two or three times."

One of Barbara's best friends in the business was Clayton Moore. "There was a group of about seven of us that were always together … Rand Brooks and his wife at that time, Lois, Clay and Sally … we spent a lot of time together. We had a joke … Clayton, Rand and I. We had a certain scene which was a hysterical thing! All I had to do was call up and say this one sentence, no matter what time of day or year and they immediately would say, 'Bobbie, is that you?' We did the first color *Lone Ranger* episode, 'Wooden Rifle' [1956]. Earl Bellamy was the director. We had this long shot of me coming out of the cabin with Rand. I come out with the rifle, walk all the way from the gate to the fence, ready to protect my husband and my son. It was a lengthy thing, but the last line was, with all humility, 'Oh, shucks, I wouldn't have shot you anyhow.' Now—everybody that knows me, knows foul words never leave my mouth! So here we are at the gate—a perfect shot, all I have to do now is pause, look back at the Lone Ranger and say, 'Oh, shucks, I wouldn't have shot you anyhow.' But, clear as day, I said, 'Oh shi...' I didn't say the *word*, but I realized 'shi' was not 'shu' and I stopped. Earl says, 'Cut.' We all went hysterical! They tried to do it again ... someone would laugh. Clayton would laugh. Earl says, 'Ten minute break' [*laughs*]. Naturally, I finally got the shot, but the sun was really, really setting. Point of story, I could call Clay or Rand on the phone and say, 'Oh, shi...' and immediately they'd know it was me. Once, Clay was in the hospital. I went down one night; I was, at that time, working in a medical office and had this nurse's uniform on. I went into the room where Clay was half asleep. He looked up and I said, 'Oh shi...' Dangerous thing. He started laughing so hard he nearly split whatever [*laughs*]."

"I was kind of angry at Clayton actually, because we had this little pact. If anything ever happened to Sally [his wife], we were going to get married. This was just all talk stuff, because of our closeness. So when Sally passed away, by then I'd made a different life here in Vegas and everything, been apart for ages, as far as the group of people, not just Clayton, but

Rand Brooks and that group. When I found out he'd married this nurse, I was really angry. I met her and I thought, 'You promised you were going to marry me.' Because, actually, in the back of my mind, I think had I been down there and contacted him and said, 'Okay, Clayton, all these years we said we were going to get married,' it might have happened."

Looking back at her career, Barbara chuckles, "I'm probably the only one you're ever going to talk to in this business that never, never, never, ever got put on a casting couch. I ran across it only one time. I was approached one time, and when it dawned on me what it was, I just started to cry and I got out of the situation. I was such a Pollyanna! I didn't let that bother me, I thought the parts would come to me anyway. When I look back, over the years, I realize I should have gone to these parties, this and that and the other ... socialization, you're in the group. They like you. They don't personally want anything from you but they promote you, they love to promote people. What was sad is that I thought I'm engaged and I don't date. Then I was married after that. I wish I had put other things aside and concentrated on doing that to build a career. I used to want to be a female Gene Lockhart, who always was the bad guy but you felt sorry for him. I always thought I was a good comedienne too. I was Lola the waitress that Harry Von Zell had a little romance with down at the restaurant on *The George Burns and Gracie Allen Show* [1950–1958]. When I look back, had I not gone to work out of the business, I probably would have gotten a series. Because everybody that stuck in there, that had any kind of worth at all, did get their time. The only regret I have is that I let other things sidetrack me."

Barbara Knudson
Western Filmography

Movies: *The Lady from Texas* (1951 Universal-International)—Howard Duff; *One Desire* (1955 Universal-International)—Rock Hudson; *The Jayhawkers* (1959 Paramount)—Jeff Chandler; *Legend of the Northwest* (1961 Rand Productions)—Denver Pyle.

Television: *Range Rider*, "The Hawk" (1951); *Sky King*, "Triple Exposure" (1952); *Hopalong Cassidy*, "Frontier Law" (1952); *Death Valley Days*, "Jimmy Dayton's Treasure" (1954); *Gene Autry*, "Stage to San Dimas" (1955); *The Lone Ranger*, "The Wooden Rifle" (1956); *Annie Oakley*, "Twisted Trails" (1956); *The Lone Ranger*, "Hot Spell in Panamint" (1956); *Sergeant Preston of the Yukon*, "Out of the Night" (1957); *Fury*, "The Baby Sitters" (1958); *Daniel Boone*, "Crisis by Fire" (1966).

Ruta Lee

Lithuanian Bombshell

Vivacious Ruta Lee was one of the two or three most prolific actresses on television in the 1960s and 1970s. She's also one of the most talented and well-liked performers in the Hollywood community. Her spirited, outgoing personality, lively wit and refreshing candor have made her a favorite for over 40 years. Beginning in the mid–1950s, she maintained a heavy schedule of guest roles throughout the next three decades, not only in westerns but in sitcoms, dramas and game shows as well. Her extensive stage work in touring companies of *Hello Dolly* and others is not to be overlooked.

Ruta tells us she was born of "Lithuanian parents, transplanted from Lithuania to Canada because they couldn't get into the United States. The quotas for any European coming into the United States was closed and their choices were Mexico, Australia or Canada. Canada was obviously the closest place to the United States where everybody knew the streets were paved with gold. That's how we wound up in Montreal, Canada, where I was born. My mother always felt I was Lithuania's answer to Shirley Temple. So she took me to dancing school, took me to music classes, all of the stuff. The idea was, when you lived in the snows of Montreal, to go to a warm climate, so she thought Hollywood would be good. This was after the war and all of the quotas for Lithuanians were taken up by displaced persons from all over the world and nobody was getting into the U.S. that wasn't a displaced person. Somehow, she persevered and we moved to Southern California when I was about eight. My mother lived her dream,

A Lithuanian out west. Ruta in _Bullet for a Badman_ (1964).

because she saw me become a celebrity in a lot of people's eyes but not in your wildest dreams would I call her a stage mother."

Under her real name, Ruta Kilmonis, she worked in little theater all through high school but the first job she had that got her her union card was on several episodes of _The George Burns and Gracie Allen Show_ (1950–1958). "The first show I did after that was a *Superman* [*My Friend Superman* (1953)] with George Reeves. These are all minuscule things. But they were fun. Then, of course, I auditioned and got *Seven Brides for Seven Brothers* [1954].

"MGM, when I did *Seven Brides*, came to me and said, 'We're going to be sending all the girls out on a tour, but you can't become a movie star with a name like Ruta Kilmonis.' 'Okay, but I want to keep the Ruta, because it's a beloved Lithuanian name. Ruta in Lithuanian is a very fragrant herb that grows in great profusion all over eastern Europe and it's the national symbol of Lithuania, it's sung about in every song, it's talked about in every poem, theater curtains have a big sprig of ruta embroidered on them, so it's a national symbol, much like the rose is to England or the maple leaf to Canada. So I wanted to keep the Ruta, and they said, well, let's kick it around. When they came to Lee, I thought, Ruta Lee works, because the diminutive of Ruta in Lithuanian or Polish or Russian or Yiddish is Rutale. So Rutale—Ruta Lee, almost the same sound. Now I go out on the tour, right? Ruta Lee doing this, Ruta Lee floating down the Colorado, Ruta Lee milking a cow, Ruta Lee playing baseball, all of this stuff, anything to make space, headlines ... then some jerk at MGM forgets to change the credit in the movie and it comes out with Kilmonis. Now *you know* all those people in Ames, Iowa, are saying, who the heck was that girl that said she was in the movie?"

The Twinkle in God's Eye (1955) was Ruta's first western feature, opposite Hugh O'Brian. "He was just a bit pompous, but then he's a bit pompous anyway. I think it's just part of his nature and I don't know that it's necessarily ego ... but oh, my dear, nobody's going to give me a bad time. If they do, I just laugh it off. That's the best."

Everyone who worked on *Sergeants 3*

(1962) seems to have a story about making the film ... an escapade, an event. "Being 'the girl,' I was exceedingly well taken care of by all the guys. I am sorry to say [*laughs*], I'm the only girl I know that has not had an affair with Frank Sinatra. And I'm sorry to say that [*laughs*]! They had already started when I went up to location in Kanab, Utah, which is just beautiful. We all stayed at a big motel-hotel kind of arrangement. There we were in Kanab, where the only thing to do was to go to the Dairy Queen after supper. But Frank worked it out so that while we were on location, which was a long time, Frank played a week at the Sands, so we went down for Frank's opening and back down for his closing. The next day we'd go down for Dean's opening and back for his closing. Then we went down for Sammy's opening and back for his closing. So it was back and forth because he had a whole fleet of planes. Never in my life had I seen a fleet of planes, coming and going all the time. I went to work on location every day, not in a car, not in a limousine, not in a bus, but in a helicopter! Isn't that marvelous? I've got a picture of the director, John Sturges, trying to get somebody's attention, because it was hysteria. This must have been a very frightening experience for him. Simply because Frank made it very clear: I don't care if you take a week to set up a shot ... fine, you set up the shot. When we come in to do the shot, we'll rehearse it once, we'll shoot it once. I don't want to hear a light went out, the dolly rattled, the floor creaked ... I don't want to hear that. You're going to get one take [*laughs*]."

In 1963, Ruta had the opportunity to co-star with not one, but two western icons, Rory Calhoun and Rod Cameron, in *The Gun Hawk*. "I was so sad, but that's our business, you have a moment in the sun and then you're out again. What made me sad was that Rod Cameron, this big,

He was the West
IN ALL ITS
UNFORGETTABLE
VIOLENCE!

THE GUN HAWK

COLOR by DE LUXE

STARRING
RORY CALHOUN
ROD CAMERON · RUTA LEE · ROD LAUREN

Ruta found young singer Rod Lauren "a bit of a pain in the ass" on *The Gun Hawk* (1963).

big, big star, in my eyes, had second billing to Rory. To me, Rory had never accomplished or done as much or had the credibility that Rod Cameron had. The young man, Rod Lauren, was a bit of a pain in the ass. Nobody ever heard of him after that. He wasn't a very good actor. He was a sweet enough guy but he was somewhat pretentious about everything and not quite as eager to have the kind of fun and everything that we would do. I mean, here we are, playing a death scene, but we'd be hugging and kissing in bed and carrying on [*laughs*] and... 'Okay, okay, it's time to shoot.'"

Although Rory was known to have a bit of a roaming eye, Ruta laughs, "Rory was married to Lita Baron at the time and

we had been friends from before making the movie. I'm still friends with her. Either there's something very unsexual about me, or it's the fact I laugh my way through everything, but nobody ever pitches me because I do the dirty jokes quicker and faster and louder and bawdier that they do, so I become a buddy rather than a hit target."

The year 1964 saw Ruta teamed with Audie Murphy in *Bullet for a Badman*. "It was a hysterical cast! We had Darren McGavin, Alan Hale, Jr., that wonderful character actor George Tobias ... one laugh after another. Everybody was fast and quick. I was the only girl on location in St. George, Utah, so everyone treated me like a baby doll and we had a wonderful time. Audie was not a laugher and a scratcher. Audie had a strange sense of humor that was strictly his own. He would make a joke and we would all look at one another and wonder—did that go over our heads? His humor was entirely different. He was on a different level. He didn't mix and mingle with the rest of us. He didn't come out to supper with us. He didn't 'play' with us. When I got to spend a little time with him, on a one-on-one basis, he was very gentle, very humble, very sweet, very much of a gentleman, but either he didn't feel secure or he didn't want to play, so I never *really* got to know him the way I did everybody else in ten minutes."

Ruta was one of the most prolific and versatile actresses on television from the 1960s to the 1980s. "I think if we counted up every appearance I ever made, guest starring, or something, it would be about 5,000. Every studio had their version of what they thought I did. Some places I was the sweet little girl with the heart of gold and other places I had the heart of gold and the teeth to match. At still other places, I was a drug addict that was in trouble, other places I was the mother of some kid. It depended on how the casting director saw me."

Because Ruta guest starred on virtually every TV western made, and because her powers of observations are so keen, we asked her briefly about each of her TV western leading men, beginning with Will "Sugarfoot" Hutchins. "A cat. A big-eyed cat that wasn't weaned yet. Absolutely adorable, charming and totally unsophisticated."

James Garner of *Maverick* (1957–1962): "Hot. Funny. Innately funny. Had a bit of a roving eye and we had to laugh a few situations off there, too, but great fun and great style. Great charisma."

Jack Kelly, the other Maverick: "Adorable. Adorable. Far more sophisticated. Very humorous also. And a gentleman, wonderful stories to spin. Also, there was an ingenuous kind of twinkle and sparkle in James' eye that Jack, being a little more sophisticated, didn't exude, you know, his was more sedate. But I'm crazy about him. Wonderful guy."

James Arness, Matt Dillon of *Gunsmoke* (1955–1975): "Mountain of a man. With a big heart, as big as that mountainous physique of his. I did several of those episodes, and in one of them ["Jenny" (1962)] I was supposed to be seducing him. Rather than a door, there was a curtain into my bedroom. There I sit, doing the whole thing. And he comes in and throws a quilt over my head, slings me over his shoulder, goes out and in order to make his way out by pulling the curtain, he swung and slammed my head against the frame of the door. All of a sudden, out I went. I came to and there was a frantic, big Jim Arness, holding me up, tears running down his face, 'Oh, my God, oh my God, have I killed you? Are you all right? Oh, my God!' He felt so terrible. I always love to remind him of that [*laughs*]."

"The rest of the cast was wonderful too. Amanda Blake, we used to do sort of bets together every once in a while. In those days, celebrities were invited to so many things, trips and cruises, whatever it was. Amanda was such fun to be with because she was a good dame and a class act. I really liked her a lot. And Milburn [Stone] was too, wonderful. Again, I think I loved all these people because they knew how to laugh. That's one of the lovely things about our business, you don't get the laughs selling insurance, or cars, or anything else, that you have in show business."

John Payne was the lead in *Restless Gun* (1957–1959): "Nice man. Sweet man. I didn't get to know him very well but he was fun to be with, he also had a twinkle in his eye and a lot of humor."

John McIntire took over Ward Bond's spot on *Wagon Train* in 1961 when Bond died. "Oh, there was a lovely gentleman. And again, humor. Able to laugh, wonderful deep voice, whole thing. Laughed at everything."

Robert Fuller came on *Wagon Train* in 1963, but also starred in *Laramie* (1959–1963): "Pussycat, full of vim, vigor, vitality and so eager to please and have a good time along the way. I'm crazy about him. You know, he's a helluva dancer too. He started out as a dancer. His father was a dancer. His father was in *Seven Brides for Seven Brothers*."

Nick Adams starred as ABC's *The Rebel* (1959–1961): "Nick was adorable. He was the new breed. He was into everything and knew everybody and everybody knew Nick, so it was like old home week if you met at Schwabs or you were on the set or something. A self-promoter, absolutely. But, somehow gently so. It was not so blatant that it turned you off. You knew he was doing it and you kind of said, hey, if you don't toot your own horn, who will … more power to you. So, I mean, he did very well."

Wayne Rogers and Robert Bray headed the cast of *Stagecoach West* (1960–1961): "Wayne Rogers was probably one of the brightest persons I ever worked with. Very intelligent. Very astute, financially. Was already talking investments and things when I was going…'What'd he say?' And he's very wealthy now. Now, I knew Bob Bray before that show because he used to do shows at the Player's Ring and the theaters I was working at in high school, so I knew who Bob Bray was. He was already a big star to me, because he'd done stuff. Beverly Garland worked at that theater too. It was fun when we became such good friends. So many people confuse us, Beverly Garland and myself. We're very similar. We're both bigger than life, we both have deep voices and full of gusto and laughter is our middle name. We were both regulars on *Stump the Stars* [1950–1963], which was the pantomime quiz show."

Eric Fleming of *Rawhide* (1959–1965): "I dated Eric Fleming, and I liked him a lot. Eric was a lovely man and he had such wonderful stories to tell. Eric had his face reconstructed. He was a very funny guy who was a bit of a loner and was always an entrepreneur. When he was in the army, he would take on all kinds of things. He would do illegal things. He would resell cigarettes and all this kind of stuff. One day, he made a bet with somebody about pressing cement blocks, or something. I can't remember what it was now … and they tipped and smashed his face. And his whole face was reconstructed. Well, I must say, it was gorgeous [*laughs*]. They did a wonderful job. Of course, we had a lot to talk about because he liked musicals. He'd done quite a few things on Broadway. He used to come up and have dinner or take me out. And Clint Eastwood of the same series, I was crazy about Clint. Always was. He was married to Maggie at that time and we all sort of hung out. He was very, very special. Very cute."

Then there was Don Collier of *The Outlaws* (1960–1962). "Charming. Not as humorous, as I remember. A little quieter. Sort of sat back and just stretched out and waited for the shot."

Clint Walker, the bigger than life star of *Cheyenne* (1955–1962), Ruta calls, "a dear soul. What a dear soul. He just made you feel so comfortable and so good and so easy. Everything was okay. And he ambled. He didn't do anything fast. He's special."

For an ensemble show, there was the whole cast of *Bonanza* (1959–1971). "I would start with Lorne Greene. Because we had a lot in common. We both had deep voices and we were both from

Canada. The *Bonanza* I did with them was a very serious one, 'cause I was playing an alcoholic who had lost her husband and children in a fire. So, I mean, we were laughing and scratching a lot, but on the other hand, I'd have to pull it together to become this kind of demented creature. And they were very helpful. It was very nice because when it came a moment to be serious, they all helped me along. The only one that was a little bit off was Pernell Roberts. Pernell was very nice to me but he could be a bit of a horse's ass. But that's okay, if he was unhappy, he was unhappy. But it took him a long time to find something else, didn't it? I bet he was sorry for a while. Now, Michael Landon had been my friend for a long time. I did a *Hitchcock* thing with Michael, so I knew him from that. Then he was married to a gal named Dodie. Dodie and Michael and I used to play a little bit together, then they were divorced."

Short-lived at Warner Bros. was Jeffrey Hunter as *Temple Houston* (1964): "He was one of the prettiest people that ever was put on the screen. God, he was gorgeous."

Also at Warner Bros., Ty Hardin was *Bronco* (1958–1962). "Ty Hardin... try harder, right? I did his test. Now there was a boy who was slightly full of himself. And he was so pretty. I mean, he really looked stunning in his outfits. The camera loved him. Later, with Ty, I did this *awful* movie called *Rooster* [1983], then it became *Claws of Death* or something. Dreadful piece of shit. But Ty was all of a sudden a different human being in this. He was always good with me, we laughed, but all of a sudden, he had a humility that he hadn't had before. Maybe it's because life hadn't treated him quite as beautifully as when he was first at Warner Bros."

James Drury essayed the part of *The Virginian* from 1962 until 1970. "Jimmy Drury turned out to be one of my really good friends. Jim Drury and I worked together, before he had the series, in a *Walter Winchell File* ["Act of Fate" (1957)]. That was the first time I worked with Jim. Then I did a whole bunch of other things he was starring in and it was always a joy to be with him. Jim Drury could be a very bad boy but he was always wonderful with me. And I have a funny story to tell. After the series, we were on the road doing plays. He would be doing a play and I would be the next act coming in, so we'd overlap the week of rehearsals and whatnot and we'd see each other. There was always a great camaraderie. Also, we were two of a very few conservatives in Hollywood. When we were on the Republican campaign trail, we would inevitably be teamed to go somewhere and do something. I don't remember who we were campaigning for, but we were up in northern California and arrived late. There wasn't any place to have dinner, there wasn't a diner or anything, so we went to the bowling alley to try to get something, but their kitchen had already closed. I said, oh, to hell with it and we went to the motel. Jimmy said, 'Good night, princess, I'll see you later,' and he took off. I thought, 'Well, he's going to go back to the bowling alley and get ten more drinks or whatever it is.' About three hours later, he turns up and he's banging on my door. I said, 'Oh, Jesus Christ, Jimmy go to bed, go to sleep, you silly drunk, we've got a lot to do tomorrow.' He said, 'I'm not drunk, open the damn door!' I opened the door and he had a big platter full of prison-made peanut butter and jelly sandwiches for me. And a big quart of milk. He had driven by the prison, pulled up to the gate and said I can't find a place around here to eat. You suppose they'd feed me? I'm the Virginian. So they opened the gate, they got the warden up, the warden's wife came down, got autographs, they got some orderly to go out and make peanut butter sandwiches

Even though it was a death scene, Ruta and Rory Calhoun were "carrying on" between takes. *The Gun Hawk* (1963).

[*laughs*]. But is that sweet? I mean, that is sweetness that he would go do that. That's my Jimmy Drury."

Robert Conrad was the fiery star of *The Wild Wild West* (1965–1969). "Bob Conrad was very good with me. I don't know that he would be good with everybody else. He, too, loved to laugh and joke around, so we were fine, but of course, the real salt of the earth was Ross Martin. So between the three of us, it was nothing but one big laugh when we were working. God, Bob Conrad had a beautiful face, and those wonderful eyes! He never got past being short, so I think, as can happen, with short, short men, they get a little bit demonic in their needs, but he was good with me."

Bat Masterson—Gene Barry is a good friend because, "Gene Barry is Lithuanian. He's Jewish, but Lithuanian. We got along just famously. I loved hearing his stories about Broadway. It was fun to just sit and listen, between takes, and talk. He liked to talk and he liked pretty women. He had a good marriage, I'm not saying he was flirtatious. We see them, six, seven times a year, probably, because they live in Palm Springs."

Even with the thousands of shows Ruta appeared on, she seemed somehow connected with Warner Bros. "I wasn't under contract to Warner Bros. and it's a mistake. An offer was made. It's truly a mistake made. But I was such buddies with Hugh Benson. My mother would bake cookies or something and I'd bring them in to the production office to the producers, Bill Orr and Hugh Benson, and I'd sit and laugh and scratch and swap dirty stories with them, so I was like one of their gang, so to speak, and they'd always put me in something. They wanted me to do a series, *The Alaskans*, and I said, 'What do I want to do that for? You'll give me $300 a week when you're already paying me $750 per episode, so why would I work for half my salary?' And they said, 'You'll be sorry, you should do it.' And they were right, because all the people under contract had the power of the Warner Bros. publicity machine behind them and if you weren't working for a studio, you had to do your own publicity or hire a publicist."

Perhaps it *was* good judgment on Ruta's part, as *The Alaskans* only lasted one season, 1959-1960, with Roger Moore and Dorothy Provine rather than Ruta. A similar series was *Klondike* (1960-1961) with Ralph Taeger and Joi Lansing. "Joi Lansing was the one whose line I stole that I dearly loved. She was very amply bazoomed. Then she'd pad in a little more and I'd say, 'Joi, what the hell' ... and she'd say, 'Please, I owe my whole career to B. F. Goodrich' [*laughs*]. Joi Lansing couldn't act her way out of anything, but she was a darling girl ... she died very young."

As for directors, Ruta has some definite views. She adored "Ted Post. Good director. I did a bunch of stuff with Ted. Chris Nyby ... great, beautiful director. I like directors that would give you just a glimmer, kind of aim you in the direction and then let you go. I like directors that said, 'I'll only talk to you if you're not doing right.'"

Some directors tried to give actors "line readings." "As a rule, you wind up doing it your way. You don't mean to be cocky but somehow you have a gut feeling about something that you have to depend on. Because it's you that's doing it. Some people like to make you an instrument for them. They will play their symphony on your instrument, and they get so friggin' artsy-fartsy that your head is spinning from trying to understand what this is all about. But I found out way back when that if you went (so sweetly), 'Ohhhhhh, you are so right. Oh, you really ... oh, my God, how could I ever have thought of it any other way?' And then you gave him the same line reading, but it was his. That worked a lot. In some cases, of course, it wouldn't work and in some cases I was probably totally wrong. Just thinking I'm right doesn't make me right. But, boy, when a director could kind of sit and play with you and laugh and then just ever so quietly say, 'Try it going from over here ... give it a little...'—it was wonderful. The directors that would scream and groan and yell... Les Martinson was a groaner and a screamer and a crier ... he was impossible. He's one of my best friends, but he's the biggest pain in the ass as a director! He would just carry on. 'What are you doing to me? You're killing me, you're destroying this whole thing. I can't do this!!!' He's wonderful ... meticulous ... wonder-ful ... but anybody that ever worked for him goes, 'Oh, do we have to work with Les again?'

"I think my best work was done on stage. I did some very nice work on television on different things. I think that *Bonanza* we talked about a little earlier, 'A Woman Lost' [1963] was good. I was very young when I did that. I probably should have had somebody put me up for an Emmy for that because, for a single segment, it was very nice work, done by a lovely director, Don McDougall, who really helped me a lot. I did some nice work on *Burke's Law* [1963–1966], the series Gene Barry did after the western. Some of it was silly and flirtatious, but it was nicely done. There again, it's not just me; it has to be that the director and the cinematographer who, above all, makes or breaks your performance and the editor, either makes it work or doesn't make it work."

Reflecting on today's heavily sex- and violence-oriented series, Ruta emphatically states, "I hate it. Everything ugly and unglamorous and undignified is where we all reach now. The uglier, the better. It's pushing the envelope all the time. We admired the comics who started it, Richard Pryor and Lenny Bruce. But that's okay because you chose to go and sit in a smoke-filled club and do that as kind of a sorority or fraternity of hip people who were going to do this. You were not putting it on the tube, where anybody can click on and be insulted, upset, hurt, shocked, whatever, by it. Of course we can click it off, but the kids don't.

"In the 1950s and 1960s, people that were running the show had expertise. They had been in the business for a long time, directors were not 20-year-old kids from Harvard or Yale. They were guys who had either been grips or were cameramen or were best boys. They worked their way into the industry and they knew it. You had a lot of respect because they knew what they were doing and if you had to do it fast, then we did it fast. 'Have you finished that shot? Fine. Turn the camera around, get this one over here, now.' You did it fast but you laughed all the way and you pulled it together to do whatever serious moment you had to do. That's all there was to it."

In looking back over the years and the enormous body of performances she's turned in, Ruta certainly believes she did some excellent work. But also, she thinks, "I would just float along and do whatever came along. I was doing a good job, yes, and I was very dependable. People could call me and know they were going to get a performance, that I wouldn't fool around. But wouldn't it have been nice if

I had been smart enough to really observe how things were done. What kind of production mechanics should be learned, learn it, and write myself a series? And collect all that money, you know, for me?" she laughs.

Much of Ruta's current time is absorbed by her charitable work with the Thalians, a fund-raising group that deals with mental health from pediatrics through geriatrics. "In lieu of dropping on my knees and praying, I get up off my ass and go do something for somebody. That's my prayer to God, and thanks for the nice things that have come my way. And it's very rewarding."

Besides her charitable work, how would Ruta Lee like to be remembered 100 years from now? "I think I'd like my tombstone to say that she put a smile on my lips and in my heart."

Ruta Lee
Western Filmography

Movies: *Seven Brides for Seven Brothers* (1954 MGM)—Howard Keel; *The Twinkle in God's Eye* (1955 Republic)—Mickey Rooney; *Sergeants 3* (1962 United Artists)—Frank Sinatra; *The Gun Hawk* (1963 Allied Artists)—Rory Calhoun; *Bullet for a Badman* (1964 Universal)—Audie Murphy.

Television: *Maverick*, "Comstock Conspiracy" (1957); *Maverick*, "Plunder of Paradise" (1958); *Gray Ghost*, "Contraband" (1958); *U.S. Marshal*, "Gold Is Where You Find It" (1958); *Sugarfoot*, "The Dead Hills" (1958); *Gunsmoke*, "Carmen" (1958); *Maverick*, "Betrayal" (1959); *Restless Gun*, "The Painted Beauty" (1959); *Wagon Train*, "The Kate Parker Story" (1959); *Colt .45*, "The Hothead" (1959); *The Alaskans*, "The Abominable Snowman" (1959); *Man from Blackhawk*, "The Legacy" (1959); *Bat Masterson*, "Death of Bat Masterson" (1959); *U.S. Marshal*, "Ghost Town" (1959); *Yancy Derringer*, "Two of a Kind" (1959); *Colt .45*, "Showdown at Goldtown" (1960); *The Alaskans*, "Long Pursuit" (1960); *The Rebel*, "Grant of Land" (1960); *U.S. Mar-

shal, "R.I.P." (1960); *Shotgun Slade*, "Killer's Brand" (1960); *Zane Grey Theatre*, "Man from Everywhere" (1961); *Stagecoach West*, "Blind Man's Bluff" (1961); *Stagecoach West*, "The Marker" (1961); *Laramie*, "Siege at Jubilee" (1961); *Rawhide*, "Incident of the Reluctant Bridegroom" (1962); *Gunsmoke*, "Jenny" (1962); *The Outlaws*, "Farewell Performance" (1962); *Cheyenne*, "Wanted for the Murder of Cheyenne Bodie" (1962); *Rawhide*, "Incident at Alkali Sink" (1963); *Wagon Train*, "The Bleeker Story" (1963); *Bonanza*, "A Woman Lost" (1963); *Temple Houston*, "Enough Rope" (1963); *The Travels of Jamie McPheeters*, "The Day of the Lame Duck" (1964); *The Virginian*, "The Long Quest" (1964); *The Virginian*, "The Girl from Yesterday" (1964); *The Wild Wild West*, "The Night of the Casual Killer" (1965); *The Wild Wild West*, "The Night of the Gypsy Peril" (1967); *The Guns of Will Sonnett*, "Trail's End" (1969).

Virginia Lee

A Silent Star Remembers

A deposed Miss America. Leading lady to Franklyn Farnum and outlaw Emmett Dalton. A descendent of Confederate General Robert E. Lee. The ideal Christy Girl. Married to the man who invented Reynolds Aluminum Foil. Any *one* of these distinctions would make a person's life memorable ... but all this and more happened to actress Virginia Lee.

Virginia was born July 14, 1901, in Mexico City, where she lived until she was eight. In Mexico, Virginia was reared under the tutelage of an old Spanish nurse. Her family then moved to Canada where her grandfather owned silver mines. In Canada she spoke mostly French. She is descended in a direct line from Confederate General Robert E. Lee and proudly owns the personal cabinet in which Lee kept his uniforms.

According to Virginia, she first posed for artists when she was 11 or 12.

Like other young girls in 1916, she admired artist Howard Chandler Christy's Christy Girl pictures. It gradually dawned on her there was something about them that reminded her of herself. Out of that grew the self-assurance that she represented either the composite or possibly the ideal Christy Girl. So, at 15, accompanied by her mother and sister, she came to New York and met the artist. He immediately agreed to have her pose for a Christy Girl picture. He called her "my most marvelous model." Virginia Lee's artistic qualifications amply justified his expert opinion: 5'4" in height, 120 lbs., slender but well-formed, with golden hair, fair skin and blue eyes. To quote Mr. Christy, "When posing she articulates grace, expression

Publicity pose of Virginia circa 1920.

and poise. Most important she is always at the studio at the hour appointed. She is never tired and never loses her temper." During World War I, portraits by Christy that Virginia posed for sold at $3–$5 million.

Lee was determined to be an actress, "I never went any place without my mother. Tallulah Bankhead, the daughter of Senator Bankhead, and I both went to New York at the same time. We started working at the same time and it never stopped. It started getting better and better all the time. I remember, now I shouldn't say this story, but my mother never was a businesswoman. She had my father and afterwards she tried to do things but she wasn't a businesswoman. That's when I got the idea I had to make money. When I would make $50 in an afternoon, I'd take $25 and hide the rest 'til I started a bank account because mother had no value at all. Everything she saw she'd spend. I knew she couldn't sew so I

hid [the money] in her sewing machine. When my mother found it, she was so naive. She said, 'Oh, toots! I found $3,000 in the sewing machine.' I couldn't tell her I was hiding it from her. She went out and spent it right away!"

As a model, "I started at the regular prices, Underwood and Underwood, a lot of those places, by the hour and then by the day, and then I got to be very good where people wanted me being seen in their clothes. Then I started in the movies—seems to me I took very fast. You know, I can't remember, but it seems to me I was making $150, $200. I was making $300 in that first Technicolor picture [*Gulf Between* (1918)] a week. Now that was a lot of money in those days! Things moved very quickly. I never was without work. I was ambitious and I loved it! I never needed a manager because I did pretty well myself. [She did finally acquire an agent later in her career.] I used every trick in the trade. I really was determined to make myself famous and I did it, without ever going to bed with any man. My hair was naturally curly. I kept it long. I could have curls down my back in a minute! I never ruined anything that was an asset to my work. People don't seem to understand how serious I was about my work."

Virginia confessed very frankly that she started in pictures as an extra but moved up very quickly with a co-starring role. "World Pictures wanted a girl to play with George Walsh and I seemed to have the energy and the right amount of enthusiasm to keep up with Walsh, the star of *Luck and Pluck* [1919]. Walsh was the brother of famed director Raoul Walsh. The comedy *Luck and Pluck* was photographed in New York's Central Park. These early films were all produced in the New York–New Jersey area." Of *The Terror* (1917) with Jack Mulhall, she says, "I didn't consider him a star. He wasn't a very

Virginia has the drop on Louis Bennison in *Sandy Burke of the U-Bar-U* (1919).

good actor and not my idea of a leading man. I didn't want to make that picture." *Oh, Johnny* [1919] for Goldwyn actually was a western based on a Broadway play, *Johnny Get Your Gun*, starring Louis Bennison. Virginia says, "It was a musical and, although there was no music actually in the movie, the piano player in the theaters would play the music."

Virginia never seemed to be without work. After *Oh, Johnny* she did *Sandy Burke of the U-Bar-U* (1919), again opposite Louis Bennison. "Louie, oh, good God, yes, he came down, he was my leading man. I introduced him to a girl on an island, I can't even remember what island it was, and before I got through making the romance, they were married. I always loved that because he was such a nice guy … but he committed suicide. I can re-

member him saying to me, 'Virginia, go home and marry that good man that deserves you, I do not deserve you.' I didn't know what he was thinking. He was a stage star, as I remember." Both Bennison westerns were lensed at the historic Betzwood studios, originally the 500-acre estate of wealthy brewer John Betz, across the river from Valley Forge National Park in Pennsylvania.

In rapid succession, Virginia did an important role in *The Whirlpool* (1918) with Alice Brady and *The Gulf Between*, an eight-reeler directed by Ray Physioc, starring Niles Welch and Grace Darmond. Her scrapbook contains early Florida newspaper clippings heralding it as the first Technicolor movie ("The newest idea of making motion pictures in their natural colors is being tried out by the Technicolor

Film Corp. of Boston, the company is headed by C. Willis."). "We went to Florida and that's what made me a star. I photographed like a million bucks in color. Four or five scientists in Boston developed Technicolor. The star was Grace Darmond but it ended up Virginia Lee was the star because I photographed so well. They treated me royal. They were four leading scientists from the college in Boston. They all became world-famous. The more successful I got, the more leading-like I became. I was gonna play the part! The higher I went the more careful I was; the more I acted like a star but with consideration. I would never hurt anyone."

While making films in the New York–New Jersey area, Virginia married a Navy man, Ensign Bill Boyer. Virginia recalls, "When my mother found out she had cancer, her doctor from Virginia said she had to be operated on right away. She called me and said, 'Are you sure you love Bill?' I said, 'I'm not going to marry anybody but Bill.' And she said, 'Well, honey, how about marrying him on Sunday?' I looked at her and said 'Mother!' She said, 'Sunday is Easter and I want to see you married, if Bill will promise to take care of you and your sister if anything happens to me after.' She was the most beautiful woman in the world, my mother was. She was so beautiful when I took her to Hollywood, there wasn't a producer out there that didn't want to star her. She was gorgeous."

After leaving Hollywood in 1928, to raise a family, the Boyers moved to Milwaukee, Wisconsin, where Bill worked for Reynolds and was responsible for developing the aluminum foil we all now use. He was with Reynolds until his death in 1975.

In 1921, while making films and modeling, Virginia actually became the first Miss America—but was stripped of the crown. She recalls, "I had my picture on the cover of every magazine in New York

City. They couldn't get over it. Miss Virginia Lee, winner of first prize of Intercity Beauty Contest Fall Pageant, 1921. Looking back on it, I must have been pretty because, my God, the world was handed to me. Lillian Russell [noted stage/burlesque/vaudeville actress] called me up to tell me I would never be the beauty my mother was. She told me Diamond Jim Brady is so crazy about Mother, every time her private train came in, he would be told and would be down at the station to see her come in. Then he would get back in his cab and go over to the Waldorf Astoria to see her getting out of her taxi cab with her servants. At any rate, I had made movies so I was fairly well known. I remember the day that an agent who had been wanting me to sign up with him called and said, 'You know, Virginia Lee, your name is in lights on three movie theaters on Broadway at one time. Don't you think you've made it?' I said, 'I might have made it but I've gotta hang on to it.' I still wouldn't sign up; I wanted to see how things went. I went ahead for two or three years and kept making more money. Doing very well. Everything just fit. Then the artists at the Hotel des Artist, who were all very, very famous artists, said, 'We have the girl we are going to send to Atlantic City.' The first pageant was not the Miss America, they didn't call it that at all. It was the Atlantic City Beauty Pageant. They sent me as a representative of New York and I won it. But they took it away from me because one of the men had a girl that he had put in. He promised her she would win it. He owned a lot of land on the Boardwalk in Atlantic City and he said there's not going to be any contest if she's not going to win it. So they picked her. But, if you call up … try it just for the fun of it, call Atlantic City and ask them who was Miss America in 1921. If they give you the other name, say, 'Tell me about Virginia Lee' and they'll tell you,

'She won it!' They are bound to tell you that I won it, because I did." Virginia has photographs in her albums with her name as winner, but she was actually stripped of the title when officials learned she was married. However, she insists, "This man was the biggest land owner in Atlantic City. He was making the rules and he wanted her to win! The next thing I knew they came back and said, 'Oh, Virginia, you won but we can't give it to you.' That's all they would ever tell me. I'd like to know what [Atlantic City officials] are saying these days. I don't want to go around saying I was a Miss America if they've taken me off and forgotten me. I'm still here and I won it hands down. They said, 'You not only won it but every judge there voted for you.' Now, you can't beat that!"

Of the pageant today, Virginia thinks, "It's now a talent as well as beauty contest. I would never have won it if it depended on talent. I think the pageants now are just wonderful. I think it gives girls a wonderful opportunity."

People in Hollywood knew Virginia had been selected as the winner so she was immediately deluged with contracts to go to California where she started making movies right away.

About *Three Women Loved Him* (1920), Virginia says, "I liked that one. That picture I stole. There were two other very experienced actresses with me."

With Marguerite Clark in *Scrambled Wives* (1921), Virginia played the part of Beatrice under the direction of Edward H. Griffith. The part was not altogether to her liking: It was a catty part. "Griffith— that man was so in love with me. He directed me in two pictures and said to me, 'Well, Virginia, I will say this: You're going to become one of the biggest stars in the industry if you continue the way you are.'

"I did a picture with Norma Talmadge, *A Daughter of Two Worlds* [1920], that I had a very good part in. Norma came over and said, 'You are stealing the picture.' She went to the front office and said she would quit the picture if they didn't get rid of Virginia Lee. They did get rid of me because she was a money-maker. Her sister Constance was married to King Vidor so she was in strong, but she was a damn good actress. She told me, 'You're a detriment and I can't take it so I'm going to make sure that you're not around.' One of the head men said, 'I'm going to make money on this one,' so he formed a company and put me in it. And I was better than ever. Also Edward Small, an agent, decided to make pictures. I was making money for them. I always cooperated and was never difficult."

Those who remember the blind girl in Marjorie Rambeau's production *The Fortune Teller* (1920) and the rollicking comedy *The Servant Question* (1920) are familiar with Miss Lee at her jolliest. Virginia smiles, "William Collier [star of *The Servant Question*] was the nicest guy. He was a very well-known New York stage actor. He was a big superstar. My name shouldn't have even been up with his. I was amazed when he asked to have me as his leading woman. I know I got good notices after *The Servant Question*. Norma Talmadge married a producer. Her husband called me up and said, 'I want you for a picture. I have another star in the picture that is a stage star.' I was always in awe of the experienced actors. I was just lucky and didn't realize my luck."

Beyond the Rainbow (1922) was a sweet story with Billie Dove, a Ziegfeld Follies showgirl. "She was in that movie and there were two or three other very well-known, beautiful girls. That was the movie when I called Clara Bow and told her to come on over to Columbia and we'll introduce you and get you in. I was the one who picked up Clara Bow and made a star out of her because I introduced her to director William Christy Cabanne."

Beyond the Rainbow with Lee third-billed, is, indeed, Bow's first film. She received $50 for one week's work, although she was cut from the release print. Subsequent to her stardom, *Beyond the Rainbow* was reissued with Bow's scenes restored and her billing about Billie Dove's.

Road to Arcady (1922) was one of Virginia's favorites. Originally announced as *Love or Money* in 1920, the Erving Cain adaptation was a big hit, "It was a love story ... a lovely one. I went to Florida on that one. Harry Benhan was my leading man. He dropped out soon after. I told him at the time, 'You're going to be a superstar,' but his name didn't go up.

"The next one we made was in Miami, too. *Destiny's Isle*. That was a very good one. Very much the action film. They flew me over to some island for the exteriors. I had first billing. That was when they said she's going to be a superstar. Every studio in town wanted me. I was a good actress. I could cry without much trouble."

Earlier in her career, Virginia had the unparalleled distinction of co-starring with Emmett Dalton, the sole survivor of the notorious Dalton Gang, in *Beyond the Law* (1918), a film based on the exploits of the Dalton gang, with Emmett playing himself. The historic botched bank raid in Coffeyville, Kansas, took place on October 5, 1892. Brothers Bob and Grat were killed and Emmett received 23 shotgun pellets in his 200-lb. body. Not expected to live, he did recover from his wounds and stood trial for the Coffeyville robbery and killings. The jury found him guilty of murder and sentenced him to life in prison. Dalton served 14½ years and was pardoned in 1907 by Governor Hoch of Kansas. Upon release, his old world gone, he married Julia Johnson (the girl who had patiently waited for him), joined a church and campaigned for prison reform. After several years as a farmer and real estate dealer around Tulsa, Oklahoma, he

came to Southern California. Upon his arrival, he ran into John Tackett, the Coffeyville photographer who had taken the pictures of Emmett's dead brothers. Forgetting the past, Dalton and Tackett teamed up to produce the film based on the outlaw gang's experiences. Press releases at the time touted, "A beautiful romantic love story written by and featuring Emmett Dalton, last of the world's most noted outlaws, published in the *Wide World* magazine from May until September, 1918. The first historical picture ever produced with any of the original characters."

Virginia fondly remembers, "Emmett Dalton—when I met him, he was about 35. I was 17. It was unbelievable the way he looked after me. He was a perfect gentleman, he wouldn't let anyone come on the set without their coat on. His wife took a shine to me. She'd struck oil in Arizona or one of those states and made Emmett a very wealthy man. He was producing this movie of his life to tell the truth about the Daltons. I played the role of Ruth Lane Young, Emmett's sweetheart. We filmed it in different locations where it actually happened in the middle west. He had so much money he could [do this]. When the picture was released, it made a lot of money. Dalton said a certain amount would go for charity. That made Emmett famous in a very good way. And it didn't hurt me either. His wife and I became very close friends. Her family owned a lot of oil. She became so rich ... she bought a ruby ring as big as this one," gesturing at one on her finger. "I'd say, 'Oh please leave that ring for me.' She said, 'I give you my word, this is going to be your ring.' It must have cost a fortune, maybe several million or something. Six months or a year later I read where she died and he had been dead and I didn't know. [Actually, Emmett Dalton died in 1937.] I didn't know what to do. I wanted to write and say, 'I bet I'm in

Virginia co-starred with Franklyn Farnum (center) for eight silent westerns in 1922, all for Merit Films of Tulsa, Oklahoma.

that will.' I used to tell Bill, 'I bet I was in that will.' I bet I was and they couldn't find me. So, I lost a ruby ring that was the most gorgeous thing. I didn't get it. Bill would say, 'Well, isn't that too bad!'"

Her stature as a B-western leading lady came about in 1921 when Merit Films of Tulsa, Oklahoma, hoping to make Tulsa a center of independent film production, hired Franklyn Farnum to star in a series of westerns. Farnum was hot with the recent success of Selig's 26 Canyon Pictures westerns and a 15-chapter serial, *Vanishing Trails* (1920). Virginia, stunt actress Peggy O'Day, Al Hart and John "Shorty" Hamilton would co-star. Francis Ford joined as director and played supporting roles in these sometimes humorous westerns, which were made over a one year period. Tulsa newspaper articles of the time

promised location work in Colorado and at the Grand Canyon in Arizona. A press release stated, "Miss Lee will be a ray of sunshine into those picturesque hills. With such an aspiring and madly alive partner as Miss Lee, Mr. Farnum ought to have a chance at further stardom." Whether or not actual filming was done in Colorado and Arizona is unknown. Virginia does not recall it. "I could ride sidesaddle or I could ride western. I did it myself. I didn't ask to be taught. I would tell directors or producers, 'I can ride sidesaddle for you. I can ride western or English,' and I meant it. I never depended on people—I did it myself! I never considered it dangerous. I loved it. I did everything. I rode horses ... they'd say, 'No Miss Lee, we can't take a chance on you,' and I'd say forget it. I'd talk to the horse a few minutes and say, 'Don't you dare hurt me.' [Ha Ha.] I've been very lucky. I recall *White Masks* [1921] ... it was very trashy as I remember. I made a lot with Franklyn Farnum. At least eight to ten. The theaters asked for them. People wanted to come back to see the combination."

It was after these westerns that Virginia decided to quit. "I had gone down to Tulsa to make the Farnum series of westerns. And there was a race riot down there. It wasn't very long after that I wanted to raise a family. Bill was out of the Navy, I'd been in films for years; I was successful and had done everything I set out to do. Now I wanted to be a wife and mother. I wanted to do it the right way. I told Bill to meet me in St. Louis. He met me and that's when we decided to have the first child. I told him I'm sure it'll be a boy and I'm going to name him William Francis Boyer; then I'm going to wait two years and I'm going to have a daughter and we're going to name her Virginia Lee Boyer. I had it all planned and that's the way it turned out. Bill was very happy. I loved the man so. All my life, there's only been one man in my life. After he died, I had several proposals. A couple of times I was tempted to remarry but I just couldn't."

Virginia was coaxed into making a couple more films, including *If Winter Comes* at Fox in 1923. "The director was waiting for me. I know I was pregnant six months and he had waited and waited until I was bulging out here," Virginia laughed, touching her stomach. "He said, 'How in the world can we start?' I said, 'If you don't start now, the minute the baby is born I'm not going to be here!' So he took me up on it! When the movie opened, there was a woman critic who said she was so tired of seeing Virginia Lee in closeups, closeups, closeups! She can't do anything but closeups. She came out to California and I wouldn't have anything to do with her. Later she said, 'I know why

she's mad, I found out that she was pregnant.'"

Lee's last film was *Adorable Cheat* (1928) for Chesterfield. Of her co-star, Lila Lee, Virginia said, "We got along great."

In the 1920s there was a extremely popular song written about her called "Virginia Lee."

Virginia has a famous painting of herself and her two children, commissioned by the royalty of England. It hung in art galleries all around the world. The deal was that it would belong to them for 18 years and at that time she could have the painting for her own. She had completely forgotten about it when one day the painting was delivered to her. She was told the owner cried; he didn't want to give it up, but because he had promised it to her, he didn't want to break his promise.

Another actress using the name Virginia Lee surfaced in 1949, but is no relation. "You see, I was forgotten. Maybe that was her real name but she didn't last. She didn't amount to much. In the pictures I purposely asked to see, she was miscast ridiculously. It was pathetic. She wasn't a good actress, so I never worried about that. You've gotta be good or you fail. She did finally get on TV ... she was on *M*A*S*H* [1972–1983] one time ... I watched her very carefully and didn't think she had anything."

Of her career and life, Virginia, smiling, reflects, "I was always eager to work ... always eager to become a superstar and I *never* became a superstar. I've often looked back on my life. I made a mistake, a very serious mistake. I loved my work. I'm a good actress. I know that I can handle any acting ... but instead of thinking of the job, most of the time I was thinking of the money. What I couldn't help, I didn't worry about. I never got sick or temperamental about it. But if I could do something about it, I did. Or if somebody else could do something about it, I stood my ground and said, 'You're going to do this or I don't play.' I'm very determined. All my life I've known what I wanted. When I fell in love, I was going to make that the big success of my life. Until 19 years ago, it *was* the big success of my life. I forgot the movies and I concentrated. Bill Boyer was, I think, the happiest man in the world and the proudest. I adored him and he was unbelievably kind. He lived to make me happy."

Virginia says she's had a wonderful life. She would not change one single thing about it. She has two children (a son and a daughter) and several grandchildren. "I can knock on wood, there's nothing wrong with me. I wouldn't even let [a recent fall] set me back. I want to live, every day is another chapter. I don't let things lag."

At the time of this interview in 1993, Virginia was 92 and living in Wisconsin. Shortly thereafter, she suffered a stroke.

She was moved to a rest home near her son in Florida, where she died January 14, 1996.

Virginia Lee
Western Filmography

Movies: *Beyond the Law* (1918 Southern Feature Films)—Emmett Dalton; *Oh, Johnny* (1919 Goldwyn)—Louis Bennison; *Sandy Burke of the U-Bar-U* (1919 Goldwyn)—Louis Bennison; *White Masks* (1921 Merit)—Franklyn Farnum; *Angel Citizens* (1922 Merit)—Franklyn Farnum; *So This Is Arizona* (1922 Merit)—Franklyn Farnum; *Crossroads* (1922 Merit)—Franklyn Farnum; *Gold Grabbers* (1922 Merit)—Franklyn Farnum; *Trail's End* (1922 Merit)—Franklyn Farnum; *It Happened Out West* (1923 Merit)—Franklyn Farnum; *Man Getter* (1923 Merit—Franklyn Farnum. (Virginia had clippings mentioning two other westerns in the Merit group, *Ghostly Rider* and *Riders of the Night*. No reference can be located on such titles. It is probable these were working titles, possibly for *White Masks*.)

Adele Mara

Republic's Spanish Beauty

Adele Mara got her big break with bandleader Xavier Cugat and went on to great fame in Columbia and Republic films. She's adamantly "all Spanish," not half–Irish as has often been written. Born

Adelaida Delgado April 28 (1923?) in Highland Park, Michigan, Adele Mara (pronounced as in Theda *Bara*) "started dancing when I was eight years old. My mom felt a girl should have some kind of

Helen Talbot, Bill Elliott and Adele Mara pose for a publicity shot on the Republic backlot. Helen was interviewed for our first volume, *Westerns Women*.

dancing. I started with tap. I loved doing it. Then I took adagio. Eventually I got into ballet and Spanish at dancing school." She was spotted at 12 or 13 by Cugat when he was trying to get another act, and the noted bandleader took her under his wing. At this young age, Adele recalls, "I could dance [in the clubs or hotels] but I could not sit in any of those places. As soon as I finished, I had to get back to our room [with her mother] where they would serve us dinner."

Upon graduation, trying her luck as a dancer in New York, she again ran into Cugat at the Paramount Theatre. "He and his wife were my guardians. When he opened at the Waldorf Astoria Hotel at the Starlight Roof, I was there. The other acts included Marge and Gower Champion. For the finale we would all go into the Congo. With Cugat, I went a lot of places. We worked theaters with Danny Kaye, Abbott and Costello, Ray Bolger. When Cugat was on the radio, I would play castanets in the background." Up until that time, Adele had worked under her real name. Cugat shortened her first name, put three last names in a hat and out came Mara. "In the meantime, I made friends and they got me a job at the Copacabana. The whole show was around me. I don't know how it happened. Everything was so easy, I cannot believe it. One of the girls in the background at the Copa was June Allyson. One night a week I would go to the Waldorf. Sometimes Cugat would give the baton to somebody and he'd dance with me. One night he said, 'By the way, you're going to make a screen test.' I knew there were nibbles for me, but the only time Cugat said okay was when Harry Cohn said he wanted to test me. Before I knew it, I was on my way to Hollywood. I got a little apartment on Gower, next to Columbia, and started working there. I think I was making $250 a week. I didn't know what I was doing! Not a thing! I went for acting lessons at Columbia and I remember a scene with Lloyd Bridges. I was supposed to be amorous, had my arms around him, and my fanny was way out there [*laughs*]. I was supposed to give him a kiss. Pretty soon, the acting coach hit me on my fanny and says, 'You can't do it that way, you have to be together.' How naive I was. I didn't know how to do anything."

One of Adele's two B-westerns at Columbia was *Riders of the Northwest Mounted* (1943) with Russell Hayden and Bob Wills. "Wills was a very thin, little guy. We were at Arrowhead; I was supposed to be in the lake and he's to come save me. He picks me up to carry me. I tell you, it was the hardest thing this man has ever had to do! I felt so bad for him 'cause I don't think he was any bigger than I was ... but a very cute guy."

She worked with Tex Ritter in *Vengeance of the West* (1942) and said Tex was, "very funny, but used to talk so country, cowboy-like, I thought he'd never had any education. Later, I met his son, John, who told me his father was quite well educated.

At Columbia I was a little unhappy because I wasn't doing things I really wanted to do ... to dance. But I was learning other things just as much fun. It was like make-believe, and I was being paid good money for it. Except I never thought I was too good at it. I tried very hard to do it, but I was finally dropped by Columbia after two years; I think for a lot of reasons. One was, I got a little chubby. I think Cohn wanted somebody that was more sexy ... and I wasn't. I didn't know what it was all about. I was getting the idea, but by that time, it was too late to be at Columbia. Harry Cohn initially took me because I was Spanish. Rita Hayworth was giving them a little trouble, and they thought, well, here's somebody that would... [*laughs*]. By the way, when I left there, I was half-blonde, because they kept putting highlights ... their big deal was highlights. Pretty soon, I was half-blonde, half-brunette."

"When I left Columbia, I was about 18. I got another agent who didn't do much for me but he *did* take me on an interview to Republic. They needed a girl to dance with John Wayne. He didn't know how to dance, so I taught him to jitterbug for *The Fighting Seabees* (1944). I said, 'You

Bill Elliott as Joaquin Murieta protects Adele from badman Dick Curtis in *Vengeance of the West* **(1942).**

just do this and I'll do the rest.' I wore my own dress, shoes—they didn't give me anything. Republic said to my agent, 'Does she do anything besides jitterbug?' They had some Hawaiian thing [*Call of the South Seas* (1944)]. Now, I knew ballet, tap, everything but Hawaiian. So I found a teacher and learned. Then I did some acting and they put me under contract [April 24, 1944–June 25, 1951]." One of Adele's first was an unbilled bit in Roy Rogers' *San Fernando Valley* (1944). "Republic gave me a seven-year contract. They give you so much every six months, then it goes to a year and they give you maybe another 50 bucks. For me, that was great, since I wasn't trying to be a Garbo or Rita Hayworth. I just wanted to work."

Adele appeared several more times with "The Duke": *Flame of Barbary Coast*

(1945), *Sands of Iwo Jima* (1949) and *Wake of the Red Witch* (1949). "I don't know why he drank so much. I think because he was one of the boys. All the group he used to hang around with were that kind of guys. If you don't drink and hold your liquor, you're not a real man. I guess after you do this long enough, you have to have quite a few drinks before you get a little tipsy. I used to see him all the time and he was one of the sweetest guys in the world. Everybody loved him, but he wasn't very talkative. He was very businesslike. I had a couple of conversations with him but no deep thinking or anything like that. At one point, when I did *Wake of the Red Witch*, I had my hair parted in the middle and pulled back very tightly in braids. He made a point of why did I do that with my hair. He was interested because he had a little money in there. He says, 'Why don't you leave it flowing?' I thought that was awful at the time because all the women … like Gail Russell … always had her hair parted either in the middle or on the side, with the waves and fluffing, like we did in that era. This was a period picture and I don't think he considered the time in which the picture was [supposed to take place]. He was more interested that the girls looked glamorous. Hair was very important to him. Must have been, because that's the only time anybody ever asked me."

According to Adele, the president of Republic, Herbert J. Yates, "was a very strange fellow. Scottish. He would chew tobacco and was always spitting in … it wouldn't go in the spittoon [*groans*]. Sometimes he'd have me come over to his office. He was always sweet but it was like he had a little yen for me. Incidentally, I would always say I was five-five. He'd say, she's not five-five, she's five-four. That was because he was short, he didn't *want* me to be five-five. He had me see the nurse. They weighed and measured me. And I was five-four [*laughs*]. Every time in his office, I'd say goodbye, I would go over to give him a hug and he would give me a kiss and … I would just go like this [indicating keeping him at a distance]. I liked him but I didn't want to have any romantic thing with him. Besides, he had Vera Ralston, whom he finally married. A lot of leading men just did not want to work with her at all. She was kind of a strange girl. Nobody understood why he did so much for her, because she wasn't exactly a beauty. She was very clumsy on stage."

Adele recalls Don Barry as "sharp, funny and quick-witted. Once, when some workers were digging up an area in front of Republic, I asked Don what they were doing. He smiled, 'Looking for Vera's lost skate key' [*laughs*]. Don was always needling me. To put him down, I said, 'Don,

do your ears pop when you take your boots off?'"

Adele fondly remembers many of the major players at Republic. "I used to tease Roy [Rogers] a lot because, although I found out later he was a real ladies man, he always came across as a very shy person, so I used to tease him. He'd get kind of a kick out of it. When he'd pass the ladies wardrobe, I would stick out my head and say something to him and he'd turn red. Everybody would be laughing and having giggles. He was very, very nice, but Dale was always there, watching her property. Really. She was no dummy. She knew what was going on all the time, but I didn't know that until I was gone from Republic and heard from quite a few people that when Roy did personal appearances, there were all these showgirls and stuff around him. He was a really sweet human being. And Gene was very sweet to me. He would say, 'You're going to have to go places and you're going to have to drink. The thing to do is to have Scotch, tall, water. That's the best thing for you. Don't have soda.' I wasn't very fond of liquor, so he said, 'That'll take a long, long time.' He would talk to me like that all the time. Bill Elliott was a very stiff person. Very rigid. When he walked from here to there, he never budged from one side to the other. I never had any conversations with him at all."

Adele vividly recalls, "Allan Lane was not as good as he thought he was. He would ask me to go out for dinner. Every night he would take me home and say goodbye. He didn't even try to kiss me or anything. After, I don't know how long, he said to the wardrobe people, 'Tonight is the night! I have got her.' You know. They weren't worried, but they told me to be sure to give him a real bad time, 'cause they thought that was pretty rotten. And … it is. So he came, he wanted to take me out to dinner. And I said, absolutely! We

Adele clings to Forrest Tucker as he confronts Sheriff Charles Kemper in *California Passage* (1950). In real life, Adele was with Tucker when he confronted Columbia studio boss Harry Cohn.

went, and he tried his best. I said, no thank you, sorry! The next day they asked him about it, and he just tried to ignore the whole thing. Everybody said, 'What happened, what happened?' They were all very anxious to find out. Yes, I remember him. I can't forget him!"

And then there's Forrest Tucker. "He was very funny. And kind of strange, but a very sweet guy. I liked him. He would try to embarrass me a lot. He would shock me, as a matter of fact! He wasn't a mean person but he was a little crazy. I remember once when he took me to Ciro's. He'd had a bad time with Harry Cohn [president of Columbia]. Now, I didn't have much of a bad time with Cohn. He did get

angry with me once when he took me out. I had told my mom I'd be home no later than 12. I said, 'Oh, my gosh, I've gotta go.' Harry said, 'You can't go now, you have to be here.' He wanted to dance with me and have pictures done. This was at the very beginning of my Columbia contract. The fact I was going to leave him was like a put-down. I didn't think of it as a put-down, but he finally let me go. So ... Forrest and I came out of Ciro's and when he saw Cohn waiting for his car, he says, 'That son of a bitch,' and all that kind of stuff and started going after him. Forrest told him what a rotten guy he was. I've heard some things about Cohn that are supposed to be pretty rotten, but you don't go out in a public place and start abusing somebody verbally. I don't think Tucker needed much to tick him off. He really hated this guy. And I have no idea why. I was so embarrassed, I didn't want anybody to know I was with him."

Republic varied Adele's roles. Sometimes she was very cute and innocent and at other times she could be very sexy. "I was a mean, nasty girl [*laughs*]. I heard from a couple of the actresses that told me when they'd go up to see Yates, he would say, 'Look, you're a very good actress, but you got to get a little more sexy, like Adele.' One told me, 'If I heard your name one more time, I was going to kill you.' And I said, 'He did? He really did?' So he considered me very sexy. A lot of people did, but I didn't think of myself as sexy. All those things I used to do; I knew how bad those scripts were but it didn't bother me. I just thought, I'll try to do better than what they are. I did my very best and I loved doing it. They used to give me scripts like crazy. I'd be working on one, on the set, and I'd have another script I was studying at the time."

Adele "loved westerns" but "I hated the horses. I loved to *see* horses, they're beautiful, but I was not a good rider. As a matter of fact, I was very, very bad. One of the things I had to do was ride English. They gave me lessons and I was doing fine, but when I went for the first day of shooting they gave me this enormous horse, huge in length and height. Just a *big* horse. My double said she was not going to ride that horse, it was a bad horse. They asked me to ride it. I said, 'Wait a minute, if *she* isn't going to ride it...' They said, 'Oh, she's just crazy. We're out here at the ranch and there's nothing we can do, we have to do this, don't worry about it, you've had enough lessons.' So I got on this stupid horse and he just roared out! Before I knew it, I was off the saddle and on his back, just hanging on to this thing. I was so scared!

After that, I only rode into a scene and out of the scene and that was it. As little as possible."

Adele at least got to demonstrate her dance expertise in a couple of Republic titles, including Gene Autry's *Twilight on the Rio Grande* (1947), becoming her own choreographer. "Republic never paid for somebody to come in. I had to figure these things out. They'd say, 'This is the music we're going to use and this is what...' they were so cheap. I never questioned it. I just went and did it. I did some dancing in *Vampire's Ghost* [1945]. I had to do it all on my own. I remember John Abbott. He's a great actor and had these crazy eyes ... he was just wonderful."

It was 1951 when Republic let Adele go. "Yates called me to his office and told me. 'We're not picking you up, not because you haven't done a good job, not because we don't like you, but we have to cut down. Television is taking over. As people keep coming up, we'll use them per picture, but not under contract any more.' I said, 'I don't think television is going to be anything.' I really meant it. I never looked at television at all, until I married Roy. I was very upset. I thought Republic was going to be my home. Like my dad worked for Ford, he thought he would be there forever. And he would have, if he had stayed in Michigan. It was very strange."

Nevertheless, it was the burgeoning television industry Adele turned to for work. "I did do some television, but every time it was lunch I would think about my little kids. I would come home in my clothes, from Warner Bros., feed Tommy and do all kinds of stuff with him and then I'd go back to work. I did that quite a bit. I did a *Markham* [1959–1960] with Ray Milland when I was pregnant, so I can always look at that and say Tommy was in my tummy at that moment."

Many people in the business fondly remember Adele's brother, Louie. "When he went to Hollywood High, he met Jim Garner. Later, dance director Nick Castle used Louie as an extra. Then Louie went to Warners as a stand-in on *Maverick* [1957–1962]. He was working all the time, at first with Jack Kelly, but he was very demanding. 'Bring me a cup of coffee, get me a sandwich…' Jim would tell Louie, 'I wish you were *my* stand-in.' They talked to Roy [Adele's husband—Roy Huggins, producer of *Maverick*]. Roy says, 'What difference does it make?' so Louie switched. Jim treated Louie very well, had a pension plan for him, did wonderful things for Louie and Louie did a lot for Jim."

As to how she met her husband, writer-turned-producer (at Warner Bros.), Roy Huggins, Adele smiles, "He was a writer, worked at Columbia, and thought I was kind of cute. He saw me first with dark hair, then blonde. Then he worked at Republic and was asking about me. I'd see him at parties and say hello." Finally, a friend arranged a blind date between Adele and Roy and they've been married 46 years. "When we got married, Roy felt my parents should live with us. They were wonderful to him and he was great with them." Looking back, the still beautiful actress says, "I never expected anything, and everything came to me … very easily. I've been the luckiest person in the world. My husband is wonderful. He thinks I'm gorgeous. He loves me very much and I love him. I love my kids and the people they're with. Everything is just grand."

Adele Mara
Western Filmography

Movies: *Shut My Big Mouth* (1942 Columbia)—Joe E. Brown; *Vengeance of the West* (1942 Columbia)—Bill Elliott/Tex Ritter; *Riders of the Northwest Mounted* (1943 Columbia)—Russell Hayden; *San Fernando Valley* (1944 Republic)—Roy Rogers; *Flame of Barbary Coast* (1945 Republic)—John Wayne; *Bells of Rosarita* (1945 Republic)—Roy Rogers; *Night Train to Memphis* (1946 Republic)—Roy Acuff; *Twilight on the Rio Grande* (1947 Republic)—Gene Autry; *Robin Hood of Texas* (1947 Republic)—Gene Autry; *Gallant Legion* (1948 Republic)—William Elliott; *Night Time in Nevada* (1948 Republic)—Roy Rogers; *Rock Island Trail* (1950 Republic)—Forrest Tucker; *California Passage* (1950 Republic)—Forrest Tucker; *The Black Whip* (1956 Regal/Fox)—Hugh Marlowe.

Television: *Cheyenne*, "Border Showdown" (1955); *Cheyenne*, "Star in the Dust" (1956); *Rin Tin Tin*, "Rusty's Romance" (1956); *Rin Tin Tin*, "Circle of Fire" (1956); *Saga of Andy Burnett*, "Andy's Love Affair" (1957); *Casey Jones*, "Black Box" (1957); *Cheyenne*, "Angry Sky" (1958); *Maverick*, "Seed of Deception" (1958); *Maverick*, "Spanish Dancer" (1958); *Wyatt Earp*, "Dig a Grave for Ben Thompson" (1958); *Bat Masterson*, "Double Showdown" (1958); *Tales of Wells Fargo*, "Wild Cargo" (1959); *Laramie*, "Day of Vengeance" (1960); *Maverick*, "The Marquesa" (1960); *Wyatt Earp*, "Wyatt's Brothers Join Up" (1961); *Stagecoach West*, "Arsonist" (1961); *Tall Man*, "Woman in Black" (1962).

Carole Mathews

An Independent Woman

Miss Chicago. Earl Carroll showgirl. Restaurateur. Travel agency owner. Registered miniature horse breeder and trainer. Actress. From humble beginnings as Jean Deifel on September 13, 1920, in Montgomery, Illinois (a suburb of Aurora), Carole Mathews has done it all and has traveled around the world with her accomplishments. But how different it all would have been if she'd followed her first aspirations—to become a nun.

Carole as she appeared on her own television western series, *The Californians* (1958–1959).

"I had no church upbringing, my parents didn't go to church. But when I went to my grandmother to be raised, I think it was because my mother divorced my father, the two boys [her brothers] went with my father and the two girls [Carole and her sister] were given to my mother. My mother took my sister and my grandmother reared me. I can't recall why, but I remember one day, I went in to my grandmother and said, 'I want to go to Catholic school, parochial school.' She asked why. 'I don't know, I just want to go.' She said okay, went to the fathers and the nuns, talked to them and made some sort of a deal and I went into Catholicism in the sixth, seventh and eighth grades. During that time, you're very impressionable. I was a very unhappy child and I thought I had found such peace in the church. I sang in the choir and this and that. I thought, in my young mind, the way to go was to become a nun. I didn't go for the right reasons, it was just a security thing. By the time I graduated from high school, I went into the nunnery. I went up to Milwaukee to St. Francis. But my grandmother pulled me out and said, wait 'til you're 21. In the meantime, I won the title of Miss Chicago. Grandma said, 'I wish I'd left you in the nunnery' after I got in show business. From one extreme to the other. Although show business is not exactly the nunnery, it's a form of giving. You give of yourself.

"At any rate, some of the kids I went to school with knew I was planning to go into the nunnery and they dared me to put a bathing suit on … $5 to put a bathing suit on and go on the stage. I took it. In those days, $5 was a lot of money. 1938. So I won that the first time I went around. Some of the men there that had something to do with the contest asked me to go to other theaters. They thought they had a winner there. So I went to about three different theaters, Miss Highland, Miss this and that, different theaters, and I won every time. On the day of the finals, my parents came home and they were absolutely against it, they wouldn't let me go. But the men talked to my parents and they finally relented and said okay. I went in and I won that title. Then, I was qualified to try for Miss America in 1938 but my parents said absolutely not, this had gone far enough. But by winning the title of Miss Chicago, I won a screen test and a trip to California.

"So my grandmother and I trained out to Hollywood. I read where Earl Carroll was advertising for showgirls, and being 5'7" I thought I would qualify. I didn't know what a showgirl really was. I tried for Earl Carroll and he said no, because I had a tan and he wanted all his girls white—you used to have to wear white makeup. He said, 'If you can lose your tan in two weeks, I'll hire you.' So for two weeks, my grandmother and I would get lemon and put it in the bath water and I'd rub lemon all over my body to try to lose the tan. In two weeks, I lost it enough that he hired me. So I became an Earl Carroll girl. Earl Carroll Vanities opened in 1938, the Christmas of 1938, and our trip didn't come around until 1939, so I was in the second show. I stayed with them and we went to Broadway but it didn't meet the critic's eye, it didn't last very long … maybe a couple weeks. Then we went on the road with it."

From there, Carole did radio in Chicago, modeling (*Vogue*, *Harper's Bazaar*) and was an extra in films before she put her heart into acting. "It was really intermingled. I modeled in Chicago before I went to Hollywood. I appeared at the College Inn in Chicago, that's how I got into show business, really. Then I had a gentleman friend who owned a lot of products … it was a health thing … and he gave me a job at WGN in Chicago, *Breakfast Time with Carole Mathews*. I had that radio show for at least four, five, six months."

As an Earl Carroll showgirl, Carole used her real name, but changed it to Jeanne Francis when she worked as an extra in films circa 1939. "I was an extra with Tyrone Power and Alice Faye in *Rose of Washington Square* [1939]. I was part of an audience. You do extra, you can't remember all the pictures. I didn't change my name to Carole Mathews until I was back in Chicago, working, dancing as a rhumba dancer in the Rhumba Casino in Chicago. I traveled back and forth to Chicago quite frequently. If things weren't working in California, I went back to do something in Chicago."

Dancing came naturally. "When I was with Earl Carroll, I was a showgirl, but sometimes they needed a dancer. They were called ponies, they're smaller, about 5'4", 5'5". Because dancing was a natural, they asked me if I could sub or fill in for somebody that became sick or ill and I did. It just came natural to me to dance."

At last firmly entrenched in Hollywood, Carole signed a Columbia contract in 1943. She remembers studio head Harry Cohn. "He didn't like me at all. I didn't like him. Actually, when I say I didn't like him, I was more scared of him than anything. He had roughness … anybody that was rough, I kind of closed … clamped up. I was really kind of independent. If I didn't like somebody, I wouldn't laugh at his jokes. My friends said, 'Carole, just laugh.' I said, 'I think they're stupid!' I was that innocent, I didn't play the game. I kind of ruined a lot of opportunities, I think, just by being me.

"The first thing I did was *The Girl in the Case* [1944] for Columbia. I was put under contract to Columbia after I did that. Max Arno, the talent person at Columbia was the one that decided to put me under contract." Good roles in *The Missing Juror* (1944), *She's a Sweetheart* (1944), *Swing in the Saddle* (1944) and *I Love a Mystery* (1945), based on the popular radio series, followed.

Carole recalls her first western. "I was so thrilled. I didn't have a script. 'We just want you to do one scene, no dialogue.' Okay. I waited all day, watching the wranglers, wondering when they were gonna get to me. Finally, around five or six o'clock at night, they said, 'Carole, time for your scene. All we want you to do is walk through the door.' No rehearsal. So I walk through the door and they turned a hose on me! They wanted my natural reaction on film. I was soaking wet! That was my introduction to westerns."

Columbia then cast Carole in two leading lady roles opposite Charles (Durango Kid) Starrett. "Charles Starrett was very congenial, very nice. But you know, I was very young and I stayed with the musicians [Bob Wills' group provided the music in *Blazing the Western Trail* (1945) and Tex Williams, Spade Cooley and Smoky Rogers were cast in *Outlaws of the Rockies* (1945)]. Tex Harding and I became friends. His father owned a butcher shop and it was during the war and we all got meat from his father's butcher store. Tex Harding was more my friend than Charlie."

Even the ladies must know how to ride if they're doing westerns, which often leads to some harrowing experiences. "Riding came naturally. I used to ride bareback in the country. I loved animals.

I had horses later on in my life. But a lot of us girls lived at the Studio Club. I was living there and got a job that required riding. I took some western saddle lessons, but I think the man was a masochist. I rode all day! I had on blue jeans. When I came home, I was so sore, I was absolutely raw. Some of the girls said they'd take care of that and they put Dr. So and So's medicine on. Well! I nearly went up to the ceiling when they did. The next day I couldn't get on the horse, but they padded me and I got through the scene.

"I very vividly remember doing one of Charlie Starrett's westerns. I was in a house and I was trying to escape. I ran out, jumped on the horse. Remember, I could ride a horse ... but I got on a horse that the stirrups were too long, they were adjusted for the wrangler, and I couldn't gain control. The horse ran right towards some trees, limbs and all that. I didn't know what to do. I held onto the horn. I lost the reins because I was trying to get to the stirrups. It all happened so fast, but a wrangler got the horse before any accident. I surely would have been killed or hurt.

"I love animals. The only thing I didn't particularly like about doing westerns was when a horse was hurt. Once in a while, they did break a leg when they were felled for a scene and they had to put them down. That wasn't to my taste."

Carole exuded strength on screen before it was the "in thing" to be an independent woman. "I thought I'd be good as another Gale Sondergaard but I never got parts like that. But I was a very strong person because of my background. When you're trussed from one house to another and one home to another and you don't know where you're going, you just have to be tough. It wasn't until later I realized that it was more of a detriment than an asset."

Columbia was one of the top producers of serials in the 1940s, and Carole

Candid pose of Carole and Charles Starrett at Columbia in 1945.

was cast as Robert Lowery's leading lady in *The Monster and the Ape* (1945). "That was just fun to do. It was like not really going to work, it was fun. We wrapped those things up [pretty fast]. Ray Corrigan was in the ape suit. He owned Corrigan location ranch in the Valley where we shot a lot of westerns. I was glad I knew Ray, because in that costume he was scary [*laughs*]. My sister had small children, and when they saw the serial at the theater, they'd cry, 'Aunt Carole is gonna die'—as I went into the fire or the ape was after me."

Some actors felt being in a serial could hurt their status in the business, but Carole sighs, "I never had a mentor, which

I'm sorry to say. I wish I had. It wasn't in the cards and I've always accepted that."

After some 16 films in a two-year period, Carole was no longer a Columbia contractee as of late 1945. "I think I had a run-in with the hairdresser. The head hairdresser at Columbia. She's the one that got me fired. I was in the B-picture level, where Columbia made so many pictures, so when I wanted to get into a higher level, I wasn't accepted. You're queen of the B's and that's it. So I went to New York [1946–1948] and studied theater and I spent some time in summer stock to learn my craft, thinking that might help.

"I was called to do *Whispering Smith* [1948] for Paramount with Alan Ladd. I came out but I was too tall for Alan Ladd as a leading lady at that time. The producer didn't want to hire me because of my height."

Another major disappointment, Carole reveals, was when "I was up for *To Have and Have Not* [1944] with Humphrey Bogart. [Director] Howard Hawks liked me. He signed me to do the picture. I remember, my husband and I went to Las Vegas for the Christmas holidays. When we came back, the writer, Jules Furthman, came to my door and said, 'I have to talk to you. You just lost *To Have and Have Not*,' which he was very upset about. He said, 'Bogie's in love with a girl named Betty Bacall and he won't do the picture unless Howard puts her in. We have to buy your contract out.' I said okay and that was that. I accepted things as they were.

"Another big turning point with my

career could have been when I did *Meet Me at the Fair* [1952] with Dan Dailey. Paul Small, who was a *very* big agent in Hollywood, called me in and said 'I want to handle you. I think you're star material.' I spoke to my agent but he wouldn't sell to Small. My contract had six months to run. Small said, 'We'll wait six months and I'll sign you then.' But he *died* within that six months!

"Then another thing that happened to me in 1942, before I got married. I did a test for Sam Goldwyn. He was interested. I did a scene from *Dark Victory*, the 1939 film. The wonderful director Lewis Milestone directed it. Jimmy Wong Howe photographed it. I never saw that test. Jimmy had a Chinese restaurant in the Valley, and that night we all went afterwards to his restaurant. My husband-to-be went along. We got tidily, drinking, and I said, 'We're both born on September 13 and we're going to get married on the 13th.' He said, 'Come on, why don't we get married now?' Las Vegas was too far to travel so we all decided to drive down to Tijuana to get married. Feeling no pain. We got married, then Goldwyn heard about it, brought me in and said to me, 'Why did you get married?' I just looked at him and said, 'Because I'm in love, I was planning to get married on the thirteenth anyway.' So he said, 'Well, you just lost your contract.' I never did see the test. Those things *do* happen in Hollywood. He got upset because I got married. I couldn't understand it."

Although that role in *Whispering Smith* didn't pan out, Paramount did use Carole's talents in a couple of other films, including *The Great Gatsby* (1949) with Alan Ladd. "Remember, I'm 5'7" and he was shorter. He stood on a box and I wore tennis shoes."

That role led to other good roles in bigger films such as *Massacre River* (1949) with Guy Madison and Rory Calhoun. "I liked Guy so much, and Rory. They were like pals. Sometimes you have leading men and all that, but they were *friends* of mine, pals. We got along very well together. Steve Brodie, playing one of the heavies, had a scene where he opened a door and was supposed to slap me. Instead of a 'stage slap,' he misjudged the distance and hit me in the face, knocking me out cold. You learned quick in B-movies, if you didn't duck, you were going to get hit. I saw Guy again when I did *Wild Bill Hickok* TV shows later. Then I did *Red Snow* [1952] with him."

Carole recalls on *Treasure of Ruby Hills* (1955), "Zachary Scott was really nice. We were just friends, but we used to go out to dinner. He was married at the time to Ruth Ford, I believe."

Another of Carole's westerns was *Showdown at Boot Hill* (1958) with Charles Bronson. "That was funny, because Charles Bronson, when I was doing that, said he was a method actor. He came out of New York. He came up to me, very nicely, 'I don't want to throw you, but I never do the same scene the same way. We rehearse it one way but I might do it another way. I don't want to throw you.' So he put me on my guard. Then he did it the same as we rehearsed it. And *that* threw me [*laughs*]."

Like most actresses, Carole moved into the burgeoning new world of television in the early 1950s. ("I rode an elephant on *The Cisco Kid* in 1952.") In the early days of live television, Carole says, "Most of the movie actors were scared of TV because it was like live theater. But I took to live theater like a duck to water and really enjoyed live television." She worked on *G. E. Theater*, *Playhouse 90*, *Kraft Theater* and others.

Many episodic western television series are a blur in Carole's memory, for good reason. "I remember *Tales of Wells Fargo* [1957–1962] with Dale Robertson. If I

Carole in 1949's *Massacre River* with her on-screen rivals Guy Madison and Rory Calhoun— who were "pals" off-screen.

liked the person, I remember them strangely enough. But if I didn't like them, I just... for instance, I was on *Rawhide* [1959–1965]. Eric Fleming was a very dear friend of mine. I knew him before he was an actor. He used to work in the studio as a gaffer on the lights. We walked New York streets together looking for jobs with Jack Kelly, who did *Maverick* [1957–1962]. The two boys and I, we drove to New York and really walked the streets trying to find jobs. We all wound up with western series, that was funny. Eric was on *Rawhide*, Jack was in *Maverick* and I was in *The Californians* [1958–1959]. Eric's name at that time was Ed Heddy. He died down in South America."

Carole's chance at a regular series came in 1958 with *The Californians* as she

joined the cast mid-season as widow Wilma Fansler, who now ran a gambling house. The role provided a love interest for series star Richard Coogan. "I was in London, doing a picture. My agent called a friend of mine about something else and told her, 'I wish Carole were here. On *The Californians*, a part like Miss Kitty on *Gunsmoke* is up.' My friend said, 'Why don't you call her and ask her if she wants to do it?' My agent wasn't going to contact me because I was in Europe and he didn't want to spend the money, I guess, for the call. But I got it. When I came back from London, they took pictures of me arriving [with my two new co-stars] Dick Coogan and Art Fleming." Coogan seemed to think the potential for a winning series was there because here was the Barbary

Coast, a different, fresh idea, but he felt the producers started retreading all the same old western stories and really missed the boat. "This is what happened to me. I did something in one series, then when I did *The Californians* I did the same story! It was a different locale, instead of the Army it was the vigilantes or something. I said, 'this is the same line, the same thing' ... all they did was change the atmosphere. I remember [former actor] Paul Henreid directed some episodes. I think he was the first one that kind of reached me. Because most directors in those days were—you move here and you move there. They never talked about interpretation or what do you think of this character or that character. It was stand here and move over here ... go there and this and that. You more or less did your interpretation yourself."

Carole was married in August of 1942. "It was one of those hit and miss things. Getting married just to be married. He came from a very well-to-do family in Chicago and I always thought they never approved of him marrying me. They were very polite, but I never felt accepted. It lasted a couple of years. But we didn't do anything about it. He went his way and I went my way." Although Carole never remarried, "I came close to it a couple of times."

That independence of Carole's began to pay off as she at one time co-owned Michael's Pub in New York. "All actors get together and you have lunch and you sit around and talk and you drink. We were at the Barbary Coast, which was a restaurant within a hotel over on Madison Avenue in New York. My agent, Gloria Sapphire, was there, Kitty Carlisle ... several others. We were sitting there drinking and it was around three, four o'clock in the afternoon and someone said, 'You know, the money we've poured into this place, meeting every Friday or something like that,

we could own our own place and it would be cheaper.' And that's how it got started. Michael Peerman was the maître d' at this restaurant we were sitting in. We called Michael over and said, 'How would you like to run a restaurant for us?' We told him our ideas and he set it up where he sold stock, you could buy shares. It was called Michael's Pub, on East 48th Street, right around by Saks Fifth Avenue. I was working at the time, going to Europe to make a picture. When I left, I bought some shares. When I came back, I was told the restaurant had opened up and it was very successful. We stayed with it 'til we sold it. We made a big profit. Out of a thousand dollars, I made 11,000. Then with this same group Michael opened up another restaurant that was called The Running Footman. That was just on the other side of Bloomingdale's Department Store and I got in on that. I didn't make as big a profit, but I made a profit. They were both successful."

Unemployed from pictures in 1961, Carole got into the travel bureau business. "This gal said, 'I'm opening up a wholesale travel agency [Hermes Travel in Los Angeles]. I'm looking for someone to write brochures for me.' I said, 'I've traveled all over. I know Europe, give me a job. See how I do.' In one year, I was the manager. I love to travel, so I loved the business. I think in all my travels, one thing I've found out is to be more patient and understanding. People that I don't understand, I stop to analyze. Where do they come from? Why are they that way? It's just a little bit more patience. Then I owned my own agency in 1971, with many celebrity accounts ... Cher, Flip Wilson, Mac Davis. I ran it up to $4,000,000 in business and then sold it in 1986. I didn't know what to do with my money. I had so much money the tax was going to take and friends said, well, invest it in something.

"This is when I got involved with my

little horses. In 1982, I was the top champion winner of miniature horses. High points. I had 13 champion mares. I had a grand champion mare, Britches, and she had a little stallion I called Son of Britches [*laughs*]."

As Carole looks back on her multifaceted life, many things give her pleasure. "For films, I like *Meet Me at the Fair*, I would have done that for nothing, and *City of Bad Men* [1953]. I liked that gal.

"On a personal level, when I was younger, I was a loner. I wasn't a joiner and I didn't keep friendships like some people do for years and years. Until I got older. Years ago, I was very serious. I talked to Jack Lord one time, we were friends. I was in his first picture [*Cry Murder* (1950)]. Jack said, 'I understand you had to take laughing lessons. I've got to take some too.' When you're unhappy as a child, you don't laugh at things. This is why I reacted as I did to all those producers, Jack Warner, Sam Goldwyn, Harry Cohn. I didn't smile that much. So someone said, 'You've got to take laughing lessons.' I took laughing lessons and, as I've gotten older now, I make people laugh because I know that's a must in one's life. Laugh at yourself. I enjoy my life. I enjoy getting up in the morning and having another day to live. I was ill for about ten years, quite ill. You name it, I had a stroke, I had several pacemakers, I had cancer, I've had this and that … I had a new hip replacement.

There were so many times I should have died, but I'm not finished yet. I've got some unfinished business."

Carole Mathews
Western Filmography

Movies: *Swing in the Saddle* (1944 Columbia)—Big Boy Williams; *Blazing the Western Trail* (1945 Columbia)—Charles Starrett; *Outlaws of the Rockies* (1945 Columbia)—Charles Starrett; *Sing Me a Song of Texas* (1945 Columbia)—Tom Tyler; *Massacre River* (1949 Allied Artists)—Guy Madison/Rory Calhoun; *City of Bad Men* (1953 20th Century–Fox)—Dale Robertson; *Treasure of Ruby Hills* (1955 Allied Artists)—Zachary Scott; *Showdown at Boot Hill* (1958 20th Century–Fox)—Charles Bronson; *13 Fighting Men* (1960 20th Century–Fox)—Grant Williams.

Television: *Wild Bill Hickok*, "The Slocum Family" (1951); *Wild Bill Hickok*, "Blacksmith Story" (1952); *Cisco Kid*, "Pancho and the Pachyderm" (1952); *Cisco Kid*, "Dutchman's Flat" (1952); *Jim Bowie*, "The General's Disgrace" (1957); *Trackdown*, "The Farrand Story" (1958); *Tales of Wells Fargo*, "The Pickpocket" (1958); *Man Without a Gun*, "Lady from Laramie" (1958); *Zane Grey Theatre*, "This Man Must Die" (1958); *The Texan*, "No Tears for the Dead" (1958); *Gray Ghost*, "Greenback Raid" (1958); *The Californians*, series regular (1958–1959); *Northwest Passage*, "The Deserter" (1959); *Rough Riders*, "Lesson in Violence" (1959); *Death Valley Days*, "A Bullet for the D.A." (1961); *Rawhide*, "Incident at the Odyssey" (1964).

Joyce Meadows

Born to the Purple

Joyce Meadows has been active in one form of show business or another since the late 1940s. Her 50-year-plus career began with a western, *Flesh and the Spur* (1957), and continues today with guest shots on *Unsolved Mysteries* (1988–), *Lois and Clark* (1993–1997) and *Days of Our Lives* (1965–), in films such as *True Identity* (1991), and many commercials. For the past 12 years Joyce put her experience as a singer to good use in Shakespearean productions of *Merry Wives of Windsor* and *Hamlet*.

The Alberta, Canada–born Joyce Burger came to California with her parents. "I always did plays in high school. I also sang up at Lake Tahoe. I was on the bill with people like Burl Ives while I was still going to high school. I worked on weekends at one of the big clubs, the Wagon Wheel, up on the South Shore. That actually stemmed from the fact I had won a Sacramento contest … and I was entertaining around. That's how I got started. I stayed in Sacramento for a year after I got out of high school and, during that time, I did about three plays. One was *Romeo and Juliet*. I had kind of a love for Shakespeare from the beginning. It seemed kind of natural for me to do that. But just getting up enough nerve to get on a bus and come to Los Angeles was a big deal for me, 'cause I had rather a protective family. There was a place called the Stu-

dio Club where I stayed when I first came to Los Angeles. Rita Moreno was there and Kim Novak. We all stayed at the Hollywood Studio Club. That shows you how much money I was earning at that time. I was in some stage shows. I was down here almost two years. An agent saw me on stage in Glendale, and represented me."

There was always some confusion over exactly which was her first film. "I had a role in *Flesh and the Spur*, but I was just a slave girl in *Omar Khayyam* [1957] which was shot first—that's how I got my SAG card. For *Flesh and the Spur* I auditioned for Alex Gordon, who was the producer and now works in the Gene Autry office. He has always had a love for cowboys. Gene Autry and Roy Rogers, a lot of those cowboys will be remembered forever. They're part of our growing up. When we [Joyce has a brother and sister] were kids, we used to go to the movies on Saturdays, while Mother and Dad were doing errands. We had a choice, whether we wanted to see Roy Rogers or Gene Autry."

Flesh and the Spur was one of Mike Connors' (Touch Connors at the time) earliest roles, but he was also listed as an executive producer. Joyce remembers him having a role in that capacity. "And his wife was on the set. He partially financed several different kinds of movies he wanted to be in at that time. Mike played a bad guy. I got murdered. Killed."

A wounded Joyce and Sydney Mason restrain an angry John Agar's *Frontier Gun* (1958).

The actual star of the film was John Agar, whom Joyce worked with three times. She still sees him every now and then at autograph shows. "I grew very attached to John. We worked very well together. He was a favorite person of most of the leading ladies he worked with. I've talked to many of them during the memorabilia shows, they all have a soft spot for him in their hearts. I think this was a very genuine person that got himself into a Hollywood scene that almost did him in. He was *first* a person, and he was adorable the way he learned his acting. He was around some very big people, like John Wayne ... he picked up his screen acting technique from the big ones. And he was well satisfied with that. He used to look at me like I was a little weird from outer

space, being so enthralled with theater and so on [*laughs*]. I thought he had a very good presence on the screen. He worked hard and was very, very in favor of whomever was working with him, to share the camera. He took me under his wing as a film greenhorn and made me feel comfortable. I was new in the business and probably stuck out like a sore thumb, but he was very helpful. So was Touch. They both were really nice, really there for you."

About a year later, Joyce did another western, *Frontier Gun* (1958), again with Agar, directed by Paul Landres. "I liked Paul a lot. I appreciated him. As I played the lead, I went to him and said, 'You know, leads like this are always ... you know.' I played a gal that fell in love with John. I was a good girl in the town. I wasn't the saloon girl. I said, 'Could we put a little sugar and spice in her, because I'm sure there are certain areas...' and he looked at me and said, 'I never thought of it like that. Do it for me, get into the scene.' So Paul liked it! In one scene, when John and I were together, somebody was shooting at us, and I got shot in the arm. John's line was, 'Are you okay?' and my line was, 'I'm just fine.' Well, I looked ... very surprised ... like oh, well, hell, I just got shot in the arm, not too badly ... yeah, I'm just fine ... like, what do you *mean*, am I all right? I remember seeing it in the theater and it always got a laugh. I said to Paul, 'Couldn't we just give her a little piss and vinegar?' [*laughs*]—that was the way I put it to him, to be honest with you. He thought it was a good idea, so he just directed me in that direction. I always adored him for working with me on that."

Barton MacLane and Robert Strauss were also in *Frontier Gun*. "Those guys all played bad guys ... and Jack Elam was another one, but he wasn't in that one. I'm telling you, a sweeter bunch of guys you never wanted to meet. I just loved sitting around at lunch time talking to them. They were just so full of fun. I used to look at all these heavies. Some of them had such a wonderful talent but only a few of them broke out of that bad guy thing. One of the worst bad guys was Humphrey Bogart. You take a bad guy like that and let the other side of him show on screen. Talk about ugly, but who cared. He became interesting, wonderful and sexy and then he wasn't ugly any more. They have such wonderful personalities and they're made to play these stereotypes on screen. I would sit there and look at Barton MacLane with this twinkle in his eye and wonderful smile ... I thought, 'What if he didn't play a heavy, what if...' ... I just started asking questions. I don't know if that was my theater background or not. I used to look at Jack Elam with one eye always going one direction and the other eye always going another direction [*laughs*]. Jack was very talented and so sweet. You loved being around him. It was hard to completely block out his real personality and be frightened of him. It was so funny watching Jack get into playing this nasty, crazy person. We were doing a scene where he murders me; I kept giggling. He kept whispering into my ear, 'You must not laugh, you must not laugh.' Of course, that would make me laugh even harder. After I spoiled three takes, we had to stop and I had to walk away from it for a little while. I finally told Jack, 'Don't say one word to me!' He said, 'You just concentrate and I am really going to scare you.' Well he did, and the final take was perfect."

All those TV westerns, but never a part in a television series. "Too bad I didn't have the opportunity to get into a series 'cause I always got involved with the crew. In those days, most of the crew had been making a living for many years off of the movies, before television took over, so you heard wonderful old stories from these guys. John Agar always used to kibitz and hang around the crew. It was everybody in there making a living and you got to enjoy each other. I was in some pilots that never sold. Lord knows, I don't even remember the names of them. I attribute it to being some of my fault, because in the 1970s I left Hollywood. I should have stayed and really tried. I had the challenge, if I could have taken the rejection, the hard knocks and all the other stuff you had to put up with, I probably could eventually have landed one. I had the talent, but I left and went on the road in the theater for ten years. So I blame that on myself. Then I did music. I just left the whole Hollywood scene. I never came back until 1984."

Yet another western feature she did was *Walk Tall* (1960). Maury Dexter was the producer-director on that one. "I just remember him offering it to me. I think it might have had to do with something I had done on television. I have a real nice picture I'll always cherish. I was in my costume, my long wig and everything, and somebody took a picture of Maury and I together, arm in arm. I've had that picture for years. That was a real action film, shot in the Sierras in the gold country area. I recall the mountains and riding the horses. Willard Parker had the lead role; we were being pursued and always on the run. It was very difficult, going up and down those hills. I had some good dramatic scenes in the film, and loved being able to handle the scenes on horseback. There was one horse who was a big ham; he'd done so many movies. Every time he heard 'Action!,' he would gallop forward, so Maury never used the word 'action' in the scenes with that horse."

Which begged the question ... does she have any horse stories and where did she learn to ride? "On a farm in Canada. But I was not a horsewoman. Even though I had been on the farm for many years, jumping up on the saddle like that was... [*laughs*]. But I felt very comfortable. But there was one ... I think it was *Flesh and the Spur* ... where I had to take the team of horses into a shot. That was kind of exciting 'cause at one point, I didn't do something right and the lead horse just kept going. He didn't run into the camera, but there's lights and gaffers and sound people all around, and I didn't stop him in time. You should see these guys scattering 50 different directions. Then the wrangler came in and stopped them. The horses weren't going that fast, but they were going at a nice little gait. They showed me what I did wrong, then I did it right. I couldn't help but laugh, because I saw these guys flitting out left and flitting out right, jumping out of the way trying to grab their lights at the same time ... mostly reflectors. Whatever kind of signal

I was supposed to give the horse, I didn't give him. Horses are really smart. When they heard 'Action!' some of those horses would just start moving. A lot of times for action, the directors would simply wave their hands, because the people were supposed to start talking on 'action' but these horses would gallop forward [*laughs*]. There was a *Rough Riders* [1958–1959] episode where we were all galloping in and one of the three leads [Jan Merlin] had a very high-spirited horse which he handled beautifully. There was a nice shot the director wanted coming through these trees. And this darn horse would reach up and grab some of the leaves and start chewing on them on the way in. No matter how the rider tried to get him to stop, he wouldn't do it. He'd reach out, or try to reach out, and grab some leaves off the trees; he was such a devil. They had to make him ride in behind us [chuckles] so the camera wouldn't see him reaching up for the leaves. Horses have their own personality."

Joyce appeared on scores of television westerns, including *Wanted Dead or Alive* (1958–1961). Star Steve McQueen often tried to upstage fellow actors, but Joyce remembers, "A couple of times during rehearsal I had to be very alert, and when I was, it didn't bother me. But indirectly, he could steal the scene, because he was into the Actors Studio thing, real heavy. At that time, instead of answering *yes* like people would do in normal life, he had to go through this whole Strasberg thing in order to get the word *yes* out. You really had to be alert about that, but as long as you were, stayed in character and used it to your own advantage, it wouldn't throw you. In a two-shot, [if you lost your character] and it was picked up in the editing room, they would cover it with a close-up of, mostly the star, which would be Steve McQueen. Once in a while, you would get your close-up, but coming upon the Strasberg approach was very different. Not that

I was against it. I didn't quite understand a lot of it. But I remember, Steve was a little airy ... so was I. I don't even know what the argument was about. It wasn't an argument, it was a debate. We were talking about something. Lord knows, it might have been about acting. It was an ongoing thing. I was going home that night and he said, 'Hey, Meadows,' from his dressing room. Some of the dressing rooms had little porches, and we were out there discussing this thing, nose to nose for about an hour after everybody should have been going home. When I got home, I remembered I had a dinner date that evening and was over an hour late. My poor date, standing on my doorstep, was not a happy camper. He was in the business, I won't give his name, but he was really upset. I said, 'Well, I was with Steve McQueen.' 'Uh-huh, yeah, talking...' 'Well, actually we weren't talking, we were kind of arguing.' 'Yeah, uh-huh, oh, boy, I've heard a lot of excuses...' An hour late and of course my date wrapped it all up in his mind we were off under a bush somewhere. Actually, he was a director. The next day he happened to be working on the same lot. Everybody knew we were kind of going together and they said, 'Boy, I'll tell you, your girlfriend was in a tiff with Steve McQueen.' Everybody going home saw us arguing on the porch! So he owed me an apology [*laughs*]."

The busy actress also did a couple of *Wagon Train* (1957–1965) episodes with Ward Bond and Robert Horton. "That was a happy set. They created, on one of their larger stages, a whole outdoor thing. They'd change it around, but whenever you'd stop moving and had camps, where the wagons were in a circle, that was always done on stage, which I thought was quite interesting. They created a whole outdoors, instead of doing that on location. What I loved about them was they were very story-oriented. In those days,

guest people got to be a good part of the plot. Now, because the cast is so huge in a regular series, if you do get a part it's, many times, not that good of a role. But these were wonderful roles. Ward Bond had a grand opportunity to be a well-rounded human being in that, as a character actor. They both were great to work with. I'd flirt with Bob all the time and he'd flirt with me."

Then Joyce did a couple of *Texan* (1958-1960) episodes with Rory Calhoun. "I remember those very well. There was a cute scene. He'd meet women, then he would always take off at the end. It was a cute thing on the end of one of them ... a little indication he would be returning ("Ruthless Woman"). Who wouldn't fall in love with that man. He had a handsome face, but he had a handsome personality too."

At Warner Bros., Joyce worked in a *Maverick* in 1962. "That was a wonderful one. I enjoyed that. Jack Kelly. But there was one I did. Was it *Lawman*? ["Detweiler's Kid" (1961)] ... where I played a gal that was a good sharpshooter. Walked into this saloon, pulled my guns and laid the law down. Calamity Jane kind of role. To get the part, I read the role and they said, 'One thing we do have to ask you, are you afraid of guns?' I said no. They said, 'Do you think you can handle a six-shooter?' 'Oh, sure.' I walked away and when the script came and I saw all this stuff, I went, 'Holy Toledo!' [*laughs*]. I wish I could remember who it was I went and panicked to on the Warner Bros. lot, to help me ... pull the gun out of my holster, put it back in. I had three days before I had to shoot the first scene and, let me tell you, I was working hard. I was supposed to be a fast draw and I had to technically do it right, reach in, pull it out and do it in the proper manner. I don't think I was ever more nervous walking on a set in my life as I was that one, because I had

Joyce with Robert Horton on television's *Wagon Train* (1961).

Warner Bros. came down, said they were upset about something. I don't know what it was, but they were making a mess of *Cheyenne* and Clint Walker ... something to do within their series. You could tell they were carrying on about something. Then Clint walked over and I noticed the whole personalities of these guys changing. When that big man walked around and said, 'You got a problem?' [*laughs*], they listened! He was the *biggest*. He reminded me a lot of my brother the way he talked ... didn't have much to say, but when he *had* something to say, he *meant* to say it."

On a personal note, "I got remarried in 1984 to a gentleman by the name of Merrill Harrington. He's a video engineer and has his own little business and does a lot of conventions. He did a lot of work for a while for a team of doctors, all in-house stuff, they talk about operations. He'd film this particular operation and produce the whole show for the doctors. The Academy Awards has a big video screen—well, he would be the one that would be operating all of those big screens. Quite talented. We met in 1982 and we've been together ever since."

The year 1984 was when Joyce came back to film. "It was very strange, but [going in to read for a part] is regular procedure for everybody. It's so ridiculous when the role is just a featured part. They'll have tons of people coming in. I've seen major stars now in their 50s or 60s, and they're in there reading."

Joyce, contemplating her hard and

given this very hearty, 'Oh, sure.' I went to wardrobe and who do I run into? The producers. They're saying, 'How's it going? Are you working with the gun okay?' Because the producers were getting a little worried. I remember responding to them, giving them all the confidence in the world and walking away, thinking, 'I'm going to faint' [*laughs*]. I had *no* idea they would speed up the camera like that, so it turned out to be just fine. Somebody could have told me [*laughs*]! I was supposed to be able to *shoot* bullets but I was *sweating* bullets on that one."

Yet another at Warner Bros. was *Cheyenne* (1955–1962). "I remember, during the episode, one of the heads of

Rory Calhoun greets Joyce and little Leslie Wenner on a *Texan* episode, "South of the Border" (1959).

fast work in the 1950s and 1960s, says, "As I look back on it, I wish I had given it more importance. I took it somewhat for granted. I just started working very easily and worked a lot. I had the talent and I could do the job, had a good sixth sense about moving around a screen and the cameras and everything, 'cause I never had any formal training about camera techniques. It was just kind of a natural thing.

I wish I had esteemed it more than I did. I probably wouldn't have gone out on the road. I would have given film much more value, would have stuck it out and probably would have had a longer career. I just didn't have it together enough to separate the good from the bad. Naturally, there was a lot of sexual harassment—we didn't have a name for it back then. There were a lot of *struggles*. A woman had a very hard struggle in those days. That's what I went away from more than anything. But had I given the work I had done more value, I think I would have found a way to get around that and withstand it. It got rougher as you started to get bigger. Political games you'd have to play ... and my psyche, as far as acting was concerned, was... I was always accused of being born to the purple, which meant I was born to be in the theater. I never left the theater, even on the road. It was such a part of me to perform. I had a hard time staying on top of all the political things, all the other stuff, to keep that in the right perspective and not be discouraged. You've heard it takes more than talent. And that's very true. Hollywood is very much a business, but it's a lot of art too. Sometimes the art gets lost amongst the business in this town. You have to learn how to cope with that. There's part of the business right now that a lot of people my age don't want to hassle with any more, especially the youth-oriented things. It's so hard to combat all of that, but for some reason, I haven't closed the doors on it. Lately, I've been on

the road with a Shakespearean partner and we do Shakespeare's sonnets, an hour and 20 minute show. And people pay us money to present this at universities! We've been in California and up toward Oregon, but we went to a booker's convention and we're going to branch out to make ourselves known to other states. Universities, big organizations."

Joyce Meadows Western Filmography

Movies: *Flesh and the Spur* (1957 American International)—John Agar; *Frontier Gun* (1958 Regal/Fox)—John Agar; *Walk Tall* (1960 20th Century–Fox)—Willard Parker.

Television: *Restless Gun*, "Sheriff Billy" (1958); *Wagon Train*, "Conchita Vasquez Story" (1959); *Tombstone Territory*, "Day of the Amnesty" (1959); *Tombstone Territory*, "Payroll to Tombstone" (1959); *State Trooper*, "Silver Spiral" (1959); *Rough Riders*, "Hired Gun" (1959); *Rough Riders*, "Last Rebel" (1959); *Texan*, "South of the Border" (1959); *U.S. Marshal*, "Kidnapper" (1959); *Texan*, "Ruthless Woman" (1960); *Johnny Ringo*, "Bordertown" (1960); *Wanted Dead or Alive*, "One Mother Too Many" (1960); *Wagon Train*, "Jed Polke Story" (1961); *Wagon Train*, "Artie Matthewson Story" (1961); *Lawman*, "Detweiler's Kid" (1961); *Lawman*, "Cold One" (1961); *Two Faces West* (semi-regular as Maggie Gray, saloon manager): *Two Faces West*, "Stilled Gun" (1961); *Two Faces West*, "The Noose" (1961); *Two Faces West*, "The Lesson" (1961); *Two Faces West*, "Doctor's Orders" (1961); *Cheyenne*, "Cross Purpose" (1961); *Maverick*, "Epitaph for a Gambler" (1962).

Colleen Miller

Bright Star

Colleen Miller, gorgeous star of so many Universal-International flicks of the 1950s, was born November 10, 1932, in Yakima, Washington. "It was sort of an Indian reservation, although I'm not an Indian. I was on the wrong side of the tracks. I remember seeing, as a little girl, Indian teepees, wood sidewalks, that sort of thing. But in the fourth grade, my family moved to Portland, Oregon, where I grew up. I had a lot of dance training. In fact, I left Portland to join a ballet company. After three seasons in San Francisco, I took a job as a dancer at the Flamingo in Las Vegas because I wanted to make more money than being in a ballet company. I was only at the Flamingo for three performances when someone saw me dancing and I was signed by Howard Hughes, thus RKO-Radio Studios. I really received my education at RKO. We went to class every day. But I only made one movie, *The Las Vegas Story* [1952] with Victor Mature and Jane Russell. I was at RKO for three years and nine months, then I went to Universal.

"Right away I went on a publicity tour for Universal, several states, and wound up back in Washington for a rodeo. I led the rodeo and the Indians there gave me the Indian name Bright Star."

As for training at the studios, "I never went to class at Universal. At RKO I had a coach, Florence Enright. She taught classes around the clock, but only for a select few people. Faith Domergue also took from her. When I did *Playgirl* [1954] at Universal, they said I didn't have to go to classes any more. They felt I knew what I was doing! But at RKO, I had a driver and I was taken to see every play; they educated you."

Colleen's first western was *Four Guns to the Border* (1954), directed by actor Richard Carlson and starring Rory Calhoun. "Carlson was a good director. He loved the business; he loved acting and actors and was a very feeling director. Rory was really very good. I knew Lita Calhoun, his wife (a.k.a. Isabelita, a.k.a. Lita Baron), before we made the picture, because she and I took ballet class together. I saw Lita three or four times a week, every week, but didn't know she was married to Rory. During the filming, I got a telegram from Lita saying, 'I don't mind you kissing Rory, but don't scratch him!' [*laughs*]. I still have that telegram!"

Four Guns to the Border was shot partly on location. "In Apple Valley. It was great, going there—the bus took us up. It was dusty, but fun and exciting. I thought it felt like we were on a real Indian reservation, with the mountains in the background. I would watch Nina Foch. She was good. I admired her in a big way. Nina is a consummate actress."

The Rawhide Years (1956) was

Colleen and Academy Award winner Walter Brennan in her first western, *Four Guns to the Border* (1954).

Colleen's next western. "Rudolph Maté was the director. He was the most delicious man. Just a joy. I see Tony Curtis fairly often, and Tony says Rudolph is one of his favorite directors. Tony enjoyed the picture and making westerns. Those were fun years. Tony has a nice lady now. They compliment each other; her name is Jill and she's a good horsewoman." As to another cast member: "Arthur Kennedy was a good actor. It was neat, watching and then playing a scene with him. The film only took three weeks to shoot, and it was all done on Universal's back lot!" The producer of *The Rawhide Years* was Stanley Rubin. "He taught me to play chess! He visited the set often, so I got to know him before he married Kathleen Hughes, who

was under contract to Universal at the same time I was."

The following year there was *Man in the Shadow* (1957), a modern-day western with Orson Welles and Jeff Chandler. "We mostly shot at one A.M. in the morning! Weird! I don't know why, but there are a lot of night scenes in the film. Orson must have liked working at night. I am not a great TV watcher, and I've missed it when it played on American Movie Classics. We see classic movies three times a week ... we go to Hugh Hefner's, where he sometimes even runs silent pictures! I really felt Jeff Chandler was out of it as a person—he was not having fun. He was, however, very personable; and looked great. Tall and handsome. I especially

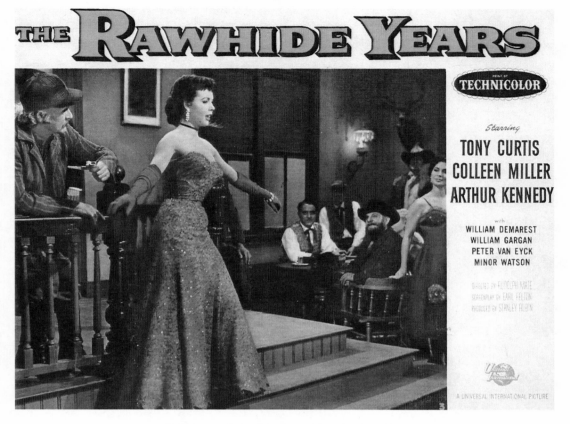

Colleen sings in *The Rawhide Years* (1956).

remember John Larch, who was the heavy—and a very good actor. The director, Jack Arnold, I knew socially because I was friends with his wife, Donna Holloway. He gave the movie the best he could, but the script was so bad, so mangled. Orson said he could fix the script but there was no time and he didn't care. During the shooting, Orson Welles taught me to play gin rummy. I loved it, and I'm very good at it now."

Miller's final western, and her last film to date, was *Gunfight at Comanche Creek* (1963) with Audie Murphy. "I went on an interview for that, but before I went, my agent wanted to see a still of myself and Tony Curtis in *The Purple Mask* [1955]. Isn't that strange? *Mask* is a period picture, not a western. Frank McDonald,

the director, looked at the still and said, 'That's what I want you to look like.' We shot that very quick—in only days! The film wasn't that good. I think it needed some more script." (Oddly, the storyline for *Gunfight...* originated in Tex Ritter and Dave O'Brien's *Flaming Bullets* [1945] and was reused in Whip Wilson's *Wanted Dead or Alive* [1951], *Star of Texas* [1953] with Wayne Morris and *Last of the Badmen* [1957] with George Montgomery.) "Audie played the guitar and would sing songs to me—and every other woman who was around. I never had any problems with him—or anyone else, for that matter. Audie always seemed reserved, though. Once, I did see Audie kick a couple of tin cans viciously. I never socialized with any actor, so I never knew him all that well."

A very sexy Colleen with Rory Calhoun in *Four Guns to the Border* (1954).

Jan Merlin was a villain in *Gunfight*. "What a good actor; a perfect villain with that child-like face and wonderful sneer!"

There *could* have been another western in Colleen's credits. "I tested for the part of Spurs in *Strange Lady in Town* [1955] for Mervyn LeRoy at Warner Bros. I really wanted it and Mr. LeRoy liked me, but Universal would not loan me out." (Lois Smith eventually played the part.)

Colleen reveals she doesn't smoke and doesn't drink, "But I paint! I have two children and seven grandchildren—five from my son and the other two by my daughter. I am married to Walter Ralphs [of Ralphs' Markets], and we have a ranch in northern California, only miles from the Oregon border. We have horses, deer, cattle, a wildlife refuge. We have a ranch manager who keeps us posted on the day-to-day activities. Because there no longer are commercial airlines near there, we have to fly to Sacramento and go up. It's a long trip, so we don't go as often as we used to."

Colleen is one star who has some of her movies—on film! "I have *The Purple Mask* and *Playgirl* with Shelley Winters on 16mm. I recently saw Shelley—she isn't in the best of health. I keep meaning to tell her I have the print—she probably would enjoy seeing it again.

"I'm just mad about my kids and my husband, Walter. I've just had a very special life. I thank my lucky stars every day."

Colleen Miller Western Filmography

Movies: *Four Guns to the Border* (1954 Universal)—Rory Calhoun; *The Rawhide Years* (1956 Universal)—Tony Curtis; *Man in the Shadow* (1957 Universal)—Jeff Chandler; *Gunfight at Comanche Creek* (1963 Allied Artists)—Audie Murphy.

Pauline Moore

Balancing Career, Marriage and Religion

Songs Along the Way is the title of a new book written by Pauline Moore, the beautiful, 5'6", sweet-faced star with an equally sweet voice, who graced the screen in the late 1930s and early 1940s. "I have about finished it, and now have to decide which stills should be used for illustrations. Then I'll be sending it to a publisher."

Born Pauline Joless Love, June 17, 1914, in Philadelphia, her father died during World War I. She took her stepfather's name after his 1925 marriage to her mother. Wanting to be an actress since childhood, Pauline racked up many stage plays at a young age.

"I, very early, took elocution lessons, so by the time I was four I knew miles and miles of dramatic poems and recitations. I sold Liberty Bonds during the first World War. In the city hall at Philadelphia I sang 'Bring Back My Daddy to Me' and songs about the flag. So I just grew up always expecting to be an actress.

"My father wanted me to go to college and dramatic arts school but I had an opportunity to go with a stock company in Pennsylvania and New Jersey. I went to New York City and through a letter to Carl Laemmle [head of Universal], at 17, Universal signed me to a contract in 1931."

That contract led to her being cast in 1931's classic *Frankenstein*. "I was only in California for three months. I went over to the *Frankenstein* set, talking to various people, when the director, James Whale, asked me if I would be a bridesmaid. It was that simple! Boris Karloff would sneak up behind a visitor on the set—like me—and would grunt or groan. When the person turned around, there was invariably a scream [*laughs*]! He would then laugh! I was on the picture for three or four days. One time, a klieg light nearly fell on Colin Clive and me. If Colin hadn't pulled me into a doorway, we both would have been crushed!"

Pauline's tenure at Universal was brief. "My stepfather wrote the studio, asking for my release—and they granted it! But I went to Broadway. In those days, if you were on Broadway, you could always get in a picture; if you were in pictures, you could always do a Broadway show. I got a job in the last show Florenz Ziegfeld did, a musical with Buddy Rogers, Bert Lahr and Lupe Velez."

In between plays, Pauline did photographic modeling for commercial advertising or illustrations posing for artists. "I was on the cover of *Ladies Home Journal*, *McCalls* and *Cosmopolitan* in the days when it was a different kind of magazine than it is now."

Pauline graces one of the most collectible of Coca Cola trays. "It was 1934—I was working on Broadway, including playing the ingenue lead in the last show

Pauline Moore and Roy Rogers get serious in *Arkansas Judge* (1941), which starred the Weaver Brothers and Elviry.

Earl Carroll did, *Murder at the Vanities*. But I soon learned when you weren't working in a show, you still had to pay the rent. So, I registered with a modeling agency. They sent me to an artist—whose name I cannot remember. I worked for him for a week. He did several paintings of me. He later sold one to Coca Cola. I didn't know about it for years. They put his painting on those trays, and used it apparently, in various other places. There are Coca Cola conventions. There was a Kansas City festival where I took a picture with the tray. I have a huge poster of that picture with no place to put it in my apartment, so the manager of this retirement complex, which only has three floors and 30 units, has it hanging in his office!

"Through modeling, I met my hus-band, Jefferson Machamer, in New York in 1932 just after my eighteenth birthday. He did cartoons, illustrations and ads for magazines like *Saturday Evening Post* and later *Life*. We married in 1934 and in 1936, my daughter Laurie was born."

In 1936, Pauline Moore attracted the heads of 20th Century–Fox, where she was placed under contract, playing in pictures with everybody from Shirley Temple ("She worked like an adult with patience and stamina") and Jane Withers ("She was a very dear, natural child who remained a child—she was playing between takes") to the Ritz Brothers in *The Three Musketeers* (1939). "Another actress had the part of Lady Constance, but Don Ameche had had an appendectomy and had to lift her, so they took her out and put me in, because I was smaller and lighter [*laughs*]. During *Heidi* [1937] I was pregnant and the studio didn't know. They kept putting off my scenes. I was getting bigger and bigger 'til I almost didn't make it."

Other superstars she worked with at Fox include Loretta Young ("A charming woman, a *real* person and a beautiful actress"), Tyrone Power ("I didn't get to know him too well—he was just beginning"), both Charlie Chans ("Warner Oland and Sidney Toler were both gentlemen") and Joel McCrea. "I had a teenage crush on Joel McCrea—I read about him in all the movie magazines. When we did *Three Blind Mice* [1938], he was so nice, so kind. My second daughter was six weeks old. His wife, Frances Dee, told him that I should always have a chair to sit in—that she once worked on a picture when her son was six weeks old, and she knew how tiring it could be." Future B-western star Allan Lane was with her in *Charlie Chan at the Olympics* (1937). "Allan had been a model in between shows in New York. He was a nice young man."

Pauline also recalls for *Charlie Chan at Treasure Island* (1939), "They made a wax image of me—a complete plaster cast dummy and used it for the levitation scene. The Westmore brothers did it. That thing looked so real you could walk right up to it and you wouldn't know it wasn't alive."

Before leaving Fox in 1941, Pauline was cast as Ann Rutledge in *Young Mr. Lincoln* with Henry Fonda. "I saw him for two or three hours—my part was that small!" This was 1939, the year of *Gone with the Wind*. Asked if 20th offered to loan her to Selznick, Pauline quickly responded, "No. I couldn't even get in to see Darryl Zanuck, who was head of the studio in California. His secretary kept telling me when he wanted to see me, he'd send for me. My agent did absolutely nothing for me, and I was too stupid at the time to think of simply firing him and getting an agent who would push for me. I especially wanted the role in *Rebecca* [1940]. Since my agent wouldn't do it, I wired Alfred Hitchcock myself. He responded with a screen test, and it was the best work I ever did. I later got the print of the test, and instead of keeping it and showing it to producers who could do me good, I sent it to my mother, where it got burned up with a lot of junk she was throwing away!"

It was at this time Pauline heard there was an opening for a leading lady at Republic. "They knew I had been in westerns at Fox and they knew about my theater background. I was told the studio had several girls, but none had my training. Actually, I should have gone back to Broadway, but that would have meant taking my two little girls and being away from my husband."

Pauline had never heard of Roy Rogers when given the leading lady role in *Days of Jesse James* (1939). "That was because he was new. They knew if Roy blew his lines, I wouldn't, whereas one of those other girls would probably flub whenever Roy didn't! The first time I worked with Roy was a scene on the steps of a home. He was to come charging up on Trigger, then rear up right in my face. It was all I could do to keep from cutting and running [*laughs*]. But I enjoyed making westerns, so it was fun for me. My husband, however, objected to my working at what he called a 'crummy studio' and he refused to drive me. So, I had to get myself a car and drive myself over the hill into the Valley each day! I never did meet Herbert Yates [head of Republic]. And I was never under contract. My private life, my family life, my personal life was in upheaval when I was working. My husband, who was a great deal older than I, did not like to go out and socialize. He'd done all that back in New York before we married. He had

Gabby Hayes, Hugh Sothern, Gaylord Pendleton and Wade Boteler check Spanish land grants as Roy Rogers holds Pauline's hand in *Young Buffalo Bill* (1940).

friends in the business, but other than my uneventful working days, I didn't get to see these people in the evening, so I don't have stories about Robert Livingston, Bob Steele and others. I didn't get to really know them. I just went from picture to picture until late in 1941, when I told them I had promised to take my children to visit my mother back east. I *had* promised my mother, and had been putting it off eight or nine months. I kept getting pictures. 'We've got something else for you, they'd say.' They explained they'd have to get another girl, which is what happened, so I never worked at Republic again."

Pauline Moore can sing, but never did sing in pictures. "I was always dubbed. People don't seem to understand that the music and songs are recorded *before* they start the picture. Then a huge machine is on the set, and the prerecorded music is played while singers and musicians lip-sync to it. So, that is not my singing in *The Three Musketeers* because I wasn't originally supposed to be in the picture. [Nor is it her voice in Roy Rogers' *Carson City Kid* (1940).] Actually, I only sing at church. I never sang in *any* pictures—someone else's voice was always used, so there was never any thought of a duet between Roy Rogers and myself."

Roy and Pauline made five pictures together. "I had no business sense, but Roy sure did. He was so very friendly to everybody. I got to know Roy very well. He was still new, still quite shy. The director,

Joseph Kane, was very helpful; a very nice man. But my husband didn't want to socialize, so we didn't—a mistake for a picture career, but he seemed dead-set against my career. I was most happy working." According to Republic files, Pauline was being paid about $300 per film.

When asked about Don Barry (*Days of Jesse James*), Pauline only says, "At the time, he was gentlemanly and very nice to me. But I remember Gabby Hayes much better! Gabby was charming! When he wasn't working, he would visit the set, but he would have his teeth in his mouth and he was dressed in smart clothes. A gentleman ... a gentle man!"

Pauline did several westerns, but was hardly on a horse. "When I started doing westerns, I learned how, because I thought I would have to know. Usually, the stunt girls—and I never saw them—did the riding, but on one picture, I'm on a wagon and Roy jumps on [*Young Buffalo Bill* (1940)]. Stunt people did the hard part— the long shots. But when it came time for the close-ups, and dialogue like, 'What are you doing?' I was breathless! They put me in a wagon when those horses were still steamed up. I had to do it under the microphones! They did put a truck across the road in case the horses got away! So, to answer any questions, I could ride, but seldom did.

"There was one picture, where the bad guy tried to grab me off the wagon. Well, he couldn't ride a horse, and we had trouble out of this. [Probably "Colorado" as Milburn Stone grabs her as she departs a stage.] Again, the doubles did the long shots, and in the close-ups the camera had to come closer than intended, so someone could boost me from below as this guy couldn't lift me up any better than he could ride [*laughs*]."

In *Carson City Kid*, Pauline played a saloon girl. "I didn't mind—a nice change of pace."

The 5'6" Pauline, asked about her many experiences with smallish leading men, is quick to point out, "I got used to them standing on a box in front of me [*laughs*]!"

In *The Trail Blazers* (1940) with the Three Mesquiteers, Pauline has lots of scenes with a baby. "I told the director no mother would go away and leave the baby in the basket on the table. He told me, 'You do it anyway.' Luckily, a man under the table caught the baby as it was about to fall off!"

King of the Texas Rangers (1941) was an excellent serial in which Pauline starred with football great Slingin' Sammy Baugh. "I wasn't a football fan. I had never heard of Sammy before we did the serial. But I do remember working on it very well. The only thing they asked me when I interviewed for the part was, 'Can you run in high heels?' [*laughs*]. I recall trying to climb up a rope ladder in high heels while a huge wind fan was blowing on me, and of course jumping out of a wagon and rolling down the hill. That was lots of fun [*laughs*]. The only really scary part occurred when Duncan Renaldo and I were in the river. For those scenes, they took us outside of Los Angeles where there was a dam [Lake Sherwood and on top of the cliff next to Lake Sherwood Dam]. Then they put the camera out in the middle of the dam and had us swim parallel to it. One of the grips shot marbles at us (standing in for gunshots); whenever we saw a splash we were supposed to dive under the water. I'm not all that great a swimmer, so for much of the sequence I was allowed to remove my heavy cowboy boots. I had on black socks so nobody really noticed. However, for those scenes of us scrambling to shore, I had to have the boots on and it created a real problem. They began the take when I was about ten feet from the bank. Right away I was in trouble. I couldn't get my feet up, so I started to sink.

Pauline, Duncan Renaldo and football star turned serial hero, Slingin' Sammy Baugh, in a scene from Chapter Ten of *King of the Texas Rangers*.

Eventually, as I was going down for what seemed like the third time, one of the grips jumped in and pulled me out. I was so tired I slept all the way back to Hollywood on the studio bus. Sammy Baugh was a gentleman and very easy to work with. I thought he was most impressive, considering this was his first time in front of a camera."

Released by Fox in 1941, Pauline went east with her daughters to visit her mother in North Carolina. "Pearl Harbor occurred when we were back east, and my husband wanted us to get a farm and settle down back there, which we did for two or three years. When we returned to California, I was into religious activities and didn't go back to films until later. My husband was against my career, so I had to endure that in addition to any struggles with the career."

In the mid–1950s, Pauline decided to give acting another try. "By then, I had lost my contacts and my confidence. I did do several TV shows, including a *Death Valley Days*, as well as a few commercials [and an unbilled bit in Rod Cameron's *Spoilers of the Forest*]. With the handicap of my husband being against my career, it was just too much. [Machamer died in 1960; she married Dodd Watkins in 1961 and was widowed again in 1971.] Mainly, I have concentrated on my family and worked in the religious area. I have written half a dozen Biblical playlets, including *The Seamless Robe*. During Christmas 1999, I went up to my son's, and at the church, I did my *Mary's Story*, about the life of Jesus through the mother's point of view. I hadn't done it in three years. I told my son I couldn't remember it any more.

But he encouraged me to do it. They wanted me back for Easter, and I agreed!

"Looking back, I'm glad I was part of something that has given a lot of pleasure to a lot of people."

Pauline Moore died of Lou Gehrig's Disease on December 7, 2001.

Pauline Moore
Western Filmography

Movies: *Wagon Wheels* (1934 Paramount)—Randolph Scott; *Wild and Woolly* (1937 20th Century–Fox)—Jane Withers; *Arizona Wildcat* (1938 20th Century–Fox)—Jane Withers; *Days of Jesse James* (1939 Republic)—Roy Rogers; *Carson City Kid* (1940 Republic)—Roy Rogers; *Colorado* (1940 Republic)—Roy Rogers; *Trail Blazers* (1940 Republic)—3 Mesquiteers; *Young Buffalo Bill* (1940 Republic)—Roy Rogers; *Arkansas Judge* (1941 Republic)—Weaver Brothers & Elviry, Roy Rogers; *Spoilers of the Forest* (1957 Republic)—Rod Cameron.

Serial: *King of the Texas Rangers* (1941 Republic)—Sammy Baugh.

Television: *Death Valley Days*, "Jimmy Dayton's Treasure" (1954).

Dorothy Morris
and Caren Marsh

Sisters in the Saddle

Dorothy Morris and Caren Marsh are "Sisters in the Saddle" with two distinctly different careers. Caren, the elder, was born April 6, 1919, while Dorothy was born February 23, 1922. Both are that rarity—native Californians as well as natives of Hollywood itself. "We were both born in Los Angeles, but that's because Hollywood has no hospital!" reports Dorothy, who kept the family name of Morris. Caren says she changed hers because "there were too many people named Morris at the time ... Chester Morris, Wayne Morris and MGM starlet Ann Morris, to name a few."

Dorothy's career came about as a result of a Hollywood High School play. "Someone spotted me and this led to a part in a 1940 experimental TV show with Ian MacDonald. We wore green greasepaint and black-brown lipstick. We looked like ghouls! Horrendous. Ian asked if I had studied at the Pasadena Playhouse. When I told him I couldn't afford it, he reminded me on Sundays they had open auditions. I landed a part in *What a Life*. I got my first

Dorothy and Carl Esmond in MGM's *Seven Sweethearts* (1942).

tiny film part in Jane Withers' *Her First Beau* [1941], dancing with Charles Lind at a party. I was studying with Maria Ouspenskaya, who preferred working with men. I was never yelled at, like a lot of the students. I couldn't afford but one semester, so the Madame put me in a scholarship. 'You can pay me back when you get your contract—I know you will get a contract.' She was right, I did! Maria Ouspenskaya looked so *old*. When I asked someone just how *old* she was, they said, 'The Madame is 55,' so I lived my whole life in fear of turning 55, because I thought I would look like *that* [*laughs*]! When I was sent to MGM to test for *The Courtship of Andy Hardy* [1942], I told them I had done the play at Pasadena Playhouse, and they *looked up* my records! They kept records on everything that hap-

pened at the Playhouse. The card said 'great actress, but wouldn't photograph.' The casting people couldn't get over that. They thought I was very pretty, and were most impressed with the 'terrific actress' line. They said talent scouts are most critical, and they should have overlooked any possibility I wouldn't photograph."

Dorothy played a wide range of parts at MGM, mostly ingenues, but sometimes a meaty role like the crazy girl in *Our Vines Have Tender Grapes* (1945), or with an English accent in *Cry Havoc* (1943), or the young lover in the anti–Nazi *None Shall Escape* (1944) on loan to Columbia. "When I was loaned to Republic for *Someone to Remember* [1943], I was most pleasantly surprised to have flowers delivered to my dressing room every day—courtesy of studio head Herbert J. Yates! He made me feel like I was a star. MGM's dialogue coach, Lillian Burns, told me 'You'll never be a star, Dorothy. You are too good an actress. You are a character actress. You get involved in the part. You need the personality to be a star. Van Johnson has the personality, but when he tries to act, he is awful.' I wanted to settle down and have kids, so on February 23, 1946—my twenty-fourth birthday—I retired. I was content staying home for years, but was out one day and ran into old MGM pal Frances Rafferty. She insisted my husband and I go to a filming of her *December Bride* (1954–1961) that night. We did, and I discovered I *did* miss it. I got an agent, and one of the very first things I did was an early *Gunsmoke* [1955–1975], before they made Milburn Stone look old. He was wonderful; a terrific, talented man. He knew me from my pictures and liked me. We had done *Little Miss Big* together in 1946. He knew all those old Colonel Stoopnagle stories. Things like 'The Nion and the Louse,' or 'The Tear and the Hortess.' That sort of thing. He could say them verbatim. It was hysterical! He was a handsome guy. I liked him a lot. He made it pleasant while you were sitting around waiting. That was so boring—I used to knit on the sets!"

Another of Dorothy's early TV parts was on *Casey Jones* (1957–1958) with Alan Hale, Jr. "I played a mother and I loved my outfit. I got to look older instead of ingenue age. At the time, I wished I had lived in those days, because of the wonderful long skirts they wore. Another show I did, in 1957, was *The Donna Reed Show*, with my old pal Donna (she got the part in *Courtship of Andy Hardy* I tested for). At MGM we were considered the same type … we had the same build, same hair. The guards at the gates would say to Donna, 'Hello, Miss Morris' and they would say to me, 'Hello, Miss Reed.'"

Among Dorothy's many television

Outside a soundstage, Dorothy is in western period attire ready for her scenes in an episode of television's *Rawhide* (1962).

credits are *Wagon Train* (1957–1965), *Sugarfoot* (1957–1961) and a couple of *Rawhides* (1959–1965). "The *Wagon Train* was memorable because of meeting the star, Barbara Stanwyck. I was only on it a couple of days, but she sure was a tough broad. She was running the show; watching her work, she was not exactly laid back. I thought to myself, 'Wow, has she always been that way?'"

As for *Sugarfoot*, "Unfortunately I remember nothing except for adorable, handsome Will Hutchins. My part was small, and I didn't get to really meet Will, which was my loss. My first *Rawhide* I don't recall at all. The second one, 'Child Woman,' was memorable because it was a good part, and because Cesar Romero was in it. He was great, terrific, very laid back and casual."

Dorothy's last acting job was on a *Dragnet* (1967–1970) with Jack Webb. "I did three of the shows … the first and second times he was very nice, but the third time—well! This was one where I played the mother of a teenage boy in trouble with drugs or something. The atmosphere on the Webb sets was so uptight; I was never on a set like that. I blew my lines and told Jack, 'I'm sorry.' Jack barked back, '*Sorry* doesn't get it in the can.' He didn't treat people nicely at all. It was most awful, and I've never said 'I'm sorry' again!"

Caren Marsh is Dorothy's older sister. "My parents wanted me to go to college, and I wanted to be a dancer. A girl in high school told me about an audition for dancers in *Rosalie* [1937], an Eleanor Powell musical at MGM. I went and I got it! This led to work in more and more pictures, mainly as a dancer. Being tiny [Caren is 5'], I was a 'pony.' The tall girls are called 'showgirls.' I worked with the great choreographers—Busby Berkeley, Nick Castle—who had given me tap dance lessons; Hermes Pan and Jack Donahue. I was a dancer in one of Dorothy's pictures, *Seven Sweethearts* [1942]. While doing one of those musicals, someone at Metro spotted me and asked for me to be Judy Garland's double in *The Wizard of Oz* [1939]. You don't see me at all. They light the set, do the camera setups, then I leave and Judy comes in. But it lasted a long, long time. And those wind machines blew hard! They tested the tornado sequence on me—inside the house when the neighbor goes by, all that sort of thing. The first time I had a real acting part was in an Army Signal Corps hygiene training film, *Pickup Girl* [1944]. I played a girl who goes out on a date with a solider. Paul Kelly was the star—but not the boy I dated. Jack Edwards played that part. I got my first closeup in *Best Foot Forward* [1943]. Lucille Ball was so nice—I was invited to sit in her dressing room, and she told me, 'You're wasting time, Caren. You're so cute and have talent. You should go to New York and then come back out here!' I later took her advice."

In 1944, Caren was seen as one of the front row dancers in *Hands Across the Border* with Roy Rogers. "The still men were always taking pictures. One day they asked me to step out from the dance line and have my picture taken with Roy. I did, and I only recently found out [from Boyd Magers] that it wound up on the title lobby card! It's my picture with Roy, instead of Ruth Terry, who was his leading lady!"

A year later, Caren *did* land a lead, opposite Bob Steele in *Navajo Kid* (1945). "Bob Steele couldn't have been nicer. I had never ever seen him in a movie—and was expecting a much taller man. He was *short*! But such friendly eyes. You liked him immediately. We shot locations in Chatsworth in the San Fernando Valley. I had a scene on a large wagon which had wobbly wheels—I thought they'd fall off, but Bob assured me they wouldn't. I trusted this well-built, two-fisted man of action. Unfortunately, because of fast shooting schedules, you didn't get to hang out with people—you'd shoot this, shoot that."

After that came a good role in PRC's *Secrets of a Sorority Girl* (1946). Another plum role arrived as Caren was selected to play Richard Erdman's girlfriend-wife in *Wild Harvest* (1947). "That was with Alan Ladd, another short man. His wife, Sue Carol, was a powerful person. I got a lot of publicity on this picture. *Life* did a layout on me that was never used, unfortunately. Some big story must have popped up. I had my picture taken with a new

Caren was merely one of the dancers in *Hands Across the Border* (1944) when she was pulled from the chorus line to pose with Roy Rogers and wound up being featured on the title lobby card.

Paramount star named Kirk Douglas. It was just great! I also had a small part as a young mother in a Bing Crosby film [*Welcome, Stranger* (1947)]. Around this time, I took Lucy's advice and went to New York. I did several things and in 1949 was signed to work with ventriloquist Paul Winchell in his show at the Capitol Theater in Manhattan! Since it wouldn't start for a month, I took the plane home to visit my folks. When the plane was over Burbank, the pilot went too low and we crashed into the side of a mountain at Chatsworth—right where I had done the Bob Steele picture only a couple of years before!" The plane broke in half on impact and erupted in flames. Of the 136 passengers and crew, only eight survived. Terri-

fyingly, Caren recalls, "I was seated on the fourth seat from the rear with an emergency exit door across the aisle. It popped open on impact. I crawled out, down the mountain about 500 yards to a fire road and collapsed. My right foot was mangled. It took over a year to recuperate! I was told I would walk again, but never *dance*. But the doctor was wrong! In 1950 I married Bill Doll, Mike Todd's press agent, and had a great life filled with travel. Bill, Mike, Elizabeth Taylor and I went to Miami for *Around the World in 80 Days* (1956). Bill and I traveled all over the world.

"Today, I teach dancing in Palm Springs, and once a month I visit stroke victims. A few months ago, a dancer friend

Sidekick Syd Saylor stops the buckboard so Caren can flirt with Bob Steele in *Navajo Kid* (1945).

called me to be in a soap commercial with him. I never saw it, but I did get a nice fat check! My life today is still very fulfilling."

Dorothy Morris
Western Filmography

Television: *Casey Jones*, "Gunslinger" (1957); *Gunsmoke*, unknown title; *Rawhide*, "Incident at Dangerfield Dip" (1959); *Rawhide*, "Child Woman" (1962); *Wagon Train*, "Kate Crawley Story" (1964); *Sugarfoot*, unknown title.

Caren Marsh
Western Filmography

Movies: *Hands Across the Border* (1944 Republic)—Roy Rogers; *Navajo Kid* (1945 PRC)—Bob Steele.

Noreen Nash

From Ingenue to Villainess

Beautiful, talented Noreen Nash was born April 4, 1924, in Wenatchee, Washington. "My real name is Noreen Roth, but after I played J. Carrol Naish's daughter in a film, The Southerner [1945], my agent suggested changing it to Noreen Nash [without the i]. Everything was al-literation in those days—Greer Garson, Marilyn Monroe, thus Noreen Nash."

Noreen's entrance into pictures was a fairy-tale story. "I was named Apple Blossom Queen in Wenatchee, and came down to Los Angeles. Bob Hope's agent saw me and got me a screen test at Warner Bros.

Noreen as J. Carrol Naish's daughter in *The Southerner* (1945).

I'd gone back home to finish high school, then came back to California. Warners didn't sign me, but MGM offered me a stock contract as a showgirl. I didn't want that, and turned it down. I was going to go back home when Louis Shurr told me to take the contract; that MGM would train you, give you dramatic lessons, the whole thing ... all expenses paid, and you earned a salary as well! So I did, and my first part was in *Girl Crazy* [1943] with Mickey Rooney. By the way, when I was 12 years old, I was on a cruise. Charles Boyer and his wife, actress Pat Patterson, were also on the cruise. He was aloof, but nice. On the last night, he asked me to dance. He thought I was 16, instead of 12. Later, I tested for the part Gloria Jean won in *Flesh and Fantasy* [1943]—and I saw Boyer again. Then, in the 1950s, I did two Four

Star Playhouse shows for him. Charles and I talked about the 20 years earlier cruise. He said he remembered me, and the incident!"

Noreen's first western was the Cinecolor *Red Stallion* (1947) with Robert Paige. "It was directed by Lesley Selander. I eventually did several films with him. He was fun. We always had a great time. The locations were great, and we always— every night—had dinner together. Les and, in the case of *Red Stallion*, Bob Paige as well. My mother was on location [near Mt. Shasta and in Dunsmuir, California] with me, as well as my year-and-a-half old son, so they were at these dinners, too. Les kept the locations going happily. Les didn't take it that seriously. We just had fun. Les had a zest for life."

It's written in the AFI catalog that

The cast of the race horse story *Red Stallion* (1947)—Robert Bice, Robert Paige, Noreen, Pierre Watkin, Jane Darwell and Daisy the dog (so named because of his appearances in Columbia's long-running Blondie series).

bad weather delayed production and cost producers an extra $500,000 but Noreen says, "We only had a couple of days bad weather. I don't know where the idea about the budget rising came from."

Selander crossed paths with Noreen again when she appeared in two of the highly popular Tim Holt westerns, *Storm Over Wyoming* (1950) and *Road Agent* (1952). "*Storm* was filmed up near Bishop, California. My husband flew into Reno so we could have the weekend together. When I went off to see him, the cast and crew would throw rice, as if we were going on our honeymoon! Of course, Les Selander and I renewed our good friendship and had our nightly dinners together. Tim Holt was an awfully nice man, but I got to know his sidekick, Richard Martin, much better. On locations, Dick and I had more to talk about—we had more things in common. Tim was sort of a loner. Dick was very outgoing and fun to be with. This was a friendship—not romantic, as we were both married. But on screen, I even got to kiss Tim Holt!"

Noreen also got to kiss her foreman and evil cohort, Douglas Kennedy, as well as play a bad girl, for a change, in *The Lone Ranger and the Lost City of Gold* (1958). "I also played a bad girl in a *Lineup* [1954–1960]. I enjoyed playing bad girls; it was fun. However, as a result, I didn't let my two sons see that Lone Ranger picture—and neither did see it, until they were big teenagers. That was mainly because of my killing Douglas Kennedy with that ax! My oldest son was in Mexico one time and saw it on TV—in Spanish. He came back and told me, 'Mom, you sure speak Spanish great' [laughs]. Then my other son was in France, and saw it on French TV! In fact, I had more to do with Douglas Kennedy than with Clayton Moore or Jay Silverheels, so I don't recall much about the Lone Ranger and his Tonto. But Clayton was a lovely gentleman. He had a lot of

dignity and charm. He was aloof, so I didn't get to really know him, but it was fun, working with him."

When reminded that Moore mentioned (in his autobiography) that Noreen's husband had doctored his black eye back in 1940, Noreen relates, "I was married to Dr. Lee Siegal, from 1942 until his death a few years ago. He was a doctor to several stars and could have told you many more stories than I can! What I remember most about the film are the changes in my personal life, because my mother-in-law died while I was on location at Old Tucson, Arizona! So, it seems like another life to me now. All the experiences were pleasant. I never had any fights or anything; just a good time."

One of her earlier films was *The Devil on Wheels* (1947) with Darryl Hickman and Jan Ford. "Jan became Terry Moore, of course, and I see her from time to time. Darryl is doing just great as a big acting coach! In fact, my grandson decided to be an actor, and I sent him to Darryl, who is a great actor himself!"

In 1948, Noreen appeared opposite Turhan Bey in *Adventures of Casanova*. "I have vivid memories of that. We shot it in Mexico. This is the one that went over budget. The Mexicans took their time doing everything from makeup to lighting. My brother-in-law brought my son down to visit me. Well, it seems if you bring a child into their country, you must also take it back with you when you leave. Otherwise they consider it a kidnapping! I had to go to court and prove I was his mother! The judge asked him, 'Who is that lady?' and my two-year-old son kept saying, 'Noreen Nash.' He wouldn't say I was his mother. So I learned to never take my child out of the country again [laughs]! Another funny thing about that picture involved Turhan Bey. He was dating Linda Christian at the time, and the president (or ex-president) of Mexico liked

Richard Martin (husband of another of our Ladies of the Western, Elaine Riley), Tim Holt and Noreen face the *Storm Over Wyoming* (1950).

Linda, too! There were threats, and Turhan had to say to producer Brynie Foy, 'I'm afraid for my life. I have to leave Mexico.' So, they rewrote the script. There's a scene where I'm crying over Turhan, who has been killed off in the script [laughs]!"

Giant (1956) is one of Noreen's biggest movies. "What I remember most is, by the time I got on the picture, director George Stevens and James Dean were at each other. Dean did his usual mumbling and Stevens kept saying, 'This script cost a lot of money. I want to hear those words!' George didn't like James' style of acting! Dennis Hopper was also in it—one of his first pictures. I've seen him around over the years. In fact, in 1996, the Academy had a screening of a 'restored' print,

and most of the cast members, who are still living, attended."

Noreen also appeared on a lot of television programs, including two *Yancy Derringer* (1958–1959) episodes with Jock Mahoney. When asked if she recalled three rather lengthy, passionate kisses with Jock, she laughed, "You know, I cannot remember that at all. I'm beginning to worry about myself, not remembering those kisses with Jock! But, this was around the time I was about to retire, so maybe that's the reason I forgot them. What I do remember about *Yancy Derringer* was that something was about to fall on me, and Jock ran and grabbed me just in the nick of time! [An incident in the script of "Belle from Boston."] I still see Frances

Bergen, who was a regular on the show, from time to time."

Noreen feels her life at home was more important than working in pictures. "I loved working; I had a wonderful time doing it. In one of my last roles, a live TV appearance, I commit suicide over Vincent Price. My son said, 'Mother, I think they're trying to tell you something' [laughs]. I thought about going to college, since I went from high school into work and marriage, but I told my son I'd be in my forties before I got out. He told me I'd be in my forties whether or not I went, so I attended UCLA and graduated after five and half years—as I still had my family responsibilities. In fact, my youngest son, who went through the same school in only three years, graduated the same year I did! In 1980, I wrote a book, *By Love Fulfilled*. My lawyer advised me about not letting it onto the internet, but this was four years ago and I think it was bad advice."

On August 7, Noreen married actor James Whitmore in a small, private ceremony at Whitmore's home in Malibu, California. "We met three years ago on August 7, 2001, and that's why we picked that date. It was just the two of us at the wedding, because there are so many children, grandchildren and family. Afterwards, there was a party and all our families came together to celebrate."

Noreen Nash
Western Filmography

Movies: *Red Stallion* (1947 Eagle-Lion)—Robert Paige; *Storm Over Wyoming* (1950 RKO)—Tim Holt; *Road Agent* (1952 RKO)—Tim Holt; *Giant* (1956 Warner Bros.)—Rock Hudson; *The Lone Ranger and the Lost City of Gold* (1958 United Artists)—Clayton Moore.

Television: *Hopalong Cassidy*, "Don Colorado" (1952); *Yancy Derringer*, "Belle from Boston" (1958); *Yancy Derringer*, "Fire on the Frontier" (1959).

Noel Neill

a.k.a. Lois Lane

Perky Noel Neill will be forever remembered by millions of television viewers as Lois Lane. But the dark-haired Paramount starlet of the 1940s had a cinema life before *Superman* (1951–1957), and westerns were a significant part of it.

Born Noel (No-**el**, as in Christmas) Neill in Minneapolis, Minnesota, November 24, 1920, the later-to-be-TV's-most-famous female reporter actually came from a journalistic background. "My father worked for three or four newspapers

Noel will always be reporter Lois Lane to millions of people. This scene from Chapter 13 of the second serial shows Kirk Alyn as Superman with Pierre Watkin, Noel and Tommy Bond as Jimmy Olsen.

in the Minneapolis area. Usually he started out head of the copy desk and then went on to another position. He was with *The Minneapolis Star Journal* a good many years until he retired."

Noel tried to act in high school plays to no avail. "I tried out and flopped each audition. I thought for certain I'd never act."

A cross-country road trip with her mother found them in California with relatives. "By chance somebody's friend said, 'Would you like to audition for a singer?' I'd sung since high school. I did, got the job and went to a thing for Bob Crosby's orchestra down at Del Mar. It was quite a place at that time for the stars and the rich

people. Of course, I met a lot of people working there. All of them were in the biz, one way or another, so I got started at Paramount. *Henry Aldrich for President* [1941] was my first. I was put under contract to Paramount after I did that Henry Aldrich picture."

The five-foot-two starlet went on to appear in over 16 films for Paramount between 1942–1946 including *Standing Room Only* (1944), *Duffy's Tavern* (1945) and *The Blue Dahlia* (1946), as well as several more in the popular Henry Aldrich series with Jimmy Lydon. During this time, Paramount also loaned her out to Monogram (*Are These Our Parents* [1944]) and MGM (*Young Ideas* [1943]).

A regular gag in the Aldrich features was for Charles Smith (as Henry's pal Dizzy) to wiggle his ears, which *he* was able to do. In *Henry Aldrich for President*, Noel wiggles her ears along with Smith, but she says, "They tricked it once, as I remember [*laughs*]. Jimmy Lydon was a very nice person. I know he went on to do many good things after that, even in production."

In 1946, when her Paramount contract expired, she claims, "I signed up with Monogram for seven of the Teenagers pictures but I only did four of them. You work pretty fast in those cheapies." In actuality, Noel's memory fails her as she *was* in all seven of the Sam Katzman–produced high school musical comedies that starred Freddie Stewart and June Preisser between 1946 and 1948. Admittedly, they weren't her favorites. "I don't care, you can say there were 20 for all I care. June Preisser was stuck up anyway. Only because she'd been in vaudeville 50 years before that, she thought she was a star. I didn't like her much. And vice versa I guess." One of the seven teenagers films, *Vacation Days*, was set on a dude ranch out west and featured western stalwarts such as John Hart, Terry Frost, Hugh Prosser, Forrest Taylor and Spade Cooley's band.

Noel's first true western was on loan-out to Hal Roach in 1943, *Prairie Chickens* with Jimmy Rogers (Will's son) and Noah Beery, Jr. "I remember working on that. We shot over at the lot in Culver City. All the 'girlies,' a couple that were fairly well-known in those days [Rosemary LaPlanche, Tommye Adams]. We called Noah 'Pidge.'"

Another western was *Over the Santa Fe Trail* (1947) with Ken Curtis and the Hoosier Hotshots at Columbia. "That's where I did the singing thing. They were trying to make Ken Curtis into another Gene Autry."

When it comes to Clayton Moore and their 13-chapter Republic serial, *Adventures of Frank and Jesse James* (1948), Noel had "no recollections" other than Clayton called her years later in an attempt to get her to appear at some autograph shows.

Republic produced a sequel to that serial in 1950, *James Brothers of Missouri*, replacing Clayton (who was by now the Lone Ranger on television) with Keith Richards as Jesse James. "Somebody sent me a picture of the two of us recently. In fact, Keith and I did a thing together in Florida, *The Greatest Show on Earth* [1952]."

Noel's westerns in the next few years with Whip Wilson, Lash LaRue, Johnny Mack Brown and Johnny Carpenter are a faded blur in her memory. "I'll tell you one thing about westerns. I never really met any of the guys. Outside of working with them, I just didn't know them. You come in and you get hairdressing, wardrobe, pages of script maybe, and sit and wait to do your thing and that's it. Sometimes you only work a day. I mean, you didn't even get a script actually, because the gals didn't have much to say. You know, get on that horse and ride and fall off or whatever you're supposed to do and then... [*laughs*]. I did see Lash LaRue somewhere a few years ago. He got into religion or whatever ... and we had a nice little conversation."

It's the unreleased *Osage* made in 1949 on the Gene Mullendore ranch in Oklahoma, that stirs a vivid memory for Noel, and for good reason. "What I remember about making that is trying to get my money. That was a problem. I wonder if [stuntman] Whitey Hughes ever got his? That was really made on a shoestring budget. Makes you wonder what you're doing down there." The unreleased, and now lost, *Osage* was directed by veteran Oliver Drake and also starred Edward Norris, former Oklahoman Bob Gilbert, singer and onetime B-western star Smith

Lash LA RUE
Fuzzy ST. JOHN

in

SON OF A BADMAN

MICHAEL WHALEN   JACK INGRAM · STEVE RAINES
NOEL NEILL · ZON MURRAY   CHUCK CASON · DON HARVEY
                          Released by SCREEN GUILD PRODUCTIONS

                          RON ORMOND   Ira Webb and June Carr
                                        Director — RAY TAYLOR
                          A WESTERN ADVENTURE PRODUCTION

Country of Origin U.S.A.   3 49/184

Showdown time for the *Son of a Badman* (1949) with Al "Fuzzy" St. John, Michael Whalen, Don Harvey, unidentified, Jack Ingram, Noel Neill and Lash LaRue.

Ballew and Johnnie Lee Wills, Bob Wills' brother. The film was produced through Sooner Pictures Inc. of Tulsa with much of the money coming from Bob Gilbert, who had appeared in B-westerns with Jimmy Wakely and Spade Cooley.

Noel's last western before turning to television was Johnny Carpenter's *The Lawless Rider* (1954), directed by Yakima Canutt. "Yak was a great stuntman. That was his original thing before he got into directing."

The role for which she'll always be remembered—ace girl-reporter Lois Lane—originally began with the first *Superman* serial for Sam Katzman at Columbia in 1948. "I saw it like *Jesse James*—something for the Saturday afternoon kids. For me, a month's work."

Noel's a bit harsh on her Superman of the serials, Kirk Alyn. "We didn't get along too well. He was a little conceited. I saw him not too many years ago on a *CBS This Morning* interview [February 1988]. He'd matured a little. He made a good Superman visually and doing stunts, I'll say that for him. But on interviews and at conventions, he'd dream up things, so to speak, to make it interesting. Many things weren't true, but that's what he had to do to make it interesting."

As for producer Katzman, Noel says, "I'd done the Teenagers and the *Brick Bradford* [1947] serial for him before that. His wife was quite a horse player. I had a lot of friends that would go to the track and we'd always see Hortense ... with her red hair, usually a fuchsia, or a lime dress and a silver mink [*laughs*], so we could all spot Hortense. She loved the horses."

Since she played Lois Lane in the two Katzman-produced Columbia Superman serials, *Superman* (1948) and *Atom Man Vs. Superman* (1950), one wonders why she wasn't immediately called upon when the TV series was being cast in 1951. Instead the role went to Phyllis Coates. "There were probably a lot of reasons. One side of town didn't know what the other side was doing. [Producer] Bob Maxwell talked National Comics into making 26 and then he did a *very naughty* (Noel *did not* explain this remark) and he was canned. So was what's her name, Phyllis Coates.

"Whitney Ellsworth was sent out from New York [as producer] to retrieve everything. He called and said, 'You were the original Lois Lane, so if you'd like to *reprise* the role...' and I said, well, why not? [*laughs*]. Thirteen weeks work ... yeah..."

According to the book *Superman: Serial to Cereal*, "the complexities of Robert Maxwell's nature soured many of the associations he maintained in 1951. He was appreciated better from a distance." Whitney Ellsworth, a pulp fiction writer in the 1930s, was hired as National/DC Comics editorial director in 1940. He had already been involved in other DC Comics-to–film projects—*Congo Bill*, *The Vigilante* and the *Superman* serials. It was he who tranquilized the violence of the Maxwell-produced episodes and brought a more comedic approach to the villains, and finally color to the series.

Noel Neill quickly became identified with the Lois Lane role in 78 episodes of the series—and still is to this day. Oddly, about halfway through the series, Noel's hair color changed and then changed back a season later. Her only explanation is: "I didn't have a hairdresser on the series. I had to get my hair done on weekends. Trying to find a hairdresser that did your hair

on the weekends was a bit of a stretch in those days. Of course, the last 52 were made in color and printed in black-and-white [because most early TVs were not equipped for color broadcast] so everything was a lot different. Wardrobe would come out red or blue or pink or whatever when they printed up black-and-white. That's probably what the problem was. And wardrobe—the hats were not my choice! Neither were the suits. That all came from wardrobe. Lot of strange costumes—the big hat I wore in the serials with Kirk Alyn, people remember that big white hat [*laughs*].

"We made a few bucks but we had the world's worst union. After playing Lois Lane off and on for nearly ten years, the most I ever pulled in was $225 per episode. The only thing we walked away with after that were the fond memories of our relationships. Back then we were doing two a week, 13 shows a year. Then basically a year off. It was impossible for me to bank more than a few thousand dollars. People think we're still getting money on residuals. No way."

As for her favorite directors, "We had three or four on the *Superman* series. Tommy Carr, nice. George Blair was really nice. Somebody else that was a real bear, but [*laughs*] Mr. Reeves spoke to him and simmered him down a little bit."

As to Noel's thoughts on the often disputed suicide of George "Superman" Reeves, "I don't know. Nobody knows what happened to him. They always say, you *must* really know. But I don't know what happened to him. I'd seen him just a couple of days before and he was happy and we were going to work again, had scripts out from New York already for another 26. He loved everybody. He was too nice for his own good. That may have been part of the problem. It was a shocker, I'll tell you."

Noel was married in 1953 "shortly

Noel staves off a severe disagreement between Jimmy Ellison and Johnny Mack Brown in the Jack Lewis–penned *Whistling Hills* (1951).

after I started *Superman*, to a gentleman named Bill Baron, from Santa Barbara. He's not in the business." They were married "about nine, ten years. I'm still in touch with him" but they had no children, "no rug rats [*laughs*]."

Yet it wasn't marriage that stifled her career. It was "typecasting. The marriage didn't make any difference in those days. Then the big studios folded and the casting directors all got laid off when the young turks from New York came out and screwed up the motion picture business. The oldies didn't have a chance. They wanted all young people, young people, young people. Jack Larson [who was cub reporter Jimmy Olsen on the *Superman* series] was into his writing, and he didn't care and I didn't care much. I'd done

enough work for a few years. So it didn't make any difference to me."

As for now, Noel says, "I'm just swamped. I'm looking at work thrown all over the floor, piled up ... out on the deck. I do PR work for a gentleman in the motion picture business. He did *Magnum P.I.* and is doing a lot of things now."

Superman made Noel Neill a household name but she sighs, "I haven't gotten a thing out of the series since 1965. I don't care if it's on or not. I don't have an ego. And the damn Internet—my name, address! God, I'm not going to have photos made. Stuff is piling up ... goes back to 1988."

In talking with Noel and discussing the amount of work she's done—and forgotten—she laughs, "It's just terrible, going so far back and realizing the movies I made over the years and thinking, gosh, what did I do that for? I don't live in the past. Some people do that, but I don't. Basically I'm just a homebody. I was probably a couch potato before the term was invented. I do enjoy loafing around. It's nice at my age."

Noel Neill
Western Filmography

Movies: *Prairie Chickens* (1943 United Artists)—Jimmy Rogers/Noah Beery, Jr.; *Vacation Days* (1947 Monogram)—Teenagers;

Over the Santa Fe Trail (1947 Columbia)—Ken Curtis; *Gun Runner* (1949 Monogram)—Jimmy Wakely; *Cactus Cut-Up* (1949 RKO short) Leon Errol; *Son of a Badman* (1949 Western Adventure)—Lash LaRue; *Abilene Trail* (1951 Monogram)—Whip Wilson; *Whistling Hills* (1951 Monogram)—Johnny Mack Brown; *Montana Incident* (1952 Monogram)—Whip Wilson; *The Lawless Rider* (1954 United Artists)—Johnny Carpenter.

Serials: *Adventures of Frank and Jesse James* (1948 Republic)—Clayton Moore; *James Brothers of Missouri* (1950 Republic)—Keith Richards.

Television: *The Lone Ranger*, "Letter of the Law" (1951); *The Cisco Kid*, "Chain Lightning" (1951).

Gigi Perreau

Everybody's Little Girl

Universal-International's child star of the 1950s was born in Los Angeles, California, on February 6, 1941. "On my birth certificate, it says Ghislaine Elizabeth Marie Perreau-Saussine. 'Theresa' was added later."

Gigi Perreau made her film debut at age two in 1943's *Madame Curie* and reached the ripe old age of eight before she made her first western, *Never a Dull Moment* (1950) with Irene Dunne and Fred MacMurray. "It was like TV's *Green Acres*, or *The Egg and I*—a city woman marries a rancher and faces many amusing situations when they go west to live. This woman has two kids—Natalie Wood and me. Natalie played my older sister. Andy Devine, who had a split in his teeth, was a very wonderful protector of mine. Natalie, *thanks to her mother*, would move this way or that way, and my face would be out of the camera. Mr. Devine would say, 'Cut. Gigi's face isn't in the camera.' That was very nice of him! I learned very early on, if you can't see the camera, the camera can't see you!

"There's an old Hollywood joke where they ask you if you can ride and the actor or actress lies and says 'yes,' and then heads for some stables to learn how! In my case, this didn't happen. My younger sister, Janine, wanted to learn to ride, so we'd already been riding. I could ride side-saddle before making this film! We took our riding lessons at Pickwick Riding Stables in Burbank. However, in the scene where I am to flip-flop over the fence, I did most of it but a double did the actual toss! However, I had to be dropped for the closeup!"

Since she was underage, a welfare worker had to be on the set. "You still had to go to school, until you were 18—Saturdays were the fun day. I loved working, but I didn't have a lot of time to socialize with the kids. They would put up a canvas dressing room, and you had to get your three hours of school whenever you could; you had to have it before four P.M. It was usually in a faraway corner where there would be peace and quiet."

Gigi was first under contract to Samuel Goldwyn. "Then I went to Universal-International. My parents didn't push—it just happened. I didn't have a business manager or any of those things people today deem necessary. At Universal, I sometimes made as many as five films a year!"

In late 1957 Gigi began work on *Death Rides This Trail*. "It was done at Universal-International. By this time, I was no longer under contract. However, they had been hiring me back again and again. They changed the title to *Wild Heritage*. We worked on it until the beginning of 1958. There was a lot of publicity about it, saying it was the first 'grown-up' picture for two former child stars, Gary Gray and myself. Also, there was a lot of publicity on the fact Gary and I were getting our first screen kisses [*laughs*]! It was also the 'first' screen kiss for Troy Donahue, Judi Meredith, Rod McKuen and Miss Sweden of 1957, Ingrid Goude."

Gigi at ten, elevated to stardom at Universal-International.

When asked about *the* kiss, Gigi amusingly smiles. "It was with Troy Donahue, on the back of a Conestoga wagon, as it pulls out at the end of the picture. I don't think you can even see it in the released print! This 'first kiss' [*laughs*] was kind of funny, and embarrassing. To screen kiss, you have to go to the corner of the mouth; cut your head to one side. It was cut and dried—not romantic at all. Also, I didn't have a *thing* for Troy. This was before he was a star, so it wasn't any big deal. Gary Gray says he doesn't even remember kissing Ingrid Goude[*laughs*]. You'd think he would remember that, wouldn't you? Also, Judi Meredith kissed Rod McKuen. Rod and Gary played my older brothers; Troy and Judi were siblings on a rival ranch."

The movie was shot both on the Universal back lot and, Gigi says, "we filmed a lot of it in Thousand Oaks, just off the Ventura Freeway, at Janss ranch. In those days, there were a lot of little areas in the

George Winslow, Maureen O'Sullivan, Rod McKuen, Gary Gray and Gigi around the campfire in *Wild Heritage* (1958).

Valley that were primitive with hills and dirt roads, so you could go on location fairly close to the studio!" In the film, Gigi laughs, "I wore those corset things under my dresses for the first time! I'd have to rest on a slant board, which looks like an ironing board, so I wouldn't wrinkle my clothes [*laughs*]!"

Asked about her many *Wild Heritage* co-stars, Gigi responds, "Judi Meredith is a pretty lady. In 1985, I was teaching at Notre Dame High and a boy came up to me and said, 'You know my mother, Judi Meredith.' We saw each other a few times at school functions. Ingrid Goude is a darling. She couldn't speak English very well and had to have a teacher." Maureen O'Sullivan? "She'd been my mother five years earlier on *Bonzo Goes to College*. I loved her, a delightful person. I used to go to her

home in Beverly Hills and play. Her son Michael, who was a couple of years older, was very nice ... and very good-looking. It was crush time. Tragically, he was later killed in a plane crash. Maureen's most famous child, Mia Farrow, was very little at this time." Will Rogers, Jr., was top-billed. "He was a simple man who was not confident with acting. It was not his thing." As for George "Foghorn" Winslow, "We went to school together. George was really cute with that funny, deep voice of his." As for her two other on-screen siblings, "Rod McKuen had the worst skin I have ever seen. No makeup could cover it up! He was unique—and already starting to write poetry back then. That was more important to him. He did some wonderful things, like writing the song 'Jean'; but acting wasn't for him. He was quiet and he was interesting, he'd tell stories—more of a storyteller than an actor. Gary Gray is like a big brother—he is close to my brother Gerald's age. Gerald later became Peter Miles, thanks to Lewis Milestone and being cast in *The Red Pony* [1949]. He now writes under the name Richard. When he got chicken pox, he was replaced in *Boy with Green Hair* [1948] by Dean Stockwell. Gary is fun, and it's nice to work with him. I still see him a couple of times a year. Gary and I first played siblings a dozen years earlier in Olivia de Havilland's *To Each His Own* [1946], for which Olivia won the Oscar! Gary was my oldest brother and Billy Gray played my other brother. Billy's actress-mother, Beatrice Gray, had to be on the set. In *Wild Heritage*, she played one of the family friends [married on-screen to former cowboy star Johnny Carpenter] saying their farewells to us, before we went west! So, I was seeing her again—but as an actress, not as a stage mother!"

Wild Heritage was given a lot of hype at the time. "Maureen's *Tarzan* pictures had just been released to TV, so that was played up big. They even said we were filming near where she'd made those films! She'd played Will Rogers' daughter in *A Connecticut Yankee* [1931] and was now playing opposite his son. The studio arranged for four of us, Gary, Rod, Judi and myself, to attend the premiere of June Allyson's *My Man Godfrey* [1957]. Gary drove, in his dad's new Lincoln [*laughs*]!"

Asked about any "real" dates with actors, Gigi states, "I had a big crush on Sal Mineo. We went to the premiere of *Six Bridges to Cross* [1955] together. Sal played Tony Curtis as a teenager in that picture. I also had a huge crush on Tony Curtis! He was the cutest thing back then. On my twelfth birthday, I was at the newsstand near the commissary. I mentioned that it was my twelfth birthday. He kissed me on my cheek—and I almost fainted!

I didn't want to wash my face again [*laughs*]!"

Gigi turned to television early on, but her first western wasn't until *The Rifleman* in 1960. "I did two of those. It was a wonderful show, and starred Chuck Connors. Johnny Crawford was this sweet, sweet kid. I remember Peter Whitney played the bad guy on one show ("Heller"). I went in to read and told them, 'I *have* to do this role! No one else can have it.' And I got it! It was so good, there was talk of a spin-off—but that didn't come together. I was abused by my father or stepfather. He's a bad man—I had slashes on my back! The girl (me) points a gun at him—he gets down on his knees and pleads for his life. It was such a meaty, wonderful role!"

Stagecoach West came later in 1960. "Wayne Rogers is very nice, but rather stuck up, a little aloof. He became an incredible multi-millionaire businessman. He rents dressing rooms to the studios!"

Gigi was back at Universal doing *Laramie*, then was cast in *Rawhide* (both in 1960). "I played a young novice nun. I have a still of me with Clint Eastwood. Clint is looking at me, in my nun's habit, chewing gum and blowing a bubble [*laughs*]!" Clint was very professional; in fact, everybody worked hard. There were no shenanigans and stuff like that. You were there on time, worked hard and knew your lines. People didn't pull *stunts* like they do today—showing up two hours late, for instance! I thought I was so lucky to be working. My parents taught me discipline. I was aware this was a job, like any other job. I enjoyed adults, and people thought of me as a little adult. Good or bad, I enjoyed being with adults."

When Gigi made *The Rebel* in 1960, "I got reacquainted with Carol Nugent, who was Nick Adams' wife. They had two kids who later played with my kids. Nick was an interesting guy, very ambitious, and a hanger-on who thought if he was around

At the dinner table in *Wild Heritage* (1958) are Eddie Parker, Guy Wilkerson, Christopher Dark, Casey Tibbs, Maureen O'Sullivan, Gigi, Rod McKuen and Gary Gray. George Winslow has his back to the camera.

these people, something would rub off on him. Nick particularly liked Bobby Darin when he was married to Sandra Dee. I'd be at their house and Nick would call, saying *he* was coming by! I'm not like that at all—not pushy and persistent, but I never had to be. In fact, it was no letdown when it was over. I have no problems like what Paul Petersen says he has. I see him every June—several former child stars go to Donna Reed's hometown—and do a workshop. Shelley Fabares, who had no problems, is the president of the Donna Reed Foundation."

From 1961 to 1962, Gigi was a regular on the ABC adventure series *Follow the Sun*, which starred Brett Halsey (*Four Fast Guns* [1959] and several Italio-oaters), Barry Coe and Gary Lockwood. "Brett and Barry were both charming, delightful young guys. Brett was dating Debbie Lowe, who had married Tyrone Power and had his child. I was newly married and didn't really socialize with them. Acting was not a passion with them. Brett was not volatile—I never saw a temper. A little moody, but always professional. Both were great guys. Gary Lockwood, on the other hand, was younger than Brett or Barry. He later dated and married (briefly) Stefanie Powers. He was kooky, pushy and very into his career; more hot and cold, but a fun guy who was dating Tuesday Weld at the time we did the series."

In 1964 Gigi was a guest on *Gunsmoke*. "Miss Kitty was wonderful—the whole cast. It was a great experience. It was a bonus, doing the show."

Gigi's last western to date was an episode of *Iron Horse* (1967-1968). "Dale

Robertson was a movie star, now doing TV. He was wonderful, but a little over the hill."

Gigi Perreau was one of the first 50 to have a star on Hollywood Boulevard. "I was at the groundbreaking ceremonies, with my gold shovel. My god-daughter, who lives in the Hollywood Hills, occasionally goes down there—and has to clean it [*laughs*]! It was taken up when they were putting in the Metro—the subway system. Now it's back, so when tourists go to Gower, then walk to Vine, they have to pass over my star!"

As to her career in general, "I thought of it as a job. I think of it as having an interesting past—it is still the past to me. I love today and am looking to tomorrow. I'm grateful for my career—I learned from it. I'm working on my book,

Everybody's Little Girl, but can't finish it until I'm no longer working full time. I now teach drama at an all-girls Catholic school, which was the school I attended. When I retire from teaching, I plan to go back to acting!"

Gigi Perreau
Western Filmography

Movies: *Never a Dull Moment* (1950 RKO); *Wild Heritage* (1958 Universal-International).

Television: *Rifleman*, "Heller" (1960); *Rifleman*, "Death Trap" (1961); *Stagecoach West*, "Land Beyond" (1960); *Laramie*, "Dark Reward" (1960); *The Rebel*, "Don Gringo" (1960); *Rebel*, "The Promise" (1961); *Rawhide*, "Incident at Poco Tiempo" (1960); *Gunsmoke*, "Chicken" (1964); *Iron Horse*, "Death by Triangulation" (1967).

Mala Powers

The Cimarron Rose

The two-gun star of *Rose of Cimarron* (1952), Mala Powers was actually a child actress. "I was born Mary Ellen Powers December 20, 1931, in San Francisco, but I never used that name. Even as a small child, whenever someone would call me Mary Ellen, I would say, 'No, my name is Mala!' My family moved to Los Ange-

les when I was eight. That summer, my mother enrolled me at Max Reinhardt, Jr.'s, Workshop and I did a play. There was a live audience. I was hooked. I later did a play, *Star Board*, which an agent saw. I was eventually over at Universal, at nine years old, testing for a role in the Dead End Kids' *Tough As They Come* [1942]. I didn't get the part—Ann Gillis got it—but I did land a small, one-day job that was written in for a second day!"

Mala was bitten by the acting bug. "I did other plays and radio as well. In fact, I played the Joanne Dru part in the *Lux Radio* version of *She Wore a Yellow Ribbon* opposite John Wayne and Ward Bond. Later, I did a *Wagon Train* with Ward."

Radio work led to Mala's breakthrough film as a "discovery" for actress-director Ida Lupino. "Ida Lupino loved doing radio, *Suspense* and so forth. I met her doing radio. She liked what I did, so I read for *Outrage* [1950] and got it. Ida even directed the portrait sittings I did for *Outrage* so I would have the look Howard Hughes of RKO, who was distributing the picture, would like. Of course, Hughes did approve. The film was very ahead of its time, because it dealt with the subject of rape ... referred to as criminal assault in the film.

"Ida was an excellent director—she would protect you. If you dared to be original and try things, she was there for you. Ida had been at Warner Bros. and got mainly pictures Bette Davis didn't want to do. Ida didn't want the rejects, so, when she refused, she was put on suspension. That meant she couldn't work for anyone else either! She'd spend her suspension time visiting other sets, learning other crafts—the camera, the way directors worked. It was never mentioned or doted on that Ida was the only female director at the time. Ida Lupino was *not* a feminist. She was wonderful. There was always a lot of laughter. I was with her when she died [of cancer]."

Mala's best remembered role may be as Roxanne in *Cyrano de Bergerac* (1950) with Jose Ferrer. "That's what is recalled by more people, although I did an enormous amount of work—especially in westerns."

Her first, and best known, western was *Rose of Cimarron* with Jack Beutel, Jim Davis and Bill Williams. "I never ran into Jack Beutel again. He was a nice man, who just seemed to disappear. Jim Davis I would see occasionally. I liked Jim very much. Bill Williams I knew quite well—I worked with his wife, Barbara Hale, on several *Perry Mason*s." When asked if she did her own riding, Mala's quick to respond, "I was told by the producer, Edward Alperson, there would be very little riding for me in the picture; that the girl who played in their last picture hardly rode at all, as she had a mask over her face most of the time. I only wore a mask in one little sequence. I ended up doing almost all of the riding! I had to learn to ride for that picture. I went riding two, three hours a day at Ace Hudkins stables. The very first day I had to ride carrying the rifle. The horse was galloping and every time we moved that rifle butt would go into my stomach. By the end of the day, I was so bruised it was unbearable. I loved horses, but it was brutal. Two great stuntmen, Tom Steele and David Sharpe, taught me how to handle guns. They worked with me two or three days each week! And the hard work shows on screen!"

When reminded stuntwoman Polly Burson was in the cast, Mala remembers, "She doubled me on the horse to train transfer—but that's about it. All the other times, I did it myself. I guess it kept Polly from earning a larger paycheck! She was a great stunt rider, so competent ... and a good, nice person."

Another western was *The Storm Rider* (1957) with Scott Brady and Bill Williams (again). "Scott and I got along just fine. Of course Bill and his wife, Barbara, were old friends by now. My part was a feisty Texas girl. She had spunk, owned her own ranch, hired and fired people. I enjoyed playing her!"

As to *Yellow Mountain* (1954), "We

To Boyd—
I've got
you in my
sights!
'Rose' and
Mala Powers

EDWARD L. ALPERSON *presents*

ROSE OF Cimarron *in* **NATURAL COLOR**

starring JACK MALA BILL
BUETEL·POWERS·WILLIAMS

with JIM DAVIS · BOB STEELE · WILLIAM PHIPPS · DICK CURTIS · MONTE BLUE · ART SMITH · LILLIAN BRONSON · IRVING BACON · ALEX GERRY · TOM MONROE
Directed by HARRY KELLER · Associate Producer EDWARD L. ALPERSON, JR.
Written by MAURICE GERAGHTY · An Alco Production · Released Through Twentieth Century-Fox

Mala, as *Rose of Cimarron* (1952), is about to avenge the death of her Indian parents.

had Mojave Desert locations. Lex Barker and Howard Duff were my co-stars. Lex was married to Lana Turner at the time, and Howard was married to Ida Lupino. Lana and Ida would come up frequently on weekends, so there were a lot of laughs."

For *Rage at Dawn* (1955) with Randolph Scott and Forrest Tucker, Mala recalls, "I was on my honeymoon during that! We went up to Sonora and Columbia, California—near Sonora. It was October and we had a wonderful Indian summer. We actually lived in Sonora. Randolph Scott and his wife had dinner with my husband and me almost every night. He was so delightful and solicitous and charming to us. I couldn't say enough nice things about him. My husband and I got this great guest cottage at the ranch of

the man who did all the catering. A stream ran right by—it was so romantic. I didn't work every day, so it was just great! Forrest Tucker was a good guy—all my 'brothers' were fun. J. Carrol Naish had a great sense of humor!" As for the color photography, "My hair photographs dark in black and white; in color, it was given a reddish tint. They often did that in those days, when you made a film in color. Never, after the first three roles I did ... *Cyrano, Outrage, Edge of Doom* [1950] ... did I ever find characters that had the depth or the interesting nuances those three characters had. Certainly in the westerns I did, there wasn't a lot of definition to the female character. I think perhaps *Rage at Dawn* had more of that because it was about a gal who had seven brothers, all bad men. I played her as

Mala is a bit indignant as Scott Brady gives instructions to her and William Fawcett in *The Storm Rider* **(1957).**

having that same kind of anger within her, except she used it in a moral direction, whereas they used it in an immoral direction. She had more complexity than other western heroines I played."

Sierra Baron (1958) starred Rick Jason and Brian Keith. "They *did* use a double on me in that, and I was quite upset with the results. I was supposed to be running around the desert—and the *man* they used was awkward—he ran through the desert in a dress like mine. I saw the rushes and was quite upset over the results. I didn't even know they were filming that sequence—they just *did it* with this guy. We shot for six weeks in Mexico, stayed for awhile in Mexico City. It was a fun trip, as again, I didn't have to work every day."

Among Mala's many TV appearances was a *Wild Wild West* episode with Robert Conrad and Ross Martin. "I used to date Ross, and I was very familiar with the show before I did it. It was fun, and a plus, working with Ida Lupino [as an actress in this]; and Patsy Kelly was an oldtimer who was also a lot of fun. I loved doing this show. There was a lot of clowning. However, I saw the new feature version of *Wild Wild West* (1999) and I thought it was just awful!"

Mala was a frequent guest star on episodic TV westerns. She calls Clint *"Cheyenne"* Walker, "very giving, a real gentleman." The same cannot be said for Steve McQueen. "Steve liked to be a bit abrasive. He kind of enjoyed that. If he

Mala in the seldom-seen *Sierra Baron* (1958).

could shock you, make you go up, he would do it. For instance, he wouldn't say someone was expecting a baby, he'd say she was knocked up. That sort of thing."

Rawhide (1959–1965) starred Eric Fleming and Clint Eastwood. "My scenes were with Eric—I didn't have any with Clint, who very nicely made a point of introducing himself and welcoming me to the show. No one *ever* does that—but Clint made me feel at home working on the show. I played a woman with leprosy, and that made it more memorable than a lot of others."

"I did a 1959 first season *Bonanza* with Pernell Roberts. We never dreamed television history was being made with that series. Michael Landon had a great sense of humor." R. G. Armstrong, a frequent co-player with Mala, was in this episode. "R. G. and I had an emotional

scene as father and daughter. He is always there for you—he supports you, he reacted to me in that scene. He is a terrific actor."

Another show was *Maverick* with Roger Moore in 1961. "What I remember best is the long, long wait we had. Roger and I were both on horses. We must have been sitting there for 40 minutes. I don't know what caused the delay, but we talked about England, Roger's life and how he got into pictures."

In the four-episode 1960 *Walt Disney Presents* version of *Daniel Boone* with Dewey Martin, Mala played Rebecca Boone. "There was a scene in a stockade—I was in close contact with a lot of children. After we shot the show, I came down with scarlet fever, which I must have contracted from one of the kids. I was already finished filming when it struck. I had a difficult recuperation. All of the episodes were made on sound stages on the Disney backlot in Burbank. I always felt the reason the show was not more successful was, we basically made the same script four times. The plots were almost exactly the same. There was little room for any character development. Nevertheless, I was sorry to see the series end. Dewey Martin I knew from when we were both at RKO. We worked hard to develop a good and interesting relationship between Daniel and Rebecca, but the scripts didn't give us much help."

Mala landed the *Boone* series because of a 1960 *Sugarfoot* she'd recently completed. "I loved that show—and Will Hutchins is a handsome doll. There was this stone statue and I got to whack the head off of it! It was a good role. In fact, in those westerns, I got to play a variety of roles—not just the sweet ingenue who has little to do. My parts had a lot of meat to them! In a *Bronco* [1958–1962] I played a real plain Jane girl—who falls for a man full of revenge."

Mala worked with John Payne in *Restless Gun* (1957-1959). "I liked John a lot, he was very relaxed. We socialized with John and his wife, Sandy. It was a pleasant set. One cowboy star I loved was Barry Sullivan, but, unfortunately, I didn't get to do a *Tall Man* with him, although we worked together out of westerns! He went out of his way to be supportive ... to help you."

Although Mala is no longer involved directly in the motion picture industry ("I would never go nude and I hate the way they kiss in pictures these days"), her life is very full and active. "I've done voiceovers, I narrate children's books, and right now am involved in two different books— a book on Michael Chekhov [Russian actor-director noted for Hitchcock's *Spellbound* (1945) and founder of the Chekhov method of acting], and a book of quotes about acting—from actors. I also teach, lecture and have written the pilot for a TV series."

Regrets? "My dream was to work with Laurence Olivier." Mala Powers is a gracious lady with lots of interesting stories to tell.

Mala Powers Western Filmography

Movies: *Rose of Cimarron* (1952 Fox)— Jack Beutel; *Yellow Mountain* (1954 Universal–International)—Lex Barker; *Rage at Dawn* (1955 RKO)—Randolph Scott; *The Storm Rider* (1957 Regal/Fox)—Scott Brady; *Sierra Baron* (1958 Fox)—Rick Jason.

Television: *Zane Grey Theatre*, "Black Is for Grief" (1957); *Wagon Train*, "Ruttledge Munroe Story" (1958); *Wanted Dead or Alive*, "Til Death Do Us Part" (1958); *Restless Gun*, "Take Me Home" (1958); *Restless Gun*, "Lady and the Gun" (1959); *Bonanza*, "Diedeshiemer Story" (1959); *Tombstone Territory*, "Female Killer" (1960); *The Rebel*, "Take Dead Aim" (1960); *Cheyenne*, "Alibi for a Scalped Man" (1960); *Bronco*, "Montana Passage" (1960); *Sugarfoot*, "Corsican" (1960); *Walt Disney Presents*, "Daniel Boone" (regular) (1960–1961); *Cheyenne*, "Trouble Street" (1961); *Maverick*, "Dutchman's Gold" (1961); *Lawman*, "Blind Hate" (1961); *Rawhide*, "A Woman's Place" (1962); *Wide Country*, "Man Who Ran Away" (1963); *Wild Wild West*, "Night of the Big Blast" (1966); *Daniel Boone*, "When I Became a Man, I Put Away Childish Things" (1967); *Here Come the Brides*, "Fetching of Jenny" (1969).

Madlyn Rhue

Beauty, Talent and Bravery

"The alienation that starts in society came into my life with great force. It was multiple sclerosis." Diagnosed with the affliction in 1974 after being one of television's most prolific actresses throughout the 1960s and '70s, Madlyn Rhue was determined the disease wasn't going to deter her career. "I didn't tell anyone because all I had was a little drooped foot. Then I had to walk with a cane. Then two canes. The wheelchair came in 1981, and I was confined to it totally in 1987." Madlyn had a recurring role on *Houston Knights* (1987–1988) playing a wheelchair-bound police officer. "Someone wrote, 'She acts better in a chair than other people do walking around,'" she smiles. There were also multiple guest appearances on *Murder She Wrote* in the 1980s, thanks to star Angela Lansbury, "who always opened her heart to the old guard because of the way Hollywood often throws away older stars like yesterday's garbage."

It was then that "painting became the second most important thing in my life. In 1980, James Cagney sent me to study with Sergei Bongart in Roxburg, Idaho. Later, I enrolled at UCLA and studied art for three years. Art has been a lifeline to all my feelings. At first, my paintings were of solitary people, isolated or turned away. Then they became realistic, my friends, children, pets. Angry abstracts turned to still life, clowns and romantic florals."

Madlyn's art has been exhibited and sold since about 1980 in many prestigious galleries around the country. Now, due to her MS, "I'm learning to paint left-handed. I've been working on one painting for a year. Some people would have said, 'Oh, I can't do that,' they would have just given up."

At this stage, completely bedridden at the Motion Picture Hospital in Woodland Hills, California, her upbeat attitude and smile are an inspiration to many—even to those who work there and care for her needs. Madlyn was excited at the prospect of this interview and relating incidents in her career.

Born Madeleine Roche in Washington, D.C., "in 1935" (she wants it corrected from many published incorrect dates), Madlyn always wanted to be an actress. After Los Angeles High School and Los Angeles City College, she went to New York to study at the Curt Conway Studios. During this time, she was also dancing at the Latin Quarter. "Curt let me teach the beginning class so I could go into the advanced class without paying. I also think he had a crush on me." She played summer stock for several years with a big break coming when she appeared in *Two for the Seesaw* at the Civic Playhouse in Los Angeles.

The name change from Roche to Rhue came back east. "I made that up in

It's been written, "Madlyn Rhue acts better in a wheelchair than other actresses do walking around." Madlyn has bravely battled crippling MS since 1974.

New York City. Well, I didn't, a PR guy named Saul Rubenstein decided to give me the name Rhue. He wanted it spelled Rue, like the street. He said then everyone would know how to say my name. I wrote to my mommy and she didn't think it looked so good. She said to put another letter from your original name in there, like the 'h' or something. So I sat down and I wrote it several ways and finally decided 'Rhue' looked the best. I changed Madeleine to Madlyn because people were calling me Madeline ... like the little girl in the cartoon." For years, publicity claimed when she was looking for a name that she recalled the James Cagney film *13 Rue Madeleine* (1946) and selected the name, since she'd grown up thinking her father was French.

One of her earliest TV appearances was an unbilled role in a 1958 *Have Gun Will Travel* episode. "Richard Boone was going with a girlfriend of mine, on the sly, 'cause he was married. And every time rent was coming up, and we didn't have it, one of us would do his show. But I can't reveal her name, because that was his foolaround."

"But in the beginning, a woman named Lillian Small took me on immediately. I went out two days later for two different jobs, and I got both. One was called *The Court of Last Resort* and the other was *Walter Winchell File*. On *Walter Winchell File* I was to play a showgirl, show my boobies and everything. But the *Court of Last Resort* ("The Stephen Lowell Case") had a lot of crying and my husband was in jail and there was a lot of stuff going on, so I picked *The Court of Last Resort*. Really, I should have done the other, but I thought about it, because I wanted to be an actress, I didn't want to be known for my boobs. But I finally got to dance in the movie *Kenner* [1969] that I did over at MGM ... with Jim Brown, the football player."

One thing stands out as you glance through Madlyn's TV credits: She seemed to basically do one of everything, seldom repeating a guest appearance on the same series. And the westerns were plentiful. "Well, I wanted to do everything. But I worked at Warner Bros. an entire year. I went from one western to another. I'd have like a week off and then I'd do the next one. I wasn't under contract, I didn't want

to be, because you got $750 if you were a guest, and if you were under contract, you got $300. El Cheapo ... Jack Warner."

From all those guest shots, Madlyn says the one that stands out is "Clint Walker, *Cheyenne* ... I really liked that ["Prisoner of Moon Mesa" (1959)]. That had a *faux pas* that was caught by a lot of people. As I went through a door, Clint was carrying me, and as we did, I changed clothes. I'd done the inside stuff in a green print dress. And I went out in another green print dress ... totally different dress. The script clerk told wardrobe to get the green print dress so wardrobe went and got the green print dress, but the wrong one!"

Madlyn could also be very versatile — an ingenue one week, a vixen the next week. Then there were the ethnic parts. "Wasn't it fun? I tried to do different stuff. When I was at Warner Bros. so much, Les Martinson, the director, got a script for *Bourbon Street Beat* [1959–1960] called 'Portrait of Lenore,' which was my mother's name. As soon as he got this script, he said, 'Get me Madlyn Rhue.' And they said, 'Madlyn won't accept this.' He said, 'Send it to her.' They did and, of course, I called them right back and said, yes, I love it, I want to do it. And that was a show where you never saw my face. It was either the back of my head or if you saw me coming forward. I had a real thick, black veil over my face. I was playing a woman who was badly scarred. I did the entire show with just my voice, which is why I jumped at it. I just thought that was such fun to do."

As Madlyn appeared in over 25 western TV series, we asked about her relationships with her various leading men, starting with *Black Saddle* (1959–1960) and Peter Breck. "He was quite wonderful. Very controlling, about everything, but, of course, you know, when a man is controlling about what he says and what he does on the set, he's said to have integrity. If a woman does it, she's a bitch. That's the way it is. So I really liked that he had integrity."

Riverboat with Darren McGavin (1959–1961). "Oh, that was the most fun," Madlyn squeals. "Vera Miles and I got so much publicity out of it because it was like 103 degrees [on the set]. I had to throw a drink at her face and she loved it. She said, 'That's the only way to cool me off.' She said, 'I don't care how many takes it takes…' And I kept throwing all this cold water on her and she was so thrilled [*laughs*]. But they got a lot of snapshots and it hit all the papers."

There was a *Rebel* episode with Nick Adams in 1959. "Oh, God … oh, yeah! He had a Bob Conrad complex. Nick did. Robert himself didn't. I tried to kind of scrunch down because my boots had heels on them and Conrad said, 'Stand up straight. I don't care if you're a few inches taller than me.' He was real sweet about it. But Nick was not. He was like, 'Have her wear flats … does she have to wear boots?' At that time I was 5'3½", but I was so long-legged … 31" inseam. I used to say I was 5'7" because that's what I looked like 'cause I was all legs. All legs and boobs. That was it [*laughs*]."

Dale Robertson starred on *Tales of Wells Fargo* (1957–1962). "That was the best. Dale Robertson also starred on *Iron Horse* (1966–1968), so I did two with Dale. Gary Collins was in *Iron Horse* … and Sam Fuller directed it ["Man from New Chicago" (1966)]. He was wonderful. He said to me, 'Don't you think this scene sucks?' I said, 'Yes, terrible.' He said, 'Well, I've written something else for it. How about this?' He handed it to me and he handed it to Gary and we said, oh, this is great and he said, 'Okay, we're going to shoot it now.' So we were learning it as we were walking up to the set. But we had it as soon as we got there, it was so much

better than what was written. Sam loved it, he knew that I could think on my feet and was a quick study and he could change things and I went with the program." Even though Fuller had a reputation for being a little bit of a wild man in his directorial efforts, Madlyn scoffs, "It didn't matter. It was Sam Fuller. You knew he was wonderful and you knew you were protected and you knew he wouldn't let you be bad. He didn't print anything he didn't like. When he said 'Print, we're ready for another shot,' then you just relaxed and went with it, 'cause you knew it was his vision."

Madlyn also did a 1959 *Gunsmoke*, which was the biggest show on the air at the time. "I loved Miss Kitty. I said, 'Did they have eyelashes back in those days?' And she said, 'No, but I'll be damned if I'm going to be filmed without them.' So I went over to the makeup guy and I said give me some eyelashes, so he gave me some too [*laughs*]."

There was a *Laramie* with John Smith called "The Pass" (1959), which takes place entirely in the snow. "Oh, God! I got my period up in the snow and John Smith said, 'You're bleeding.' I said, 'When I get up, cover it, and stay right behind me.' My mother had come to see me on the set and John walked with me, like Cary Grant and Katharine Hepburn in that movie where her skirt was torn, and he walks up right next to her. Well, John was right on top of me, with his hand around my waist and we walked off to the ladies room off the set. Bless his heart … and we walked past my mother and my mother was horrified. This was racy show folks [*laughs*]. Her mouth dropped open and I could see this look on her face like, what *are* you doing? I taught you better than this. I went to the bathroom, got all fixed up and cleaned my skirt and everything, then I went back and told my mother why we were doing that. Then she

Besides her extensive western television credits, Madlyn appeared in scores of other programs including the short-lived CBS series, *Executive Suite* (1976–1977) with Percy Rodrigues and Mitchell Ryan.

said, 'Oh, well, he's so sweet...' I said, 'Yes, he was.'"

The one western TV episode Madlyn really enjoyed was the one she did with Sam Peckinpah of *The Westerner*. "Sam Peckinpah directed 'The Painting' [1960]. He came over to me the first day and said, 'Do you want some coffee or something?' I said, 'Oh, yes, please, with lots of milk and a sweet roll.' Well, he got it and brought it back and sat down next to me and he said, 'What is it?' I said, 'What's what?' He said, 'Why do I feel I have to take care of you?' And I looked him straight in the face and I said, 'Because you do.' He said, 'Yes, I do.' After that, he just took care of me. All day long [*laughs*]. He kept in touch with me by phone. In-

terestingly enough, he was always kind of drunk. But he'd get on the phone and call me and he'd say, 'I was just thinking of you.' He also did some funny things. He came over to me one time and said, 'Madlyn, do you know that that's the worst Spanish accent I've ever heard? Not only that, it sounds familiar. Who were you doing?' I said, 'Katy Jurado.' He said, 'Oh, my God, you're right. That is her.' I said, 'That's how I do my accents. I pick a person and I imitate them.' He laughed, 'You're right, I've worked with Katy, and I hate the way she speaks.' I said, 'Oh, I didn't know that or I would have picked someone else, Rita Moreno or somebody."

Later in Madlyn's canon of westerns came *Hotel de Paree* (1959–1960) with Earl

Holliman. "Earl and I have remained friends. I went to the Emmys with him one year. Earl Holliman is one of the great dancers of all time, ballroom dancing. I mean unbelievable. We danced at the party afterward, and the bandleader played an extra round of the song because everyone kind of backed away and left a big space for me and Earl to dance in. We were so good together. I never forgot that. It was like the best time I ever had. That's Earl."

Bonanza was one of TV's most popular westerns from 1959 to 1975, 430 shows. "In one I did with Ricardo Montalban ["Day of Reckoning" (1960)] we played Indians. I loved playing with Ricardo. It was right after the writer's strike and in the unemployment line was Ricardo, myself and Inger Stevens. We all three came at the same time for unemployment, when the writer's strike was on. We made a deal, whoever got the first job had to take the other two out to dinner. Then Ricardo and I were hired for the same *Bonanza* episode. I told him, 'If we play this right, we just have to take Inger out once.' He started laughing."

Will Hutchins was, in person, very much his character of *Sugarfoot* at Warner Bros. Television. "The next time I saw him, I was doing *Streets of San Francisco*. We had a circus background and there was this circus in San Francisco. Will Hutchins was a clown with that circus." Hutchins actually traveled all over the world with that clown act.

As for Robert Horton, while filming an episode of his *A Man Called Shenandoah*, Madlyn recalls, "A guy from *TV Guide* came to do an interview, do an article on Bob, and he said to me, 'Do you find it difficult to work with a temperamental actor like Mr. Horton?' And I said, 'No, no, no, no, no, no…' He said, 'No, you don't find it difficult?' I said, 'No, I'm not going to answer that question. No matter how I answer it, you could then say I don't find it difficult that he's so temperamental, and I didn't say that.' So instead, he gives me short shrift in the column and prints something like, 'As his leading lady this week Horton has the multi-layered eyelash lady.' I mean, something really nasty … I loved it [*laughs*]."

Some egos in show business are larger than others. "Fess Parker didn't have one at all. He and I used to play and kid around and joke and laugh. We had the best time. I loved him. He was very special. He has vineyards and what have you. Too bad he couldn't invest well [*laughs*]. He and I were both with the same business manager."

Madlyn tells me *Stagecoach West* (1960–1961) "was very important to Wayne Rogers and I, because Wayne got sick the first day and he had to take medicine throughout the night. So I sat up in the chair in his room, stayed up all night long and set the alarm so I could get up and give him his medicine so we could work the next day. It worked out fine 'cause the medicine worked. He slept. I was falling asleep at four o'clock the next day; I couldn't keep my eyes open. Then an ex-boyfriend of mine came on the set and just made me so unhappy. I think it was Vic Damone. So Wayne returned the favor and let me cry on his shoulder."

When Madlyn worked with a then up-and-coming actor named Clint Eastwood, she noticed his potential. "The only thing was, the show I did was the last show of the season and they were both clenching. They couldn't look at each other without laughing. Eric would get out a line, Clint would go to answer and he'd start to laugh. Clint would get out a line and Eric would start to laugh. So when it came time for my closeup, we started and the two of them were punching each other and laughing so hard, I said, 'Get them out of here!' So I ran the lines with the director

THEY CRIPPLED HIS GUN HAND and left him nothing to face them with... but his COURAGE!

...OF GUNS

...ONS ...BITED

ROCKLIN, ...HAL

HE RIDES TALL

TONY YOUNG · DAN DURYEA

JO MORROW · MADLYN RHUE · R. G. ARMSTRONG

CHARLES W. IRWIN and ROBERT CREIGHTON WILLIAMS · R. G. SPRINGSTEEN · GORDON KAY · a UNIVERSAL Release

Madlyn and Tony Young were married from 1962 to 1970. They only worked together in *He Rides Tall* (1964).

and the script guy. Because I couldn't do it with them, they just kept laughing and I'm the worst, if you start me laughing, it's over [*laughs*]. When I did *I Spy*, I started laughing around four o'clock and Bill Cosby and I and Bob Culp laughed until 5:15 and they finally said, 'Stop this for the day.' We were still laughing. We never got the shot as it should have been. We got bits and pieces. Then when they opened up the door, the air came in and we all sobered up. What had happened was, there was no air on the stage and it was really hot out, so it was close and once we started laughing we didn't stand a chance.

"We had such fun back then. They don't have fun now. Every once in a while, I'll see a couple of actresses shopping together or being together having lunch and

laughing or something, but when Susie [her friend Suzanne Pleshette] and I were young, and when we were working, if we didn't think we were right for a job, we'd call up the actress we thought should go in. We were very sharing and caring and giving with each other. Now, it's like ... cut your throat. There's not the play any more. At one time there was a group of us. Me and my husband [Tony Young], Connie Stevens and whatever guy she was going with, and Dorothy Provine and the guy with her. We all went on picnics and shot photographs together and had a good time. Even if it was for a magazine article or whatever. We had good times. They don't do that any more."

Madlyn's husband was Tony Young, whom she co-starred with in *He Rides Tall*

(1964). Young starred on the short-lived *Gunslinger* TV series (1961). "I remember meeting at Warner Bros. But he said he met me coming out of a theater, but he was so shocked by my language, 'cause I used the 'F' word. I was so angry at the theater people that I went to the manager and told the manager why. It was a Marlon Brando picture and that theater let people come in during the last ten minutes. They kept coming in with their 'I can't see, can *you* see? There's a seat over...' I was so angry because I missed the end of the picture. I was really involved with it. I went and screamed and yelled at the manager. When I got out, when we met Tony and some other people, I was still swearing and angry and his guests were too. I was just so furious! So Tony was glad I didn't remember meeting him. 'Cause he thought I was a bad girl [*laughs*]. We met in January of 1962 and we got married in December of 1962. We were married when we did *He Rides Tall*. As a matter of fact, he came home with the producer [Gordon Kay] and they were just groaning and groaning and I asked what's wrong and they said, 'The girl we hired to play this, she's bad, she's so bad.' Tony said, 'I wish you would...' So I did it. I wasn't supposed to do it and I didn't like working with him because there was another girl in the story [Jo Morrow] and I was jealous. 'Cause she was sexy and she kept playing up to my husband, or I thought she was ... my green eyes got greener and greener and greener." Tony and Madlyn were married for eight years. They divorced in 1970.

Madlyn feels strongly about others who are in a disabled position such as hers. "I think all people who are in a differently abled position have a choice. You can either be down and sad and grumpy and whiny or you can be up and smile and be happy to see everyone who comes to visit. Smile, 'cause no one wants to visit with a grumpy or whiny person."

Madlyn Rhue
Western Filmography

Movies: *He Rides Tall* (1964 Universal)—Tony Young; *Stranger on the Run* (1967 Universal TV Movie)—Henry Fonda.

Television: *Have Gun Will Travel*, "Deliver the Body" (1958); *Have Gun Will Travel*, "Hunt the Man Down" (1959); *Black Saddle*, "Client: Reynolds" (1959); *Riverboat*, "About Roger Mowbray" (1959); *Cheyenne*, "Prisoner of Moon Mesa" (1959); *The Rebel*, "In Memoriam" (1959); *Tales of Wells Fargo*, "Woman with a Gun" (1959); *Gunsmoke*, "Tag, You're It" (1959); *Laramie*, "The Pass" (1959); *The Westerner*, "The Painting" (1960); *Hotel de Paree*, "Sundance Goes to Kill" (1960); *The Alaskans*, "Disaster at Gold Hill" (1960); *Pony Express*, "The Last Mile" (1960); *The Outlaws*, "Ballad for a Badman" (1960); *Bonanza*, "Day of Reckoning" (1960); *Sugarfoot*, "A Noose for Nora" (1960); *Stagecoach West*, "Fort Wyatt Crossing" (1961); *Rawhide*, "Incident at Rio Deloroso" (1963); *The Virginian*, "A Portrait of Marie Valonne" (1963); *Daniel Boone*, "The Hostages" (1965); *A Man Called Shenandoah*, "Special Talent for Killing" (1965); *Laredo*, "The Would-Be Gentleman of Laredo" (1966); *Iron Horse*, "Man from New Chicago" (1966); *Wild Wild West*, "Night of the Bubbling Death" (1967); *Cowboy in Africa*, "Work of Art" (1968); *Guns of Will Sonnett*, "The Straw Man" (1968); *Men from Shiloh*, "Jump-Up" (1971).

Elaine Riley

Classy Lady

Of direct Irish descent, Elaine Riley (her real name) was born in East Liverpool, Ohio. Studying music and appearing in high school theatricals at 16, Elaine was chosen Miss Chic at the Cleveland Exposition. Traveling to New York at 18, she was a Powers and Hattie Carnegie model. Then, as she told me, "A judge that sat on General Sessions court invited me out to dinner. We met Tim Whelan for dinner that night, a director who was doing Frank Sinatra's first picture at RKO. During the evening, Whelan said to the judge, 'I think your girlfriend should be in Hollywood.' So they arranged an interview on top of the RKO building. Of course, I knew how to model, so it was a shoo-in. I mean, I knew how to handle myself. They signed me in New York City.

"At the time, I was signed to be in Frank Sinatra's first picture, *Higher and Higher* [1943]. I was one of the bridesmaids in the show along with Dorothy Malone.

"From there, the first big part I had after I'd been in Hollywood, probably two weeks ... I was in a scene with Bob Ryan. I was his girlfriend and we pulled up to a curb in a convertible Ford and he kissed me goodnight [*Gangway for Tomorrow* (1943)].

"On my second or third day at RKO, a talent fellow that took young talent around, so you could orient yourself, took me down on the set of Pat O'Brien's pic-

ture. They sat me up on one of these high stools to watch what went on in pictures. Pat O'Brien came over and started to talk to me and he knew Richard Martin, my future husband, who I didn't know at the time. Pat asked me to lunch at Lucy's, right across the street from RKO. So we went over and had lunch and while I was sitting with him, Judy Garland came over and I was introduced to Judy ... and I'd only been in Hollywood three days! It was fun, an exciting time.

"But certainly one of the most exciting things that happened to me was the first day I was on the set at RKO when I saw Richard Martin come through a door. That's the most exciting thing that *ever* happened to me. I was at the commissary for lunch. It held probably 250 people. I'm sitting probably 50 feet from the door, facing the door, and all these people were walking in. I remember Dorothy Dandridge and Harry Belafonte walked in together and, oh, what a gorgeous picture. I mean, there were two beautiful people. All of a sudden I looked up and here come two fellows through the door dressed in tuxes. I didn't know at the time who it was but there was Richard Martin and I thought who is *that*? That's the best looking fellow I've ever seen! My friend Bea turned around and said, 'Oh, he's just one of our young players.' And I said, 'Oh, he's really nice looking.' So I went back to my

Elaine, Tim Holt, Elaine's off-screen husband Richard Martin, Marshall Reed and Dorothy Vaughn in *Rider from Tucson* (1950), the only western pairing of Elaine and Dick.

lunch, but I'm thinking to myself ... what's wrong with you, you don't even know who this is, why are you feeling this way? About ten minutes later, over my right shoulder, I heard this voice say, 'Well, Bea, why don't you introduce me to the young lady?' I turned around and there he stood. I thought, of all these people, why is this happening?

"Well, Richard was going with somebody but I used to see him on the lot and he was always dressed so neat. I just thought that was one appealing fellow. But we never even talked about a date until ... it had to be eight months afterwards ... they took 130 of us to a lodge at Pebble Beach for Pat O'Brien's picture, *Having Wonderful Crime* [1945]. They put us in what they called Canary Cottage, a beau-

tiful place. The first night out, we were all going to have dinner in the lodge. I was in the cottage combing my hair. Everybody had gone to dinner and I thought gee, you know, it would be nice if I would have dinner with Dick Martin tonight. And I thought, well, that's ridiculous, we'll all be eating together, so that's out. I walked downstairs, there wasn't a soul around, walked around the building and sitting on the wall all by himself is Richard Martin and he said, 'I think it would be nice if you and I had dinner tonight.' Well, that was it. It was incredible ... just incredible.

"We were supposed to be at the lodge for ten days, but clouds every day, so we couldn't shoot. We were there three weeks. And we had the time of our lives. It was just such fun. Anyhow, we came back and he had to call his friend and I called my friend, the judge, and that was it. We started to date. We were married three years later [1946]. And it was perfect." The couple was married until Dick's death from leukemia September 4, 1994.

Elaine was under contract to RKO for about four years. "I was in a lot of pictures at RKO. When you're under contract, they put you in everything. I call it 'stuff.' I did Leon Errol and Edgar Kennedy shorts for Hal Yates."

Writer-director Yates came to RKO's shorts department after 20 years with the legendary Hal Roach and managed to breathe new life into the Errol and Kennedy comedies by both writing and directing. His idea was to make the shorts move so fast, even if they weren't funny, no one would have time to notice. As it was, Yates' entries *were* funny. Two of Elaine's best are *He Forgot to Remember* (1944) with Leon Errol and *Alibi Baby* (1945) with Edgar Kennedy.

"I was kind of brand new, and I thought, 'Gosh, if I can work with Hal Yates'; and here he was asking for me. I wish I could have done it all the time."

But suddenly, Elaine's tenure at RKO ended. "Finally, options are dropped or whatever, they just had no plans. They would regularly drop somebody or several, when your contracts come up. But I signed at Paramount before my option ran out. When I went to Paramount [in 1946] the first thing they did was loan me out to Hopalong Cassidy" (*Devil's Playground* [1946]).

Via four films, Elaine became one of William "Hopalong Cassidy" Boyd's most frequent leading ladies. "The first Hoppy I did was *Devil's Playground*. I looked at myself and I just wanted to die. It was the first time I had ever seen myself do a picture ... at least that big a part. I had never had any acting experience. My mother had given me elocution lessons. She didn't want me to have a New York accent

[*laughs*]. I had done a lot of plays and things in school. I had been exposed to that, and of course I had a musical background since the time I was five. So I was exposed to the public and it didn't bother me. But talk to painters. They say their painting is never done; that's why they never hang them in their house. So when I saw myself, I thought, 'Why'd I do that?' But now when I see them, I think, okay. I wouldn't have maybe spoken that rapidly or I wouldn't have done this or done that...

"But I just loved Hoppy's sidekick, Andy Clyde ... I loved Andy. He was such a neat guy. And of course Rand Brooks was a neat fellow. Still is. He used to have an ambulance service. We shot a lot of Hoppy's up at Lone Pine. Bill and his wife Grace would stay out there. She would bring brownies over on the set. There was a classy lady. Oh ... charming. And Bill Boyd was a very classy fellow too ... and very handsome. And a gentleman." On the films, Boyd had all of the say, Elaine states emphatically. "He obviously did, because he made all the decisions."

Another decision maker, according to Elaine was "the little French person Gene Autry used to have around. George Archainbaud directed I don't know how many pictures. That's somebody who really did call me back to work. I think partly because I could get the horse on the mark and there weren't too many gals who could.

"I learned to horseback in Central Park, New York City, English saddle. Never had been in a western saddle until I came to Hollywood. To learn western, I just got on a horse and Hank Potts [a wrangler] said, 'Kiddo,' he called everybody Kiddo, he said, 'Get on the horse, put your feet out and ...'—what else was it ... something else, I've forgotten. But English saddle, you ride with your knees. It was totally different. But I used to get on, ride with the posse with Carl Andre and those cowboys. I did all my own riding.

James Craven, William Boyd and Elaine in Hopalong Cassidy's *Strange Gamble* (1948).

"In fact, I remember replacing Beverly Garland in a picture. [Most likely 1953's *Texas Badman* with Wayne Morris.] They called me up and said she fell off the horse, she won't get back on, can you come up? And I said *fine*. It was a good part. Wayne was a neat guy. Really down to earth. I did that picture with him not too long before he passed away. I don't think he took very good care of himself. He was a little overweight, but a nice fellow." Morris died of a heart attack in 1959.

Who were some of the more interesting actors Elaine worked with over her years in Hollywood? "I loved Charles Laughton. And he loved me. He used to call me Chubbins. You meet somebody you have a rapport with ... it was kind of a fatherly type of thing, he was just so nice to me. I appreciated that. I did *The Big Clock* [1948] with him at Paramount but I ended up on the cutting room floor. Laughton loved people with class. He was a classy person. Miserable to get along with ... nobody liked him, but he took a liking to me. He put me in *The Big Clock* that Maureen O'Sullivan was in. Well, she and I really didn't look any different, two Irish gals, you know. She had dark hair and I had dark hair. The director was John Farrow, who was married to Maureen. Farrow wanted me to bleach my hair, which I wouldn't do, but I did wear a blond wig. I had the second lead in that picture, but when it came out, it was just totally gone. So, you know, I was younger than she was. She'd had seven children by then, but she still looked great. What a lovely person. You saw her on the screen and that's the way she was. But Charles Laughton. Wow, I just love him. His wife Elsa Lanchester was a neat gal. She was also in *The Big Clock*. They had a strange kind of marriage. They each had a wing in the house. They loved one another, but they didn't live together. When they'd greet one another, it was like dating. He was a very complex person.

"I also worked with Joseph Schildkraut, who was very strange. But very interesting to sit and talk to. Barbara Stanwyck. I did a picture with her. She was so professional, so down-to-earth.

"Another great time was when I had a part with Joseph Cotten on his television series that didn't go [*On Trial* (1956–1957)]. He was so nice and his gorgeous wife, Patricia Medina, was one beautiful woman. But what a gentleman.

"Then there was Charlton Heston. As I walked in on the set, he started looking ... interested in who I was. Lots of times, I've thought if I had been an aggressive woman, which I'm not ... I am in certain ways, but I never ran after a man or went after anybody in my entire life. If Richard Martin hadn't come up to me, that would probably have been the end of it. My mother just made me an independent woman. To me, it would be demeaning to do that. And Peter Graves ... whenever we'd work together in a scene, he kept looking and looking and I was looking at him too. The class ... Charlton Heston's a classy fellow."

Elaine worked with Gene Autry in one film and three TVers. "He was a sweetheart too. I have about two people in my mind, maybe three, that fell short of what I would say was, you know, nice. Not for any personal reason, anything they did to me, just statements they made. But aside from that, I got along with every-body. I think actors are a special group of people. Actors have a charisma about them, even the people in the craft part of the industry, as far as the sets and designers, they're all special. But Gene Autry is a doll. I spent a lot of time with Gene and [his sidekick] Pat Buttram on location in Pioneertown."

Pioneertown being a remote location, Elaine remembers, "We didn't have a personal phone. They had one probably in the studio, but at night anybody that wanted to use the phone, if Gene were going to town, Twenty-Nine Palms, he'd take you. So I'd always go down and call Dick. I'd drive down with Gene ... and he was just a nice man. Neat. I didn't go to dinner with Gene but I did go a couple or three times with Jocko [Mahoney]. He and I laughed. And Dick Jones. When I first met Jocko, they were making his TV series [*The Range Rider* (1950–1953)]. George Archainbaud was directing. And I thought, what a great guy Jocko is. He's tall and he was in shape. I think he had just come off being a stuntman type of thing. And oh, we laughed ... between him and Dick Jones ... a sweetheart of a man."

Elaine's memories of her *Leadville Gunslinger* (1952) co-star Allan Lane aren't so pleasant. "Smart aleck. I remember being in makeup one morning, we'd been in makeup together two or three times. I really didn't like him, which is very difficult for me to say. But I remember the makeup man was talking to me about Dick. I always talked about Dick in glowing terms, because it was true. And Allan said something about 'Oh, listen to her, making this marriage thing wonderful and all this.' And I turned and I said, 'You know something, I've always thought you'd probably make somebody a great boyfriend, but I think you've made some girl very lucky by staying single.' Then he'd get on the set and he would be nasty. Not to me, because I wouldn't take it. To

Elaine worked frequently with Gene Autry, as here in *Hills of Utah* (1951), also with Onslow Stevens.

people around him that couldn't talk back, he'd say something like, 'That wasn't right, you had the door wide open ... you can't do this.' I think what it was, was an expression of insecurity ... afraid he wasn't doing it right, so he'd be nasty in order to cover it up. He just made things nasty when there was no reason to have it that way."

Upstaging is another problem actors have to deal with from more ambitious, egotistical actors. Elaine's problem came from future senator George Murphy. "I thought, this is sad. Here he is a star and I've got probably five lines and I thought, this is stupid. Of course, I'd been warned by my coach, but the best actors aren't worried about doing that. They're into their scene. But my career was not life and

death ... I have another life, thank goodness, so it never was all-absorbing."

Completely the opposite, where some people had upstaging problems with Steve McQueen, Elaine told me, on the 1960 *Wanted Dead or Alive* episode she did, she "never had a moment's trouble with him. When I saw Steve McQueen, it was like Bob Mitchum ... they're not actors—it's personality and it's there. Bob Mitchum was Bob Mitchum. I knew Bob Mitchum. I did *Girl Rush* [1944] with Bob at RKO. The first time I'd ever seen him, he came on the set of that Frances Langford picture, and somebody said he's going to be the next big star. And I thought, oh? And he certainly turned out to be in *The Story of GI Joe* [1945]."

The other problem for a woman is

unwanted advances from male co-workers. "I don't know that I was ever made a pass at except one executive at one studio. I'll just go that far."

These situations aside, possibly Elaine's worst experience came from the Arizona heat while filming an episode of *26 Men* ("Man in Hiding" [1958]). "Hot? My goodness! I remember getting out of the airplane and it was like somebody had opened up the oven door. It was in July, or something. I'd never felt such heat before. It was just incredible. I remember we had an assistant director on that show that was a task master. Even with all that heat, you didn't have a chance to take any time off. I'd never passed out in my life before. Awful. They had me learning to drive a buckboard with two horses, a team, by myself. When I wasn't working, I had that team of horses out and I had all those heavy clothes on, a bonnet, the whole thing, taking these horses up and down trying to get the team to cooperate. I remember the director was fighting to get the scene because the sun was going down. I had to get out of the buckboard and run to the back and say something to somebody. I think it was the second take, I was running. *Now* I know what was happening to me but I didn't know then because I'd never felt that way. I got disoriented and had a headache that—oh! And I never had a headache. I remember jumping out of the buckboard, running back, and that's all I remember. That was it. I was laid out on the ground. That was the only time."

In 1958, Elaine appeared on a *Texan* episode with Rory Calhoun. "I remember Rory had an ego. [In certain scenes for the] cameraman he took his hat off, shook out his curls, put the hat back on. We were doing a closeup of the two of us and the cameraman said something about my blue eyes and his gorgeous blue-gray eyes, you know. I don't think he liked it. He wasn't too friendly with me."

In nearly 50 years of marriage, Elaine only managed once to work with her husband, Richard Martin, who from 1947 to 1952 was Tim Holt's sidekick, Chito Jose Gonzalez Bustamonte Rafferty, in an above-average string of B-westerns at RKO. The film was *Rider from Tucson* in 1950. "Working with him was great. You know something? This sounds like Pollyanna, but all the years that we were married, we were on a honeymoon. I mean, it was just wonderful. In fact, one night we were out dancing somewhere and a middle-aged couple stopped us and the lady said to me, 'Would you please excuse us, but I'm having a discussion with my husband. He says you're not married.' And I said, 'Only for 15 years.' So she said, 'See, I told you.' He said, 'I can't believe you two are married.' Because we always had something to say to one another. We'd go out to dinner, we'd walk down the street holding hands, it was wonderful. And we didn't argue.

"The biggest problem we ever had … the only one I can really think of … was when we moved here, to Newport Beach. I was upset. *I was upset!* I did not want to move down here. I loved my home in Encino. It was just gorgeous. It was my dream place. He really didn't discuss it with me. He just wanted to retire. He liked to fish, so he had an ocean here two blocks over. So that was a severe moment in our marriage. I took off with the King Sisters, friends of ours forever and ever and ever. They were going on a month's tour on a cruise ship. I said, I'm going on this vacation. That was the first time in my life I'd ever been away from him. I got on the ship. One night I'm sound asleep in my cabin and the phone rings, I guess it was three o'clock in the morning or something. It was Dick. Of course, there was never a thought of leaving him. I was just angry with him. I was angry because I really enjoyed my home. But he was an easy man to live with.

Meticulous about himself, about the house. Never had to pick up a piece of clothing. We had no children, which we planned. And it was right for us. So we had no stress. Life was a honeymoon."

Tim Holt was not only Dick's co-star, but a close friend as well. "They loved one another. Tim stayed at our house for eight months," Elaine explained. "What a sweetheart. And for me to let somebody stay in my home for eight months... [*laughs*]. But he was so thoughtful. It was after he and Alice broke up. I think that's why he came." Tim Holt was married to Alice Harrison from 1944 to 1952, but they were legally separated in March 1948. Tim's romance with leading lady Nan Leslie had begun in 1947.

"Tim's father, Jack. Oh, what a gentleman. That was a beautiful family. Look at Jennifer. But oh, Tim and Dick had a real camaraderie. They really did. And boy, Tim really did fabulous things ... got Dick raises ... he was just wonderful. Just incredible. I wasn't close to him when he moved to Oklahoma. He married Birdie and we kind of didn't keep in touch, but I think Tim finally found some happiness there."

Elaine kept her career going until 1960, whereas Richard Martin, with a couple of special exceptions, was typecast as Chito and quit acting when the Tim Holt series ended in 1952. "When Howard Hughes [of RKO] didn't pick up Dick's option, he decided he had to find himself something in life to do and Lee Bonnell [Gale Storm's husband] talked him into going into the insurance business. And, of course, it was great. He did real well. I just wanted to keep working. I was financially independent, so we didn't have to worry about that. Dick was making a nice salary. He was working in insurance and was making a lot of money. And I'm a great one for investing it and doing this and doing that with it.

"Basically, what happened, I took a live soap opera at CBS, *For Better or Worse* [1959–1960] and I was on that eight months. They were more or less theater actors rather than motion picture actors. I was wondering, 'How did I get this? My agent must have gotten it for me.' Obviously. I went over on CBS and read for Hal Cooper, who was the director, genius, oh, what a director! Got the part and never worked so hard in all my life! I lost 11 pounds ... my clothes were hanging on me. I was getting up at four o'clock in the morning. You'd come in to makeup and as soon as you got finished, you had a dress rehearsal. Then they'd break for breakfast! And at four o'clock in the morning when I'd get up, I was learning the script for that day. And the script would be *that thick*! There was no way you could learn the lines. So you had to rely on one another. You learned your cues more or less but there was no way you could learn everything. I'll never forget one morning, this was the first thing, the opening line of the script. This fellow and I were in business together and he was to run in and say either we had a robbery or a fire, I've forgotten which. Whatever he was supposed to say, he said the other one. Every time! That went on all the time, because people would blow their lines. It went on for eight months and I thought if I don't stop this, I'll... [*laughs*]. Also, when I was doing that, I had a sick father and he needed a lot of attention. I had too many avenues going. I was so glad to just get out of it. That's when we moved to Newport Beach."

Elaine certainly has no regrets about her career or her life. "I've had a Cinderella life. I met a great love in my life. Many people never have it. I didn't have to work at my marriage. We just were meant to be. And why that happened, I have no idea. When I hear people that can't get along because of their careers, I just simply don't understand it. I feel I'm very lucky. The most important thing in my life?—being happy. If you have a happy attitude ... that old saying, your attitude determines your altitude, I believe that. When Dick passed away, I'd heard so many widows say, 'Oh, I feel like a fifth wheel.' I have *never* felt like a fifth wheel. I have all kinds of invitations. I'm invited to parties. I'm invited to dinner out. I think I have something to offer. I read a lot, I know the current events, I read the paper for an hour and a half every morning. I think it's your approach to life that determines what happens to you. I've never been lonely in my life. I have missed my husband, but I have not been lonely. He would not want me to be lonely. No, he would not want me to. Again, I feel I'm very lucky."

Elaine Riley
Western Filmography

Movies: *Girl Rush* (1944 RKO)—Frances Langford; *Devil's Playground* (1946 United Artists)—William Boyd; *Sinister Journey* (1948 United Artists)—William Boyd; *False Paradise* (1948 United Artists)—William Boyd; *Strange Gamble* (1948 United Artists)—William Boyd; *Trailin' West* (1949 Warner Bros. short)—Chill Wills; *Rider from Tucson* (1950 RKO)—Tim Holt; *Hills of Utah* (1951 Columbia)—Gene Autry; *Leadville Gunslinger* (1951 Republic)—Allan "Rocky" Lane; *Texas Badman* (1953 Monogram)—Wayne Morris; *Pardners* (1956 Paramount)—Dean Martin and Jerry Lewis.

Television: *Range Rider*, "Six-Gun Party" (1950); *Lone Ranger*, "Gold Fever" (1950); *Range Rider*, "Gunslinger in Paradise" (1951); *Range Rider*, "Indian Sign" (1951); *Range Rider*, " False Trail" (1951); *Range Rider*, "Shotgun Stage" (1952); *Gene Autry*, "Bullets and Bows" (1952); *Gene Autry*, "Six-Gun Romeo" (1952); *Gene Autry*, "Sheriff Is a Lady" (1952); *Range Rider*, "Old Timer's Trail" (1953); *Hopalong Cassidy*, "Outlaw's Reward" (1954); *Cisco Kid*, "Schoolmarm" (1955); *Cisco Kid*, "Gold, Death and Dynamite" (1955); *Stories of the Century*, "Jack Slade" (1955); *Lone Ranger*, "Six-Gun Artist" (1955); *Fury*, "Joey Sees It Through" (1956); *State Trooper*, "Jail Trail" (1957); *26 Men*, "Man in Hiding" (1958); *The Texan*, "Jail for the Innocents" (1958); *Wanted Dead or Alive*, "The Partners" (1960).

Kasey Rogers

Isn't That Laura Elliott?

Call her what you may, she's given us hours and hours of entertainment on the big screen as Laura Elliott and on the small screen as Kasey Rogers.

The future co-star of Paramount A-westerns, Hitchcock's *Strangers on a Train* (1951), TV western guest star roles and long-running character roles on

Kasey was still known as Laura Elliott when she starred in the cult classic *Two Lost Worlds* in 1950 with James Arness and Bill Kennedy.

Peyton Place (1964–1969) and *Bewitched* (1966–1972), she began life in Morehouse, Missouri (circa 1926), as Imogene (long I) Rogers. Her family headed to California when she was two and a half. Studying piano from age seven, she switched to accordion and performed at the Hollywood Bowl, the Orpheum Theatre and other venues in an accordion band. First married at 19 ("for two or three years ... a wartime thing"), she had her first child, then became an Earl Carroll showgirl. Off that she was signed to a Paramount contract. It was here she gained the Laura Elliott moniker. "The song 'Laura' was just out and I thought it was beautiful." Laura was immediately put into the lead of the Pine-Thomas–produced *Special Agent* (1949) with William Eythe, a former Fox

star now making his final films before writing *Lend an Ear* which became a Broadway success with Carol Channing.

Other roles quickly followed including the female lead in the cult classic, *Two Lost Worlds* (1950). "It's such a kick with volcanoes and dinosaurs, and the leading man was James Arness. I understood at the time it was his first film." (Actually, Jim's first was *The Farmer's Daughter* in 1947 under his real name Aurness. *Two Lost Worlds* was, however, his first lead.) "Jim was very tall. When he met [producer] Boris Petroff for the first time, Jim's agent told him to sit down—and don't stand up. 'No matter what you do, don't stand up!' Because he would have towered over Petroff, and sometimes, if you're too tall, that's not good. So Jim sat through the whole interview, and he got the role [*laughs*]. Jim was a good actor to work opposite. We got along fine but never saw each other again. I didn't realize at the time they [the moviemakers] were matching things [from *One Million B.C.*, 1940] and were going to intercut. We shot some stuff in Red Rock Canyon in the northern California desert ... running. I was barefoot and Red Rock is a series of small pointed rocks ... sharp rocks! Talk about hurt. We tried taping the bottoms of my feet but it wouldn't stay on. Nothing worked. So I just ran across the rocks. It was uncomfortable to say the least [*laughs*]. Also, at lunchtime, I used to climb the nests of those big ships in the picture. I *was* a bit of a tomboy." Bill Kennedy was the third co-star in *Two Lost Worlds*. "He was always trying to upstage me. One time he had his arm around me as we were watching the volcano and he tried to bury my face in his shoulder. There were a couple of situations like that. That's where I learned about upstaging and how to protect yourself."

Laura was fortunate enough to work with legendary directors such as Capra, Stevens, DeMille and Hitchcock. On loan out to Warner Bros., she's most proud of her work in Hitch's *Strangers on a Train*.

In 1951 and 1952, Paramount teamed Laura with Edmond O'Brien in two A-westerns, *Silver City* (1951) and *Denver and Rio Grande* (1952). "Eddie was always outgoing and active. He had his family on location."

Laura had no problems with *Silver City* co-star Yvonne DeCarlo, whose future husband, Bob Morgan, was one of the many stuntmen on the film. But tomboy Laura told us, "I don't think *I* ever had a stunt double. *Silver City* was shot around Sonora, California. I'm jumping in the logging ponds, logs rolling out ... gee, you could slip and fall under and they'd never get you out of there.

"I learned to ride on *Denver and Rio Grande*. I was good enough to do all my own riding with all the guys."

Sterling Hayden as a ruthless engineer opposed O'Brien in the classic railroad film. Laura recalls, "He was very quiet and reclusive ... writing something. After work every day, he'd come back to his little bungalow and write, write, write."

Producer Nat Holt permitted director Byron Haskin to destroy full-size trains in the only train-wreck scene of its kind ever filmed. Laura was there. "The day before, 150 members of the press congregated, waiting for these two trains to crash. The sun was not right, it was too overcast. It was disappointing to Nat Holt that the press had to come back the next day. Then the sun was out and we all gathered umpteen hundred yards away from the trains because they were rigged with dynamite. Two engineers started the trains from opposite ends, and as they gathered speed, six to ten miles an hour, they jumped with the controls locked down. Stuntmen didn't know how to drive the trains. The special effects people had the trains rigged with dynamite to make it really explode when they crashed. Well, once the trains are put in motion on the track, they're not going anyplace else. When those trains hit, *man*, the smoke went and the fire and everything! Hunks of metal flew as far out as we were, although no one was injured. It was emotional. Those engineers just cried. They'd driven those trains for 50 years. It was very exciting. I'm very lucky. I have one of those gorgeous, big, brass-and-copper original chandeliers from one of the cars. It was filmed outside of Durango, Colorado. We stayed in Durango, then took those little narrow gauge track trains for an hour every day up into the mountains. I told you I was a tomboy. At night, coming in after work, I'd get up on top of the train cars with the stuntmen and run along and

The cast of *Silver City* (1951)—Edmond O'Brien, Yvonne DeCarlo, Michael Moore, Kasey (Laura) and Richard Arlen.

jump the cars. Oh, Nat Holt would have killed me if he'd seen me up there."

Laura thinks affectionately of Holt. "In making those two, I got to know Nat—a lovely person. He was a distinguished, white-haired ... I don't want to say 'old southern gentleman,' not that type, just a nice businessman. Obviously, very good at what he did, the action-western type things. I met his daughter Jackie, though we really didn't get to know each other. Years later, I did *Bewitched* [as Louise Tate, 1966–1972]. Interestingly enough, I never worked with Bernard Fox [Dr. Bombay] on *Bewitched*. About six years ago we had a little reunion and I discovered Jackie, Nat Holt's daughter, is married to Bernard Fox. So the four of us

have been very good friends ever since." (Holt produced several top flight Randolph Scott films—*Badman's Territory* [1946], *Trail Street* [1947], *Return of the Bad Men* [1948], *Canadian Pacific* [1949] and *Cariboo Trail* [1950]—along with many A-westerns: *Warpath* [1951], *Flaming Feather* [1952], *Cattle King* [1963]. He also produced Dale Robertson's *Tales of Wells Fargo* [1957–1962] TV series.)

The name change to Kasey Rogers came "when I left Paramount in 1953. I'd grown tired of being called something else; Kasey was my nickname and Rogers is my maiden name, so I took the name Kasey Rogers and in mid-career changed my name. So almost all my films are Laura Elliott and all my television is Kasey

Rogers. It's like two different actresses and very few people associate the two. I don't know how smart it was but at least I kept on working."

In checking credits, the actress was still billed Laura Elliott on screen as late as 1955 in a *Lone Ranger* episode. "That may have been the first TV show I ever did. It probably was what got me into television, because, in those days, you kind of looked down your nose at TV. 'Oh, I do pictures, I don't do television.' But having a little boy to support and, by then, being a single mother, I probably took the *Lone Ranger* job to put bread on the table. From then on it opened doors and I just worked, worked, worked. The only difference [with TV] is it's much faster. Film is so precise with lighting and reflectors and everything. I remember on some of these TV shows, the director, trying to pick up the pace, saying 'Action,' and as you're starting your first line, the guy is running up, putting a reflector in place, shoving it up so it's reflecting on your face [*laughs*]. 'Okay, print, next shot.' It's very fast. I did every type of role. It was interesting. For one casting director I would always be the saloon girl. For another I would always be the loving mother. For another I would be the society girl ... they just had their vision of the way I looked and that's what I did for them."

Before leaping headfirst into TV work, just after leaving Paramount, Laura/Kasey tried her hand at screenwriting. "I had written a screenplay and sold it to Universal and wanted to get some publicity about the writing. That's how I met my second husband who did public relations in the industry. It was written for film, for Audie Murphy. Since he was not available, they did it as a *Wagon Train*, which I didn't know until years later. I never saw it. My title was 'Little If,' but I don't know what title they finally used. It's the story of a young white man raised by an old Indian after being found or saved from a wagon train massacre. He's been taught to read but the only books his parents had were Shakespeare, so he speaks with a Shakespearean accent."

One of her first TV westerns as Kasey Rogers was a *Wyatt Earp* in 1956. "With what's his face, Hugh O'Brian. I don't want to eat these words later, but he had a monumental ego. We all grow up. That was just *his* growing-up period."

As for other TV cowboys, Kasey found Robert Culp (*Trackdown*, 1957–1959) a "nice man" but fell in love "with Dan Blocker of *Bonanza* (1959–1971). Not literally. I just adored him." She thought Gene Barry (*Bat Masterson*, 1958–1961) "appeared to have an ego, but was really a nice person. Gene was very well equipped to handle [being the star of a series]. It's a heavy load. I saw him inter-relating with some clients one time and he was wonderful." She "got along great" with Steve McQueen, the star of *Wanted Dead or Alive* (1958–1961). "We raced motorcycles together. He became a really fine motor-cycle racer. At one point, he went to Europe on the six-day international trials ... a very big thing, only six representatives from the U.S. go to compete. And you don't get chosen because you're Steve Mc-Queen, you go because you're good. We used to race over at Indian Dunes. I used to have black boots, with all white leathers, white shirt and white helmet. I'm on the track and I hear this great big bike coming up behind me. It roars by, the guy gets in front of me and grabs the throttle, which sends up a shower of rocks. They really pelted me in the chest and the face guard. When I got to the end of the course, I pulled off. All of a sudden, over comes Steve and says, 'Oh, my gosh, Kasey, I'm so sorry, I didn't know that was you.' That's the way boys play rough with each other. I raced for seven years, the Women's Nationals, I loved it."

There is some danger working very fast on TV westerns. Kasey frowns, "I don't recall which series it was, but there were two older gentlemen and myself and they were going to hang us. They put this foot-wide board out from a [hanging] platform and balanced it at the far end with a big barrel under it for support. We have to walk out on this 12-inch board and stand there while they put nooses around our necks, all three of us. I'm in the middle; they placed the nooses around our necks. We're standing there, waiting to hear 'Action,' and all of a sudden, one of these guys nudged me. His hands were tied so he motioned with his eyes—a 'look behind you' movement. I looked back and this prop man is tying down the nooses, which means, if a horse kicks over the barrel, we'd have had three hung actors. I told him to unloosen it! They weren't exactly thinking! You have to look out for yourself. Then I got myself shot in the leg once, with a full load wad, on camera. I was doing a fast draw talk show guest appearance against Art Linkletter's son. I used to do fast draw, twirl the gun and things of that sort, which I learned from stuntmen on *Denver and Rio Grande*. My gun had broken that morning, so I took my husband's, which was not a fast-draw gun. It was hard to pull back the hammer. When you do a fast draw, you slap for the gun, you don't just reach for it gingerly. I slapped, shot myself right in the leg, four inches from where it came out of the barrel. I still have powder burns on my leg from it."

One of her last TV westerns is one of her favorites, a *Maverick* spoof of *Bonanza*: "Three Queens Full" (1961). "[Jack Kelly] was thrilled to death to be brought in on a major series, so well established, right in the middle of it. I was seven months pregnant when I did that show. I went on the interview, said, guys, I'd love to do this, but I'm pregnant. They asked,

Dropping the Laura Elliott moniker, Kasey appeared on over two dozen television westerns.

'How pregnant?' 'Pretty pregnant.' But I always carried babies close in as opposed to out like a huge mountain. But if you'll notice in the scenes, I'm leaning over the back of a sofa ... or always have a big fan in front of me or a shawl walking down the street. They used to call me Little Mother. A month after Mike was born, Warner Bros. called: 'Kasey, what shape are you in? We have to do the fight scene over and we need you.' I said, 'I've had the baby, I can come to work.' When I walked on the stage, one of the girls said, 'What do we call you now that Mother is a dirty word?' [*laughs*]. That's the only scene, in the barroom fight, where I dropped the fan and had a full figure shot."

From there, Kasey became a regular on the popular night time soap, *Peyton Place* and segued right into *Bewitched*. Later, with her husband in public relations, she did a lot of writing ... from press releases to travel and fishing-oriented articles for *Holiday* and *Sunset*. "I ghosted a story for Merle Oberon in *Vogue* or one of the big magazines."

A revival-updating of *Bewitched—Bewitched Again*—is one of her current projects along with *Son of a Witch*, which she's written in the same genre. As to how the lady views her career: "With amazement. If I made a mistake in my life, it was not planning a career. My career just happened. I was in two classic series and at least one or more classic films where I had a major role. I was so blessed and so fortunate. I loved every minute of it and I want to do it again, but this time I may be behind the camera. The writing and producing, that's my goal at this point."

Kasey Rogers
Western Filmography

(As Laura Elliott) Movies: *Silver City* (1951 Paramount)—Edmond O'Brien; *Denver and Rio Grande* (1952 Paramount)—Edmond O'Brien.

Television: *Lone Ranger*, "Trigger Finger" (1955); *Frontier*, "Tomas and the Widow" (1955).

(As Kasey Rogers) Television: *Wyatt Earp*, "Bat Masterson Wins His Star" (1956); *Jim Bowie*, "Jim Bowie Comes Home" (1956); *Sgt. Preston*, "Underground Ambush" (1957); *Maverick*, "Third Rider" (1958); *State Trooper*, "Joker's Dead" (1958); *Colt .45*, "Rare Specimen" (1958); *Trackdown*, "Matter of Justice" (1958); *Trackdown*, "The Judge" (1958); *Trackdown*, "Every Man a Witness" (1958); *Yancy Derringer*, "Marble Fingers" (1958); *Bat Masterson*, "Two Graves for Swan Valley" (1958); *Colt .45*, "Return to El Paso" (1959); *Wanted Dead or Alive*, "Railroaded" (1959); *Bat Masterson*, "Election Day" (1959); *Rough Riders*, "Death Sentence" (1959); *Wanted Dead or Alive*, "Matchmaker" (1959); *Restless Gun*, "Trial for Jenny May" (1959); *Lawman*, "Shackled" (1959); *Sugarfoot*, "Blackwater Swamp" (1960); *Colt .45*, "Strange Encounter" (1960); *Bat Masterson*, "Masterson's Arcadia Club" (1960); *Bat Masterson*, "Dakota Showdown" (1960); *Wanted Dead or Alive*, "Three for One" (1960); *Wyatt Earp*, "Until Proven Guilty" (1961); *Maverick*, "Devil's Necklace" (1961); *Maverick*, "Three Queens Full" (1961).

Jean Rouverol

The Road Back

Jean Rouverol is best known to B-western watchers as a leading lady to Harry Carey, Hopalong Cassidy and Gene Autry. Her second career, and one she prefers, is as a screenwriter—*So Young, So Bad* (1950), *Legend of Lylah Clare* (1968), *A Face in the Rain* (1963) (with her husband), and those uncredited while she and screenwriter husband Hugo Butler were blacklist victims of the Communist witch hunts during the McCarthy era (*Autumn Leaves* [1956], *The Miracle* [1959]). Her personal life holds more drama than all her onscreen work combined.

Jean suffered through the worst period in film history, the McCarthy era, and survived.

It began in 1916. "My father was hooked on theater. My mother, as an actress, met him when she was on the road with *Little Women*; she played Meg, following Alice Brady on Broadway, then on the road. She was about 30 when she got to St. Louis. She didn't want to get married, but she wanted children. While she was there, Henry Hull and his wife were in another production; they made a threesome for bridge, always looking for a fourth. My father had been in enough little theater plays to have a big crush on the stage, but he was a teller for a bank. He made a good fourth for bridge and told sharp, funny stories, so, the Hulls were rooting for mother to marry him. Mother thought, 'Well, reddish curly hair, it would look nice on a child. ' ... so she married him. Then the Hulls' show left, leaving Mother married to Joe and they didn't have a thing to talk about. There I was, born in St. Louis, Missouri, in 1916. Actually, the name is spelled Rouveyrol."

We wondered if Jean ever thought of simplifying her last name. "A numerologist friend said, with the 'y' in it, it's unlucky, but with the 'y' out, it's lucky. There were some complaints [from studios]. They said it was too long for a marquee, but my mother had already done it honor and I felt strongly there was something hazardous to the health of one's sense of self in Hollywood ... about getting swept into the mores, standards, the values. You really had to work hard to retain who you were and what you were. Anyway, by the time I was three, Mother decided she had to get us out of St. Louis, she was afraid something would happen to her and we would be raised by her in-laws, whom she did not respect because they used bad grammar. She framed my poor father into thinking her brother and she were just taking us out to the Rockies for the summer. That was it. From then on, Mother supported us. I didn't see my father again 'til I was 30.

"Did you know my mother created the Hardy family? [Aurania Rouverol wrote the Broadway play *Skidding* in 1928. MGM picked up the property in 1937, giving credit to Aurania for creation of the Hardy family characters.] She wrote under her married name. Her maiden name was Ellerbeck, the eighth child of a Mormon family. Metro hired her and I think she did a little work on the first Hardy picture. But Metro didn't know what to do with her. They put her to work writing a gangster picture, Joan Crawford and Clark Gable, *Dance, Fools, Dance* [1931]."

Jump cut to 1934. After several plays in New York, Jean was now under contract to Paramount with one line in *Pursuit of Happiness* (1934). "I had seen the play in New York. There was a charming Czech actor, rather slight, who was brought out for it [Francis Lederer]. I was turning 17 that summer. I did a drama club play in high school [Palo Alto]. It went to the Palo Alto Playhouse and I did the lead. I went from one play to the other. And while I was doing that, I was taking screen tests at Paramount. I wasn't interested in Hollywood *per se*, I was more interested in stage. Hollywood dropped in my lap. I'd wanted to go to Stanford because I'd been admitted. My contract ran six months on and six months off, so I could have a quarter at Stanford in between times. First time anybody had thought that one up. It got a lot of publicity."

Paramount, not having work for Jean, sent her to producer-director Max Reinhardt, who was casting *A Midsummer Night's Dream*, to be produced at the Hollywood Bowl as a play. "Gloria Stuart was supposed to play Hermia but she never showed up. So I started rehearsing Hermia with Gail Patrick and Bill Henry, whom I'd known slightly from Pasadena Playhouse. He was silent, very nice and agreeable. He ended up in landscape gardening, I believe. He married one of [child actor] Junior Durkin's sisters. There was also a very nice English girl who was understudying me … determined she was going to get in this production. We got to be friends, I really liked her. Then Paramount says, 'We want you for a W. C. Fields picture. Show up Monday.' After weeks of rehearsals, I'm pulled out and my understudy gets the part—and it's Olivia de Havilland." (Who later did the film version as well.)

Soon, Jean was cast with Fields in *It's a Gift* (1934), for which she's fondly remembered. "I kept thinking, 'They took me out of Shakespeare and want me to work with this drunken vaudevillian?' I'm still trying to educate myself, so I'm reading *Men of Art* by Thomas Gray. When I'm not acting, I'm sitting someplace with my nose in the book. Learning nothing about motion pictures. If I had only opened my eyes to the matter at hand, I might have done a better job. As it is, the only reason I'm any good in it is because I was so straight. I didn't know what was going on and that worked fine."

In 1936, Paramount cast Jean in her first western, a Hopalong Cassidy film, *Bar 20 Rides Again*. "We were going to be shooting up in Lone Pine, the place where the entire church-going population was wiped out when there was a Sunday morning earthquake in 1906. It's a weird country. I remember somebody in the company telling me that around Lone Pine, all the cattle are musclebound from stepping over those damn rocks. I didn't know I'd be required to ride a horse, but I thought I'd better learn fast, so I took riding lessons from a little stable out in the Valley, and had a wonderful time, except I was taught on an English saddle, to post. First time I was confronted with a western saddle and you can't post; I didn't know what you did when a horse trotted."

Jean found William Boyd "very nice, but I was the ingenue opposite James Ellison, whose real name was James Ellis Smith. I remember we went to the preview of the picture out in Glendale … and they had him up on the marquee … James Ellis Smith. I remember this kid, 'Gee … look at my name!' He was a good-looking young man; also married one of Junior Durkin's sisters, Gertrude. I remember in one shot … I was supposed to sing with Jimmy and they listened to it over the sound and said, 'Jean, why don't you just

One of Jean's wardrobe test photographs for the Hopalong Cassidy western *Bar-20 Rides Again* (1936).

hum?' So I hummed. There was a quick conference off-camera and the director, Howard Bretherton, came up and said, 'Jean, your mouth looks funny when you hum, why don't you just *listen*.' I can't carry a tune [*laughs*]. 'The Moon Hangs High' was the song."

As to *Western Jamboree* (1938) at Republic, Jean says, "I remember only that Gene Autry was as white as a flounder. I have never seen a western actor who looked less like one. He was white and soft and I thought, 'What in God's name ever enabled this man to become a star?' The music helps.

"I was shooting a scene with Smiley Burnette, who was the comedian: I couldn't understand how I always managed to end up with my back to the camera. The cameraman called me over and said, 'Don't let Smiley do this to you. He's upstaging you.' I didn't know enough about camera ... and I probably wasn't narcissistic enough to care, but I was puzzled ... that never happened on the stage. The cameraman said, 'Don't let him. Complain.' So I did, aloud, to everybody! I learned, subsequently, Smiley did that to everybody he worked with. *Everybody*! That's the only time in my experience it ever happened. I never saw it again with anybody else."

Jean had an excellent role in *Law West of Tombstone* (1938) with Harry Carey and Tim Holt. "My mother was very indignant about it. She said afterwards, 'Jean, this is the first picture I've ever seen where you were self-conscious.' And I thought I was beginning to get a sense of what was going on. I was having fun with that one. Harry Carey was wonderful ... and subsequently, when I was being politically active, he was one of our speakers ... Valley Democratic Committee. He was campaigning for Henry Wallace, for president, for Heaven's sake. And his wife [Olive Carey] was magnificent. There was something majestic and wonderful about her. Intelligent. I thought Harry was gorgeous. But Tim Holt, I had very little to do with. I watched his subsequent career with great interest. I couldn't tell anything about him really, other than he was a good actor."

Two of Jean's friends in the business were Olivia de Havilland and Anne Shirley, but "my best acting friend is Jeff

Corey and his family. Lovely people. He knows more about theater than anybody." Robert Blake studied with Corey and Jean tells us, "My son, Michael Butler, worked with Robert Blake. He wrote for *Baretta* [1975–1978]."

So how did this wonderful actress-writer meet her husband and become involved with the political McCarthy witch hunts of the 1950s? Jean explains, "I had become radicalized when, to a degree, I was kind of recruited by a producer's son that my mother picked up. I was 17, in *Growing Pains*, which was Mother's play she'd written for me. It had run three weeks and flopped. We were on our way home on the Chief and my mother had seen this young man typing. Having no shame, she peered over his shoulder and discovered he was typing a dramatic poem. She decided to pick him up and introduce a nice young man to her daughter. What she didn't know was, he immediately recruited me into a left wing study group. When he was blacklisted out of the business, he ended up on the faculty at Dartmouth. Anyway, I was interested for a while, but it was all this dull reading and I knew if I wanted to be a writer, which I did, I had to be reading pretty serious stuff. I thought it would be better to be spending my time with Tolstoy than with the wage labor. So I drifted away.

"Then, about the time I married Hugo, we got interested [together]. Hugo Butler proposed to me in December 1936. We met at the MGM Commissary. Waldo Salt introduced us. [Salt later wrote *The Philadelphia Story* (1940), *Rachel and the Stranger* (1948), *Serpico* (1973), *Midnight Cowboy* (1969), etc.] Hugo was absolutely enchanting. I had just come back from another flop in New York. Well, it lasted two weeks [*laughs*]. One of our mutual friends said, 'Oh, Jean, if you haven't seen Waldo yet, he's a junior writer at Metro.' This girl said, 'He's got the cutest friend, his name is Hugo Butler.' Well, I got in touch with Waldo 'cause I knew he would invite me up for lunch at Metro. That's where I met Hugo, in this little group of junior writers. I just found him a dream. He was Canadian, his parents were English and he had a certain kind of behavior which was awfully nice. And he was so funny. Hugo telephoned me a few days later and suggested he pick me up for a party. He said it would obviate my having to find my own way there. I thought any man who uses the word 'obviate' in casual conversation is the man for me! We were married in May of 1937.

"Hugo was still under a junior writer contract making $50 a week. I was making 200. I had done *Stage Door* [1937], *The Road Back* [1937] and *Law West of Tombstone*, then I did two MGM shorts. It was an intensely political period in American history. During one of the flops in New York, I remember walking to the subway stop from the theater with my mother. It was cold, it was November ... and seeing men in threadbare coats huddling in doorways to get out of the wind. I had never seen poverty before in my life. We hadn't been rich but we'd never been poor. It was shocking to me. Then of course, Hitler was on the rise by now, 1936, 1937. Mussolini had already taken over Italy and the Spanish Civil War was going on. That was a very heartbreaking period and the only people who seemed to be worried about it or doing anything about it were the Communists. Also, apart from the New Deal, the rise of the union movement had a big effect on the country. It did restore a certain level of hope to union members, to workers; and the Communists were active, trying to boost a lot of the union movement. We got interested together. We were focused on the idea of social justice. Without quite realizing the extent of it, a lot of my friends started joining. Waldo dropped around one afternoon and invited

us to a meeting. Hugo said we'd think about it. I thought about all those books I'd have to read. Otherwise, I had no misgivings about it. Hugo had gone to a Writers Guild meeting and come home. As he got into bed, he said, 'I gave Waldo the nod, okay?' So he made the decision. Hugo and I were instantly put in different groups. Hugo is put in a group that meets in Beverly Hills, all the important writers. I, being only the wife, am shunted out to a group in the Valley ... wives, dentists and story readers. Even there, I discovered the Communist party was just as sexist as anybody else. As literature chairman, I had to go to the left wing book store and come back with a box of literature and sell it at every meeting.

"I was already working on the *One Man's Family* radio show. They auditioned about 200 girls for it. I knew radio was a good, fun way to make a living. So for a while, I was acting on *One Man's Family*, working as a junior writer at Metro and pregnant. Rich, full life. I started *One Man's Family* [as Betty Carter] in 1938, didn't leave until June or May of 1950. That was one of the reasons we didn't flee to Mexico straight away, when [politically] things began to bubble up around us. We knew we would need every penny we would earn. I wasn't earning very much, something like $75 a show. By then, we were taping three shows once a week and two shows another part of the week. By that time I was also getting jobs as a writer."

The character of Betty Carter had not existed before Jean came on *One Man's Family*. "She existed off-stage. They'd never had her voice." Jean recalls, "Carlton [E. Morse—creator of that great American radio serial] was amiable. Very much the father figure with the whole group, this creation of his. He was a good technician before he created the family, a good radio writer.

"By now Hugo and I are working on a little picture called *The First Time* at Columbia. Hugo was a real screenwriter. I had some magazine articles published. When he was in the Army, I turned to short stories and published my first novella. Hugo was in the Army getting $35 a month and I sell my first novella for $5000 to *McCalls*. Hugo had tried to get in the Navy, as a officer, 'cause he was a sailor. They turned him down, possibly because they knew about our politics. Hugo was indignant he had been turned down and said, 'Oh, hell with it, let them draft me.' We had two children and I got pregnant during his Army service. The third baby got him out of the Army. When Hugo entered the Army, he was automatically given a leave of absence from the Communist Party because Communists didn't want any sense of divided loyalty ... they wanted your whole heart and soul to be in the war effort.

"When Hugo came out of the Army, the question of rejoining came up and somebody asked him, how about me? By that time I was on the board of the YWCA, metropolitan board, the PTA and I was writing and selling stuff to magazines. Hugo said, 'God, I'd never see you.' So we decided I would not rejoin. I went into a ladies auxiliary sort of thing. When Hugo rejoined, he became a vice-president of the Writers Guild. His status in the industry was rising but he was also turning out a lot of wonderful movies which eventually gained him two Academy Award nominations [*Edison, the Man* (1940) and *Lassie, Come Home* (1943)]. He also was the person in charge of handing out the writing awards when his father [Frank Butler] was Oscar nominated for *Going My Way* [1944].

"Much earlier, around 1922, Hugo's father had come down from Canada, after he divorced Hugo's mother, and worked as an extra, then as a bit player. He was

doing moderately good small parts; he played Rudolph Valentino's brother in *Son of the Sheik* [1926]. [Butler was also in *Fighting Buckaroo* (1926) with Buck Jones, *King of the Wild Horses* (1924) with Rex.] With *No Man's Law* [Rex, Oliver Hardy, 1927], he got his first chance at writing; that's what he really wanted to do. He wrote most of the Hope-Crosby road pictures." Frank Butler also wrote *Montana Moon* (1930), *Babes in Toyland* (1934), *Bonnie Scotland* (1935), *Rangers of Fortune* (1940), *Wake Island* (1942), *California* (1946), *Perils of Pauline* (1947), *Whispering Smith* (1948), and many others.

"Anyway, Hugo and I are working at Columbia on *The First Time* (1952). Hugo one morning said that the U.S. marshals had begun serving subpoenas and it might be smart for him not to come home that night. We had a dinner date. I said, 'I'll meet you there.' We had our day at work and that night we went in two cars; he went one way and I went home. The doorbell rang, 6:30, quarter to seven on a cold January night. I knew when the doorbell rang who it was. I went to the peephole, looked through, and it's two men with hats. Now you know California. How many people do you ever see wearing a hat? I know they're from out of town. They say 'Is Mr. Butler here?' And I say no. They said, 'Where can we find him?' I said, I don't know and they glanced at each other and said, 'Well, when will he be back?' I realized they've got to have some excuse for why I, his wife, don't know where he is, so I said, 'We've had a little disagreement and I don't know where he's gone or when he'll be back.' I was so terrified, tears were on the verge. They looked at each other and said, 'We'll be back,' and off they went. I had to let Hugo know, but I knew they might be watching the house. They might have tapped our phone. I shouldn't telephone from the house. So I asked our housekeeper to put

Jean was not impressed with Gene Autry or Smiley Burnette. In this scene from *Western Jamboree* (1938) are Smiley Burnette, Jean, Margaret Armstrong, Kermit Maynard and George Wolcott.

the kids to bed, made up a bundle of laundry, called a taxi, figuring we're less traceable in a taxi than in our car, and I take a taxi to the local laundromat." Jean then contacted Hugo's parents who stayed at their house with the children while Hugo and Jean slept at the unoccupied apartment of Ian Hunter.

Afraid U.S. marshals would show up at the studio the next day, they proposed finishing the script in Palm Springs. Working there for two weeks, Jean realized they only had $70,000 in the bank. "We knew it was going to last us, perhaps forever, might be the last money we ever made, so we didn't want to lose one cent

of possible income." Jean and her two youngest children moved in with her mother. Hugo's mother took the two oldest children. "Hugo was traveling from motel to motel. We kept having these romantic little rendezvous. I was going in once or twice a week to tape *One Man's Family*. The nature of your friendships, I think, determines your behavior. Two of our friends were in jail. For the guys that became friendly witnesses ... and Dave Braxon said it better than anybody, he said, 'Every day of my life, I question myself and my behavior and my motives and I wonder whether I didn't have the courage.' This just seemed to me so terrible. It had to be so destructive. The only person who didn't for a second mind, apparently, was Eddie Dmytryk and he was so frankly opportunistic that he never questioned the things underneath. But I think other friendly witnesses suffered."

Jean and Hugo soon decided to flee to Mexico rather than face Senate questioning. "The guys who had been to jail were terrified they were going to be re-arrested, re-subpoenaed, asked the same question as before, and convicted on a brand new charge of contempt. They were terrified. Albert Maltz's wife met him at midnight when he was released, with a car already loaded to drive straight to the Mexican border. So they went down first. [Maltz was screenwriter of *This Gun for Hire* (1942), *Destination Tokyo* (1944) and *Two Mules for Sister Sara* (1970).] One of the reasons I hadn't wanted to leave California until summer was that I didn't want the kids to lose any school. But in the meantime, Dalton Trumbo found there was a very good school in Mexico City, the American School, and living was cheaper. All this time, we've been evading the marshals. Our stuff was still in the house, we were still paying rent. One day I have the car radio on, the news comes on with names of those people they have been unable to find. They list Hugo Butler. I know now, we've got to make a move. We had decided with the Dalton Trumbos we would rent a house in Ensenada and see how we liked it. We can kind of get the feel of Mexico and see if this is something we can bear to do." It turns out they loved it. Hugo continued to write and they stayed in Mexico 12 years. "What you couldn't do in Mexico was be political. There was an article in the constitution, you had to be completely apolitical. If any foreigner does anything political, they can be thrown out of the country without a trial, without a hearing."

Jean and Hugo stayed in Mexico 12 years, eventually leaving for Italy. "Then Hugo's personality began to change. He was finding it harder to work, he was feeling weary. Our doctor prescribed Methadone, on the theory it was not addictive, but his disposition was changing and I was in full denial, refusing to recognize there was anything wrong. In Italy, everything broke loose. Hugo seemed angry with me all the time. Finally, he committed his first infidelity ... and he told me about it. I was struggling to keep the marriage together ... just awful. We came back to Mexico for about a year and a half because we weren't sure whether we were ready to make the move back to the States. The Trumbos stayed down there almost three more years. Trumbo and Hugo went to bullfights together. Hugo became an ardent fan of the bullfights and ended up writing an Oscar-nominated documentary on bullfighting called *Torero*. Trumbo ended up writing, under the table, *The Brave One* [1956]. Those are two aspects of the same bullfight. We just couldn't decide whether to come back to this country. Hugo worked on several jobs for director Robert Aldrich, doing some polishing. I was reading books for Aldrich, sending up resumes. Hugo was beginning to have serious personality changes. Finally, he just went to bed and stayed for several months. When he died he was 53. I was 51. January 1968.

"After Hugo died, I started reading biographies of women who have made it, to shore myself up ... Eleanor Roosevelt, Louisa May Alcott. I was on the board of the InterGuild Federal Credit Union [for 18 years]. I was on the board of directors of the Writers Guild of America. I was on the documentary committee of the Motion Picture Academy." Jean also served on the Board of Governors of the Academy of Television Arts and Sciences from 1990 to 1992. In the 1970s and 1980s, Jean wrote for several soap operas: *Bright Prom-*

ise (1969–1972), *Guiding Light* (1952–), *Search for Tomorrow* (1951–1982) and *As the World Turns* (1956–). She's authored biographies of Harriet Beecher Stowe, Pancho Villa and Juarez as well as writing "how-to-write-for-daytime-drama" books. She's also taught and lectured on writing at UCLA. Jean is now working on her autobiography.

In retrospect, Jean smiles, "Essentially, Mexico was so dear, so magical for us in those days and the experiences … unbelievable. You look back on your life and it has been so enriched by the experience. I take a certain pride in it." As to her screen work with Hoppy, Harry and Gene,

"It left me feeling somewhat in ignorance of my craft. I still thought it was more honorable to be a stage actress. I was always vaguely embarrassed about being a movie actress." Today, Jean is proudly hard at work restoring credits to films penned by various blacklisted screenwriters.

Jean Rouverol
Western Filmography

Movies: *Bar 20 Rides Again* (1936 Paramount)—William Boyd; *Law West of Tombstone* (1938 RKO)—Harry Carey; *Western Jamboree* (1938 Republic)—Gene Autry.

Ann Rutherford

Serials, B's and Classics

Vivacious Ann Rutherford is possibly best remembered by the general public today as Carreen, one of Scarlett O'Hara's sisters in *Gone with the Wind* (1939), or as Andy Hardy's girlfriend Polly Benedict in the popular MGM series from 1938 until 1942. However, it's the Golden Boot award winner's westerns opposite Gene Autry and John Wayne for which she's fondly recalled by western devotees.

Born on a November 2 in Toronto, Ontario, Canada, the daughter of a former Metropolitan Opera singer, John

Guilberty, she laughs, "That was a stage name. His real name was John Rutherford—he changed it for professional reasons, so family members wouldn't find out what he was doing."

When told her bio mentions she did several plays as a child, starting at age five, she reveals, "That was poppycock. Studio publicity. I did do plays as a kid—but just school plays like everybody else."

Her bio also states *Carnival of Paris* was her first film. "Baloney. That was a short I did at Metro, after making some 18

Ann is best known today for her role in the classic *Gone with the Wind* (1939).

After school, my sister [Judith Arlen] and I would go by radio station KFAC and watch the radio actors perform every day. I noticed how they'd take their scripts, and highlight their parts. How they turned away from the microphones when they had to turn the page. All those things. When I was 12, I went in and was asked, 'What have you done?' Well, I named every play I'd ever seen—whether or not it had a child in it! A month later, I had just come home from school when my mother asked me if I had been making a nuisance of myself—that KFAC wanted to see me. There were two lines of kids—one for girls and one for boys. Being a smart little girl, I naturally got in the line with the other little girls [*laughs*]. When given a script, I took a pencil which I kept in my long hair over my left ear, and underlined my part. From watching those radio actors, I knew how to stand, how to keep from rattling papers when changing pages—all the things you need to know—and I got the job! The show was called 'Nancy and Dick and the Spirit of '76.' We did it for two years. Dick was played by future actor-director Richard Quine! One radio show led to another—so it grew from there.

pictures before. My first movie at Metro was a short, *Annie Laurie*, with Stanley Morner—who later became Dennis Morgan."

Motion pictures were not her initial entertainment medium. "I began my career on radio—by lying about my age! My family lived in San Francisco, and every Saturday afternoon the local Henry Duffy Players, a stock company, presented plays. They had companies in both San Francisco and Los Angeles. We moved to Los Angeles when I was nine, so I was still able to see every play they did in town. I loved the theater and watching the people act.

"One day, there was a call at the station for me—'Do you want to be in pictures?' I had heard about these type of guys so I said, 'I'm sorry, they're calling me' and hung up on him! When I got home, sitting in the living room was this relaxed agent—a friend of Nat Levine of Mascot Studios. It seems another actress, Anne Darling—the shepherdess in 1935's *Bride of Frankenstein*—had eloped that day with Artie Steppins, an insurance big shot. So I stepped into the leading role in *Waterfront Lady* (1934) at Mascot. It was my very first movie—and I got my name before the title!"

In 1935, Ann Rutherford starred in *The Fighting Marines*. "That was a serial. The script looked like three New York City telephone directories! By the time you've scrambled through this huge script and dog-eared the pages on which your scenes appear, they start sending the pink pages and blue pages—those are changes. So it doesn't really pay to learn a lot. Grant Withers and Adrian Morris were the stars. Adrian was Chester Morris' brother. He was on the road to getting fat by this time. He even drank a lot. This was right after prohibition and those guys thought it was a very jock thing to do—live it up, drink and smoke. Yakima Canutt did all the stunts in the serial. Because of the pressure of shooting a serial, there are usually two directors, and neither one remembers what the other one did. Sometimes they'd be so pooped out they'd sleep all day, letting the other director work. Suffice it to say the directors were far more interested in keeping the action going than dialogue. There was always an airplane flying overhead ... they'd not retake a scene for that. You did a wild line later—a loop—to fill that part of it in. There were virtually no rehearsals except you sort of walk through in a hurry for the cameraman so he'll know what he's aiming at. We lined up for the cameras and tried not to blow our lines or be out of camera range. There was one scene where I was required to drive an open four-door touring car through many ruts and rills and go on my way. Somebody had

just killed my brother and I'm rushing off. There were a couple of scenes where I drove a car. I asked the director, 'Which scene is this? Where is it in the script?' He said, 'I don't know. Just get in the damn car' [*laughs*]. I said, 'One more thing—I don't drive!' He said, 'Oh, that's all right, I'll put a guy on the floor. You steer and he'll drive [*laughs*]. Well, I'll tell you, this guy leans on the gas and we take off! I'm smiling all the time. Well, there was one scene where I was supposed to be smiling—I'm going to meet my lover ... but I didn't realize this was the scene where I'm going to find my brother's murderer. I'm going right through there, smiling like an idiot [*laughs*]. Then I hit a terrible bump, the guy lying on the floor bounces right up into sight ... *that* they never re-shot [*laughs*]. They left it in the picture! There was another scene where I had to change my clothes. I had a summer dress on with slits in the sleeves to let the air in. They were hurrying me so, I stuck my arm through the slit and the sleeve was hanging down from my armpit. They shot that sucker ... they shot that scene right then [*laughs*].

"And we were on location and that is not lots of fun in the summertime. They take you to funny, dusty, dirty places with rocks and all sorts of terrible things ... no plumbing, accommodations, no nothin'! You just stay out there all day and you get dirty. And in those days, we did not have the protection of the Screen Actors Guild Union. You'd work 48 hours a day! Now you work five days a week. The reason these companies took you on location was so they could work you seven days a week and hurry right back. The big banner cry was, 'Fighting light.' That meant hurry up, for God's sake, the sun's gonna go down and we can't shoot anything. Sometimes people would get klieg eyes—red sore eyes from those big klieg lights. They'd put cold raw potatoes over their eyes to help them. They sliced 'em real thin, one for each eye. The prop man carried the potatoes around. We would start in at first light in the morning—which meant for a girl, if she wants to wear makeup or comb her hair, she had to get up an hour and a half earlier than the first call! And your hair got so dirty on location. It was messy! If you had to wash your hair, you did it from midnight 'til two in the morning [laughs]. There was no restaurant, they'd bring a chuck wagon out and spoon up some slumgullion stew or something. And this went on *seven days a week*! It was an interesting experience and I choose *not* to repeat it again! I think it's one of the reasons the Screen Actors Guild rolled up its sleeves and started protecting the players.

"Also at that time, the Humane Society was not large on the sets. I remember from my westerns how horrified I was when I saw my first running W when they rigged a horse with wires going crossways and they'd pull them, causing the horse to fall down. I've seen horses be injured. But these directors—Yakima Canutt, Breezy Eason—were action men. Some of them were Eastern men and did not understand about horses. They had no idea a horse couldn't run all day. How dare he stop to breathe and be winded [laughs]. It's an era that is mercifully over, but I'm glad I was a part of it."

Ann recalls Buster Crabbe taught her to swim underwater for a role in Mascot's *Down to the Sea* (1936). She'd embellished her aquatic skills to get the part and then, luckily, found Crabbe to teach her. "I was never more scared in my life!"

Asked about her many early Gene Autry oaters, Ann is proud to announce, "I made more money than Gene Autry! I was earning $150 a week; Gene only got $100 a week while Smiley Burnette received $50. And that's the only time I ever made more money than Gene Autry [laughs]! Gene was a lovely man, but he

was one cowboy who couldn't ride a horse! He virtually invented the 'singing cowboy.' Actually, he wasn't a cowboy at all—he worked as a telegraph clerk at a train station in Oklahoma. He had a radio show, and when Will Rogers came by, Gene asked him to 'tune in and hear me.' Gene had a good quality to his voice. He wrote Nat Levine, head of Mascot, who didn't answer his letters. But Gene was persistent—eventually Nat Levine himself stopped off—at the radio station—and heard Gene and Smiley and the gang. They had a young flavor about them that Levine liked. He bought them all for peanuts [laughs]! He started Gene off in a science fiction serial at Mascot, *Phantom Empire* [1935], just before it turned into Republic.

"Smiley Burnette [Gene Autry's comic sidekick] was the most talented young man, musically, I ever met, with the possible exception of Mickey Rooney. I can see him now with his accordion—what he called his 'Stomach Steinway'—and his guitar or 'git-fiddle.' There wasn't an instrument he couldn't make music out of."

Ann later signed with MGM, who loaned her back to Republic for Autry's *Public Cowboy No. 1* (1937). When asked if she received a bonus for this outing, Ann screeches, "Are you out of your gourd [laughs]?"

As for Republic in general, she's pleased to say, "It was not Poverty Row. I watched it grow from two soundstages when Trem Carr turned it into Republic. He built it up. It had a good western street. It was located out in the San Fernando Valley—and that was in the country back then. Property was cheap and you could buy an acre for $100. That's how Bob Hope and some of the others made so much money—buying up Valley property at low prices and developing it!"

Asked about some co-stars, "Fern Emmett was a nice actress—we worked

Gene Autry and Ann don't really think Smiley Burnette can ride Buck, do they? *Melody Trail* (1935) was Ann's first western.

together more than once. And Robert McKenzie—I knew the whole family. His wife Ella was a character actress, and their daughter Lolly was married to the comedian Billy Gilbert. Their other daughter, Fay McKenzie, worked with me in *Student Tour* [1934]. [Fay also co-starred with Gene Autry in several features.] My sister, Judith Arlen, was a Wampus Baby Star of 1934. Those girls appeared at World's Fairs. Once, when she was out of town, I was doing radio under my real name, and when she received a call for *Student Tour*, I told them, 'Judith can't come—I am Joanne Arlen—can I come instead?' So I went and they picked me to be one of the students! Herman Brix (later Bruce Bennett), Dave O'Brien (who later

did those Pete Smith shorts), June Storey, Douglas Fowley—lots of people were in it. The singing cop, Phil Regan, was the lead."

Could she ride a horse? "Of course *everybody* claimed they could ride, but *nobody* could—you'd see the air full of people falling off horses. Thank God for pummels! I always rode side-saddle—but I wanted those pummels to hold onto! In one of those movies, I almost drowned! [Most probably John Wayne's *Oregon Trail* (1936).] I'm in a wagon with a little girl and an old man, near a stream. We were supposed to ride this wagon over the shallow spot. Naturally, the wagon turned over! I grabbed the little girl, who was about six, and told her to hang on. It scared the liver out of me! Today, unions would have protected us against such things—but not then! In those westerns, they'd be doing shots of men riding hell-bent for leather. Then they'd stop—have makeup put on them to look like Indians—then they'd start riding again—chasing themselves [*laughs*]!"

George Montgomery was in Gene Autry's *The Singing Vagabond* (1935), "but he didn't mention it to me when we did *Orchestra Wives* [1942] together seven years later! He didn't want me to know he was George Letz at that time [*laughs*]. George was a good-looking kid; a good actor; fun; wonderful, dear and sweet with two wonderful kids by Dinah Shore! His talents are unlimited—as a sculptor, furniture maker—whatever it is, George is excellent at doing it!"

It wouldn't be Republic in the 1930s if Ann hadn't worked with John Wayne. "John Wayne was always so relaxed. He wanted them to stop making him sing—and he didn't sing in our pictures. [Wayne's singing voice was dubbed in by Bill Bradbury, Bob Steele's brother, for *Riders of Destiny* (1933), and later by Jack Kirk for *Westward Ho* (1935).] He was a very nice man. I liked him a lot and it didn't surprise me when he became a big, big star. He was charming, and so attractive. He was a good father, even then. He let his kids come on the set! But I didn't bump into him later on. Once a year, someone will ask me if I have a copy of *The Oregon Trail* [1936], our 'lost' picture. The last ones to ask me about it were John's kids! Even John Wayne didn't have a copy of it, unfortunately! John Wayne had about him an aura—a presence. The only other person I know who had that was Clark Gable. Wherever he sat, it was the head of the table. He was dearly loved by every member of the cast and the crew. I don't think I've ever heard anyone say an unkind thing about John. He ate lunch

with the grips and the crew and his loyalty is absolutely legendary. He always used Ward Bond, Yakima Canutt, Paul Malvern, Ed Faulkner ... as long as John Wayne had a job, his friends had a job. If you were gonna work, he'd see to it that you did. He was a special man. I cherish the thought I worked with him."

Legendary stuntman Yakima Canutt doubled Wayne in those early B-westerns as well as often playing a heavy. "I loved Yak; he was unbelievable! He could do anything! He'd do running W's on a horse. I'd get upset over the way horses were treated in those days. Yakima was miraculous—he could hold on, under eight galloping horses. He practically made the impossible possible!"

Ann Rutherford has been friends with Rand Brooks for over 60 years. "We met on a Hardy family picture—he played a bandleader. He was so nice, and he still is! My mother loved him and my grandmother loved him! He is the first person I knew who bought a big black car—then removed all the chrome. He has class! He is so darling. We did four or five pictures together. The second was *Dramatic School* [1938]. Then, of course, *Gone with the Wind* [1939]. He got the part of Charles Hamilton before I landed my role. Louis B. Mayer at MGM told me, 'David [O. Selznick] wants to borrow you, but I said no, because your part doesn't drive the story.' I begged and beseeched Mayer. Nagged and wept and carried on until he finally let me do it—but only when I got time off from MGM and when I wasn't needed on a picture! David O. Selznick thought I closely resembled Barbara O'Neil, who played the mother. Our profiles did show a resemblance. Two brunettes in the picture—that allowed Evelyn Keyes, who had lighter hair, to be cast. The original picture was longer—Selznick shot 12 hours, so scenes that didn't 'drive the story' *were* cut—and that means *most*

In this scene from *The Lonely Trail* (1936), Etta McDaniel consoles Ann over the death of her brother Dennis Moore, which is being "staged" to fool Union troops. Fred "Snowflake" Toones, to Ann's left, was one of the most prolific black actors in films of the 1930s and 1940s. McDaniel was the sister of Academy Award winner Hattie McDaniel, with whom Ann worked in *Gone with the Wind* (1939).

of my scenes! Plus, they tightened up the scenes that I *was* in! Every 15 to 20 years, we've had reunions—the best one was in 1968. Vivien Leigh had died, but Olivia de Havilland came over from Paris for it. The last one was in 1989, in Atlanta. Somehow, Frank 'Junior' Coghlan got overlooked in the invitations—he was not happy about it [*laughs*].

"Because of *Gone with the Wind* and *The Wizard of Oz*, most of the Technicolor cameras were tied up in 1939. At MGM, I was in *Pride and Prejudice* [filmed 1939, released 1940] with Greer Garson and Laurence Olivier. They wanted to shoot it

in color, but couldn't because of *Oz* and *Wind* going way over schedule. I thought Adrian, the costume designer, was going to kill himself—he had designed such colorful costumes that would have looked great in color. As is, even the Jane Austen Society still prefers our version to the BBC eight-hour mini-series or the English remake."

Asked how she got from Republic to MGM, Ann reveals, "My mother had to go to court and swear I had lied about my age when I signed the contract. This made the contract null and void and I was able to take MGM's offer! I was supposed to play Polly Benedict in the first Hardy family movie, *A Family Affair* [1937]. They had a good-looking young boy, Frankie Thomas, positioned to play Andy Hardy. I was taller than he, so I left for awhile and came back in flats with my hair flat on my head. The studio liked the idea that the girlfriend was taller than the boyfriend. Unfortunately, that summer, Frankie Thomas had a growing spurt—he grew six inches, so he was 'too tall' for Andy. They scrounged around, got Mickey Rooney, and brought him in. Then, I was doing a picture, *The Devil Is Driving* [1937], at Columbia with Richard Dix. Well, Mr. Dix was long in the tooth. One day he tripped and broke his arm and couldn't finish the picture. So I wasn't through with *The Devil Is Driving* when the first Hardy picture began shooting. Margaret Marquis replaced me, but just for that one time."

Ann smiles, "The Hardy family pictures had such a wonderful outlook on life that they caught on with young people, as well as old, which is partly attributable to Mickey Rooney, a gifted dynamo who had some wonderful ideas over and above what was in our scripts.

"I started at MGM at $350 a week, and always got my raises! I went up to $500 a week and so forth. But I kept hearing these stories from girls saying Mr. Mayer called them in and told them he wanted to keep them, but couldn't afford to give them their raise. So, when it was time for my trip to his office, I was prepared. I brought my bankbook—and showed it to him. I explained I was saving money to buy a house for my mother and grandmother. He got misty-eyed—anything about mothers made him emotional. He thought mothers should look like May Robson, *old*. He put a bun on Fay Holden, Mrs. Hardy; and Lewis Stone [Mr. Hardy] was so *old* he looked like a grandfather more than a father! Mayer was so

pleased I was buying my mother a house that I always got my raise! A contract at MGM was like the White House. They treated you so beautifully. I learned the ropes: Be available. Once you finish a picture, go to the publicity department. Do beach, leg art, portraits. Have lots of pictures that could be sent to magazines, newspapers, whatever, for publicity! Also, if they thought you were unavailable, that's when they wanted you for something. Les Peterson or Howard Strickling in publicity would call my agent and get me radio shows in New York. The Super Chief stopped off in Chicago, so you'd do a stage show where your latest movie was playing. I never paid a hotel bill. I stayed at the Hampshire House in New York—gave interviews and plugged MGM products. Most theater managers would even stop the movie for your appearance. They'd put your name out front, stating you were making a personal appearance. I was Queen of the Cotton Festival, and later Queen of Mardi Gras during the War. I traveled the U.S. with Charles Laughton. We missed nothing—we hit every war plant in the country, selling war bonds."

Unfortunately, one such incident cost Ann Rutherford her MGM contract! "There was this gig at the Great Lakes Naval Station—officers, women and kids came by. One kid climbed me like a tree. He was a pretty little boy. His mother said, 'Alvin got out of his sick bed to see you.' Well, he had German measles! Ten days to the day, I came down with them! I was scheduled to appear in *Seven Sweethearts* [1942] and for the only time ever, I went to Mr. Mayer and said I was not happy and I didn't want to do it—the part was too small. He insisted anyway that I had to do the film! Shooting started on the very Monday I came down with German measles! My mother called the studio and told them I was sick—they didn't believe us. That very day, 20th Century–Fox called, wanting to borrow me for *Orchestra Wives*. MGM made a deal to sell my contract to Fox, with the stipulation they would agree to loan me back for any Hardy family or Whistling picture [comedies with Red Skelton as a radio detective named the Fox]. I *hated* 20th Century–Fox. I did *not* do the publicity for them. I missed MGM. They sold me down the river!"

Before leaving the MGM lot, Ann was borrowed by Universal for *Badlands of Dakota* (1941). "I enjoyed that and all the actors in the picture—Robert Stack, Broderick Crawford, Lon Chaney, Jr., etc. Frances Farmer was lovely. I was so very impressed with her."

When I informed Ann she was scheduled to have played a follow-up part in 1942's *Men of Texas*, she was unaware of it. Anne Gwynne was told she was being given the role after Ann's contract mess-ups. "Anne Gwynne was so nice—we worked together in 1941's *Washington Melodrama*. I was so grieved when she had her stroke."

Ann Rutherford's first "western" at MGM was *Out West with the Hardys* (1939). "In the Hardy pictures, I was only in at the beginning or ending—there was some excuse for either Andy or me to leave town. I was the rich girl, so usually I was the one who was gone. In this one, the Hardys take a vacation out west, but I wasn't around for any of the western things."

Ann's only Grade-A western at MGM was 1940's *Wyoming*. "We had fun locations in Jackson Hole, Wyoming. I loved being there. Marjorie Main had this big machine she brought, some sort of juicer that made vegetable juice out of everything she squished in it. What a character she was! She'd wear bloomers and would put those white undertaker gloves in those bloomers. She was a fanatic about dirt and dust, so whenever she needed to open a door, she'd take out those

gloves and put them on before she would open the doors [*laughs*]! One day, I didn't have to work, so my mother and I were going to drive to nearby Yellowstone National Park. Marjorie wanted to go, and when she got to the car my mother was sitting in the front seat. Marjorie shouted, 'Hey, put Mom in back. I throw up if I don't ride in front!' We weren't gone five minutes when she cracked down the window and stuck her head out, inhaling and exhaling. She loved doing that! It wasn't long before she didn't have a hairpin left. Her long, long hair fell down, making her look like Gravel Gertie [of the Dick Tracy comic strip] [*laughs*]! Her hair was waist-length! She took her shoes off, so her bare feet were on the floorboard. 'Oh, that feels so good,' she'd say! It took us two hours to get there. We were at Old Faithful and a gang of people were standing around it. Although it was a large crowd, Marjorie Main pushed her way through the people up to around the ring. Then it erupted. Marjorie raised her head and screamed, 'Great God Almighty! It's the coming of the Lord!' [*laughs*]. She dropped to her knees—she was a Holy Roller, I think! She was praying on her knees. We were there two hours and I was a wreck!"

Asked about Wallace Beery, the star of *Wyoming*, who was infamous for being uncooperative, "I don't like to speak ill of the dead. But this poor soul—he would steal scenes from that lovable child actor Bobs Watson! He would take to scratching his crotch, or pick his ear and examine the wax. Anything to get attention on himself and off the other actors. We had a scene together. We rehearsed it and when we shot it, Mr. Beery did a monologue—saying both his and *my* lines! He took all my dialogue and I said, 'Cut! I didn't know this was a monologue,' and I went to my dressing room. I was right. This was an old trick of his! He was also a kleptomaniac—he would take stuff off the set before we were finished with it. They'd need to shoot at a different angle and things would be missing—he'd swiped them! He drove the script girls crazy!"

Following her tenure at MGM and Fox, Ann returned to Republic for 1946's *The Madonna's Secret* as well as the all-star *Murder in the Music Hall*. "Vera Hruba Ralston was in that one. Herbert Yates, the head of the studio and her future husband, put a full-page picture of her in the trades once a week, with a caption underneath the photo stating she was the most beautiful woman in the world. I know this embarrassed her. She is dear, sweet and kind. But she married the old toad. At lunch, he would muffle himself up so they could go to the ice rink—she never ate lunch with anybody else. She *earned* whatever money she got out of him!"

For the 1949-1950 season, Ann was *Blondie* on radio in the role originated by Penny Singleton. She was also heard regularly on *The Eddie Bracken Show* as Eddie's girlfriend, Connie, between 1945 and 1947.

By the early 1950s, Ann had slowed down her career. "When my baby preferred the nanny's company to mine, I fired the nanny and stayed home with my daughter." She did continue to make occasional films and TV shows. "Just to keep my hand in. I was friends with Gail Patrick [executive producer of the *Perry Mason* TV series (1957–1966)] and her husband Cornwall Jackson, as well as *Perry Mason* author Erle Stanley Gardner. Erle had a kind of factory at his home—there were five little cottages filled with secretaries. He'd dictate all day, or until he got tired, in one house; then go down to the next one and work on another book! So I did a few of the *Perry Mason* TV shows." Among her other TV work was a *U.S. Marshal* ("I don't even remember that show") and a *Tales of Wells Fargo*, both in 1959. "That was a western and that was

fun. Dale Robertson was a very nice man. He was gorgeous then, but he's let himself go to pot. I swear to God, he now looks like Wilford Brimley!"

A rather well-publicized accident has left Ann Rutherford with a permanent defect. "One leg is shorter than the other! On May 10, 1999, I was to spend two hours narrating a tribute to Mickey Rooney. I didn't return home for two months! July 14, 1999, in fact. Next door neighbors Steve Lawrence and Eydie Gorme had sold their house—and the new owners had torn it down by the time I got home! I went to a one-story recording studio. The guy said, 'Go in the other office,' and I went flying through the air. There were two steps, but no railing or warning signs. It was an illusion, due in part to being carpeted. I shattered my leg, knee, everything! I've been out $75,000 of my own money and the Screen Actors Guild Pension and Health Plan, plus Medicare, have paid dearly as well. For the first and only time in my life, I am suing. I want to reimburse SAG and Medicare—they shouldn't have to pay for someone else's negligence. A doctor said I could have another operation and remove the pins and metals they inserted, and then my knee—which bends out like James Whitmore's—would straighten up. But another doctor said, 'Why do that? You could be fixed, but you could also possibly have a stroke or even die from the surgery!' I don't want to be like poor Anne Gwynne, and I certainly don't want to die, so I've had to throw out all my shoes and only use flats with one being built-up! I wear slacks and long dresses, I don't want that knee to show! This hasn't stopped me. I still travel to New York, go to the annual Lone Pine Film Festival, and still enjoy life to the fullest!"

Ann Rutherford
Western Filmography

Movies: *Melody Trail* (1935 Republic)—Gene Autry; *Singing Vagabond* (1935 Republic)—Gene Autry; *Oregon Trail* (1936 Republic)—John Wayne; *Lawless Nineties* (1936 Republic)—John Wayne; *Comin' Round the Mountain* (1936 Republic)—Gene Autry; *The Lonely Trail* (1936 Republic)—John Wayne;

Public Cowboy No. 1 (1937 Republic)—Gene Autry; *Out West with the Hardys* (1938 MGM)—Mickey Rooney; *Gone with the Wind* (1939 MGM)—Clark Gable; *Wyoming* (1940 MGM)—Wallace Beery; *Badlands of Dakota* (1941 Universal)—Robert Stack.

Television: *Tales of Wells Fargo*, "Branding Iron" (1959); *U.S. Marshal*, "A Matter of Friendship" (1959).

Karen Sharpe

Challenging the System

The pretty lass who would become Don Durant's leading lady on *Johnny Ringo* (1959–1960) and *High Noon* (1952) director Stanley Kramer's leading lady in real life, was born Karen Kay Sharpe in San Antonio, Texas, "in September" (circa 1933).

Karen's mother put her in ballet and dancing as a child. "That led me into ice skating. I came to California in the summertime to study skating. But my mind was not on that, it was really on motion pictures. I went to see *The Jolson Story* [1946] at least 48 times. I was crazy about that story, Larry Parks and that whole era. Whatever it did to me, it was important. In those days, you could not get into a major motion picture studio; it was just another world we were not privy to. The very first two days I was in Los Angeles,

I only dreamed about one thing, meeting Larry Parks. On the third day ... and we had no connections to the business ... I went to the Beverly Hills Hotel as part of a skating entourage and ran smack into him. That was like an omen to me, a good one. I went to his house the next day. He and Betty Garrett were married at that time, and he signed my scrapbook. Then I went home to Texas and made life miserable for my family so I could come back out here.

"By the time I was in high school, my mother had brought me to California and I was living here, going to Schwabs, trying to be discovered on a drug store stool, like Lana Turner, but of course, that was not a true story. I believed everything I read. When it wasn't happening, I began to think, 'Maybe I need to learn how to

Don Durant was Marshal Johnny Ringo and Karen was his love interest and store owner Laura Thomas on the very popular *Johnny Ringo* series (1959–1960).

act!' So I did all kinds of plays … playing much older than I was … and was discovered by an MGM talent scout. I did a screen test at MGM when I was about 16 or 17 years old and failed it. I was not

picked as a contract player, which really broke my heart. I thought my whole career was over. Then I was picked up by Columbia and tested for a contract in a film opposite John Derek. But the man producing it was Donna Reed's husband ... and the part went to her. It didn't look like I was going to be a studio contract player, which was really the thing to be in those days. I also tested at Universal with Tony Curtis and Piper Laurie, who was in my school, and also failed that test. I was not the blonde pretty type they were looking for. I was more of an Anne Bancroft type of actress and just didn't fit their criteria. I just did what I did in theater and worked like a little son of a gun to be good at anything I did.

"I was very lucky in one thing. I went to study with a drama coach, John Morley. In his building was an agent who would only accept ten clients, that's all he would ever take. Leon Lance. He started Terry Moore's career, Diane Baker, Kim Hunter and James Arness. He liked me, and took me. But if there was somebody who'd been with the agency longer, you had to wait until that person was set for Lance to work with you. We were required to have dinner every Sunday night with him as a family. He had no children, no wife, nothing; we were considered his family. A great agent, he really cared about his clients and protected you from the casting couch or from anything that was wrong. He was very old-fashioned, very strict and very good for me. He took me to a photographer, Willinger, who has become quite famous because of all those pictures he did with Marilyn Monroe, and I became a photographic model for magazines. I didn't really want to be a model, but I had a good face, I guess. Paul Hesse was *the* photographer in the business. Willinger was a small-time photographer, but Hessey did [most] all the magazine covers. He liked me and used me in beer commercials ... he would take pictures of me and they'd draw me. I did car things. I was a cover girl. *Cosmopolitan*, *Pageant*, I don't remember half the things I did. Hessey got me to Hal Roach, where they did

a little children's program for television called *The Angel and the Devil...* I was dressed as the angel but was really the devil. That kind of got me started. I did a lot of things for Roach when I was just a teenager.

"Then I was given an award by *Photoplay* magazine. It got in all the movie magazines, which led to a little film at Allied Artists, *Army Bound* [1952]. Actually, before that, I went to MGM and did a little part because the talent scout was so upset I'd failed my test; he really thought I should be at MGM. He got me a two- or three-line role as Janice Rule's younger sister in *Holiday for Sinners* [1952]. That led immediately to *Bomba and the Jungle Girl* (1952). I liked Johnny Sheffield. He really did not want to be in this business ... how smart he was [*laughs*]! He wanted to be a brain surgeon, I think. I went with him in his pickup truck, which was very unusual; we just didn't go in pickup trucks in those days.

"Then I met Lynn Stalmaster, who was casting some very big TV shows ... *Big Town* (1950–1956) and others. I was lucky to get some very good roles. I was never good at playing ingenue roles. I just didn't know how to do that. I was much better as a killer, neurotic call girl. You know, as a lead; they were more interesting parts for me. Incidentally, Lynn was an actor who was with UCLA, and just didn't make it apparently, and went into casting. He was a virtually independent casting director. He was tough but very sweet and very selective. The first time I saw him with *Big Town*, I fell madly in love with him and went after him, dated him, almost married him. But that didn't mean he was going to cast me. We kept it real separated. If he thought I was right for something, he'd have me in on it, but have two other actresses besides me. He'd pick me up for dinner, but he could never mention anything about my work. If I got it, I got it, if I didn't, I didn't. I respected him but it used to irritate me. Anyway, we're very good friends today.

"That led to a lot of other things. My agent's office was very close to Batjac, John Wayne's company. He took me over to see Andy McLaglen, at that time an AD [assistant director]. Andy said I would be really right for a major motion picture *The High and the Mighty* (1954) they were doing and to be there for testing the next morning. The director, Bill Wellman, was not happy at all with Andy's decision. He had a fit. How dare Andy say I could test when he, the director, had never seen me. He was really a very gutsy, crusty, egotistical kind of man. He said, 'Just call her at home and tell her not to come.' But I'd already left for the studio. They planned to send me home and not even run any film on me. But my agent was with me and he'd already signed the contract. You had to sign your contract in advance of the test in those days. For me, a very lucky thing was, there was an actress who was kind of a very rich woman [testing opposite John Smith] whose agent, Henry Willson, didn't think the money was good enough for her. So, at the last minute, he pulled her from the test. I didn't know *any* of this, of course. Luckily for me, I ended up testing with John Smith 'cause there was no girl to test with him. That's how I got in. Not knowing I was axed before I even started. Wellman never let you rehearse. He always believed in putting film on you the first time you did the scene. You'd try to remember everything he told you and hope you knew the lines. The minute we finished the test, he said, 'That's it. I've found my Nell Buck and I found my Milo Buck. I don't care about anybody else.' I was signed to *The High and the Mighty* before they even saw the screen test. That picture sort of catapulted me into a different arena.

"Before that, I did *The Vanquished* [1953], where I met Jan Sterling. I met her again on *The High and the Mighty* and she really took me over. She really was my mentor. She took me to Louise Long, the masseuse that used to mold the stars.

"Another film that came along was *Man with the Gun* [1955] … Sammy Goldwyn, Jr.'s, first film to produce and they didn't want me. The girl really needed to be reminiscent of Jan Sterling and I wasn't. I had kind of honey-blonde hair at that time. Jan knew I wasn't going to get the part, so she dyed her hair darker. She went in with a kind of honey blonde color and said, 'Now can Karen play the part?' Which I did. Jan was also, at that time, mistress of ceremonies for the Golden Globes. I was up against Shirley MacLaine, Kim Novak and a lot of people, but I got the award as the most promising newcomer, based on *High and the Mighty*. Jan gave me the award, which was really lovely. That began a whole lot of work for me.

"I did a *Stagecoach West* with Bill Campbell and Lee Van Cleef [1961]. I did a lot of westerns which I never felt I belonged in, they were just not my type. But they had more character … so you worked, you just did it and never said no. I hated westerns, I just didn't ever feel they were what I was capable of doing. I never felt I got the opportunity to do things I would have been better at doing. But it was leading me to improving my work constantly. I got very hooked on the work, more than hooked on becoming more important."

In the mid–1950s, appearing in a TV show directed by Ida Lupino, Karen met an actor who would later become instrumental in her career. Karen says he was "a funny little guy from Texas with bug eyes—nobody would have him in their pictures. But I took him under my wing and was very good to him." When this failed actor became producer Aaron Spelling, he remembered Karen. "When Aaron got his very first break as a producer on

Robert Mitchum, Karen and John Lupton in *Man with the Gun* **(1955).**

Johnny Ringo, the pilot was made with Marilyn Erskine, Stanley Kramer's first wife [*laughs*]. Isn't that strange? Anyway, [when it sold as a series] Aaron said, 'I want Karen to play that role.' I didn't want to play it as it was written. The reason I walked out of the series is because I didn't see the role the way Aaron did. I didn't want to play Laura Thomas as Linda Evans was playing her role on *Big Valley* (1965–1969), as a sweet little thing. I wanted to play Laura more as a tomboy; I thought it would be more appealing. I wanted to cut my hair off and play it like Shirley MacLaine. I thought that would be much more endearing. I didn't want to be glamorous. I wanted to go against the grain. Laura would be much more unique in jeans. So we fought! Aaron, in the beginning, allowed me to start out that way. That was my own long hair by the way—

but I wanted to cut it off. There was a lot of [office] intrigue on that series I did not like. I don't want to knock Aaron Spelling because I was probably very difficult at that time because I had a vision of that series. We began to have fights about it and finally they let me out of the series. They began to focus on Mark Goddard as Cully. He was playing what I wanted to play. I wanted to play a young tomboy who was not that pretty but more in trouble and a more interesting character for Don Durant [as Johnny Ringo] to work off of. When I saw the shows, I was very unhappy. I felt it just wasn't my best work. They changed me around and I was stuck playing this pretty little girl, so I balked. I kept trying to insinuate lines I felt were more appropriate. I would change lines and they got absolutely furious with me, which they had every right to get because that's not very professional. But I was the *only* real professional on the show. Don had never done very much of anything … Mark Goddard had never. I was the only one who had ever done *anything*. I already had the Golden Globe, an Emmy nomination, and I really thought I had the right to dictate in certain ways how that series should be. But understand, Aaron was on shaky ground, it was his first thing. Since then, he's done pretty well. I could have followed [what he wanted] if I'd felt comfortable with it, but from the very beginning I was not comfortable. I think I didn't have the power to insist. I always saw it differently than it was written.

"Women are never written well in the character for the most part, particularly in westerns; you're just decoration or a story plot. I want that person to come alive, be more believable. I'd get different impressions when I'd read the script. I'd try to insinuate my performance and my look into that. I would be much more comfortable as a Shirley MacLaine … that kind of offbeat quality. I thought [ingenue] roles were boring. But you don't get that kind of stuff on television [*laughs*]. So, *Johnny Ringo* didn't end happily for Aaron and myself. I liked Don very much … and Terence DeMarney, who played my father. Don was a doll, really. I just think there was a communication problem because Aaron was insecure. At that time, he had every reason to be. He thought (when I was hired) I'd be very dutiful about the whole thing. I meant to be, but we had different ideas about how Laura should play. I think he said I could do it my way as influence so he could sign me. Then, I think, he got pressure from the head office and the network 'cause they were more comfortable with the standard performance. I was grateful he gave me the role, but since it was his first time out, he couldn't fight for me any harder than perhaps he fought. It taught me an awful lot.

I was grateful for the opportunity to learn, even though it was a negative."

Although Karen appeared in *The Sniper* in 1952, she never met the producer of the film, Stanley Kramer, until she was appearing in Jerry Lewis' *The Disorderly Orderly* in 1964. "It took Stanley a year to get a date." Married in 1966, the couple moved to the Seattle area in 1978 and only recently returned to Beverly Hills where she oversees their production company, International Films, and is in charge of the Kramer Library Group. Her most recent project was the remake of *High Noon* with Tom Skerritt which aired on TBS in August of 2000. (Kramer died on February 19, 2001, at 87.)

Karen's philosophy is, "I always have to do things different … against the stream, not with it. I always like a challenge. I married a man who certainly challenged the system and I certainly was challenging it myself many times. In Shirley MacLaine's acceptance speech at the Golden Globes, which I love, she said she was trying to please every director she ever worked with although, she, for the most part, never agreed with anything they told her to do. I felt like saying, 'Isn't that the truth?' She was on a bigger scale and was luckier and had better tools and maybe deeper talent to get that done. We're all a little masochistic, because it's a hurtful business. I call it 'the trouble.' You get up every morning with 'the trouble.' You have that unrest. You see what other people are doing; it upsets you and you want to do it too; you want to get *that* part but it goes to somebody who's totally wrong for it and you get cast in something you're totally wrong for, and you've got to make it interesting.

Acting is all about discovering yourself. When I took a part … words on a piece of paper…, I had to find the backbone of that person and insinuate myself, my ideas, my beliefs and my vision and

Karen, seen here discussing a script with Don Durant, had her own vision of how to play her character on *Johnny Ringo* (1959–1960).

make that a real person ... one you can bring to other people to be fascinating enough to look at or to feel something for that person. It's your own gut that cre-ates it. As you do it, you learn a lot about yourself and you learn about other people too."

Karen Sharpe
Western Filmography

Movies: *The Vanquished* (1953 Paramount)—John Payne; *Man with the Gun* (1955 United Artists)—Robert Mitchum.

Television: *Range Rider*, "The Chase" (1953); *Death Valley Days*, "Claim Jumpin' Jennie" (1956); *Gunsmoke*, "Sweet and Sour" (1957); *Gray Ghost*, "Humanitarian" (1957); *Trackdown*, "Young Gun" (1958); *Desilu Playhouse*, "Ballad for a Badman" (1959); *Rough Riders*, "Wilderness Trace" (1959); *Yancy Derringer*, "A Game of Chance" (1959); *Northwest Passage*, "The Killers" (1959); *Texan*, "Private Account" (1959); *Johnny Ringo*, series regular (1959–'60); *Overland Trail*, "All the O'Mara's Horses" (1960); *Bonanza*, "The Ape" (1960); *Stagecoach West*, "Never Walk Alone" (1961); *Laramie*, "Handful of Fire" (1961); *The Americans*, "Reunion at Blazing Rock" (1961); *Rawhide*, "Gold Fever" (1962); *Rawhide*, "Incident of the Black Ace" (1963); *Dakotas*, "Crisis at High Banjo" (1963); *Gunsmoke*, "Dry Well" (1964); *Wild Wild West*, "Night of the Flaming Ghost" (1966); *Wild Wild West*, "Night of the Ready Made Corpse" (1966).

Marjorie Stapp

Working Actress

The leading lady to Charles Starrett in 1949's *Blazing Trail* and *Laramie* was born in Little Rock, Arkansas, one September 17. "When I was in the seventh or eighth grade, my family moved to California. Originally, I was placed under contract to 20th Century–Fox, although I made no pictures for them at the time. They loaned me to Goldwyn for the Danny Kaye movie *Kid from Brooklyn.* [1946]." When asked why she's in that movie so little, Margie states, "I wanted to go to the University of Chicago, so I wanted out of the picture. Samuel Goldwyn was furious with me—so I was cut out of the opening number and other parts, although you can still spot me at the train

station, greeting Danny. I told Goldwyn he'd already fired two other girls, and was getting along fine without *them*, so he could get along without me ... but he was not happy. I only stayed at the University six weeks, then I returned to California!"

Margie's first leading role was with Charles Starrett, the Durango Kid. "That was on freelance. I was acting in theater, always doing plays. I'd let the casting people know I was in a play and they'd come. I changed agents frequently—I was impatient. With each new agent, we'd make the rounds of the casting people. In those days, there were 5,000 actors and only a few casting people—the studios all had their own. Now it's 100,000 actors and so

Marjorie surrounded by Charles Starrett, Smiley Burnette and Fred Sears in *The Blazing Trail* (1949). Sears served as both actor and director in many Columbia westerns.

many hassles—you even have to read and get call-backs on tiny parts these days, which is ridiculous. That's how I got the part in *Blazing Trail*. Charles Starrett was such a gentleman. He would help me up on the horse, every time! And there were many times when I had to be on a horse! The grips would have done it—but he was always right there. I liked him very much. He was a charming man, so helpful to me." Smiley Burnette was different. "He *did* ignore people—I didn't talk to him at all! But, he was always joking, the few times he was there!"

She worked for director Fred Sears several times "but never had personal contact off the set." The director who *did* im-

press her was Fritz Lang, who directed the film noir classic *The Blue Gardenia* (1953). "Fritz Lang was a top, top director, but very temperamental—yelling at grips, Anne Baxter, everybody. But, he knew how to handle me—he said, 'Dear Margie—take it easy now; relax.' He yelled at everybody but me! He came to see me in a play and said, 'You're a very fine actress.' If he hadn't been so old, he'd have used me in other pictures. Most directors would tell me, 'Okay, bring it up' or 'Bring it down'—but normally I didn't need direction."

Early on, Marjorie worked as a receptionist ... for Bugsy Siegel! "But I didn't know it, until he was murdered and

I recognized his picture in the paper! The Flamingo Hotel in Las Vegas had an office on Sunset Boulevard in Hollywood. They had four phones (which never rang) and I was to take reservations. All the filing cabinets had nothing in them. But it was a big, plush office. I got so bored doing nothing, I started going on interviews. I'd take two, three hours or more for lunch. One day, the man who hired me had to wait on me for two hours, then he fired me [*laughs*]! Earlier, he'd introduced me to Mr. Siegel (no first name or nickname was given). He was just like George Raft, he had bodyguards—just like in the movies!"

Margie worked with many of the top cowboy stars of her day, but not always in westerns. She appeared in *Battle of Bloody Beach* (1961) with Audie Murphy. "I twisted my ankle once—Audie was near and caught me before I hit the ground. He always asked how the ankle was. It was a very nice relationship. I don't understand the stories you hear about Audie Murphy."

As for Hugh O'Brian, TV's *Wyatt Earp* (1955–1961): "Hugh was dating my girlfriend, Lorna Thayer, when I did that. She was jealous of her boyfriends, so other than mentioning my knowing Lorna, nothing much was said or done. Hugh was easy to work with."

Nick Adams of *The Rebel* (1959–1961) "was a dear man. Nick said to me, 'Margie, you should be a big star. You should send your picture to every producer; send them your résumé. If you'd do that, you'd go places. You are so good. You really should do that.' But, I couldn't push myself that way… Nick and I worked well together."

Tim Holt starred in *The Monster That Challenged the World* (1957). "I didn't get to know him too well. He thought the little girl [Mimi Gibson] who played Audrey Dalton's daughter was good and mainly paid attention to her."

Jeffrey Hunter starred in 1957's *Gun for a Coward*. "He asked me out, but un-fortunately I was going with somebody, so I didn't go. I liked him a lot—a very attractive man!"

Margie worked with Randolph Scott and James Garner, but "they didn't impress me. The biggest star that *did* impress me was Burt Lancaster. I was in *Elmer Gantry* [1960]. When they shoot things, they do the master shot, the two-shot, then the closeup. Well, we did the master, the two shot and Burt did his closeup. When it came time for my closeup, Burt stood there and gave me my lines! Big stars don't do that—usually it's the script girl who gives you bad readings that aren't helpful. But Burt did it; what a guy! The director, Richard Brooks, was a nut. He'd only give you your scene, not the whole script! I never had that happen before—or since!"

Rory Calhoun starred in *The Saga of Hemp Brown* (1958) but Margie was more impressed with the main villain. "I am friends with Claudia Bryar, who is the wife of John Larch. John murdered me in the picture! A few years ago, Claudia appeared in *Psycho III* [1986] with my husband, Robert Alan Browne—and John was on the set, but having trouble getting around."

Remembering *The Far Country* (1955), she says, "Walter Brennan was a real character. At four in the afternoon, a pretty, young boy, who was a grip, was standing there. Walter grabbed him by the crotch and laughed, 'I couldn't help it—it comes over me this time of the day.' So, I avoided Walter Brennan each afternoon around 4:00, that's for sure [*laughs*]!"

Good billing, but Margie is hardly in the 1949 Columbia serial *Adventures of Sir Galahad* as Queen Guinevere. "They cut out 90 percent of what I did. I was captured by the black knight—and the horse I was riding didn't have the saddle properly fastened underneath. It was not tied at the bottom. It was a grip's fault. I was

Steve Darrell, Steve Pendleton, Marjorie and Charles Starrett are amused by Smiley Burnette's antics in *The Blazing Trail* (1949).

riding side-saddle and sliding off as I was galloping up that hill. I held onto the reins for dear life! I was so mad, I was telling everybody off. I yelled at anyone and everyone. It apparently made them angry at me, because most of my part was cut out! Dialogue, if not entire scenes. They were really angry at me, but I was furious about the situation! Lois Hall was the other female [the Lady of the Lake], and I found her to be both beautiful and talented. I wish we'd gotten to know each other better. Sir Galahad, George Reeves, was a bit of a jolly ... making jokes, things like that."

An early marriage ended in divorce, but produced a daughter. "She lives in New York. That's where I met Bob, my present husband. I did *The Subject Was Roses* on Broadway, and we met at a vocal class. When we returned to California I started doing TV things, like three movies of the week, *Quantum Leap* [1989–1993], *Jake and the Fat Man* [1987–1992], *Columbo* [1971–1977]. I have several of the films I made. I have a copy of my *26 Men* [1957–1959]. Tris Coffin was so handsome—such a good actor. And the same can be said for his sidekick, Kelo Henderson. I was surprised Kelo didn't do more— he should've gone further."

Margie and her husband moved to North Carolina a few years ago and, in October 1998, attended the Asheville Film

Marjorie obviously sees through Smiley Burnette's disguise in *The Blazing Trail* (1949).

Festival. But recently, they relocated to California. "I wanted to go back home. We took an apartment on the ninth floor of a building next to the Farmer's Market, across from CBS Studio Center. I now intend to return to my great love—acting!"

Marjorie Stapp
Western Filmography

Movies: *Blazing Trail* (1949 Columbia)— Charles Starrett; *Laramie* (1949 Columbia)— Charles Starrett; *Rimfire* (1949 Lippert)— James Millican; *The Far Country* (1955 Universal-International)—James Stewart; *Gun for a Coward* (1957 Universal-International)— Fred MacMurray; *Shoot-Out at Medicine Bend* (1957 Warner Bros.)—Randolph Scott; *The Saga of Hemp Brown* (1958 Universal-International)—Rory Calhoun; *Wild Westerners* (1962 Columbia)—James Philbrook.

Television: *26 Men*, "Incident at Yuma" (1957); *Wyatt Earp*, "It Had to Happen" (1958); *Californians*, unknown title (1958); *Tales of the Texas Rangers*, "Ambush" (1958); *Rebel*, "In Memory of a Son" (1960).

Olive Sturgess

Ingenue

Bubbly, vivacious Olive Sturgess first came to prominence playing Carol Henning, girlfriend to Chuck MacDonald (Dwayne Hickman), Bob Cummings' nephew, on the *Love That Bob* comedy series of the 1950s. Born October 8, in Ocean Falls, British Columbia, Canada, she smiles, "I am only 5'2" tall; which reminds me of the *Wagon Train* I did with Mickey Rooney ["Wagons Ho!," the fourth season opener in 1960]. I had to take my shoes off so I would look shorter than Mickey in the marriage scene. I had low heels but was still taller than him. It was muddy on the Universal backlot, where the wagons were put in a circle. So, there I was, getting my feet muddy in that scene [*laughs*]. As for the kissing, it was hard to kiss him. It wasn't much of a kiss— he gave a funny look at the camera which I didn't know until I later saw the show. It came off all right—we were working together on a par. He was wonderful to be with. It was thrilling working with Mickey Rooney. Imagine, being able to work with Mickey Rooney, the one and only! He is such a professional. I'd seen him in the movies since I was a child! On the show, he was always doing his own thing—being with the director, that sort of thing. We didn't socialize—Mickey was a bit distant from me. Years later, when he wrote his book, I got his autograph—but he had such a line and was so busy, that we didn't

speak and he didn't know it was me. When he finished, he and his entourage left immediately!"

Character actress Ellen Corby also appeared on that *Wagon Train* episode. "I worked with Ellen many times—she was a short person, like me, with a wonderful sense of comedy. I wore the wedding gown Elizabeth Taylor had worn in *Father of the Bride* [1950]! I don't know how many times the gown, which was beautiful, was

You may not know the name of Olive Sturgess at first, but you've seen her in dozens of television westerns in the 1950s and 1960s.

recycled, but I got to wear it with very few alterations. It needed shortening only two inches! My daughter is still always talking about that dress."

As for the star of *Wagon Train*, "Ward Bond was hard to get to know, but he was good to work with."

Of all the programs she appeared on, only one involved a bad accident, and it was on *Wagon Train*. "I rolled down the hill—it was the scene where I'm to be picked up and lifted on a sling. They carried me up a hill. They shot the scene as high as they could—then I fell off this stretcher or sling. I also got scratched on another show where I was driving horses. I pulled my arms—the stunt girl should have done the driving!"

In the mid–1950s, Olive landed a contract with Universal-International. Like Olive, Clint Eastwood had a small role in *Lady Godiva* (1955). "Clint Eastwood was under contract to Universal at the same time I was. He even did my screen test with me. Clint told me he was going to be a western actor; he planned that, although we were doing different things at the studio while under contract. Things like taking lessons in horseback riding, fencing, learning how to shoot guns, even voice and dancing lessons! All the things you learn as a contract player. So, when I went on to do westerns, I could do all that stuff! Clint wanted to be a western actor—and he really ended up being just that!"

One TV show Olive fondly recalls is *Sugarfoot* (1957–1961) starring Will Hutchins. "I had a mad crush on Will. He was so handsome, so charming, just great! I wonder why that show went off the air— it was a good show. Will is kind of like Henry Fonda in his way. It was a real treat to work with Will Hutchins. His show had stories—not violence! *Sugarfoot* was a wonderful show! Myron Healey was also in the episode I did. He always seemed to

play such a heavy—he was in lots of stuff I did."

Another of the Warner Bros. westerns Olive guested on was *Cheyenne* (1955–1962). "Clint Walker was wonderful, and famous. People in those days weren't vegetarians, but Clint was! This 6'4" man would be eating nuts, bananas, health food! I always seemed to work with actors who were either very short or very tall! Clint is an excellent person!"

Olive was one of the busiest actresses in Hollywood in the 1960s. When asked about all her various leading men such as *Have Gun Will Travel* (1957–1963) star Richard Boone. "He was funny, different, wonderful. He had large potholes in his face—such bad skin. I only had a very small role in the show, but I found 'Paladin' to be friendly, and pleasant!"

The *Destry* TV series (1964) was an offshoot of the famous Max Brand movie western. "John Gavin later went into politics. He was interesting. Such a handsome man! John Abbott and Charlie Ruggles, two terrific character actors, were great with the comedy in this episode."

Bonanza (1959–1971) was an early color show. "Maybe the first of the nighttime color westerns. Denver Pyle was in my episode—he played a corrupt sheriff. The thing I remember most concerns Hoss—Dan Blocker. He had terrible language! He used foul language—it just came out! Michael Landon I had worked with before. He was very nice, but at this time, he seemed preoccupied. Of course, by then, he was a 'star.' Lorne Greene and I are both Canadians. Lorne was a very famous radio announcer in Canada before he came to the United States. He was very well known, so I knew him when I was a little girl."

For *The Tall Man* (1960–1962), which was shot at Universal and starred Barry Sullivan as Pat Garrett and Clu Gulager as Billy the Kid, Olive and Judy Nugent

Rod Cameron and Olive in a publicity pose for *Requiem for a Gunfighter* (1965), the Alex Gordon production that cast, to the delight of viewers, such former western stars as Cameron, Tim McCoy, Johnny Mack Brown, Bob Steele, Lane Chandler, Raymond Hatton, Dick Jones and Rand Brooks all in one production.

played tomboy sisters, May and June McBean, in three separate episodes. Old timer Andy Clyde was their father. There was talk of turning the McBean clan into a series, but the idea never came to fruition. "My husband-to-be, Dale Anderson, would see me on the screen in this and other shows, like *Laramie* [1959–1963], that I did at Universal. This is because he is a studio musician. When they would do the *Tall Man* themes, he'd play in the orchestra and there I'd be on the big screen that projected the film as it was being scored! "He played on the score for

Titanic in 1997. He did *The Dinah Shore Show* [1951–1957], *The Dean Martin Show* [1965–1974], all the John Williams movies.

"Clu Gulager was fun—he worked and planned the accent he used as Billy the Kid, that manner of speech. As for my acting, it was like the English actors—I was told I was a character actress because I could do a variety of things, whatever they tossed my way."

When asked if Clu, or some of the other actors, asked her for a date, Olive states, "Clu did not ask me out—he might have been married at the time." However, she did date a couple of actors. "I went out with Johnny Wilder a couple of times; I also went with Nick Adams twice. I did two episodes of his series, *The Rebel* [1959–1961]. Judy Lewis was on one show—she is Loretta Young's daughter by Clark Gable. People would say, 'Shhhh. Don't tell anybody. Judy doesn't even know this.' But everybody else did. Nick and I had done two or three different shows before this—*Matinee Theater*, a *live* program, was one! When Nick and I went out, it was a casual thing—no great love or anything like that. Nick took me to visit Natalie Wood, who was married at this time. I think Nick was in love with her. I knew who Natalie Wood was since I was a little girl. I had no idea she would know me, even though I had done a lot of television. Natalie told me, 'I think you are one of the best actresses going right now. I wish I could be half as good as you.' That was very gracious of her to say that! As for Nick, I thought he was very troubled, even then. You could feel he was troubled. It was in the manner he had—that *was* the way he was in real life, always brooding. It was what was in style at the time and it was the way he was in person! When we went out, it was never on his motorcycle! That's one trick he couldn't pull on me. We always went in a car! Incidentally,

Nick married Carol Nugent, Judy Nugent's actress-sister."

The Rebel is also special to Olive for another reason. "My nephew, Leonard Sturgess, played my baby on an episode called 'Scavengers.' When they said they needed a baby, I told them I could provide one. He was six months old at the time. He was so cute—he'd look at the ceiling, things like that. He cried when I showed him the video of it recently!"

Maverick (1957–1962) was one of the biggest shows on TV when Olive guested. "Jack Kelly was another old friend from Universal. A lot of the guys made it really big. Like David Janssen, who was there with me, and his future wife, Dani Crayne. Jack Kelly was always busy. Such a good actor. I played a Quaker girl on one—I thought it came off very well, too!"

The Texan (1958–1960) is yet another of the many programs which guest starred Sturgess. "Rory Calhoun was so nice—and regardless of what his wife Lita Baron said about him [claiming, during divorce proceedings, he slept with many women], he did not come on to me. Rory couldn't have been a nicer guy, a gentleman. He was flirtatious, but this was harmless fun. I always seemed to play ingenues, or somebody's daughter or granddaughter. I often didn't play the romantic type, so maybe that was it."

For ABC's *Lawman* (1958–1962), "Peggie Castle played an Amanda Blake 'Miss Kitty' type. As for Amanda, she was smoking all the time! She told me when she landed the *Gunsmoke* series that she wasn't sure she wanted to do it. Later, she was glad she did. She was a perfect Miss Kitty! I thought she'd died of lung cancer, until I recently found out it was actually AIDS, which she contacted from her [bisexual] husband, who also died of the disease! I knew Rock Hudson in the 1950s and I never knew he was a homosexual. It was really a shock. In fact, in my screen

Olive as she appeared in *Requiem for a Gun-fighter* (1965).

test for Universal, I was testing for a role as Jane Wyman's daughter in her second picture with Rock, *All That Heaven Allows* [1955]. I had been seen on TV and the studio felt I would be right for the part, but Jane Wyman didn't think I was right. Gloria Talbott got the role, but I got a contract!"

The Virginian (1962–1970) was the first 90-minute color western. "I like it because it was one of the first shows where I was 26 and not playing 16. I could finally play older parts!"

One of the last series Olive appeared on was *Wide Country* (1962–1963), which starred Earl Holliman as rodeo rider Mitch Guthrie. "Earl Holliman is a special person, and so handsome. I stopped working when my daughter was born. Of course, my husband was still working, and when Earl would see him, he'd ask why I didn't go back to work. I was up for *Flipper* but I told them I didn't want to go to

Florida and leave my baby. But Earl Holliman is such a good actor—a very down-to-earth person. That's why he goes on and on!"

Reflecting upon her only western feature, *Requiem for a Gunfighter* (1965), Olive tells us, "Rod Cameron was making sort of a comeback at this time. He was very gracious, and very kind. You can see it in him in the scene when we are having dinner—his look. He was a professional man, with his lines learned. I played a city girl from Chicago in that. The director, Spencer Bennet, was so good. He was so experienced in directing westerns. He wanted authenticity. And the same can be said for the producer, Alex Gordon. Alex was very authentic. He liked to use the old stars. He'd get all the wonderful mature actors, like Rod Cameron. He'd get all of them together and make a good movie. I enjoyed knowing Alex Gordon. I felt he was a nice man, and I was so grateful he cast me in the movie. I was a newlywed and had never done anything but small parts in features—but a lot of TV. It was a highlight when he cast me. The actors he chose were so equally balanced. Rod Cameron and Stephen McNally and the others. Mike Mazurki was wonderful—Alex was clever in his casting, so smart. Mike Mazurki brought humor to the picture. With his cauliflower ear, his looks and attitude were like *Guys and Dolls*. Mike Mazurki was an innocent guy but a bad guy at the same time. Remember in the film the snake Mike had which he put in the saddlebag of Rod Cameron's horse? It was a rubber snake, but he worked over and over until it looked real—putting it in the saddlebag. It was remarkable how he did that. And Alex Gordon was always there, making it look real! I wish he'd make another western. They are like the backbone of this country. You learned the history of this country through western films." Tim McCoy also appeared in

Requiem. "Wasn't it marvelous to see Tim McCoy? He had such dignity and poise when he rode. You felt strengthened and confident with people like that!" Dick Jones played the gunfighter in *Requiem.* "He has the most marvelous laugh—I wish I could laugh like that. He is so good like that. My very favorite movie, incidentally, is *Pinocchio* [1940]. My three-year-old granddaughter loves it, too. Dick, then Dickie Jones, played Pinocchio! But we never talked about it."

In between westerns, Olive was involved in a rodeo. "I was Grand Marshal of the Rodeo in Whittier. I learned to ride on a single footer horse at Universal-International. However, the rodeo people gave me a cow-roping horse. I was leading it around the circle, going fast up into the middle, then stop. He was going so fast, I had to hold onto the horn of the saddle. The horse stopped so fast, he threw me over his neck while I was holding onto his mane! My mother was laughing so hard— my behind was showing! My bottom was in the air! To the whole audience! I managed to get back on the horse's saddle, without ever touching the ground! The audience laughed and whistled, stomped and applauded."

Reflecting on her illustrious career, Olive muses, "In those days [the 1950s and early 1960s], they had good stories. In a recent *Hollywood Reporter*, Mary Tyler Moore said it exactly right. She said writing for television today 'is like writing shorthand. There is no depth to anything.' We used to have stories that had a begin-ning, middle and an end; stories that made you feel good after watching them. Not those terrible, shallow shows of today— they are just not funny. Back in the 1950s and 1960s, we had stories that were genuine, stories of the west done with humor or drama and romance. A good show you looked forward to seeing. You really felt good when you saw the TV shows of those days."

Olive Sturgess Western Filmography

Movies: *Requiem for a Gunfighter* (1965 Embassy)—Rod Cameron.

Television: *Tales of Wells Fargo*, "John Wesley Hardin" (1957); *Cheyenne*, "Renegades" (1958); *U.S. Marshal*, "The Threat" (1958); *Sugarfoot*, "Short Range" (1958); *The Texan*, "The Ringer" (1959); *Rawhide*, "Incident at Chubasco" (1959); *Have Gun Will Travel*, "The Chase" (1959); *Lawman*, "The Huntress" (1959); *Buckskin*, "Mary MacNamara" (1959); *The Rebel*, "Scavengers" (1959); *Laramie*, "Company Man" (1960); *Wagon Train*, "The Benjamin Burns Story" (1960); *Wagon Train*, "Wagons Ho!" (1960); *Maverick*, "Last Wire from Stop Gap" (1960); *The Rebel*, "The Pit" (1961); *Maverick*, "The Golden Fleecing" (1961); *Tall Man*, "McBean Rides Again" (1960); *Tall Man*, "Reluctant Bridegroom" (1961); *Tall Man*, "Millionaire McBean" (1961); *The Outlaws*, "The Sisters" (1962); *Bonanza*, "A Hot Day for a Hanging" (1962); *Wide Country*, "Girl from Nob Hill" (1963); *Destry*, "Deputy for a Day" (1964); *The Virginian*, "Big Image ... Little Man" (1964); *Bonanza*, "Lothario Larkin" (1965).

Ruth Terry

Republic's Singing Sweetheart

Ruth Terry, the multi-talented star of movies from the late '30s to late '40s was born Ruth McMahon October 21, 1920, in Benton Harbor, Michigan. "My mother played the piano, I sang at home. There were amateur nights at local movie palaces, and the winner received a dollar! That would buy me tickets to ten movies—they cost a dime in those days. I won every week, and they finally told me I couldn't sing anymore! So I entered a contest at WLS Radio in Chicago and won a contract to sing with the Paul Ash Theater Orchestra. I was billed as 'the Youngest Blues Singer' as I was only 12. In 1933, I went with the Paul Ash Orchestra to the Chicago World's Fair, playing at the Pabst Blue Ribbon Casino." From Benton Harbor were the Capps Family—an acrobatic dance team. "The Capps and the McMahons were friends—and they took me as part of their fairs and vaudeville. I must also mention that my aunt was private secretary for many years to Irving Berlin. I got a job at his music publishing house. People would come into this Tin Pan Alley–like place, pick up sheet music that Mr. Berlin had written, and I would sing it. If they liked it, they bought it!"

The versatile Ruth did other things as well. "I appeared in nightclubs with Ed Sullivan, who couldn't pronounce words even then [*laughs*]! But he was a famous newspaper columnist for the *New York Daily News*. I was in his column so often that I developed 'a name.' It was Walter Winchell who gave me my new name—Ruth Terry—after Babe Ruth and Bill Terry, both famous baseball players of the day. I was booked into Jack Dempsey's in Miami, and it was there 20th Century-Fox first saw me. Later, at the Chez Paree in Chicago, they heard me again and offered a screen test. My daddy told them to either sign me or forget it—no screen test. So, I got my contract, with options of course, in 1937, at age 16. I had one line in *International Settlement* [1938]. It was so God-awful. It was made first but, *Love and Hisses* [1937] which starred Walter Winchell was released first. I was making $400 a week, and given lessons every day—drama and singing. My singing coach was Jule Styne, who later wrote so many standards—but at this time he was only a piano player. Fox offered to keep me on, at the same salary, so I left them to freelance."

Around this time, Ruth was put under contract to Howard Hughes. "Hughes loaned me—exclusively—to Republic. That's how I got at Republic." It was there that singer Ruth Terry appeared in many musicals, and westerns *with* lots of music. "I did *Call of the Canyon* [1942] with Gene Autry, my first western. Two things I remember about the picture and Gene Autry. First, I *never ever* talked to the man! He

Ruth co-starred with Roy Rogers in three B-westerns at Republic in the 1940s.

did speak to the fellows on the picture, but not with the girls. I never said *anything* to him, nor he to me. I don't even recall him saying 'Good morning.' We just did the scenes and that was it. The other thing I remember is he kept us waiting one night.

Gene was a very big star then, and he had it in his contract he wouldn't have to work after six P.M. Gene was punctual, knew his lines, always there in the morning. But on the last day of shooting, they needed another two hours. They didn't want to bring

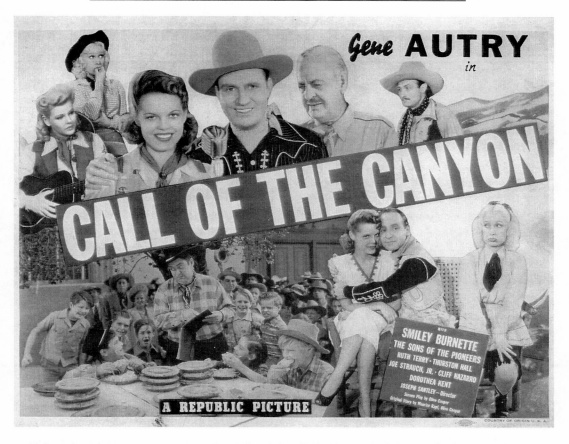

Although a romantic screen team, Gene Autry hardly spoke to Ruth during the lensing of *Call of the Canyon* (1942). Others shown on this title lobby card are guitarist Jean Lucius, Dorothea Kent, Thurston Hall, John Holland, Smiley Burnette and double talk artist Cliff Nazarro (with his arms around Ruth).

everybody back the next day for just a couple of hours shooting. They argued with Gene about breaking his rule, just this once. He firmly said, 'No.' Finally, he said 'Okay, let's eat dinner.' He never came back! He left us all there, waiting on his return—which didn't happen until the next morning! A lot of people got an extra day's pay as a result, but not me as I was under contract to Hughes."

An unbilled extra in Ruth's *Youth on Parade* (1942) at Republic was Yvonne De-Carlo. "She was just starting at that time. She said, 'Oh, Ruthie, if I could just do the things you're doing, I would be so happy. I want to act so badly and I want

the fame.' Well, she wanted it and she got it."

Heart of the Golden West (1942) was the first picture Ruth did with Roy Rogers. "It was a lot of fun, because Roy was a lot of fun. He joked with us; he was so sweet. Gabby Hayes, Smiley Burnette and the Sons of the Pioneers were all in it—all people Roy had worked with over and over; so he was comfortable. It was one of the films I made in Lone Pine. Roy never changed one little bit over the years."

One incident Ruth recalls vividly. "Roy and I were on location at Lone Pine. We were a distance away on horseback and were supposed to ride into camera range.

We were out there waiting for the shot when all of a sudden Trigger reared. Roy, being used to that, hung right on. He looked around to see what had frightened Trigger and it was a rattlesnake. Roy took out his gun and—bang! Now, they were all blanks of course, but a blank can cut right through you. And it did. He hit that rattler. Jumped off his horse, grabbed that snake and went on into the scene and said, 'Wait a minute.' With that he took his knife and slit right down the middle of that rattlesnake, took the skin off, dried it the next day and he had it wound around his hat the following day. True story!"

Speaking of horses, Ruth jokes, "I never understood them and they never understood me! But I coped. As long as somebody was down there out of camera range holding on to the reins while I said my lines, I was just fine [*laughs*]!"

"I made *Lake Placid Serenade* [1944] at Republic, and in Roy's obituary, I noticed they said he was in it. I don't recall that. He must have been in a specialty or something. [Ruth is correct. Roy sang "Winter Wonderland" in the 1944 musical.] Vera Ralston was the star."

Ralston was the Czechoslovakian-born actress Herbert J. Yates fell in love with, signed to a contract in 1943 and promoted to stardom, as best he could, in the films of John Wayne, Bill Elliott and others. Yates eventually married Vera. Ruth recalls, "We [the rest of the actors at Republic] were never allowed to approach her, speak to her or have any contact with her whatsoever. That was the *law* from Yates. Yates worshiped her and protected her. So I only met her for the first time a few years ago at the Lone Pine Film Festival! It was nice to finally get to know her—she's a dear! She still talks with an accent, of course, and is a lovely person."

Another Ruth Terry western at Republic was Roy's *Hands Across the Border* (1944). "[It was] Republic's answer to the Broadway smash, *Oklahoma*. They wanted someone who could sing as well as act. That started a whole series of musicals that were so-called westerns."

By this time, Hughes had sold Ruth's contract to Republic. "Howard was notorious for having women stashed all over town. When he found out I wouldn't give him anything, he sold me to Republic."

Ruth Terry's most famous picture, and her signature song, was Republic's *Pistol Packin' Mama* (1943). "People still remember me from that film. It was a good little picture. I like it a lot. A lot of hit songs came from those little pictures—'I've Heard That Song Before' by Sammy Cahn and Jule Styne from *Youth on Parade* [1942], for instance."

Robert Livingston was Ruth's leading man in *Pistol Packin' Mama*. "Bobby never understood why he didn't rise higher. He was very bitter toward Republic. He thought he deserved better films, and he did. But Roy and Gene were there—strong competition. Bob died a very unhappy man, actually. He did not like what they had done to him."

Ruth's final western was at Columbia, *Smoky River Serenade* (1947) with the Hoosier Hot Shots and Carolina Cotton. "I did it on freelance, and remember hardly anything about it. It was two years after I left Republic—I had been doing a lot of USO war work in the meantime."

Specifically asked about Republic president Herbert Yates, Ruth frowns, "He was a mean man—very cheap—a tyrant—especially when it came to money! I guess Vera ended up with all his money—she earned it, for putting up with him all those years!"

Circa 1947, Ruth married and moved to Canada for a number of years. After her divorce, she returned to the States in 1957. "I did a *Donna Reed Show*, and other things, like a bit in *Hand of Death* [1962]. I met my present husband, John Ledbet-

Eddie Parker approves as Ruth Terry slaps down hoodlum Joe Kirk in an opening scene from *Pistol Packin' Mama* **(1943).**

ter, and we were married January 29, 1966. I've been retired ever since, and my career today is taking care of my husband."

Ruth Terry
Western Filmography

Movies: *Call of the Canyon* (1942 Republic)—Gene Autry; *Heart of the Golden West* (1942 Republic)—Roy Rogers; *Man from Music Mountain* (1943 Republic)—Roy Rogers; *Pistol Packin' Mama* (1943 Republic)—Robert Livingston; *Hands Across the Border* (1944 Republic)—Roy Rogers; *Smoky River Serenade* (1947 Columbia)—Hoosier Hot Shots.

Television: *Maverick*, "People's Friend" (1960); *Cheyenne*, "Greater Glory" (1961).

Lyn Thomas

Beautiful, Bright and Witty

"I'll tell you right now, I don't sing any more, I don't dance any more and I don't ride a horse. And I hope I never have to ride a horse again [*laughs*]!" But Lyn Thomas—who many people tell, "You're funny," as soon as they get to know her—does honestly enjoy reminiscing about her fun-filled screen career. "I'm an egomaniac, just like all actors and actresses. If they say they're not, they're lying [*laughs*]."

Lyn started life November 2, 1929, in Fort Wayne, Indiana, as Jacqueline Rose Thomas. "I was a Gerber baby. I've been working since I was three months old [*laughs*]. Then I went into modeling and children's things locally, then into teenage modeling, but in the interim, I got involved in the children's local theatre. Kind of like stock, because we would take the show to another city, which I don't think they do any more. You learn by making an ass out of yourself, which I did many times [*laughs*]. At that point in time, they had talent scouts that would go around and check all these little theaters. One of them saw me and said, 'Oh, my God, she's fantastic! Cap your teeth and come to Hollywood' [*laughs*]. So Metro-Goldwyn-Mayer brought me out in 1947 under contract for six months. I was 17."

"I was in a lot of classes with Elizabeth Taylor, and Roddy McDowall was a friend of mine forever. That whole group was there at the time. But I wouldn't go to bed with Mayer so I didn't do very well [*laughs*]. I said, no way. Louie B. Mayer [head of MGM] was just the crummiest, oldest creep, as far as I was concerned, but unless you go to bed with somebody, you didn't do anything. I was too young and too dumb. Later, I just gave it away—that's stupid [*laughs*]. At MGM, you weren't allowed to do anything ... you were their chattel, but they gave you a background. They really did."

That "background" led to her first role at Monogram in 1947, *Stage Struck*, about girls trying to get to Broadway but winding up as entertainment pieces in seedy nightclubs via a shady talent agency. Lyn co-starred with Audrey Long, Pamela Blake, Wanda McKay and "Conrad Nagel! I don't know many women alive today that ever made a picture with Conrad Nagel. I think the rest of them are all dead [*laughs*]."

Home in San Antone, still under her real name, Jacqueline Thomas, followed in 1948. "That was at Columbia. I didn't go to bed with Harry Cohn either. He didn't like that very much. My leading man, Bill Edwards, was very nice but he was the lousiest actor in the whole world. I mean, he was terrible. I kept trying to help him in scenes and kept trying to do things, but he was like a wooden stick. He wouldn't move, he wouldn't bend. I said, 'Listen to me when I talk to you ... that's how you act, you have to listen to what

I'm saying. Don't just wait for the cue.' And he wouldn't. It was a shame, because he was a nice-looking man. He just wouldn't listen, he wouldn't do all these things that you want, and you have to have this.

"I was kept at Columbia as kind of a threat to Joan Caulfield, who was under contract then. We were very much similar at that age. Whenever anything would go wrong, I'd go make tests. Of course, I never got the pictures, 'cause I didn't go to bed with Harry [*laughs*]. And as far as I'm concerned, these gals all did. They must have, because I was all set to do *Mighty Joe Young* [1949] at RKO and Terry Moore ... Howard Hughes got that for her. She's weird, just weird. Very pretty, but weird."

Lyn was under contract to Hal Wallis following MGM; it was he who changed her name. "He said I could have Gwen or Lyn, and I said, 'I'll take Lyn because it's the last half of Jacqueline.' I was under contract to Hal Wallis in late 1949,

Lyn appeared with Roddy McDowall in *Black Midnight* (1949) and *Big Timber* (1950).

1950. He had put me under contract and chased me around the desk a few times. Wouldn't do that, either [*laughs*]! I left Wallis because he didn't pick up my six month option."

Another six-month run, this time at 20th Century–Fox, found that studio using Lyn as a "threat" to June Haver should she give them trouble.

In 1948, Lyn was reunited at Monogram with her "classmate" from MGM, Roddy McDowall. "He said, 'My God, we're back together again!' Budd Boetticher directed our *Black Midnight* [1949]. Budd lives right down below me in Ramona, so I called him when Roddy died and said I want to come down to see him. 'Oh,' he said, 'I'm so busy right now, I'm getting ready to do the picture of my life' and all this ... and I said, damn, he hasn't changed one bit, he's so full of himself. He's got the biggest ego ... but, oh, Roddy and Budd. We had so much fun on location. But Budd's just got a deal with ego."

Lyn learned to ride horseback while filming *Black Midnight*. "The wranglers were teaching me how to mount and dismount without a mounting block and get my butt over the side of that horse. God, I'm used to hoisting a highball glass, not putting my leg over a horse [*laughs*]! They always gave me a horse that was too wide so I couldn't control him with my knees. The crew took me out one night after shooting and we were playing pool. You know how sometimes you have to hike one leg up on the table to make a shot? I fell off the pool table [*laughs*]! Everyone the next day said, 'She's all tired because she's been trying to get on this horse' ... they all covered for me. Which I thought was so cute. The whole crew, 'Oh, no, she's just been having an awful time with the horse.' What happened was I fell off the pool table [*laughs*]! So horses and I have never gotten along real well. I had one scene where I had to ride on the back of the horse with Roddy. I got on that horse, but what they didn't know, because it was a western saddle of course, was that every time the horse bounced it was hitting me right in the hoo-hoo and I kept yelling 'Roddy, we gotta stop! We gotta stop!' Finally, I just slid right off the back of the horse. They said, 'Cut, cut, what's the matter?' I said it was killing me!

"I had a double who did all my horse riding in *Black Midnight*. Budd fell in love with her and they had a big romance. How long can they romance for 12 days [*laughs*]? She was rooming with me and she said, 'Oh, we're going to get married,' and I said, 'Boy, if you believe all that, you are a sad, sorry little girl.' Her name was Ann Robinson. She did several things later. She was my stunt double because she was a great horsewoman. She was excellent, really great. And Budd was good. I like Budd, but he was temperamental and egotistical and, boy, you do what he said, so I said, later Charlie. Fortunately, his sights were set on her instead of me, so I breezed through that one."

Completely the opposite was the producer of *Black Midnight*, Lindsley Parsons. "Wonderful, adorable, sweet man. I made many pictures with Lindsley. He always had me on the show, he kept thinking he was going to get me in bed. I kept promising I would and I never did. But I let him think I was going to. We went to Mexico, to Acapulco, for a picture and all this. He was just an adorable man, very soft and gentle and never pressured anybody. That's the only way I could describe him. Just a doll."

Lyn recalls that eventually her agent got her an interview with Howard Hughes. "He was going to do *My Forbidden Past* [1951] at RKO with Robert Mitchum and Ava Gardner. Howard Hughes met me and said, 'She's pretty good.' Of course. I'm not endowed like Jane Russell, not by any means [*laughs*],

so he had a special corset made for me, to make my boobs look like Jane Russell. It took two weeks to get me ready just for the test. Billy Wilder did the test I made with Ava Gardner and she was a doll, I just loved her, she was wonderful. After the test, I was told I had to go meet Mr. Hughes at his house in Beverly Hills for dinner. So his henchman drove me up there and I sat in Hughes' house and I waited and I waited. Finally, Howard Hughes came in, in his sneakers and rope belt. He really did wear a rope belt. But he was very neat and clean. We had dinner in front of the fireplace. He thought the test was very nice and he had plans for me and this and the other ... and now we were going to go in the other room and discuss it. I said, 'What other room? Come on, you're not going to pull that routine on me?' And he said, 'Well, that's part of show biz.' He didn't say it in that manner, of course. I also realized everyone said that he was deaf, but he heard what he wanted to hear at that point in his life [*laughs*]. Maybe *later* he couldn't hear anything at all, but he heard what he wanted to hear. And I said, no way Jose, just forget it. A fellow came up in an old Chevrolet, picked me up and took me home. Never saw Hughes again. My test with Ava Gardner sat on the floor for one year in Hughes' office and he would not let anybody have it to show it. It was a good test, it really was. When I finally got it, a year later, I got some other jobs off of it, but he was pissed. Janis Paige got the role eventually. I figured, either I'll do it my way or forget it. Besides, I never could have gone to bed with him. No way at all. He was creepy. That was my personal opinion. Very bright. We had marvelous conversation at dinner and he was surprised I had the intelligence I had, I guess, at that age, and that really spurred him on, but he wanted to go to bed. Dumb, dumb, dumb ... I should have. I would have ended up with

Lyn was one of Rex Allen's last leading ladies at Republic.

a contract forever, like Jane Russell. I don't really regret it, but I know darn well if I had, it would have made all the difference, because I had all the opportunities in the world with Hal Wallis and Cohn, Mayer and Howard Hughes. I mean, how many big guys can you have? I know darn well any one of them could have made me a star tomorrow. Any one of them. Because I had the ability to know how to handle it if I would have had the opportunity. But I crucified myself, I guess you would say. Because I said, no, I'm not going to do it that way. Besides, they were so unappealing."

Lyn came to Republic towards the end of the B-western cycle, but made one film each with Allan "Rocky" Lane, Monte Hale and Rex Allen. "My agent got me

those. He was trying to get me under contract there, but they had several girls who were very similar to me, so it didn't work out. But [Republic president] Herbert J. Yates, there's another one. You can put him on the list too. Except for, he had Vera Hruba Ralston by the time I got there. Oh, first day on the set, flowers from Mr. Yates, which I understand he did for everyone, but I don't care who sends them, I love them."

Other co-workers had experienced problems with Allan Lane, and Lyn was no exception. "He was extremely egotistical. I just kind of gave him a lot of room, because he was the king of the mountain. He never made any overtures toward me or anything. I mean, he was nasty to the director, everybody in the crew. I was a big crew person. They're the ones that made you look good. They're the ones that help you. I was a gal that was always with the crew when we were on location and things. Everybody else would go to dinner with the producers and all this, but I was out shooting pool with the crew. And I had a ball [*laughs*]. They always thought I was the funniest ... I'm basically a comedian but nobody every let me be a comedian on film."

As opposed to Lane, Monte Hale and Rex Allen were "very nice. Extremely nice. I had a crush on Rex. If he hadn't been married, Rex Allen, Jr., would be my son [*laughs*]!".

In the Republic westerns, Lyn admits, "They kept casting me as the sweet little thing, but I wanted to do comedy so bad. I really did, and I always thought [producers] missed their thing, not letting me do a 'Doris Day type thing.'"

Suddenly, a change of pace: Lyn is a brassy saloon girl in *Frontier Gun* (1958) with John Agar. "Well, they finally let me be me [*laughs heartily*]. But I would have to say John Agar is a blur because that's the way he was ... blur. He was very nice, very sweet, but I got nothing from him to work with him. It's a shame, because he was attractive and he was nice and he had a little bit of ability but he just was blank. That's an awful thing to say ... but he was. He was just ... a wet noodle. You want him to get in there and do it and he just didn't."

One of Lyn's best friends in the business was Steve Brodie, with whom she co-starred in *Three Came to Kill* (1960) (a loose remake of *Suddenly* [1954] with Frank Sinatra), *Here Come the Jets* (1959) and *Arson for Hire* (1959). "Steve and I were just the most simpatico people you'd ever want to meet. Steve and I were together three or four times, and we just had a ball. He had a great sense of humor. I was a nut too, and we would play jokes on

each other. I'll never forget, one really interesting thing, when we were in Mexico City. He was on a picture and I was on another picture and we ran into each other ... 'Oh, my God! Steve, you're here!' I said, 'Steve, come up to the room, we'll have some drinks.' Well, he came up to the room, and five minutes later the manager came up and said the gentleman has to leave. I said, 'What do you mean? This is my brother.' He said, 'I'm sorry, but no men are allowed in the ladies' rooms.' 'Oh, come on, this is my brother, we're working on pictures and all this ... but they made him leave. So Steve snuck up the fire escape to get back in the room and then we sat and drank [*laughs*]. But this is the kind of thing Steve and I would do together. So funny.

"When Steve and I did *Here Come the Jets*, we had a scene in a wind tunnel and all of a sudden he had to kiss me. He says, 'You ready?' I say, 'Yeah, knock them on their butt! Don't let go, and I won't let go either.' So he's kissing me and kissing me and kissing me and finally the director said, 'Cut, cut, cut, cut!' We were just playing it right to the hilt! Of all of the fun times, I never had any sexual relationship with him. He was just the funnest guy. We just had a ball, every picture we did."

Lyn found Jim Davis, her leading man in the 1960 western *Noose for a Gunman*, "was pretty impressed with himself. To me, when you don't have the personality and the charm, you are not very good-looking. It has to come over ... because there are a lot of people who are not very attractive, who become very good-looking, because of their charm, and this man just did not have it. But I'll tell you one that did. Forrest Tucker. We became very good friends and Forrest had that charm ... just unbelievable. Another was Lyle Talbot. He became very attractive because he was charming. He could tell stories. Charming and fascinating, and well-read.

Lyn found Jim Davis "impressed with himself" during the making of *Noose for a Gunman* (1960).

People like that become very attractive. Douglas Fowley was the same way. He could recite anything and he was so charming and well-read, well-versed and ... an actor, when it was being an actor and not just a pretty face. Doug was going to become a priest, then he got involved in theater and decided that was his life."

Lyn even made one film, *Triple Trouble* (1950), with the inimitable Bowery Boys and found them not at all difficult, as others had. "They were wonderful, really great. And very good. Leo Gorcey was extremely well-read. And very intelligent. A lot of people thought he was just a dumb-dumb, but he was just really very interesting. You used to have a lot of time,

to sit around and talk and things like that, and I found him extremely interesting. Huntz Hall was also." However, some actors and actresses have stated that they just kind of winged it as the Boys didn't go by the script and they just pretty much had to jump in with their lines where they could. Lyn agrees. "But if you've got some semblance, if you listened to what they were saying, you know how to answer them. This is what I always say: If you listen to them and look at them, then you know what to say. If it isn't the line, you make up a line. The same way if you're waiting for a cue ... forget it. But if you listen to what they're saying, you can hop in. Usually, too, if somebody's up, as you call it, if they've forgotten their lines, you fill in and carry on the conversation and they don't have to cut.

"I was with Abbott and Costello also. A very small thing on one of their television shows. They were dull. Very dull. They just weren't very interesting and weren't any fun. Of course, in those days, you always had fun on the set."

In the early 1950s, most actresses and actors began to appear in the onslaught of westerns being made for TV. Lyn was no exception. "I did several *Cisco Kid* television things. The crew thought I was a kick in the pants. They would pull jokes on me and do things you wouldn't believe. We just had a ball. They were just so adorable to me. First time I used a gun was on that series. I had to knock out a window and shoot all these people. I kept saying, 'God, I can't even hold the damn thing up, it was so heavy' [*laughs*]. The prop man and everybody's helping me... 'all you have to do, 'cause it's a breakaway window, just hit it and shoot.' I said, 'Do I get to practice?' 'No, you don't get to practice.' Time comes and I'm going to do it. I knocked that window out and I shot that gun and the whole crew collapsed. They just roared! [Duncan Renaldo and Leo Carrillo] were both considerably older. Leo was in his sixties at least when he was doing that show, but Duncan looked very good, as long as he put his girdle on."

After three *Sergeant Preston of the Yukon* (1955–1958) episodes, Lyn smiles, "The dog was wonderful! But [Richard Simmons] was very full of himself. 'I'm the star.' Well, swell, that's great. I don't care if you are the star. Let's do it and get it over with."

As a contradiction, most people found Dick Simmons very easy to work with and Hugh O'Brian, of "Wyatt Earp" (1955–1961), just the opposite. However, Lyn considers Hugh one of her best friends to this day. "He's very big with his Hugh

O'Brian Youth Foundation ... HOBY. He's done wonderful work with that. My very best friend is his right hand gal Virginia, and she travels with him to all these HOBY things. Every year they have a HOBY dinner in Beverly Hills that we attend. Every year, she gets on one side and I get on the other side with Hugh in the middle and I say, 'Pull in your stomach.' It's a little bit roundy [*laughs*]. Hugh is a very hard man to understand. He's very, very shy. You wouldn't believe that, but he's extremely shy. A lot of people don't realize that. He's a very private person. I don't think he ever got married because he didn't want to share his life with anybody. He's just that kind of person."

For *26 Men*, Lyn laughs, "We went to Arizona. We had a ball on those. I remember Tris Coffin was very nice. I had so much fun with those shows, but it was awfully, awfully hot. Anybody that says they want to take a stagecoach across the desert has got to be out of their mind [*laughs*]. I even had to drive a stagecoach and all this. It was miserable. Just miserable. And you had to wear all these dumb period clothes [*laughs*]."

One of the last things Lyn did was with producer-actor Jack Webb. "I was engaged to Jack at one time. He was divorced from Julie London and had started going with Jackie [Loughery] and I was kind of in the middle there. I did a lot of *Dragnet* shows with Jack, because every time he'd get stuck, it was, 'Can you come over and fill in?' He called me one day and said, 'We're going to do this picture with a lion. We're going to do it next week. How's your period?' I said, 'Just fine, thank you, how's yours?' [*laughs*]. He said, 'Well, we can't have anybody on the set that's in their menstrual' ... and I said, 'No, I'll be fine.' So I did this picture with this lion for Jack's veterinarian series with Paul Burke, *Noah's Ark* [1956–1957]. 'You're going to be an animal trainer and your lion won't work any more and you have to take it to the vet and all this.' I got on the set and all of a sudden around the corner comes this great big lion, 350 pounds. The trainer said, 'Don't make any quick moves and just be calm.' This lion's not in a cage, just walking around with this chain link leash. I said, 'Okay, fine' [*laughs*]. The lion came over and the trainer said, 'Don't let him lick you because it will take the skin right off your arm' [*laughs*]. The next day I came in and here's the damn lion. Every time I turned around, here's this lion. I said, 'Why is this lion following me?' And the trainer said, 'He likes your perfume.' I said, 'Well, I *won't* wear it tomorrow.' Every time they brought the lion on the set, half the crew would go up in the catwalks [*laughs*]! Now, I had this scene where I had to get between the lion's legs and pull on his mane to try to make him work for me. 'You sure this lion likes me?' And the trainer said, 'He loves you, he loves your perfume.' So I said, 'Okay, we're going to do this in one take 'cause I ain't going to do this twice.' So I get down and I pull on the mane and that lion's looking at me in the eye and I said, 'You son of a bitch, I'm going to look you right back because you ain't going to get me.' We got the scene and afterwards, Jack said, 'I wouldn't have done that if you'd paid me a million dollars.' Thanks a lot! [*laughs*]. The lion was not declawed, he had his claws. But he did like me and he kept following me around. He was cute and I love animals."

On a personal note, Lyn tells me she's been married six times. "My twenty-first wedding anniversary is coming up and I say, if he doesn't shape up, ain't going to be 22 [*laughs*]. You couldn't total the others and make 21 [*laughs*]. Some of them were bisexuals, you know, which was interesting [*laughs*]. When my father walked me down the aisle last, he said, 'This is the last time.' I said, 'Dad, I'm going to keep doing it til I get it right.'"

Looking back on her career, Lyn is proudest of "the fact I didn't go to bed with Howard Hughes and Mayer and Cohn ... because I still had fun and worked. I didn't become a star, and I don't think I could have handled it if I would have, because I would have been a real ding dong. But it was such fun and it was a wonderful time of my life, which I'll never forget. I want to write a book one day but I have to wait for a lot of people to die before I do. I've met a lot of very, very interesting, wonderful people. It's been tremendous. I wouldn't change it for anything."

Lyn Thomas
Western Filmography

Movies: *Home in San Antone* (1949 Columbia)—Roy Acuff; *Black Midnight* (1949 Monogram)—Roddy McDowall; *Big Timber* (1950 Monogram)—Roddy McDowall; *Covered Wagon Raid* (1950 Republic)—Allan "Rocky" Lane; *The Missourians* (1950 Republic)—Monte Hale; *Red River Shore* (1953 Republic)—Rex Allen; *Frontier Gun* (1958 20th Century-Fox)—John Agar; *Noose for a Gunman* (1960 United Artists)—Jim Davis.

Television: *Cisco Kid*, "Phony Heiress" (1951); *Cisco Kid*, "Ghost Story" (1951); *Cisco Kid*, "Water Well Oil" (1951); *Death Valley Days*, "Which Side of the Fence" (1953); *Sergeant Preston of the Yukon*, "One Bean Too Many" (1955); *Sergeant Preston of the Yukon*, "Trapped" (1956); *Sergeant Preston of the Yukon*, "Skagway Secret" (1956); *Death Valley Days*, "The Sinbuster" (1956); *Colt .45*, "The Gypsies" (1957); *26 Men*, "The Big Rope" (1957); *Ford Theatre*, "Quiet Stranger" (1957); *Jefferson Drum*, "Law and Order" (1958); *26 Men*, "Tumbleweed Ranger" (1959); *Man from Blackhawk*, "Gold Is Where You Find It" (1960); *Wyatt Earp*, "Wyatt Takes the Primrose Path" (1961); *Whispering Smith*, "Stake-out" (1961).

Martha Tibbetts

Ranger Lady

Bob Allen's two-time leading lady, Martha Tibbetts, was born Martha Thorndyke Tibbetts in Melrode Highlands, Massachusetts, in 1912. She grew up in Winchester, Massachusetts. "I started dancing as a child. From the time I was about ten, I would appear in veteran's shows and at hospitals, where they have kids dance. That's how it started. My parents were both very intellectual. My mother graduated from college, which was unusual for women in her time. There

Martha only made two westerns, both with Bob Allen, but the wholesome beauty she brought to both are well remembered today.

were three children in the family but I was the one who hated school. I was just interested in the dancing, plus horses.

"I began riding as a child. I rode in the westerns, did all my own riding. Buzzy Henry played my little brother in one film. I was very friendly with his mother. I knew him up til he was a teenager. His mother had a big riding stable, and the horses I had I kept there, as long as I was in Southern California. I learned to ride and went to Steamboat Springs, Colorado, to study for the summer in one of those theatrical camps. I rode there. I was never on an English saddle until, in San Francisco, I began to ride more and wanted to jump; you can't jump on a western saddle.

"I graduated from high school around 16½ or 17 years old and when I was 18½ I went to New York to visit a friend I'd met through dancing and went to a chorus call of a New York show. I was what we called a modern dancer then. They picked 18 girls out of probably about a hundred. They asked my name and I got up and had to do a time step or something; anyway, I was one of those chosen. I went home and told my parents I had been picked for a show in New York, to be a chorus girl, and they were horrified. I said, 'If I can't get out of the chorus in two years, I'll get out of show business. I'd rather do that than go to one of these damn dramatics schools.'

"For three seasons, I was in three Broadway shows. *Say When* with Mary Boland. That was in 1932. My second show was *Let Them Eat Cake*, a sequel to *Of Thee I Sing*. I had walk-ons and understudies and things like that. I wasn't anybody, I was just in the show. The third was Bob Hope's first Broadway show. Walter Winchell used to write remarks about me, 'Watch the girl on the left,' things like that. Warner Bros. read that, saw the show and took me to Hollywood and signed me up.

"Warner Bros. put me in one or two small things to get me in front of the camera [*Special Agent* (1935)]. But then, I couldn't tell you whether Jack Warner tore up my contract or I did, but he and I had a fight. He was the head of the studio, the one Cagney fought with all the time. Warner fought with everybody. He was impossible, to be very blunt. Anyway, they all wanted to go to bed with me. And I wouldn't go to bed with anybody. I told Warner to go to hell. He'd told me I was supposed to be at a private party at one o'-clock in the morning! So anyway, I was out of the studio.

"Then Howard Hawks was looking for someone, I can't think who it was, she was supposed to make *Ceiling Zero* [1935] with Cagney and O'Brien and the role is the one that's married to O'Brien. But this actress dropped out. Hawks was looking at film tests of people in the studio. He was looking at a test of somebody else, saw me and asked who I was. They told him and he said, 'I want to see her.' He was informed by the head office, 'You don't want her in that!' Hawks told me this later when I got to know him. They said she won't play ball with anybody, you don't want her on the picture. But he'd made up his mind that if I had a harelip and a lisp, he was going to put me in the picture. To make a long story short, that's what he did. He cast me but I was no longer under contract. He didn't know that and they didn't tell him. I worked in the picture two weeks before he knew I wasn't under contract. He told me later I could have held them up, they'd been shooting for weeks. He got his brother Bill to be my agent. I said, 'I don't want to be under contract to Warners.' He said, 'We'll make the contract for the picture. We won't tie you up for after the picture.' He was the one who sent me to Columbia. That's why that was my only good role at Warners.

"Pat O'Brien, when he wrote his autobiography, sent me one and wrote in the front of it, 'My favorite ex-wife' and put in parentheses, 'That is, in the film. Then he said, 'When you walked out on us, darling, we lost an actress,' which I thought was very sweet of him. Of course, Cagney was in a row with Warner all the time. He didn't work for a year because he wouldn't work for Warner. He was in a battle from beginning to end with Warner."

Producer Larry Darmour made Martha's Bob Allen westerns independently and released them through Columbia. "I was under contract to Columbia and they told me they'd like to put me in a couple of westerns. At that time, of course, I was pretty well fed up with Hollywood. But I loved making the westerns. I adore horses and the outdoor country and loved all that. That was a big kick, and it was good training."

Child actor and expert rider Buzz Henry was only about five when he appeared in Bob and Martha's westerns. "He was absolutely the most sensational little horseman you ever saw. I don't think today they would ever allow a child to do the things he did, that his mother did with him. She was a real interesting gal. And knew what she was doing. She trained him. She was divorced from his father and she had a boyfriend. Then, as I said, she made her living with a horse stable she had out in the San Fernando Valley. He was a terrific little boy! In the second picture, I was driving that covered wagon and the horses ran away. Bob Allen jumped through the air and landed on the horse. Well, I had an Uncle Harmon who was born and raised as a cowboy, and he married my aunt, a New England schoolteacher. He was a real character. When they finally came East, he gave up being a cowboy. Harmon and she went to the movies, to see this western I'd made. When they came to the scene near the end, where I was driving that runaway wagon, Harmon rose right up out of his

seat and at the top of his lungs, hollered, 'That's my niece driving that wagon. Look at my niece... I didn't know she knew that much. With that, my aunt yanked him by the seat of the pants and got him down [*laughs*].' I kept in touch with Buzz Henry's mother. I went to San Francisco after the war started and it was shortly after that I was divorced. Buzz used to come and see me. Then, of course, I was out at the stables where his mother was, but he never had an acting career after. I thought he would."

Buzz Henry became a stuntman until he was killed in a motorcycle accident in 1971. "It's a wonder his mother didn't kill him. She really did the most fantastic things with him around the stables. She'd seat him on a bucking horse when he was about seven or eight years old."

As for Martha's remembrances of the star, Bob Allen, she exclaims, 'He was fresh. I had to tell him off the first day. But I'll say this for him, at the end of that first picture, he came to me and wanted me to go to dinner and apologized for the way he was when he first met me. As I look back on the whole thing, if I had known then what I knew later, I would have handled Bob differently. Probably a lot of that was a reaction to what I'd been through at Warner Bros. I thought, 'Oh, boy, here I am out in the middle of the desert at Kernville, back into this rat race again.' Though the picture was corny as the devil, I enjoyed making those two pictures more than I enjoyed anything I ever did in show business, including the dancing. Boy, some of the things they did and some of the accidents that happened while they were making those, to the fellows who were riding those bucking horses and things."

If Martha enjoyed making the westerns so much, why didn't she continue? "I married a man who was second in charge of one of the largest advertising agencies

"Don't mess with Martha," Bob Allen seems to say to veteran heavy Walter Miller in this shot from *Ranger Courage* (1937).

in the U.S. I wasn't interested in falling in love … then all of a sudden he just wanted to marry me. I *thought* I was in love. His career later blew up in his face but it wasn't until he was 60 that it did. He was ten years older than I. He married me under a false name. He was a complete phony. He never went to the college people thought he went to, he never did anything anybody thought. But of course he had a brain or he couldn't have done what he did in handling advertising. But he was an absolute no-good bum. He had more women; he was absolutely woman crazy. I knew I'd made a terrible mistake. The day I left him, was in New York. We'd rented a house in Turtle Bay, because he was going to be doing a lot of work there. I

had a dinner party for about 24 people and my trunk was packed and he didn't even know I was ready to go. The next morning, we were having breakfast and I said, 'I'm leaving, I'm going back to Massachusetts.' He tried to stop me. He didn't think I'd divorce him, but I did. Fortunately, my father was an attorney, so I was taken care of correctly. I just set my jaw and figured I want out. It finished me on romance, I'll tell you that."

One would assume she'd have obvious regrets, not only about the marriage, but about not continuing her career. "After I was divorced, Bill Hawks wanted me to come back. He said I had a typical background getting established, and wanted me to start over again. But there was a problem in our family. My sister, who is 11 years younger than I, was taken very, very ill, and going to have a baby. Also, I was about to have a federal lawsuit against my ex because he'd forged my name and taken money I had earned and everything else… he was just no good. I had a federal case that involved property in Hollywood, Los Angeles and San Francisco. I had been divorced over two years. The case was pending. Anyway, my mother was not able to take care of my sister. I had to go down to New Jersey and never got back 'til six months later and brought my sister and her baby with me because her marriage broke up too. Then the federal law case came up and I had to postpone it, because I couldn't go. That put it off another couple of years. So I had to call Bill and say, 'I can't come to Hollywood, I'm tied up.' I was still waiting on the federal case when I met the next man I married, who is one heck of a guy. He had never been married … busy building a career. I knew I couldn't marry him and have a federal lawsuit after I married. I told him I loved him, no question about that. He just said, let your father and me handle it. And so he did. He was extremely wealthy. To try to sum it up, what made him what he was, what he grew into, was that he founded the first industrial center on the East Coast, in Lawrence, Massachusetts, and it was at the heart of the Depression. He was also involved in the Essex Museum of Salem, Massachusetts, the oldest maritime museum in the country, now in a tremendous expansion which my husband started. The whole maritime section is now named after him. He was everything under the sun. Russell Knight … and he's well-known. In the town, he's what they call a Header. He was born in Marble Head, Massachusetts. His people settled in Marble Head in 1620. In our town hall, all the old famous paintings there, he gave them. He gave them Marble Head Public Library. He lived to be 91 and was active right up to the end. The most marvelous person you ever met in your life. I married him on his forty-eighth birthday. I was 38. We were married all that time and we had different religions, he was Episcopalian and I was Christian Scientist. Russell used to tell young people, which I think is a wonderful thing, and I do it now but I quote him when I do it … he would say, 'Everybody makes mistakes, everybody has bad judgment at a point, but you are that much richer, mentally, when you admit openly you've made a mistake. You've learned something. You're smarter than you were yesterday. Nobody that's honest, that has any brains at all, can say they could go through life or career and not make mistakes. That's how you learn. That's why you don't make the same mistake again.'"

Martha Tibbetts
Western Filmography

Movies: *Unknown Ranger* (1936 Columbia)—Bob Allen; *Ranger Courage* (1937 Columbia)—Bob Allen.

Yvette Vickers

Western Vixen

In talking with Yvette Vickers, one quickly finds she's no "dumb blonde." Bright, intelligent and witty, her sexy good looks typecast her as the sultry siren of numerous drive-in cult flicks (*Attack of the 50 Foot Woman* [1958], *Attack of the Giant Leeches* [1959], *Reform School Girl* [1957]). Yvette continued to fight for more serious roles, but even when they came in Paul Newman's *Hud* (1963) and on TV in *The Rebel*'s "Shriek of Silence," she was still cast as the sensual vamp. "That became the role for me. I used to think, yeah, I can do *50 Foot Woman* and then drop it ... go on and get serious parts. But it really doesn't work that way. People judge you very harshly—especially women."

Her myriad of romantic entanglements, two husbands and a long running on-again off-again affair with actor Jim Hutton also complicated Yvette's struggle for more rewarding roles.

Today, in retrospect, that kittenish vixen typecasting has come full circle and pays innumerable rewards for Yvette. She's well remembered and respected at film festivals for those roles as well as the westerns in which she appeared. She is even hoping to cash in on her swaggering, sultry image by starring in a one-woman show about an earlier screen sexpot, Mae West.

Born Yvette Vedder in Kansas City, Missouri, her parents headed for California after "my grandfather smashed me against the wall. I had great parents, though. I was very blessed. I'm one of those few people you hear say had a happy childhood. I lived in Malibu. Paradise Cove was my sandbox."

Yvette changed her last name when she first started working at a little musical

Yvette's sexy image in several films belies her intelligence as an actress but probably stifled her career in A-films.

review in San Francisco. "I was about 15. Interviews ... radio shows ... they spelled it wrong ... pronounced it wrong. So I wanted to make it something easy to say and remember. I got the phone book... The V's are good. V–V–Vickers. That's how it happened. My father never liked it. But I like it. It has *stuff*."

Yvette's parents were also entertainers. "They toured and played in lounges all over the country. I've produced and released a CD of nine songs they wrote. I chose all the tempos and style. 'A Tribute to Charlie and Maria!'

"I did a couple of musicals here in town before I did TV or anything. A casting woman saw me at the Players Ring in a little musical review and called me in to do a White Rain commercial, which turned out to be a big bonanza in 1955. It ran on and on and on and on ... the World Series every year. It was a national commercial, which means you get paid about a hundred or so dollars every time it runs. I was getting checks like 2,500, 2,000 a week... I like this [*laughs*]! Later in the 1970s, I did a couple of cigarette commercials, and I don't even smoke."

Yvette's first major film was *Short Cut to Hell* in 1957. "I was playing in *Bus Stop* at a local theater. The people at Paramount saw it and brought me to producer A. C. Lyles and director James Cagney. He was judging my acting in our conversation, how I reacted to things he said. He suddenly looked at me and said, 'Do you want to do this picture?' 'Of course.' 'You've got the part.' He didn't have me read; he had his way to see how I responded to things. He was just an angel. There was a lot of publicity about my being his discovery, which I loved. He worked with you and rehearsed the scenes. For instance, in a phone booth when a guy has a gun on me, I had to be really scared and I wasn't quite up to the intensity. Cagney picked a fight with me. He said some kind of an insult.

I idolized him and all of a sudden he's putting me down. Then he pushed me in front of the camera ... 'Now! Let's go!' When I finished the scene he smiled, 'Good work, Yvette ... are you still mad at me?' And I went, 'Oh, I get it!' You know you can only do something like that with somebody that's just starting out. The old pros would catch it. Unfortunately, the film didn't make it. He directed it as a favor to A. C., who was a good friend of his. They went sailing together. For whatever reason he did it, after that he thought it was just too much responsibility. Maybe he was disappointed too at the way it came out. It was a remake of an Alan Ladd film. Well, you can't have an Alan Ladd film without Alan Ladd. They were thinking this guy [Robert Ivers] would have the charisma and it turned out, wonderful guy that he was, he didn't have it, it just didn't come across on the screen."

Other actresses (Joan Collins, Marilyn Monroe, etc.) had posed nude for *Playboy* magazine, so in 1959 Yvette did also, thinking "the national publicity would help me get better parts. Sure wasn't doing it to get dates, boyfriends; I had so many hanging around [*laughs*]. I was already doing sexy parts. I liked doing them for that time but I would have liked to have graduated on to some romantic comedies, or really heavy drama. I loved to do all kinds of parts. I wondered if people would just see me as this degenerate sex goddess and I'd get this horrible reputation or something. Marilyn Monroe didn't have any problem with it. That's the argument everybody always gives you, so when they called me back, I said all right. I still to this day have no idea whether it was the right thing to do or not."

Yvette did win a Broadway show from it. "I went to New York to do *The Gang's All Here* with Melvyn Douglas and E. G. Marshall, all males. I was the only girl, center of attention, which turned out

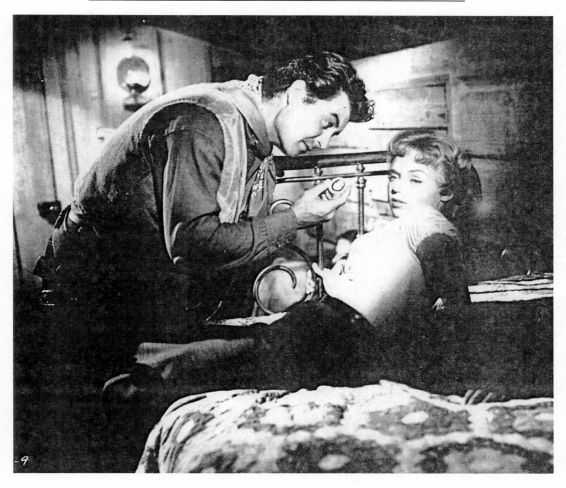

Charming, with a sense of humor, is how Yvette found Rory Calhoun while filming *The Saga of Hemp Brown* in 1958.

very well for me. The playwright and the producer did want the publicity, and they admitted it. They had hundreds of actresses in New York that could have done it but they wanted me because of that centerfold. And because it was that kind of part.

"More recently, Sharon Stone did something similar for the same reason. Most actresses, if they so something like that, it's definitely a career move, they're not doing it to get men in their life. I think most actresses, especially when you're starting out, if you're working a lot, you meet so many people and almost every-

body wants to go out with you. It's like anybody that's doing well at anything, everybody just wants to be around you, even if they can just say they know you very well [*laughs*]. I hear about so many affairs I had where I didn't even know the guy. Why are they doing this? I will admit to the real love affairs, but when people start making up stories, that does get on your nerves."

Yvette's first experience in a western was opposite Rory Calhoun in *The Saga of Hemp Brown* (1958). "Rory Calhoun was involved in the production. It was so cute, I went on the interview and most producers play it cool, 'We'll call you,' but they just said, 'We want you.' I just loved that. Rory was charming. If he hadn't been married, no doubt about it, I would have gone right away with him because he was not only good-looking and charming but he had a great sense of humor. He could make you laugh. That's number one in my book. That's what got me all hung up on Jim Hutton later; he's one of the funniest men I've ever met. Rory was like that, he had that charm and just full of life and loving every minute of it. You know, later on the *Texan* episodes I did, he used to tease me. He and [producer] Vic Orsatti would come behind my trailer, pretend like they were peeking in, they couldn't see anything, but they were giggling back there, and I'd say, 'Get away from here, you guys, go on now.' But we were all laughing. It was adorable, the fact that they would want to see me dressing. I thought that was so cute. I know a lot of people who say, 'You think it's cute, somebody peeking in your dressing room?' But the way they did it, they were harmless. They just liked to tease me, and I liked the attention, but I couldn't take it any further because … not only was he married, but I was going with somebody.

"That's the way I always felt. If I was in love with somebody, I was completely faithful. If I was married, I would do the same. But I was a little abrupt in breaking things off, if I really knew it wasn't going anywhere. I think a lot of people got angry about that. I told my second husband [a Hollywood-based writer] over breakfast, this isn't really going anywhere and he wasn't contributing to the household, that was another problem. Financially. That marriage was only a couple of years. My first marriage lasted four years. He was a nice guy, it was just the wrong time. He was traveling, a musician out on the road all the time. I was working, one of my busiest times, and we never saw each other. At a certain point, we both just looked at each other and said, 'I'm never going to get to know you, am I?' And so we both agreed, 'It's not the right combination.'"

Richard Carlson, the director of *Saga of Hemp Brown*, "was another darling guy. So charming and so open. He listened to every word, everything, and watched every expression. Very intent. As a director he wasn't like Cagney, he was more hands off. He pretty much let us go with whatever we came in with."

Yvette has mixed emotions about the biggest budgeted (and best received) film she was in, *Hud*. Director Martin Ritt and Paul Newman gave the public as rotten a human being as can be found on screen in a modern western that's closely linked to others of its ilk—*The Lusty Men* (1952), *Lonely Are the Brave* (1962), *Junior Bonner* (1972)—all dealing with the passing of the old West in one way or another. Great plaudits were given to Newman for his frighteningly evil portrayal of Hud Bannon. "My agent sent me out on an interview to the set, they were already shooting. I met Marty Ritt, Newman and Patricia Neal. They were in the midst of this scene and they brought me over and she looked up… I'll never forget her, adorable woman. Just looking up at me, she said, 'She's perfect!' Paul didn't say much. Then they wanted me to do the scene. We were rehearsing and Paul and I got into this kind of improv thing where he was chasing me around the set and there was a photographer there, shooting us, like this was going to be a real sexy relationship, which it was. There were originally four scenes, two in the motel room, one by the pool at the motel and the one where my husband catches us and we end up having this fight. I don't know whether this is true or not, but years later, I was told Mr. Newman's wife, Joanne Woodward, heard there was some kind of vibration going on between us ... and they cut those scenes. All that's left is the moment where we come in to meet his father and brother. What I thought was going to be a real jump start in A-movies, turned out just to ... well, it hurt me in the sense that most of the interviews I got after that were only for small parts, instead of starring roles. Up til then, I'd been doing lead roles. So I started turning everything down and that's when the whole thing kind of took a dive and I started working in the theater again. I just felt the movie business shut me down. It wasn't going the direction I wanted to go.

"I think Joanne Woodward cut the scenes in an emergency knee-jerk reaction, thinking that Paul may be attracted ... but it was an innocent flirtation to do with the part in the movie. It was our fitting into the parts. She was absolutely wrong if she thought I was going to initiate anything, it would never have happened. You've got to remember, she's an actress and they'd been criticized for not having any chemistry together on screen. Very few married couples do. It's funny, but they don't on-camera. I guess maybe it was a sensitive thing at that time for somebody else to have that chemistry with him. For instance, Hepburn and Tracy, who never got married, are magical on screen, they're just a kick in the pants. But who knows, if they had been a married couple, who knows?

"I was dating Ralph Meeker at the time. I loved him. He showed me New York. I had never been there before and he literally romanced me, took me on the Hansom cab ride around the park, took me to the Oak Room, Hotel Plaza, and all these landmarks, and the best restaurants, all the best places. It was spring. It started out on cloud nine and it remained that way for a long time. Later, he came out here to film and we hung out together, we played tennis, we worked out together ... we were pals too, as well as lovers. It was a great re-lationship, heavy-duty. But neither one of us wanted to get married. I'd had two marriages, he'd had one. He loved to kibitz. He again has a wonderful sense of humor, but very serious. When I started bitching about 'Hollywood won't give me any chance' and all this ... he said, '*They* won't?' He used to bawl me out for that. '*You* make it happen!' He was very, very strong about that. The actor had to be the one to change it, make it go his way. And he showed me how to do it."

Like everyone, TV provided a great new opportunity for work in the 1950s. Yvette's sexuality came into play on an episode of *Bat Masterson* (1958–1961). "Again, the wife. You always wonder, why are they worried about me? Of course, they don't know me. They don't know I have all these great principles. I'm a flirt. I admit that. But I'm a friendly flirt. I just have a flirtatious nature, but I have no intention of doing anything. And these guys know it. Ask anybody. If he was still alive, you could ask Lee Marvin ... Darren McGavin would know. These guys who showed an interest in me were married. I even had dinner with Lee while we were shooting. But anything too personal, I would tell them I was seeing somebody and you're married and that means you can't do anything about it. Sorry. But these guys are great. They could get another date two minutes later. They don't have to worry. But it's awfully flattering to have an attraction going on. I admit that.

"So, meanwhile, I'm having this love scene with Gene Barry in *Bat Masterson* ["Double Trouble in Trinidad" (1959)]. The guys in the crew, they know everything ... they're behind the scenes going, 'Has she gotten here yet?' Sure enough, Gene's wife walks onto the set. I didn't know what was going on. All I could hear was little titters. And so Gene, he's a great guy, he whispered to me, 'My wife always comes on the set when I'm doing a love scene.'"

Having mentioned friendships with Lee Marvin and Darren McGavin, Yvette compared their two varying personalities. Lee Marvin was "butter. Like warm butter, just mellow and easy and yummy. He was so sexy. I was attracted to him. When we'd done *M-Squad* [1957–1960] we had these incredible vibes going on. That voice and everything about him. I thought he was marvelous, not only as an actor but as a guy. He took me riding on his motorbike. He was adorable and somebody I would have loved to date if either one of us had been free.

"Now Darren McGavin impressed me as a very dedicated actor. Very, very into the work. I didn't expect any personal attention from him. We were doing *Mike Hammer* [1958–1959]. I liked a lot about him, he had a lot of integrity. The suits, guys from New York, came out here one day and kind of swaggered around. Darren mentioned it before they arrived. 'The hatchet men are coming in from New York'—he had all kinds of names for them [*laughs*]. 'They're going to tell us what we're doing wrong.' We all were kind of laughing when the guys showed up and did all the things he said they were going to do and tried to change everything. We were kind of joking about it later on the way to our cars and he said, 'How about dinner or something,' and … just for a second, I thought, why not? But I had the feeling, I don't know what it was … *don't go!* I did know he was married. Something stopped me. But at that moment, I don't know how to say it, there's a twinkle or something that men get and he had it. It could have been very innocent. I should have gone."

Yvette worked with Jan Merlin on two episodes of *The Rough Riders* (1958–1959). "I loved working with him. He was real supportive and has a terrific smile. I loved his smile. Genial, and a gentleman. And he shared things about his trips to Africa. I'm an animal lover and an animal rights person, so I listened with objectivity because I understand people have interests like that but it's very hard for me; I couldn't do a hunting thing. But I admired him. People have to be honest about their likes and dislikes and I thought he was a terrific guy."

Yvette's role on "Decision at Sweetwater" for Nick Adams' TVer *The Rebel* was one of her best performances. There is a scene in the episode where actor Donald Buka manhandles Yvette quite realistically. "He was a fine actor, and we got into it. We were both on a high-energy plain, almost like it was really happening. And he did bruise me, he actually did. But I didn't mind, because I knew it was happening. There was no way I was going to stop the scene. Yeah, he was very rough. But we went out later. He was adorable."

As for the star of *The Rebel*, Nick Adams, "I liked Nick. I didn't get to know him too well but I used to run into him at cocktail parties and all kinds of events in Hollywood. I didn't see that part of him that was troubled. [Adams died of a drug overdose February 5, 1968. Some say it was suicide.] On the set, I had no indication. To me, he just seemed like a really together guy who was very career-conscious and wanted to make it big time. Everybody knew that about him and he presented himself as a very dedicated actor. I don't remember who I was seeing, but if I would see Nick in a social setting, sometimes at his home, invited to parties, he seemed to me very balanced. I just didn't know anything about the other stuff. I have the feeling it was some kind of an accident, because most people with that kind of ambition, there's very little that can tear you away from that. I think the big problem with these people who have accidental overdoses, is that they drink, and when they're drinking, they can't remember what they've had."

Although she did westerns, crime dramas and A-films such as *Hud* (1963), Yvette's career defining role will no doubt always be as Honey Parker (with William Hudson) in *Attack of the 50 Foot Woman* (1958).

In Yvette's other *Rebel* episode, "Shriek of Silence," she has to use sign language for the deaf. "They were teaching me what it meant and I would... I didn't just do a circle and then move a finger [*laughs*]. I'm just amazed when I see it. I look like I knew what I was doing. So whatever intelligence I show in that, I feel very proud of it."

For a *Tales of Wells Fargo* in 1962, the ever blonde Yvette wore a dark wig. "I wanted to look like a character actress, like really unattractive. I'll show them I can really look ugly [*laughs*]."

When Yvette guested on *Shotgun Slade* in 1961 with well known ladies' man Scott Brady, "Everybody started kidding me on the set. They knew immediately what Scott was going to do when I arrived. Sure enough, by mid-morning we were out on the back lot and he came moseying around ... how are you and blah, blah, blah ... he was adorable. I was smiling and laughing and at a certain point, I thought, should I tell him or shouldn't I ... I was dating Ralph Meeker, and they knew each other. So when I mentioned Ralph's name, he just looked at me and backed off [*laughs*]. But I think it's kind of natural. It's also kind of a game to see what happens. With my sense of humor, I think a lot of this mystery of men and women relationships and the war of divorce and marriage and all that, is fun. I can't really take it that seriously, even though I do take a relationship seriously. My feeling about it is, have a sense of humor, unless the person is really, really doing something disrespectful to you."

Among her many male acquaintances was Ben Cooper, who worked in such westerns as *Johnny Guitar* (1954), *Rebel in Town* (1956), *Arizona Raiders* (1965) and *Duel at Apache Wells* (1957). "Ben was one of my first boyfriends. That was a long relationship, we were very involved. It looked like marriage for a while, then all of a sudden, something happened with his career."

Yvette never had the opportunity to appear on *Sugarfoot* (1957–1961) but would have liked to. "Will Hutchins was so sweet, such a gentleman. A good friend who was dating my girlfriend."

Although she never worked with John Wayne, Yvette did meet the legend. She was seriously involved with actor Jim Hutton when he was filming *The Green Berets* (1968). "When Wayne got back from location [Ft. Benning, Georgia], they were shooting over on the Warner Bros. lot. I made an appointment to meet Jimmy and he put a pass out for me. Closed set, but they let me on. When I came in, Wayne was just crossing as I was coming toward Jim. Wayne stopped and looked at me and said to Jimmy, 'Wow! Now I can see why you wanted to get back.' I was so flattered, you know ... be still my heart. Everybody loved John Wayne and Jimmy was just glowing, his face just lit up when Wayne said that. And so we had a few minutes chat. But another weird thing, when they were having a death scene where Jimmy gets strung up by that trap, I was standing behind the camera, and I felt these vibes. Then a cigar appeared and this hat, then Wayne comes over and says, 'Hey, hiya Pappy'—it was John Ford! Such buddies and hugging. Ford just showed up. I was thinking, my

God, what a day I'm having! Ford just had a powerful presence."

Over the years Yvette had romantic liaisons with Hugh O'Brian, Edd Byrnes and one with Cary Grant she simply describes as "mystical." But the true love of Yvette's life was actor Hutton, with whom she had an on-and-off relationship for 14 years. "It was love at first sight. I came back from New York. I'd just done a Broadway play. We got together and just never looked back for years. It just went on and on and on. There was a problem of fidelity at a certain point and he broke it off around five years into the relationship. He told me about [his infidelity]. He felt terrible. We'd already talked about marriage. He said, 'This is something that ruined my first marriage.' And I didn't know what to do. I was very confused. But we broke up.

"I got married first, went off to Las Vegas and married somebody. Jim and I would then run into each other and be very civilized as if we never had a relationship. Then *he* ran off and got married. Then we both got divorced and got back together. Both of us would say how we messed this up, we were crazy. We kept going back. You're just tangled in each other's lives.

"At the very end, I didn't know he had cancer when I called him. I went to the hospital. They'd just told him he had lung cancer with about six months to live. Jim said, 'I always thought, when we were old and couldn't kick around any more, no matter what we did in between, that somehow we would end up together.' He was very upbeat, he said, 'I want to read a lot, I've leased Mary Tyler Moore's house in Malibu and I want you to come out there and spend some time with me and I will go walking on the beach at sunset with you.' I went straight into denial. 'You're going to be all right. But I'll do whatever you want.'"

Unfortunately, this was to be their last time together. Although Hutton went home, he was soon back in the hospital where he died June 2, 1979, at only 45. "His last words were, 'We'll be happy at Malibu again, and walk into the sunset.' I had a hard time getting over it. I moved to Palm Springs. I just changed everything in my life. Now I concentrate on my creative energy, singing, recording, producing the CDs on my parents, writing a book of memoirs and doing the one-woman show about Mae West."

Yvette Vickers
Western Filmography

Movies: *The Saga of Hemp Brown* (1958 Universal-International)—Rory Calhoun; *Hud* (1963 Paramount)—Paul Newman.
Television: *Rough Riders*, "The Imposters" (1958); *Rough Riders*, "The Electioneers" (1959); *The Rebel*, "Shriek of Silence" (1961); *The Rebel*, "Decision at Sweetwater" (1961); *Shotgun Slade*, "Lost Herds" (1961); *Tales of Wells Fargo*, " Return to Yesterday" (1962).

June Vincent

Fetchingly Frosted

There are several ways to break into pictures. June Vincent, a minister's daughter, did it uniquely. "I was a model—someone saw my picture—and I landed a stock contract at Universal. Because of my experience, I received a higher salary than the other girls starting out. And during my first week in Hollywood, I got to meet and have dinner with Greta Garbo!"

Reminiscing about her westerns, June recalls, "I never did a western while at Universal unless you call my small part as David Bruce's girlfriend at the beginning of *Can't Help Singing* [1944] a western. I did a variety of roles, including *The Climax* [1944] with Boris Karloff. There is a huge painting of me in the film. When it was over, Ernest Pagano, one of the producers, put it up in his office. It took up most of the wall! I wasn't happy because people thought we were having an affair—which I never have and never would do.

"At Columbia I was in *Song of Idaho* [1948] with Kirby Grant. We'd known each other at Universal. We were to play romantic leads in *Babes on Swing Street* [1944]. For reasons I cannot recall, I was taken out and Anne Gwynne put in. Anne even wore the gown Vera West designed for me. Kirby was a nice fellow, with a good singing voice that we seldom got to hear.

Unidentified player, Hezzie Trietsch, Gil Taylor, Ken Trietsch (of the Hoosier Hot Shots), June, Kirby Grant and Tommy Ivo (sporting two Buck Rogers air-popper space pistols) in a scene from *Song of Idaho* (1948).

"In most of my westerns, in fact most of the movies I did at Columbia, I was the meanie, the bitch. Like *Colorado Sundown* [Republic, 1952] with Rex Allen and even the musical, *Arkansas Swing* [1948] with the Hoosier Hot Shots, a terrific quartet who were also in *Song of Idaho*. Off-screen, I was friends with people I was nasty to in pictures. Judy Canova and I were friends. There's a terrific line in *WAC from Walla Walla* [1952] where she's trying to pick out a shade of lipstick. I walk by and say 'window shade' [*laughs*]. Judy played the star bit to the hilt! She had an entourage that followed her around. One woman held an umbrella over Judy's head to keep the sun off her."

For several years, June sported a dis-

tinctive white streak in her hair. "It was my idea to 'frost' the streak in the front. I was searching for a different look." Producers liked it so she kept it for awhile but eventually they said, "Either be blonde or brunette. But don't be brunette in the back and blonde in the front."

As early as 1947, June began freelancing and appearing on TV. "I did a *Public Prosecutor* with John Howard and Anne Gwynne—the first filmed TV series. I left Universal after doing *Black Angel* [1946] with Peter Lorre and Dan Duryea [a big flirt]. Universal was like a family. When I was having a terrible time during my pregnancy, they came to my home and built sets right in my bedroom so I could finish the few scenes I had left in *That's the Spirit*

June says she was "a meanie, a bitch" in most of her westerns such as *Colorado Sundown* (1951) with Slim Pickens and Rex Allen. Mary Ellen Kay, another of our Ladies of the Western, was also in this Republic film.

[1945]. But Columbia—that was work! I did a lot of crime pictures and another horror called *The Creeper* [1948]. When it was time for those cats to be all over my dead body, I yelled for a stand-in. I couldn't stand having dozens of cats walking all over me. It gave me the shivers! Around this time I did a picture called *Zamba* [1949] with a very young Beau Bridges. I like him so much—I've followed his career ever since."

In the 1950s there were several appearances on series like *Perry Mason*. "Producer Gail Patrick used me so much as a villain I finally told her, 'They'll know it's me the moment I show up!'" Abbott and Costello: "I worked with them in *Here Come the Co-Eds* [1945]—it was fun to see them again" and *Boston Blackie*: "Kent Tay-

lor was Blackie and Lois Collier was Mary. Lois and I worked together in *Ladies Courageous* [1944] ten years earlier. We were roommates on our location shooting. I had a blind date and when Lois and I were going up the elevator with some servicemen, she pointed to a very handsome guy and said, 'I'll bet that's him.' And it was! We've been married over 50 years now! I used to see Lois every week at church but lost touch after we moved south." Lois Collier died October 27, 1999, at 80, of Alzheimer's.

A western series June guested on five times was *Have Gun Will Travel* (1957–1963). "A nice man recently sent me a tape of the episode 'Strange Vendetta.' I played a Mexican woman and wore a dark wig. We've been showing it to the kids and

June tries to explain the fine points of harness racing to Ken Trietsch, Stuart Hart, Gil Taylor, Mary Eleanor Donahue and Hezzie Trietsch in _Arkansas Swing_ (1948). Donahue changed her name to Elinor Donahue and appeared on six television series, including the very popular _Father Knows Best_ (1954–1960) where she was Betty (Princess) Anderson. Ken and Hezzie Trietsch, Gil Taylor and Gabe Ward comprised the popular musical group known as the Hoosier Hot Shots.

friends. Several have told me I should dye my hair black, but I'm not about to do that!"

After guesting on _Maude_ (1974–1978), June Vincent retired. "I didn't like what I was seeing, so I decided that was it. I never thought I was a good actress in pictures—but later I became an actress on TV. I kept every W2 for every show or film I did. I had them in a huge box which I took to SAG, dropped on their desk and asked for my pension! Thank God for SAG and their insurance. Ten years ago a cart full of groceries was dropped on my

foot and crushed it. It's caused me constant pain and developed into arthritis and everything else, including, eventually, Parkinson's Disease. Lately life hasn't been pleasant—but SAG came through on all those medical bills! I have three children, grandchildren and a wonderful husband. I like our quiet lifestyle down here in Lake San Marcos, and I do enjoy being remembered by the fans."

June Vincent
Western Filmography

Movies: *Can't Help Singing* (1944 Universal)—Deanna Durbin; *Arkansas Swing* (1948 Columbia)—Hoosier Hot Shots; *Song of Idaho* (1948 Columbia)—Kirby Grant; *Colorado Sundown* (1952 Republic)—Rex Allen; *WAC from Walla Walla* (1952 Republic)—Judy Canova; *Miracle of the Hills* (1959 Fox)—Rex Reason.

Television: *Screen Director's Playhouse*, "Cry Justice" (1956); *Have Gun Will Travel*, "Strange Vendetta" (1957); *Have Gun Will Travel*, "Colonel and the Lady" (1957); *Have Gun Will Travel*, "Black Sheep" (1960); *Have Gun Will Travel*, "Everyman" (1961); *Have Gun Will Travel*, "Broken Image" (1961); *Zane Grey Theatre*, "Wire" (1958); *Trackdown*, "The Wedding" (1958); *Wanted Dead or Alive*, "Double Fee" (1959); *Rifleman*, "The Visitors" (1960); *Riverboat*, "End of a Dream" (1960); *Tales of Wells Fargo*, "The Wayfarers" (1962); *Great Adventure*, "Testing of Sam Houston" (1964); *Virginian*, "Dead Eye Dick" (1966); *Virginian*, "With Help from Ulysses" (1968); *Kung Fu*, "Way of Violence Has No Mind" (1974).

Beverly Washburn

Queen of the Criers

In the 1950s, talented child actress Beverly Washburn replaced Margaret O'Brien as the screen's "queen of the criers." "I am very emotional. I'm told I even cry at supermarket openings."

Born Thanksgiving Day, November 25, 1943, in Los Angeles, the youngster began her career in modeling. Why would she want to be an actress at such a young age? "I just thought it was fun. My parents got me in it, but didn't force me. It was like playing pretend."

Stuntman-actor Jocko Mahoney was instrumental getting her into pictures. "I met him when I was six, doing a benefit with my sister. She was an acrobat and I

would occasionally sing. We were in Long Beach and met there. He asked my mother about me, things like that. My agent had sent me on interviews, but I never got anything. I never had a 'credit' to use—saying I had already done a part. A couple of months later, I was at Columbia, to audition for a role in *The Killer That Stalked New York* [1950]. My mother noticed the character, Walda, was described as a brown-eyed girl with long brown hair, and told me I wouldn't get the part... I wasn't right, but to do my best. In comes Jocko—under contract to the studio at the time. He walked through the lobby and recognized me. When he was told what we were

Clayton Moore as the Lone Ranger, Beverly and her screen mom, Bonita Granville, in Warner Bros.' big-screen production *The Lone Ranger* (1956).

doing there, he went into the other room and told them, 'Oh, she's done this, she's done that, she's done everything' when I really hadn't done *anything*! But, they took me on his say-so. It was the first part I ever had, and it had lots of lines."

Beverly is well-remembered for playing the daughter of Bonita Granville and Lyle Bettger in the feature version of *The Lone Ranger* (1956). "We stayed at Parry's Lodge, on location in Kanab, Utah. Real Indians were used as extras in the movie.

Bonita Granville was very nice, but the main thing I remember about the picture was a trick played on Clayton Moore. If you've ever seen any *Lone Ranger* shows, you know his outfit was *very* tight. In the scene where we're with the Indians, Clayton Moore jumps onto his horse. When he did, those pants split wide open [*laughs*]! This isn't the worst of it. Because the pants were so tight, it made it necessary for Clayton *not* to wear any underwear, because underwear lines would show. So, when those pants split—at the back, his whole butt stuck out! No one in the crew, cast or anyone, told him, and the director let the camera keep rolling—for a gag. It was hilarious [*laughs*]."

Beverly actually worked on television more than feature films. One of her earliest was a *Zane Grey Theatre* with Ralph Bellamy and Gloria Talbott in 1956. "But I most remember James Garner, because I thought he was really cute. I had a crush on him."

There were two appearances on *The Texan* (1958–1960) with Rory Calhoun. "I had a really fine role in one of them. Rory was a really nice man. He and I danced in one of them. I liked him a lot." Michael Pate was also in that episode. "Michael was just great; I liked him as an actor."

Perhaps Beverly's most famous TV appearance was her second on *Wagon Train*, "The Tobias Jones Story" (1958). "Lou Costello was a doll. I loved working with him. It was his first dramatic appearance—away from his comedy partner Bud Abbott—and he was so nervous. But so nice. At the time, an article came out on the show and he mentioned me in the story—he said, 'There was a little girl in the show, Beverly Washburn, and without her I couldn't have done it.' That was so nice. Actually, because of the comedy things, Lou was used to ad-libbing and not following the script. But on this he *had* to follow the script. There was no free

rein. He had a hard time memorizing those lines. When he would go up on his lines, he would stare at the camera and say, 'So how are you, Ward?' [*laughs*]. He was cute. There's a scene where Lou is drunk, and I am to push him into the wagon. Lou said, 'The way to do it is, I'm gonna bend over, and you push my biscuits right up into the wagon' [*laughs*]."

An earlier appearance on the series was the premiere episode, "The Willy Moran Story" with Ernest Borgnine. "I was a big fan of Ernest Borgnine before doing this; I had good rapport with him." As for other cast members, like Marjorie Reynolds and Andrew Duggan, "A lot of actors and directors you meet, they do the job and leave. When you are little, it doesn't mean anything—then later, you look back and think about who all you met and worked with and wish you had known just who they were when you were with them."

As to locations: "Most of the *Wagon Train*s were shot on the soundstage, but we did go on location to Iverson's Ranch, and also Lake Sherwood."

As to Ward Bond: "He was great; he gave me an 8 × 10 which says, 'To Beverly, the finest little actress.' Ward Bond did have a foul mouth [*laughs*] and the schoolteacher—from the Los Angeles Board of Educators—they called them welfare workers then—she threatened to pull me from the set because of the swearing. They reprimanded Ward. She had every authority to pull me from the set, but fortunately she didn't, as it would have caused a lot of trouble—delays, wasted money, that sort of thing." About Robert Horton, "He was cute, very nice to me."

One of Beverly's best and most famous roles was in Disney's classic *Old Yeller* (1957). "That was fun to do—although I knew it was a sad movie. One of the greatest enjoyments was getting to be on the Disney lot, going to school with the

Beverly as she appeared in Disney's *Old Yeller* (1957).

Mouseketeers. The school was in a big red trailer on the lot. I didn't think I'd get the part, because Disney had so many kids under contract. But I read for it, and got it! I'm still friends with a lot of the kids I met during that film."

The most famous film Beverly did was the classic western, *Shane* (1953). "I was eight years old and I got very ill—they thought I had polio; but they didn't replace me. They used a double, Gretchen Steinbrook, for the long shots—I was sick for a week and a half with a high temperature. It turned out to be a strong form of flu."

Dealing on *Shane* with another child star, Brandon De Wilde, was no picnic for the youthful actress. "Brandon was a brat! So precocious. He didn't like girls, and he would pull my pigtails and chase me around the set."

About *Shane* he-man star Alan Ladd: "The movie was shot on location in Jackson Hole, Wyoming. Alan Ladd and I both went up the chair lift to the top of a

mountain. I went down the lift by myself, but Ladd was too *scared* to come down! Finally, they sent a helicopter to rescue him; he was too chicken to go down. The cast and crew never let him hear the end of it [*laughs*]. Jean Arthur was reclusive, not a whole lot to say, but Ellen Corby, who played my mother, was a doll, and Edgar Buchanan, my father, was very nice. We took a train to get to Wyoming. It was a great experience."

Beverly appeared on a *Fury* episode in 1956 that turned out to be one of her most memorable adventures. "Bobby Diamond and I are still friends. He's an attorney now. But as for the show, it was the most dangerous time I ever had. I was running away and there's a scene where I fall down a cliff. The horse brings a rope to rescue me to safety. It was a fake mountain—but two stories high. My double was a midget—she had on this wig and duplicates of my clothes. She climbed up the steps to the top of the mountain, then refused to do the stunt. They were so upset, so angry. The director asked me if I'd do it. I was too afraid to say no—because I thought he'd get mad at me. I didn't want to, I was scared—but I didn't tell. My mother asked, 'Do you want to do it?' and the welfare worker said, 'No, absolutely not!' The director said, 'It's fun.' I knew it would hold up production [if I didn't do it] and the director told the welfare worker, 'She wants to do it.' She asked and I was afraid to say no. So, I finally climbed to the top of the mountain. They rolled the camera—the director said, 'Take your time, then jump.' I was petrified! Finally, I did it but it was terrifying! The crew applauded and I was so glad it was over with. Later, I realized I should never do something that even a professional stunt person wouldn't do. After all, I was given a double to ride on the pony in *The Lone Ranger* [1956] and I *could* ride!"

In the mid–1960s, Beverly starred in

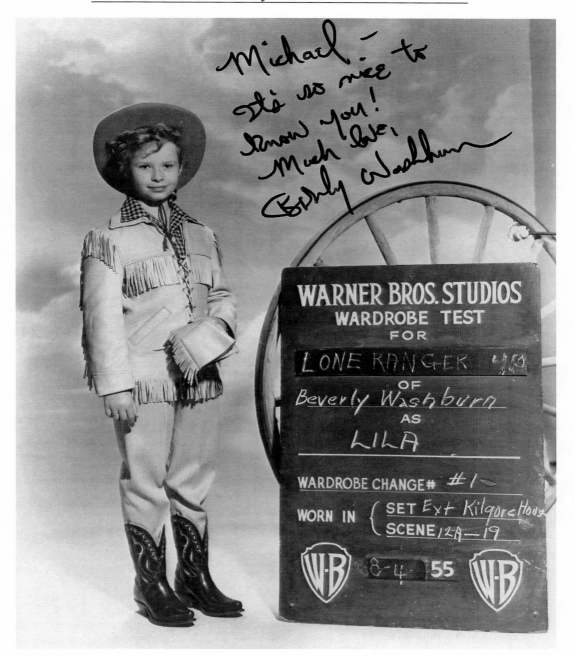

A rare shot of Beverly's wardrobe test at Warner Bros. for *The Lone Ranger* (1956).

what is now a cult film, *Spider Baby* (1968). "I liked it because the part was good, and I got to play somebody unlike me—she kills people and stuff like that. Also, I got to meet Lon Chaney, Jr., which was ex-

citing. But the film had no budget, I think they spent six dollars on it [*laughs*]!"

As to her favorite director, she immediately responds, "Herschel Daughtery. He did a lot of *Wagon Trains*, and so many shows. Whenever he directed and there was a part for me, I got it—without even having to read. Unfortunately, he's since died. My husband and I moved to Dallas in 1987, when he was transferred; then on to Reno and finally back to California about six years ago. When I returned to Los Angeles, I called the Directors Guild wanting to talk to Daughtery, but he had just passed away."

Beverly was, at one time, the sister-in-law of child western star and later stuntman Robert "Buzz" Henry. "My late sister, actress Audrey Allen [*Son of Sinbad* (1955), *The Lion in Winter* (1968)] was married to Buzz. She told me, although she was happily remarried with a good husband who was a wonderful father, that she hadn't gotten Buzzy out of her system. She still loved him. A few months later, Buzz and I had lunch together. Naturally, Audrey came up. Buzz told me, although he too was happily remarried, and that [his current wife] Pat was a wonderful wife and mother, he never got Audrey out of his system. He said he'd always love her. I told Buzz that was so weird, so chilling, as Audrey told me the same thing in reverse, practically verbatim. Later, that same afternoon [September 30, 1971], Buzz went drinking and was killed in a motorcycle accident."

The bubbly, warm, friendly Beverly Washburn keeps in touch with many of her friends from her acting days. "Jack Benny I kept in touch with until he died. I did one of his early live TV shows, then a couple of his radio shows. Later, I traveled with him (and Iris Adrian—that wonderful, wise-cracking blonde) in a vaudeville-kind of act. I also did several of the *Loretta Young* shows [1953–1961]. When she did the later *New Loretta Young Show* [1962–1963], she picked me to be one of her daughters. I spoke to her on the phone once a month—she was a very special person, and went through a lot in recent times. In 1997, her two sisters, her brother *and* her husband, the fabulous designer Jean Louis [pronounced John Lou E], passed away. But she was very religious and endured until her death August 12, 2000, of ovarian cancer. I really loved her very much. I miss her, she was my idol. She was like a real mom to me, so gentle, sweet, lovely. Sharon Baird, from the 'Mouseketeers,' is a good friend; and Annette Funicello is an angel, so sweet and so giving. Very down to earth—her medical problems with MS are such a shame. I also keep in touch with Tommy Kirk and Kevin Corcoran from *Old Yeller*."

Beverly's two-cassette audio book, with fascinating anecdotes from one of the most talented child actresses of all time, is *Hollywood Child: The Beverly Washburn Story*, available through Barnes and Noble. Her Top 40 single from 1963, "Everybody Loves Saturday Night," is on the audio tape.

Beverly Washburn Western Filmography

Movies: *Shane* (1953 Paramount)—Alan Ladd; *The Lone Ranger* (1956 Warner Bros.)—Clayton Moore; *Old Yeller* (1957 Buena Vista)—Fess Parker.

Television: *Fury*, "Joey Sees It Through" (1956); *Zane Grey Theatre*, "Stars Over Texas" (1956); *Wagon Train*, "Willy Moran Story" (1957); *Wagon Train*, "Tobias Jones Story" (1958); *Wagon Train*, "Cassie Vance Story" (1963); *Texan*, "No Tears for the Dead" (1958); *Texan*, "Badman" (1960).

Marie Windsor

Western Noir

The first thing you notice are her shadowy eyes. As an actress for over 50 years, Marie Windsor appeared in some of the finest B-westerns and *film noir* productions ever made. Beyond her well earned image as a sexy, tough broad, her acting versatility is her most remarkable trait. The exotic beauty was a tall (5'9") beauty contest winner ("I was even Queen of the Covered Wagon Days") before going to Hollywood. She began her career in the early 1940s at RKO. "Then, I was under contract to Metro-Goldwyn-Mayer [1942–1948], where I did bits both at the studio and on loan out, as well as a short, *The Lady or the Tiger* [1942]. I used to go to Clark Gable's ranch to ride."

Marie worked as a telephone girl and even a dancing teacher before hitting the big time. She studied drama for two years at Brigham Young University in Utah. "I was trained in dramatics by Maria Ouspenskaya. I lived at the Hollywood Studio Club, where one of my friends was Carole Mathews. I was very fond of Carole." The actresses worked together in *Swamp Women* in 1956.

By 1949, Marie was getting leads. "Did you say laid?" When I explained the word was l-e-a-d-s, she had to agree. "I'd rather star in B-pictures than do parts in A-films." Her first western was *The Fighting Kentuckian* (1949) with John Wayne, Vera Ralston and Oliver Hardy. "It was the first time I worked with John Wayne and it was a great pleasure! He was young, fun and feisty in those days. He introduced me at a party as one of his ex-wives [*laughs*]."

As to director George Waggner: "A lovely man. He later went to the Motion Picture Home. I am on the board of directors. Oliver Hardy was a joyful, sweet fellow. My part was all done at Republic on the set. No locations for me; Vera did her chase scenes someplace, but I never knew where."

As to the studio itself, Marie smiles, "Republic was a cozier and smaller studio." *Hellfire* (1949) soon followed. "I have three favorite pictures—*Hellfire*, *Narrow Margin* [1952] and *The Killing* [1956]. I loved *Hellfire*. I was so thrilled to get that well written part of a *female* bandit, Doll Brown [*laughs*]. Adrian Booth went to Mr. Yates, because she wanted to play it. I felt badly, because by rights, the part should have been hers. She was under contract to the studio. So, I sent her a dozen roses. Adrian was at the 1999 Golden Boot Awards, and we talked about that. [Marie won the Golden Boot in 1984.] There were a lot of good actors in *Hellfire*. The gentleman cowboy, Bill Elliott, taught me how to twirl a gun and holster it quickly. Bill had a high academic and social background. He couldn't hide that quality whatever western clothes he wore. At his

Forrest Tucker, Marie and Bill Elliott in one of Marie's favorite films, *Hellfire* (1949).

own expense, Bill set up an opening publicity tour in Salt Lake City for *Hellfire*. As for horse riding, it was wonderful being taught no-stirrup mounts! Recently, I received a package of negatives—a couple of them show me doing the leaping mount—onto the butt of the horses! Actually, Republic was especially pleased that I had been at home on a horse since I was a child. It was a great advantage in getting parts such as this."

As for any accidents, Marie recalls, "I never had any. And I did most of the stunt work."

Dakota Lil (1950) was next on her western schedule. "We shot this on location somewhere in Nevada. I had Rod Cameron's sister as my double, but she couldn't ride a horse! I'm from Utah [born

Emily Marie Bertelsen December 11, 1919, in Marysvale, population 300], and I learned to ride horses bareback, because my family didn't have enough money for a saddle. My horse's name was Silver. I was a good rider in my younger days. However today, I can't even ride a merry-go-round! On June 2, 1997, I had a back operation that left me paralyzed. My third or fourth lumbar was like a rat's nest. After extensive surgery, I can drive and walk with a cane."

As for anything further regarding Rod Cameron, "We did another picture, *The Jungle* [1952] on location in India. At that time, he was married to a part–Portuguese, part–Chinese woman. Rod and I had dated slightly prior to this, so it was an odd relationship there. The producer offered to give me a monkey. Rod's wife made such a fuss, because she wanted it, that I finally said, 'Take it!' She had a terrible time getting it into the United States. And, it messed up her house pretty bad [*laughs*]!"

George Montgomery was the other star of *Dakota Lil*. "George has arthritic problems like me, but he still manages to make various functions. George was a good actor and good on a horse. I always felt he was more serious than other western actors; very meticulous. Perhaps it's the artist in him, but he didn't let his hair down, if you will." (Montgomery died December 12, 2000). Marie always stated that Marni Nixon, a popular dubber of stars' singing voices, sang for her in *Dakota Lil* although 20th Century–Fox records indicate it was Anita Ellis, who sang for Rita Hayworth in *Gilda* and Vera-Ellen in *Three Little Words*.

Frenchie (1950), a Technicolor remake (with many changes) of *Destry Rides Again* (1939), was Marie's next western. "I had a great fight in it. There were no doubles. Shelley Winters and I talked it over and decided to do it ourselves. Everybody was happy we did. The fight scene took a day and a half to shoot. We didn't get punched on the nose—but there were a few accidental scratches! I had another fight—with Dolores Dorn, in *Bounty Hunter* [1954] with Randolph Scott. We had a fight in the dust that was very dirty—literally! Randolph Scott was such a gentleman, and as for Ernest Borgnine, I sure like that man—he's a good actor, too!"

In *Frenchie*, the star was Joel McCrea: "A sweet gentleman. A guy like John Wayne—ready and professional. He did everything—and he was so nice to the crew. I met his wife, Frances Dee, later and we talked about the movie, and Joel."

The Showdown (1950) was a murder mystery as well as a western. "It had the same producer and director as *Hellfire* and

a wonderful cast, too. I didn't go outdoors—all my scenes were shot on the set. I don't even know if the campfire scenes were done on a set or on location. Probably on a set." *Hellfire* was written and executive produced by Dorrell and Stuart McGowan, produced by William J. O'-Sullivan and directed by R. G. Springsteen. The McGowans adapted *Showdown* from an *Esquire* story as well as directing it under producer O'Sullivan and Elliott himself.

Little Big Horn (1951), produced by Charles Marquis Warren, was next. "Lippert made the movie. They announced on the set they were out of money. They tore pages out of the script—so we finished early and without certain scenes! The same thing happened to me a couple of years later on *Cat Women of the Moon* [1954] [*laughs*]."

The posters for Ron Ormond's *Outlaw Women* (1952) (released by Howco) proclaim: "Meet the Babes Who Put the *Bad* in the Bad Men." "That was an exciting picture. There were two sets for us—I had more change of wardrobe than I did acting. I would run from stage to stage! I was quite annoyed about the picture, though. Jacqueline Fontaine was the girlfriend of the producer or some big shot, and she got privileges she didn't deserve. Richard Rober, that poor guy, was killed in a car wreck before the picture was released." Rober, also in *Sierra* (1950) and *Man in the Saddle* (1952), died May 26, 1952, in a Santa Monica auto wreck. *Outlaw Women* was released in June 1952. "Allan Nixon, who was also in it, was a very sweet man. The makeup man was Carlie Taylor. I went to the makeup department and sat there a little while. Finally, he asked, what color makeup did I want. I applied the makeup myself. When I finished, someone asked for me. Until then, Carlie didn't know *I* was the *star*!"

Marie has the ability to change her

Walter Brennan, Bill Elliott and Marie in Republic's *The Showdown* (1950).

appearance from film to film, whether in hair color or hair style. "Mostly, that was my own idea. Once, I changed because of Andrew McLaglen. The only time I wore a wig was in *Support Your Local Gunfighter* [1971]. I replaced Marilyn Maxwell. They didn't think she had the feistiness the part required. I felt badly about it. Marilyn and I had known each other since the early 1940s and our days at MGM together. Also, we had done a TV movie, *Wild Women* [1970], only a year or so earlier. I ended up wearing the red wig she was supposed to wear."

The Tall Texan (1953) starred Lloyd Bridges. "We did that in New Mexico, in an area where the dust was so fine that when we drove out to location, we'd be covered in this fine dust, even if the windows were rolled up tight [Deming, New Mexico, City of Rocks State Park]. It was very, very dusty. Lloyd and I had done *Little Big Horn* a couple of years earlier, and I was a friend of the family. His wife Dorothy brought the kids on the set. Years later, I did a picture called *Hearts of the West* [1975] and the star was Jeff Bridges. I knew him as a little kid, and worked with him when he grew up!"

Another for Lippert, *Silver Star* (1955), starred Earle Lyon but was headlined by character actors Edgar Buchanan and Lon Chaney, Jr. "They were all nice men. In fact, on *Silver Star*, Lon Chaney, Jr., wasn't drinking at the time! I understand he was quite a boozer by this time, but on the film, and around me, he was always sober!"

One of Marie's lesser westerns was *Two Gun Lady* (1955) with Peggie Castle

WARNER BROS. present **RANDOLPH SCOTT 'THE BOUNTY HUNTER'** Colour by WARNERCOLOR

with DOLORES DORN · MARIE WINDSOR

Screen play by WINSTON MILLER · Directed by ANDRE de TOTH · A Transcona Enterprises Production · Distributed by Warner Bros.

Marie has the drop on Randolph Scott—momentarily—in *The Bounty Hunter* (1954).

and William Talman. "I'm not fond of the picture—it was lightweight, and done in a hurry!"

Golden Boot supporter Buddy Rogers both produced and co-starred in *Parson and the Outlaw* (1957). "Buddy and I were friendly before we did the picture. He was a sweetheart—I am so sorry we lost him. Sonny Tufts was in it also. He'd been in *Cat Women* with me. Sonny was a nice big fellow who tried to be very friendly. I don't think he ever cared much about acting, though."

At Universal-International, Marie played the girlfriend of outlaw Christopher Dark in *Day of the Bad Man* (1958), produced by Gordon Kay. "It was wonderful, working with Fred MacMurray. I

made a good try, doing the character. I enjoyed that movie very much."

It would be six years before another western feature, this one with comedy dominating, *Mail Order Bride* (1964). "That was directed by Burt Kennedy. Burt and I remained friends and he used me later on other films. As for Buddy Ebsen, I liked him both as a person and as an actor. He is one of my favorites."

In 1969, Marie worked for Burt Kennedy again in *The Good Guys and the Bad Guys*. "Working on this with Burt, and with Robert Mitchum—could I ask for anything more? I was invited to Burt Kennedy's seventieth birthday party, and I definitely went!" *Support Your Local Gunfighter* (1971) was yet another Burt

Kennedy directorial job. "I loved that. James Garner, who was honored at the Golden Boot, was just great! Outgoing and warm." *Cahill, U.S. Marshal* (1973) was the actress' last film with John Wayne. "It was directed by Andrew McLaglen, who had directed me in *One More Train to Rob* in 1971. McLaglen was a good director. This film was shot down in Durango, Mexico. The food was lousy! You would look out the dining room window and see a lamb tied to a stake. You knew what you would have for dinner, and you didn't like it!" In the film, Marie operates a boarding house on top of a hill. "There's a shot where I'm driving a wagon with two children. The longshot picks up at a distance from the house as we come down the hill. We got halfway down the hill when Andy McLaglen yelled, 'Cut! Marie, take off those damn sunglasses' [*laughs*]."

Marie has had a long and successful career, which includes the *Look* magazine award as best supporting actress of 1957 for *The Killing*. Her television work is so extensive, it would make for yet another long interview. "On TV, I wish sometimes they didn't take the attitude, if you get all the words in, they print it. I did enjoy working in the various series Warner Bros. produced." One of her favorites also is the title role of "Belle Starr" in *Stories of the Century*. Married for over 45 years to Jack Hupp, a Beverly Hills realtor, Marie Windsor's *film noir* credits continue to get good play on TV and at theaters. "In August 1999, the Egyptian Theatre in Hollywood ran *Narrow Margin* one week and *The Killing* another. I attend the screenings, then answer questions afterwards, followed by a long autograph session. It was very rewarding!"

A few months after this interview, Marie died December 10, 2000, one day short of her eighty-first birthday.

Marie Windsor
Western Filmography

Movies: *Romance of Rosy* Ridge (1947 MGM)—Van Johnson; *Fighting Kentuckian* (1949 Republic)—John Wayne; *Beautiful Blonde from Bashful Bend* (1949 20th Century–Fox)—Betty Grable; *Hellfire* (1949 Republic)—William Elliott; *Dakota Lil* (1950 20th Century–Fox)—George Montgomery; *The Showdown* (1950 Republic)—William Elliott; *Frenchie* (1950 Universal)—Joel McCrea; *Little Big Horn* (1951 Lippert)—Lloyd Bridges; *Outlaw Women* (1952 Howco)—Richard Rober; *Tall Texan* (1953 Lippert)—Lloyd Bridges; *Bounty Hunter* (1954 Warner Bros.)—Randolph Scott; *Silver Star* (1955 Lippert)—Earle Lyon; *Two Gun Lady* (1955 Associated)—Peggie Castle; *Parson and the Outlaw* (1957 Columbia)—Anthony Dexter; *Day of the Bad Man* (1958 Universal)—Fred MacMurray; *Mail Order Bride* (1964 MGM)—Buddy Ebsen; *Good Guys and Bad Guys* (1969 Warner Bros.)—Robert Mitchum; *Wild Women* (1970 Spelling Productions–TV)—Hugh O'Brian; *One More Train to Rob* (1971 Universal)—George Peppard; *Support Your Local Gunfighter* (1971 United Artists)—James Garner; *Cahill, United States Marshal* (1973 Warner Bros.)—John Wayne; *Hearts of the West* (1975 MGM/United Artists)—Jeff Bridges.

Television: *Stories of the Century*, "Belle Starr" (1955); *Cheyenne*, "Decision at Gunsight" (1957); *Cheyenne*, "Mutton Puncher" (1957); *Californians*, "Regulators" (1957); *Maverick*, "Quick and the Dead" (1957); *Yancy Derringer*, "Ticket to Natchez" (1958); *Bat Masterson*, "The Fighter" (1958); *Rawhide*, "Incident on the Edge of Madness" (1959); *Tales of Wells Fargo*, "Warrior's Return" (1959); *Deputy*, "Back to Glory" (1959); *Shotgun Slade*, "Salted Mine" (1959); *Alaskans*, "Winter Song" (1959); *Rebel*, "Glory" (1960); *Wyatt Earp*, "Wyatt Earp's Baby" (1961); *Rawhide*, "Incident of the Painted Lady" (1961); *Whispering Smith*, "Trademark" (1961); *Bronco*, "Equalizer" (1961); *Lawman*, "Wanted Man" (1962); *Maverick*, "Epitaph for a Gambler" (1962); *Destry*, "Nicest Girl in Gomorrah" (1964); *Rawhide*, "Incident of the Rusty Shotgun" (1964); *Branded*, "That the Brave Endure" (1965); *Legend of Jesse James*, "The Quest" (1965); *Bo-*

nanza, "Five Sundowns to Sunup" (1965); *Gunsmoke*, "Trafton" (1971); *Alias Smith and* *Jones*, "High Lonesome Country" (1972), *Hec Ramsey*, "Green Feather Mystery" (1972).

Jane Withers

Top 10 Star

Jane Withers was a Top 10 Box Office champ during the late 1930s. "Dixie's Dainty Dewdrop" was born in Atlanta, Georgia, April 12, 1926. Jane had her own radio show in Atlanta, but before long, was in Hollywood, making casting calls with a lot of other kids. Her big break came when Fox needed an opposite "type" for Shirley Temple's *Bright Eyes* (1934). The rest is history. First given her own picture, *Ginger* (1935), the star quickly rose to the top of the box office standings.

"Westerns and musicals have always been my favorites. I always longed for a western-themed picture, and I first got one in *Wild and Woolly* [1937]. Walter Brennan played my grandfather. I adored him; we worked together many times later—even in *The North Star* at RKO in 1943. That one took so long I had two birthdays and graduated from high school before it was finished! Walter's daughter Ruth was an excellent equestrienne. She played two roles in the film. Riding, of course. I adored Walter, and since I received cast selection and approval, he did many pictures with me."

Child star Jackie Searl (*Skippy* [1931], *Oliver Twist* [1933], etc.) was in *Wild and Woolly* as well. "One of my all-time favorite people—I put him in *Ginger, Small Town Deb* [1941], anywhere I could. I was lucky that way. I put as many of the kids in my pictures as I could—I'd get jobs for the children who used to make the casting calls with me, before I made it! I really loved Jackie Searl. He didn't like to sign autographs, but one time I called him and asked him to please co-sign some pictures for the fans, and he did!"

Pauline Moore was in both *Wild and Woolly* as well as *Arizona Wildcat* (1938). "I love her, too. A very sweet lady."

Leo Carrillo was Jane's co-star in *Arizona Wildcat*. "Goodness gracious, Leo was so much fun. He was exactly the same off camera as on, although his accent wasn't as exaggerated. He was full of fun and always smiling, very much the gentleman. He was well read, and I really liked him."

Jane Withers was a unique child star, with privileges not granted most any other star—child or adult. "I was the only child star I know of who was given the

Jane Withers was a Top Ten box office draw when she co-starred with Gene Autry in *Shooting High* (1940).

opportunity to sit in with the writers on story conferences—and I got to come up with some of the dialogue. They didn't like too much slang, like the word 'swell,' but I had to sometimes tell them I would say what they mean, but in a child's way of saying it—the dialogue sometimes seemed too grown-up."

It was Jane who was responsible for *Shooting High* at Fox in 1940. "Joseph

Leo Carrillo and Jane share a joke as Rosita Harlan holds Leo's coat in *Arizona Wildcat* (1938).

Schenck was then head of 20th Century–Fox. I wanted to do a film with Gene Autry, so I called Mr. Schenck. He told me Gene was Republic's biggest star and they'd never loan him to Fox. So, I asked if he would loan me to Republic but he told me I was the number six box office draw in the country, and Fox would never loan me to another studio. He did agree it was a great idea, it would be box office dynamite! I just had to do a picture with Gene Autry, so I put it in my prayers. Then I called Republic. When the studio operator answered, I told her I would like to talk to the head of the studio. I didn't even know his name at the time. She said, 'Little girl, a lot of people would like to talk to Mr. Yates, but he's a busy man.' I told her, 'Well, I'm a busy girl. My name is Jane Withers, and could you please connect me?' The operator screamed '*The* Jane Withers, the actress? I am sure Mr. Yates would be thrilled to speak with you.' Mr. Yates was in an important conference, but she said she'd take a note into him; he'd definitely want to talk to me. I waited for awhile and finally he came on the phone. 'Hello, is this little Jane Withers? I'm Herbert Yates and I am a big fan of yours!' I told him I had a terrific idea—I wanted to make a picture with Gene Autry—and he said he'd love to borrow me. I had to explain that Mr. Schenck wouldn't loan me and thought he wouldn't loan Gene, but that I had a great idea and that, honest Injun, I would not take up more than 15 minutes of his time. He had a board meeting, but I was getting out of school at noon and could meet him around 2:30. He said he'd explain to the others and leave the

It was Jane who brought Gene Autry to 20th Century–Fox on loan-out from Republic for *Shooting High* (1940).

meeting when I arrived. True to his word, Mr. Yates left the meeting. I explained that perhaps Fox could loan Republic two or three of their stars in exchange for Gene, since neither studio would loan us to the other, outright. He thought that a good idea, so we called Fox. Mr. Schenck's secretary said he was in an important meeting. I told her if she went in and slipped him a note, saying Jane Withers was at Republic in Mr. Yates' office, he might come out and talk to us. And he did! I wouldn't take no for an answer. Not when I knew this would be good for everyone concerned. I was afraid Mr. Schenck would be mad at me, but he wasn't! He thought it a wonderful idea! Mr. Yates told him he had a very determined young lady

with a very credible idea! It was like having a baby—it took nine months to put the deal through, but three of Fox's stars were loaned to Republic in exchange for Gene. And, as I thought, the picture was enormously successful! It was one of the biggest box office pictures of the 1939-1940 season. I was happy as a lark to finally get to work with Gene Autry. We remained friends ever since. When he would be on the road, he would carve things and send them to me. I have a little slide ornament he made from the horn of a cow—it is white with two turquoise eyes. I have it beside a little gold watch with engraving he gave me, which I haven't worn since I was a little girl. I kept the little box he sent it in. The inscription reads 'For

Janie—love and kisses from two-gun Autry.' I have three scarves he wore in *Shooting High*. He got all his costumes after his pictures. I have Gene's shirt—embroidered, and a pastel plaid and a brown earth-colored one."

When Autry died, Jane attended his memorial, held at the Autry Museum. "I had a table with Dickie Jones and his wife, Sammy McKim and his wife and son, and Betty Lynn."

The most famous western Jane appeared in was *Giant* (1956). "Well, since the storyline goes on for such a long time, I guess it could be considered a kind of modern-day western. I became good friends with Rock Hudson, a movie buff. One night *Imitation of Life* [1934], the Claudette Colbert version, was on TV. Rock called and asked if I were in it! You bet, I was one of the kids in the schoolroom. Mercedes McCambridge, Robert Nichols and of course, dear Monte Hale, have been close friends ever since. During the so-called restoration of the film, Bob, Mercedes, Carroll Baker—but not Elizabeth—went to Texas for the re-premiere. I still have the pink shirt James Dean gave me to wash, the day before he died. He asked me to hold it for him, and I have kept it all these years."

Jane Withers is a legend—and she makes a terrific guest at any festival or movie-related event.

Jane Withers Western Filmography

Movies: *Wild and Wooly* (1937 20th Century–Fox)—Walter Brennan; *Arizona Wildcat* (1938 20th Century–Fox)—Leo Carrillo; *Shooting High* (1940 20th Century–Fox)—Gene Autry; *Giant* (1956 Warner Bros.)—James Dean.

Index